INDIAN and CHRISTIAN

Changing Identities in Modern India

INDIAN and CHRISTIAN
Changing Identities in Modern India

Papers from the First SAIACS Annual Consultation
9–12 November 2010

Edited by
Cornelis Bennema and **Paul Joshua Bhakiaraj**

SAIACS Press
BANGALORE—INDIA
&
Oxford House Research Ltd
OXFORD—UK

SAIACS Press
SAIACS, 363 Doddagubbi Cross Road
Kothanur, Bangalore-560077, India
www.saiacs.org
saiacspress@saiacs.org

ISBN-13: 978-81-87712-26-8

Cover design: Nigel Ajay Kumar
Cover Photo: Mridula Dwivedi
Layout: Primalogue Publishing Media Pvt. Ltd

Printed and bound by Brilliant Printers Pvt. Ltd, Bangalore

SAIACS Press is the publishing division of
South Asia Institute of Advanced Christian Studies

Contents

Religion and Culture

Pastoral Theology and Psychology

Foreword

This book is the fruit of SAIACS' first annual consultation. We plan to have many more because they offer significant value for the Church in South Asia. Through these consultations and through an open call for papers each year, we want to participate in current academic debates, signalling in a small way that we are part of South Asia's public sphere. We want to facilitate discussion especially among those who are members of the Christian community at large. While we don't have all the answers, we want to provide an influential evangelical voice on a broad topic in South Asia at large.

Stimulation, encouragement and direction. We need these if we are to make progress. We need these for life; in fact, they are proof of life. If something cannot be stimulated, encouraged or directed it is inert or dead. Without such interaction, we cannot fulfil our calling or contribute to the common good.

You will have noticed our purposes spring from our identity. SAIACS is evangelical and academic. We stand for excellence in mission. SAIACS is Indian and Christian and the question of how we construe our identity and live it out is an essential part of the adventure of life before God and before the world. Who we are is both a commitment and a question.

It is so appropriate then that for the topic of our first annual consultation we have: 'Indian and Christian: Changing Identities in a Modern India'. The sixteen essays in this volume explore Indian and Christian identity. The aim is to arrive at a mature and balanced attitude to Indian-Christian identity. It is noteworthy that the participants, by and large, do not do several things. We should appreciate that they:

- Do not define Indian-Christian in terms of opposition or contradistinction to other communities;
- Do not make a hasty dash for Bible verses;
- Do not oversimplify the task;
- Do not oppose or play off 'Indian' and 'Christian'.

There is an appreciation of the complexity of the task, of the need for communal conversation and of the provisionality of attempts to answer.

What fascinates me, as a theologian, is how Christian identity stems from who *our* God is. What can be said of Indian Christian identity should not be able to be equally said of *any* community. Even to claim Christian identity as 'a divine gift' is unclear in the South Asian context. As it turns out, it is crucial to clarify *who* is the giver of this 'divine gift'. It is the Christian God.

Some quick reflections mainly based on the book of Galatians demonstrate the point. Christian identity is both the gift and the demand of the Christian God. Moreover, that identity is provisional because it 'not yet clear what we shall be' (1 John 3.2).

Christian Identity is a *Gift* of God the Father—Through Jesus Christ and by the Spirit

The identity of the Triune God is important for Christian identity. Paul, in Galatians, insists there was no human source of his gospel (1.11). What turned Paul from his non-Christian past was, he says, the fact that 'God chose me and called me . . . and revealed his Son to me' (1.15). Christian identity does not consist in birth (2.15), nor in keeping the law (2.17). It is defined by faith in Jesus Christ (2.16) whom God the Father sent. Christ died, that is the *objective* basis of Christian identity. Paul declares that his old self has died, it has been crucified with Christ and now union with Christ is the determining factor in his new existence (2.20). Christian identity is enjoyed and appropriated by the Holy Spirit whom God the Father gives (3.5). It has its *subjective* basis in experience by the Spirit (3.3, 5.5, 25). We are those who are 'living by the Spirit [and who] follow the Spirit's leading in every part of our lives'.

This gift demonstrates the *dignity* of Christian identity. It is not a dignity that belongs inherently to us, but to God the giver. Because the liberality of this gift–this grace–is undeserved, Christian identity is evidenced supremely by *loyalty* to Jesus Christ. We give ourselves to him who was given for us; we love him who first loved us.

How this Christian identity is also distinctively Indian needs to be unfolded, but it begins from the dignity that Indians have of equally being God's creation and of equally having the opportunity of being God's redeemed people *in this particular context*. It means representing Christ our maharaja and guru. *Indian-ness* finds its true meaning in relation to Jesus Christ (Eph. 1.10) and will always exist as his particular delight (Rev. 7.9).

Christian Identity is also the *Demand* of God—Living Like Christ by the Spirit.

Christian identity is what God expects of Christians. Paul talks about 'so-called Christians' (Gal. 2.4) who claim to be Christians but are not really. He also speaks of Christians who behave badly, acting 'according to the flesh' (5.19ff.). Christians are identifiable, he implies, by their ethical behaviour and by the character qualities of the fruit of the Spirit (5.22f.). 'Those who belong to Christ have nailed the passions and desires of their sinful nature to his cross' (5.24). This demand demonstrates the challenge of Christian identity. It is evidenced by ethical behaviour. We must *live up to* our identity. We *must* live 'by the Spirit'.

Again how this Christian identity can be distinctively Indian also needs clarification, but it begins with living Christianly as an Indian *in this particular context*. It involves fulfilling 'the cultural charge', being fruitful, celebrating God's creation, discovering and using God's laws in nature and looking after what God has entrusted in this particular context. It means serving and obeying Christ our maharaja and guru. It means living holy and obedient lives as an Indian community of Spirit-filled Christ-followers, and as such, serving the peoples and nation of India.

Christian Identity is *Provisional*—Because it is Eschatological.

Christian identity awaits its final clarification when God's goal in history is achieved. Paul talks of the process of transformation (6.15). Those who live by the cross of Christ 'are the new people of God' (6.16). It is the cross of Christ that is at the heart of our identity, not our confidence in ethnic identity. 'Circumcision' and 'uncircumcision' do not count as much as the transformation brought about by Christ's cross. The ethnic identity marker 'Israel' is here used as a metaphor to undermine ethnic supremacy—'we are the Israel of God'. No ethnic identity is superior. All find their proper place before God. Our ethnicities are brought into harmonious relation in God's new humanity.

Indian Christian identity is evidenced as we work with God towards his new creation as Indians, in India and for India; at least for the India which will be found in the multitudes gathered before the throne of God (Rev 7.9). This is where history is heading. This is no violent hegemony of one culture's metanarrative, no new colonialism; for the One who is seated on the throne is the Lamb.

Christian identity, Paul reminds us, centres on the cross of Christ. The cross of Christ clarifies our identity in terms of loyalty, ethics and our view of history. Indian Christian identity is no foreign import; it is the response of *Indians* to the One who *made* them, *calls* them and *awaits* them. What it means to be Christian and Indian will emerge as Indian Christians engage with *that* gift, *that* calling and *that* hope, all the while dialoguing with all Indians, interacting with all the disciplines of knowledge and living by faith *in the particular context of India*.

Read on. These sixteen essays will contribute to answering *for you for today for this particular context* the questions posed by the title 'Indian and Christian: Changing Identities in Modern India'. And in doing so they will point the way to what it means to be human. Or at least make you look forward to next year's SAIACS annual consultation!

Ian W. Payne
Principal, SAIACS

Introduction

SAIACS stands for excellence in academics, ministry and missions. One way to promote and achieve this is through a consultation of top-notch thinkers, and so the idea for a SAIACS Annual Consultation was born. The overall purpose of the consultation is to stimulate, encourage and provide directions for academic, evangelical and missional thinking in South Asia. The specific objectives are:

- to provide a platform for addressing critical, pertinent issues that the Church faces in the changing context of South Asia;
- to promote and advance evangelical scholarship, and provide the Church in South Asia with resources, by producing a book from the presented papers.

The SAIACS Annual Consultation strives to be unique by aiming for excellence, holding together theory and practice within an evangelical framework, and being relevant for the Church in South Asia.

The first SAIACS Annual Consultation took place during 9–12 November 2010 at SAIACS in Bangalore, and had as its theme '**Indian and Christian: Changing Identities in Modern India**'. The consultation was co-sponsored by the Institute for Religion and Society in Asia (IRSA), based in Oxford, UK. Each session in the consultation consisted of an academic paper presented by a specialist in the relevant field (whether academician or practitioner), followed by a response and an open discussion. The specific outcome of the consultation is the present book, co-published by SAIACS Press and Oxford House (a global expansion of IRSA).

The book starts with the **keynote address** given at the consultation by the Very Reverend Dr Christopher Hancock, Director of Oxford House (previously of IRSA). He explores how 21st century Christians in India reconcile the tension between the acts and givens of their history, and the problems and opportunities of their identity. Subsequently, the book covers four areas:

- **Biblical Studies**: three essays (H. Dharamraj & A. Rotokha, S. Samuel, C. Bennema);
- **Theology and Philosophy**: five essays (K. Kevichusa, P. Joshua Bhakiaraj, B. Prince, M. Amaladoss, N. Ajay Kumar);

- **Religion and Culture**: four essays (J.A. Kumar, A. Gangatharan, R. Jayakumar, S. Oliver-Dee);
- **Pastoral Theology and Psychology**: three essays (I. Joshua, R. David, S.K. Kiran Kumar).

These essays attempt in their own ways to attend to the already complex issue of identity, which is made even more complex by the perspectives that religion and national affiliation bring to the discussion. The first section draws from and reflects on the Bible as it relates to identity construction. The essays in it affirm together that the attempts of our forebears and the patterns they established are indeed rich resources that could assist us in the contemporary project of identity construction. Havilah Dharamraj and Angukali Rotokha correlate the role the Chronicler played in the writing of Jewish history with the controversial altering of history books that was promoted by the NDA collation government at the centre. Similarly Simon Samuel looks to the apostle Paul and his attempts at identity construction as a model for the contemporary project. Cornelis Bennema sees in the life and practices of the early Church a model for identity formation today.

The section on Theology & Philosophy contains papers that deal with both theological/theoretical issues as well as historical/practical ones, illustrating that the particular context we inhabit is necessarily an important conversation partner. It affirms that our theology of and for identity construction is not a matter of providing ready-made answers that have been sealed for all time. Rather it is a matter of developing a conversation with the teaching of the scriptures, our spiritual traditions, our particular histories and our contemporary situations, as complex as they may be. The complex and multiple practical issues that we face therefore can be engaged with and evaluated employing these resources. From his Naga context, Aniu Kevichusa analyses what would be the best word to use so as to connect the two terms 'Indian', 'Christian'. Paul Bhakiaraj identifies that the larger macro-narrative of the scriptures represents the theological foundations for the project of identity construction for Indian Christians, yet a foundation that encourages the building of identity with Indian materials. Analysing conflicts in India, Brainerd Prince employs Ricoeur's work as a resource within the conflicts of our times. Michael Amaladoss notices how particular examples of a unique inter-religious engagement can be found as some people create identity straddling two religious traditions. Nigel Kumar casts his eye over history and observes that in the declining of the communal award Christians were really seeking to integrate within the mainstream and serve the nation as responsible citizens. In this section the papers suggest that theology is a dynamic and rich undertaking that can and ought to contribute to the church's contemporary life and perhaps more importantly even to the building of the nation, as it fits and equips the Christian community to honour and serve the nation and its people.

The people of the nation, men, women and children, with their differing religious affiliations and socio-cultural preferences have surely benefitted in the past from Christian presence in the nation, and indeed can continue to do so in the days ahead. By the same token the Christian community can benefit from studying how these communities have attempted to create an identity. This is the contribution that the essays in the Religion & Culture section make. Arun Kumar analyses the contentious issue of conversion and affirms that in a democratic and secular nation this prerogative should be open for all. A. Gangatharan analyses the relationship of caste and mission as the background to his study of indigenous churches which he interprets as an attempt to create a liberative identity in Christ that affirms the dignity of the individual who is ostracised by the caste system. R. Jayakumar observes the ambiguous role women are granted in society and challenges the church to serve them in the spirit of Christ. Sean Oliver-Dee seeks to study Muslim engagement with such issues as a valuable part of any study of identity and change, for it could teach us valuable lessons in a democratic polity.

The final section offers us an instructive study on the need for sensitive analysis of practices that we find on the ground. These practices occur within the Christian fold, in between Christian and Hindu/Muslim/..... traditions, and within the Hindu fold. I. Joshua alerts us to the dilemmas that some people face as they yield to Christ's person and message and desire to maintain allegiance to their family. After studying aspects of the background to the current debate, Ravi David suggests that Christians maintain both a constructive and critical stance in their process of identity construction. Kiran Kumar offers a valuable analysis of identity from the perspective of *Sanātanadharma,* which he then correlates to the perspective of transpersonal psychology, affirming the need for and benefit of a comparative perspective. This essay rounds of a section that brings fresh light from various sources to the complex subject of identity.

These essays are clearly not homogeneous in their views. In fact some hold diametrically opposite views. For example, while C. Bennema's essay eventually denies the possibility of dual religious identities, M. Amaladoss and J. Iyadurai uphold that concept. They suggest that it is not only possible but also acceptable to be a Christian and Muslim or Hindu at the same time. This book intentionally does not seek to resolve such issues but intends to inform the reader about the complexity and breadth of the debate. We then leave it to the reader to make up her or his mind. In line with what SAIACS stands for, participants are normally evangelical in a broad sense but are not limited to a particular denomination, academic affiliation or country. Sometimes, however, an even broader participation, as is the case here, may be beneficial even necessary to sharpen the thinking, stimulate wider dialogue and gain broader acceptance. While SAIACS does not necessarily endorse all views represented in this volume, it desires to promote dialogue and mature conversations across disciplines and religious traditions.

Overall this volume affirms and represents such a pursuit. Through the discussions that were conducted in a cordial and academic atmosphere and the resultant book, we seek to promote the health of the Christian community, engage with those from other religious traditions and together serve the nation by affirming and promoting its secular and democratic credentials. We thereby assert that religion can and should contribute to civil society and from that platform work to the building of an inclusive society and nation, thus also affirming its constitution and its place in the international community. It is with such a desire that the consultation was held and this book is published. We present it to you with the trust and prayer that it achieves those goals.

We would like to express our thanks to several people and organisations that have contributed significantly to the completion of this book. We are grateful to SAIACS and the Board of Trustees for their enthusiastic support of this initiative. We thank the staff of the SAIACS CEO Centre for successfully hosting the consultation. We are especially grateful to Dr Chris Hancock, Director of Oxford House and previously of IRSA (UK) and the Slavanka Trust (UK) for largely funding the consultation. We thank Mrs Selena George, Mrs Susan Bennema and Mrs Mary Varughese for their able editorial work, Mr Nigel Kumar for the cover design, Mr George Korah for the layout, and Mrs Shilpa Waghmare, the SAIACS Press manager, for effectively coordinating the production of the book. We must also thank a donor who wishes to remain anonymous and generously provided a large donation towards the production of this book. Above all, we thank God for his help and hope that he can use this book to further his work in this world.

The Editors

The Burden of History and the Gift of Identity: Reflections on Christianity in India

Christopher Hancock*

1. Introduction

I count it an immense privilege both to take part in, and, as Director of the Institute for Religion and Society in Asia (based in Oxford, England) to co-sponsor this historic gathering. We should all be immensely grateful to the Slavanka Trust in the UK whose generosity has helped to make our meeting possible.

I see this event as providing the best kind of opportunity for mature, academic dialogue between scholars around *sensitive issues* that relate to the past, present and future character of the Christian community in India. It also provides an invaluable chance to explore together *vital questions* about the coherence of Indian national identity, in a society and world of many faiths and conflicting ideological interpretations of our shared global reality. I am delighted we have friends here from inside and outside the Christian community in India to help us think together critically and creatively on these immensely important subjects.

The theme of this paper—and, indeed, I believe, of the whole Consultation—is this, *How do 21st century Christians in India reconcile the tension between the acts and givens of their history and the problems and opportunities of their identity.* It is a great topic and one that will, I hope, shape and challenge our conversations over the next few days and in the years ahead.

2. Initial Observations

Let us be clear about a number of things at the outset: unless we are, much that follows in our meeting will be misleading or misdirected.

* The Very Revd Dr Christopher Hancock is Director of Oxford House, an international affairs think tank, focusing on politics, religion and global affairs, based in Oxford, London, and Washington DC. Oxford House is a recent, global expansion of Dr Hancock's previous work as Director of the Institute for Religion and Society in Asia.

First, *not all history is burdensome*. Many of us have a sense of pride in our ancestry, however humble or obscure. Not all of us can name sixteen generations of forebears, as one of my dear Ghanaian friends did one day when I asked him a naïve question about his knowledge of his ancestors! My roots on my father's side are deeply Welsh, going back many centuries. On my mother's side, we name the poet Lord Byron among our relations, with the De Burun family present in the Norman Conquest of Britain (of which the poet was unnaturally proud, I should add!). Mine is, like many families built on a mixed history — and not all of it is burdensome.

I say this at the outset because I know how easy it is for the Indian Christian community (in all its tribes and traditions) to feel tainted and tarnished by internal conflict and the confusions of political and religious ideology; when, in fact, of course, there is an immense amount to be proud of in their history. I wish Indian brethren could be a little more like their Chinese Christian counterparts (that I study and know well), who are awakening to a new sense of appreciation for their unique history and commendable communal identity — and, as a consequence, are growing in public confidence and private self-respect.

Secondly, *not all identity is a gift*. My years growing up in a medical home, and later as a pastor, have made me acutely aware of the pervasive problem of *self-loathing*. Indeed, it is clear that individual and communal identities can be the source of immense pain, disappointment, psychological trauma, and self-loathing. It is not uncommon for an incident, story, rumour, or physical flaw to ruin a person's whole life; for on top of that issue they grow the horns of hatred and the brittleness of bitterness. I think of a dear Indian friend whose world-view is the product of his suffering and exile in the 1970s purges. How very sad.

I say this by way of introducing my overarching hope for this paper and for the symposium as a whole; namely, *to develop a mature and balanced understanding of Indian-Christian history and identity*. That is, one that faces the present situation of Christians in India, in light of an honest, open attitude towards the Christian community's past; in order that it can build on that a new clarity, and confident communal narrative for the future.

3. Indian-Christian History: On Developing Self-Confidence and Self-Awareness

In this section I want to explore some of the problems and possibilities of researching, writing and re-appropriating Indian-Christian history. First, a word about some *hindrances* to this.

3.1. Hindrances

What *hindrances* exist in developing a mature and balanced attitude towards Indian-Christian history? I suggest four, not all of which are unique to India.

We have touched on the first hindrance already, viz. *the assumption of a burdensome past*. If we are not careful, the pervasive cultural assumption shaping Indian historiography—including Christian historiography—is that Indians are habitually 'victims' and their country and culture that of the 'victimised'. This is both tragic and wrong. The four thousand year history of India's development as a nation—especially since the end of British rule—is one of extraordinary richness, complexity, variety and beauty. Not all good or worthy, no; but no less flawed than any other nation—and I say that from the perspective of post-imperial, post-Christian Britain! But, as a reasonably knowledgeable outsider, and friend of many Indians, I am constantly surprised by India's strangely insecure, vulnerable attitude to its past, which generates at times an unnecessary defensiveness or over-protectiveness to all things Indian. Why so?

The second hindrance is, I believe, *the barrier of post-colonialism*. Again, if we are not careful a compulsive tendency towards 'victimisation' (something Muslim scholars in the UK identified within the Pakistani communities I worked with in Bradford in my previous job) reinforces, and is itself reinforced by post-colonial ideology. Though increasingly passé in the social sciences in the West, I recognise this ideology continues to be a significant driver in Indian intellectual circles. The reason for its persistence here is plain to see: it feeds off the deeper cultural inclination towards 'victim-hood' and the national predisposition to handle questions of community and identity in only superficially confident ways.

The third hindrance I would name is *the compulsion to praise or blame*, which is spawned by a culture of victimisation and the persistence of post-colonial ideology. We enter here the psychologists' professional domain, and I risk straying as an amateur onto the complex scientific fields of psychology and psycho-therapy. That said, I would argue that it is all too clear that the development of 'a mature and balanced attitude to Indian-Christian history', is necessarily compromised by psychological 'compulsions' to attribute praise or blame to individuals, events, institutions and new ideas; especially when those 'compulsions' (reactions) are not submitted to careful, critical analysis and robust, academic cross-examination. We know the risks and temptations of working off 'impression' or 'hearsay', 'rumour' or 'prejudice', rather than engaging in the solid, responsible activities (albeit sometimes counter-cultural) of research and dialogue, debate and balanced reporting.

Fourthly, I would see *the difficulty of finding or refining data* as the historical corollary of the hindrances above: for, in addition to these 'hindrances', the historiography of Christianity in India is complexified by the difficulties surrounding access to accurate data. As I know from studying Christianity in China, the range of possible sources and resources available to scholars (including the rich mine of missionary archives inside and outside the country) is immense—and, for that reason, problematic. Put simply, who can, or should, the historian trust to provide the right kind of perspective? Who provides what information, and to what ends can, or should that material be put? Missionary sources have value (as often a primary, written corpus of cultural commentary and description); local sources have value (as correctives to cultural distortions and grass-roots commentaries)—but neither are consistent, unbiased, coherent or comprehensive. The task of finding, and refining data, is essential to the quality of the historiography of communities in India (generally), and to Christian-Indian history (too). And yet the historian's task is, as my dear friend Professor Tao Feiya, of Shanghai University, puts it, simply *'to set the record straight'*. To those in the West who imperialistically claim Christianity should not be in China, I adduce the balance, energy, vision and directness of Tao Feiya's approach to local, Chinese Christian historiography. His is, surely, a model for India. To those who question the story, or doubt the evidence of Christianity in India, I would say, 'Study the material, set the record straight.'

3.2. Historiography

The second issue I want to comment on is that of historiography. For, before we go too far, we should remind ourselves of the character of historiography. Writing the history of Christianity in India is made even more difficult when we are unclear, or disagree, on what we are trying to do, and how, therefore, we should do it. Consider some of the ways historiography is understood, and the implications flowing from these different perceptions of the historian's work.

To some, *the narrating of history is an art*. It is a matter of telling a story, the story of a place, person, event, crisis, process, or community. Part of the power and beauty of history is that it tells this story and enables the reader to see and feel for themselves the events described. This can be an immensely attractive, creative and powerful historical form. But we need to be clear, narrative history — popularised in historical fiction and Christian biography — is subject to the twin temptations of manipulating the evidence (to make a good story) and/ or manipulating the reader (to make them believe what they read). That said: local oral histories and inherited community 'myths' are a rich resource for the historian, and narrative history often attracts a larger audience and thence distributes data and perception (for good and ill) more effectively.

To others, *the writing of history is a science*. It is about handling evidence and presenting facts, just as a scientist would write up an experiment, or a lawyer martial evidence for her case. Having taken a first undergraduate degree in modern history from Oxford in the early 1970s, I know that *the science of history* has, however, changed dramatically in recent years. It has moved away from the grand, meta-narrative, or even the more restricted narrative sweep, to the detailed, analytic work of economics and demographics, family structures and feudal ties. As a consequence, historiography in the dusty world of the Western academy is now rarely the stuff of the artist and interpreter: it is more the domain of the scientific historical sociologist and the committed examiner of cultural and political minutiae. Not surprisingly, this approach disturbs Christian writers predisposed towards hagiography and secular historians favouring post-colonial ideology. To neither of these two groups is the objective criticism and impartial representation of data found in scientific historiography entirely welcome.

To others, thirdly, *the shaping of history is a political prerogative, or a social responsibility*. In both cases, it is a benign or noxious, exercise of power. Nowhere is this use of historiography more evident than in China, where history has for 5000 years been the tool of the ruling elite and historiography, to a greater or lesser extent, the servant, or stooge, of the state. The reasons for this are obvious. When an imperial, or totalitarian regime writes history, it has power to rewrite the past and justify the present. It positions itself to receive praise and resist blame from both the past and the present. Historiography is a prerogative the state is slow to surrender. But, as China slowly comes to terms historically and politically with the Communist-Maoist era (from 1949–1979), it has to balance its (political) desire to nuance the mistakes it sees and admits in the past with the (psychological and social) reality of popular resentment and populist perceptions. It has to manage the evidence to ensure political integrity and social stability are both procured. But historiography is, in reality, always to some extent power-laden: when it tells *my* story in *my* way, I exercise control. If I control the news, I control perception. So the issue is not really, *does history exercise power?* But, *whose historiography is trusted, and which writer/s, or sources are entrusted with that power?* Seen in this light, the responsible historian will always be more concerned to speak truth with integrity and report evidence accurately than to succumb to political pressure or perpetuate falsehood and prejudice.

Finally, to some, *the teaching of history is a duty*. It is a time-honoured method of defining and preserving identity and of refining and communicating culture. We might even argue that one of historiography's most significant roles is to preserve culture and define, or enliven identity. In short, we are who we are, because we know our forebears—for good and ill!

So, the rhetorical challenge I lay before those of you who are engaged in different ways, and from different perspectives, in understanding and interpreting Indian-Christian history is this, Will Indian-Christian scholars tell new stories (change), write good history (research), act responsibly (lead), and communicate effectively (transform)?

3.3. Virtuous History

I want to end this part of my paper by issuing a plea for 'Virtuous History'.

There are a number of issues to be addressed here. First, as we have begun to see, *history is never value-neutral*. Indeed, we might argue, this should be more often and openly recognised, for then the power of history, for good and ill, will be the more clearly seen.

Likewise, I would maintain, *historiography is a moral venture*: that is, in the work it does or does not do, it should not presume, or claim, to be morally blind. The historian has to take a view on things. Like any other person, he or she is a moral being with a moral conscience and a set of moral obligations. When we set out on a historical journey, we see things to praise and blame, to commend and censure. That is life. To suggest otherwise, is to imply or project a moral blindness in the historian which is unworthy of any observer of human behaviour. This does not mean all history will be moralist (written in order to make a moral point): it does mean history will be morally alert because life is morally potent. The historian will encounter things that offend neutrality and challenge moral impartiality. Genocide and prejudice, injustice and barbarity are morally offensive; to suggest otherwise renders the claim to write good history meaningless or offensive.

But we may go further, and should understand, thirdly, that in a particular way, *Christian history makes judgements*. It has *moral sight* and articulates *moral insights*. This is not to claim anything new or especially distinctive. As we have already seen, history, because undertaken by moral subjects, makes moral judgements. On this basis, *Christian historians should not deny to themselves what other historians permit themselves, viz. the making of moral judgements.* Indeed, Christians—like other religious interpreters—might justly claim more acute moral sight than those who repudiate religion and commend an amoral world-view. The Christian historian is not technically superior to a historian who rejects, or discounts religion, no: he or she is, or should be, more adept at moral discourse and more habituated, through conviction and experience to making moral assessments. This is not to deny to non-believers moral consciousness, far from it; it is to challenge the believer to own a moral identity professional peers may wilfully deny to them.

Lastly, *Christian history passes moral judgements and submits to moral scrutiny*. If Christian historiography argues that life's moral potency requires it be ready to pass judgement and express praise and blame on individuals and institutions, it also renders *itself* accountable to moral judgement. Not all it does is accurate, and not all it reports is worthy. This is surely self-evident. So, too, is the fact that Christian history's moral duty — shared at times by people of good will in other faith traditions — is an inalienable responsibility. Christian historiography has a high and holy calling to demonstrate Christian veracity and Christ-like humility in the way it treats the evidence and assesses facts.

Before leaving this discussion of 'virtuous history', two important qualifications to what I have said above. First, *history is always an incomplete and imperfect science*. At no point can we say, as historians in the late nineteenth century sometimes argued, 'We've done it! We've discovered all there is to know about the past.' The historian, like the believer, 'sees through a glass darkly': knowledge is partial, perception distorted. Secondly, *Indian-Christian history cannot change the past: but it can re-write it*. My point is simply this: in light of the multiple hindrances we have seen, the historiographical variants we have acknowledged, and the obligations we have noted with regard to writing 'virtuous history', we should understand ourselves to be re-empowered for confident, but humble, engagement with the delicate, but vital task, of re-writing Indian-Christian history — and to do this before others, with less personal investment in the project, undertake that historiography for us, and project onto the story 'truths' we deny!

4. Indian-Christian Identity: On Developing a Mature and Balanced Attitude

The theme of this Consultation reflects in part the contemporary national discussion of 'Indian identity'. I am acutely aware of how inappropriate it is for me, as an outsider, to say much, if anything, on such an immensely important and complex subject. However, the concern of this specific gathering — and one in which I am personally invested as a regular visitor/teacher here — is, as indicated at the outset, to develop a mature and balanced attitude to Indian-Christian identity, as a sub-set of the larger national conversation. On this, I have a little more entitlement to speak: for discussion of Indian-Christian identity, or identities, is part of a global conversation about Christian identity or identities in a rapidly changing world. You are part of something bigger: your issues are part of a global discussion.

Let me begin, then, by setting the Indian question in a larger context. First, some general observations on 'identity':

1. Identity is neither self-generating, nor self-sustaining: it is, we might say, *learned and loaned, given and received, projected and perceived*. If I am left to define myself, or insist that my identity is something over which I alone have control, I risk delusion or myopia. Identity is never satisfactorily, nor consistently, *self*-generated. We are products of other peoples' opinions and perceptions, prejudices, and preferences. The elephant may think he can dance, but woe-betide the ant at his feet!

2. Identity is both *fixed and fluid in 'form' and 'content'*. As is often pointed out, we are best understood as both human 'beings' *and* human 'becomings'. The word 'identity' is in reality a *misnoma*. We are all product of our own and other peoples' evolving identities. Postmodernism did not create the fragmentation of human identity: it named it and then proceeded to laud it. Talk of multiple, or fluid, identities is as true of a community as it is of an individual. Indeed, in social commentary, as much as in psychotherapy, the real issue is not about defining an 'identity' as recognising and reporting its fragmentation, inevitable growth and transformation.

3. Identity has *one and many faces*. We have 'one' and 'many' identities in a complex world. The problem of identity becomes more acute when set in the larger matrix of global cultural transformation and local, social evolution. At any given point in time, all of us inhabit (consciously and unconsciously) different worlds of identity. Think of the young village boy who does well at school, goes to college in Bangalore and joins a hi-tech international corporation. How many worlds does he inhabit? How does he manage his multiple identities? And, crucially—something my colleague Dr Mayjee Philip and I reflect on often—how does his inherited religious identity manage the transition to a new, urban world of meaning and value?

In this light, to speak of Indian-Christian identity is necessarily to engage with a complex, dynamic phenomenon to which the observations of the sociologist and historian are as relevant as those of the theologian and psycho-analyst. To suggest otherwise, is to deny our own complexity or to project simplicity artificially.

We may go further and posit *six particular points* about Indian-Christian identity.

First, *it is inherently complex*, because it is multiply sourced. Though 'identity' *per se* is complex, the argument could be made (as I have just illustrated) that Indian-Christian identity is unusually (though *not* exceptionally!) complex. The confluence of historical traditions, ethnic diversity, regional variants, denominational distinctions, language differences, and multiple spiritual dimensions, involved in identifying Indian Christianities, render the definition of 'Indian-Christian identity' virtually impossible; or, at least, we need to be intensely circumspect, or suspicious, if we encounter claims for *an* Indian-Christian identity.

Secondly, *it is essentially unique*; and, as such, it is both a treasure and a trust. The corollary to recognition of the rich, cultural bio-diversity of Indian-Christianity is its precious uniqueness; like a finely balanced tropical rain forest, or endangered Amazonian butterfly, Indian Christianity can lay claim to distinctives not found elsewhere that warrant eco-theological and social protection. Mapping the DNA and cultural heritage of this ethnically and religiously diverse community, at this time of immense, globalised change in India is, surely, one of the most pressing obligations on scholars attentive to such things.

Thirdly, *it is corporately owned*. Let us be clear. Indian Christianity should not allow itself to be co-opted or coerced from within, or from without. A treasure to all inside and outside India, it belongs to none, be they Western tele-evangelist or Dalit insurgent, denominational leader or local pastor. Part of the character, and tragedy, of Indian Christianity, is that it has not managed well its cultural bio-diversity. It has been as inwardly self-destructive (through conflict and rivalry) as it has been outwardly manipulated (by alien theologies and ideologies). Mapping the multiple identities of Indian Christianity might be an early — indeed, an essential — step, on the road to better ecumenical self-understanding, and thence to greater self-confidence; through both of which the corporate character and strength of Indian Christianity can be safe-guarded.

Fourthly, *it is, like every form of Christianity, negotiably defined*. Those who claim they possess what it is to be Christian do themselves and others a disservice: we see 'through a glass darkly'. In the process of identifying Indian-Christian identity/ies, it is clear there needs to be a greater willingness for that identity — like every form of personal and Christian identity — to be amicably negotiated and corporately constructed. Dye-hard partisans, or compulsive power-brokers, will find the exercise painful: they may need to be skilfully wooed by the grander prize of a coherent Christian voice speaking into the debate about India's national identity. For we are not only accountable to ourselves as Christians, we are accountable to the world as Christ's ambassadors. Our cacophonous voice and conflicted personality does us and him no service.

Fifthly, *it is continually developing*. There is a 'provisional' nature to every instantiation of the church. We are, as the French would say, members of *l'église provisoire*, the provisional church *en route* to fulfilment and perfection in heaven. As such, every enculturated form of the church is a provisional reality. We should claim no more. The task of becoming Church, like the task of becoming human, will never end this side of heaven. In theological terms, Indian-Christian identity shares the journey made by every form of Christianity around the world towards the perfected identity and full communion of all God's saints in his heavenly kingdom.

Lastly, *it is ultimately a divine gift*. Like all of life, Indian-Christian identity is a gift of divine grace: it comes as a responsibility and a duty to discharge, imbued with a power for good and ill. We should, in reality, never see identity as something *we own* or determine: it is given to us as we recognise the gift, and more readily receive it. Indian-Christian identity is ultimately no more and no less than the embodiment of the culturo-spiritual (and presently imperfect) characteristics that God has given, and is giving, Indian-Christian communities, as their contribution to the glorious diversity of the children of God. As a divine gift, and cultural discharge from God, Indian Christianity has within itself the seeds of good that human effort alone will never be able to match: herein lies its essential power. It is the recognition of God's active presence in this set of Christian communities and identities that can, and will, add untold richness to India's broader discussion of its identity, and national development in the future.

5. Conclusion

At the outset, I said that the theme of this paper, and indeed of the whole symposium is, *how 21ˢᵗ century Christians in India reconcile the tension between the acts and givens of their history and the problems and opportunities of their identity.* Our aim being: *to develop a mature and balanced understanding of Indian-Christian history and identity.* This symposium is, then, simply the beginning of a process; or better, perhaps, the beginning of the end of the time when Indian-Christianity is unclear about its identity and vocation, and clearer about its history, gifts and distinctiveness. The task ahead is both important and immense. There will be an on-going need for scholars to enter into a vocation to speak into, and out of, the life of the church and society. Their ultimate goal, and ours, being to promote better mutual understanding among Christians and others in India, and to advance the 'common good' of all in this great land that stands on the brink of a remarkable new global profile.

BIBLICAL STUDIES

History, History Books and the Blue Jackal

Havilah Dharamraj and Angukali V. Rotokha*

The *Panchatantra* tells the story of Chandarava the jackal. In his search for food he strayed into the city. Beset by dogs, he fled into a dyer's courtyard and hastily leaped into a vat of indigo dye. Since his new *avatar* defied identification as any known beast, the blue jackal was elevated to kingship over the animals of the forest. He proclaimed himself to be Kukudruma, the heaven-sent. One day, the howling of a pack of passing jackals fell on his indigo ears. Instinctively, he raised his head and howled a response. His cloak of anonymity fell, and so did he. Without pressing the parallels too far, it can be suggested that the Indian Christian is, metaphorically speaking, a blue jackal, in that he is unsure who he is—Chandarava or Kukudruma, or both. What voices from his past does he need to hear to help him recognize himself?

This paper proposes that (especially) in times of crisis, group identity can be mobilized[1] by appeal to that group's history as mediated to it through its popular history books. We first establish this through the use of the Chronicler's history by the Jewish community of the Second Temple Period as the basis of identity negotiation with their specific historical context. We then test the theory, *mutatis mutandis*, on the two communal groups that have, over various periods, had political control over the sub-continent—the Hindu and the Muslim—to see if this is indeed so, and draw from this an answer to whether history-writing is a part of fixing of the Indian Christian group identity.

The socio-psychological phenomenon of 'cultural identity' may be defined as 'a group's basic way of organizing experience through its myths, memories, symbols, rituals and ideals'.[2] We will use it, as psychoanalyst and cultural commentator Sudhir Kakar does, as inclusive of language, ethnicity and religion,[3] since as such, it is a

---

* Havilah Dharamraj is professor of Old Testament and Head of Department at SAIACS. Angukali V. Rotokha (MTh, SAIACS) is lecturer in Old Testament at Oriental Theological Seminary, Dimapur.

[1] A term preferentially used by Sudhir Kakar, *The Colours of Violence* (New Delhi: Penguin, 1995). The paper implicitly clarifies its use.

[2] Kakar, *The Colours of Violence*, 184.

[3] Kakar, *The Colours of Violence*, 192.

convenient catch-all term. In everyday existence the individual is largely indifferent to cultural identity. This indifference is breached under situations of external crisis such as persecution, war or riots; or, under internal crisis as in the identity-seeking phase of life, usually adolescence. This moves the individual to seek safety in groups that have sufficient stores of 'myth, memories, symbols, rituals and ideals' — commodities that can best be located in 'primordial' identities such as 'Hindu' and 'Muslim'.[4] While, primordial identities may also be created on the basis of say, tribal affiliation, we can agree that the dominant phenomenon is religion-oriented. At points of crises, the individual becomes particularly vulnerable to what Amartya Sen describes as 'the imposition of singular and belligerent identities . . . championed by proficient artisans of terror',[5] examples of whom we shall see.

Our particular interest lies in that organizing factor of cultural identity that Kakar calls 'memories'. Visions of the past are crucial to the way any community perceives itself and constructs its identity vis-à-vis the 'others'. Such visions are preserved and/or presented in the national historiographies which, although seemingly unchanging, are often reflections of the existing dominant ideology. As Jon Dorschner and Thomas Sherlock state, formation of national identities depends on narrations — the telling and retelling of the past — that are conceived to be true and invest in the group a sense of 'meaning, direction and cohesion'. Over time, these seemingly timeless narrations come to be either displaced or reinterpreted to reflect the current political ideology and the elites who construct the dominant ideology, thus gradually shaping our understanding of the self and the 'other'.[6]

Before we consider the role of popular history books in India, let us demonstrate a case of group identity directed by a history book — the Book of Chronicles and the Jewish community of the Second Temple Period (STP).

---

[4] Kakar, *The Colours of Violence*, 185–95.

[5] Amartya Sen, *Identity and Violence: The Illusion of Destiny* (London: Allen Lane, 2006), 2.

[6] Jon Dorschner and Thomas Sherlock, 'The Role of History textbooks in Shaping Collective Identities in India and Pakistan', in Elizabeth A. Cole (ed.), *Teaching the Violent Past: History Education and Reconciliation* (Maryland: Rowman and Littlefield, 2007), 276.

1. The Chronicler's History and the Formation of Cultural Identity

Postulating the fourth century BCE as the date of Chronicles,[7] the context of the Chronicler would be Israel under the Second Commonwealth. By this time, Israel had undergone significant changes, including the schism and two major national tragedies—exile of both the northern and southern kingdoms—marking the end of old Israel as a political entity. The return of the exiles under Cyrus in 538 BCE resulted in further hardship and frustrations—both physical and spiritual—for repatriates and residents alike.[8] There were fundamental questions regarding continuity/discontinuity with the past. In monarchical Israel, self-understanding was more political, vis-à-vis the Davidic dynasty. This self-conception was however severely challenged by the Babylonian conquest and exile which deprived them of such a geo-political-based identity. Further, in the restoration under Cyrus, they faced an even greater dilemma—the restoration was affected not by a Davidide as expected, but by a pagan king under whose dominion they continued. Thus the reality of the Jewish post-exilic community called for a reformulation of the basis of their cultural/national identity.

The Chronicler's representation of the monarchial history is an attempt to meet this need by presenting an identity based not on the geo-political statehood contingent on the Davidic dynasty, but rather on the temple and its cultus, an institution stretching beyond David to Moses, the nation-founder himself. According to the Chronicler, what defined Israelite identity was not the Davidic dynasty but her faith. The Chronicler communicates this by a twofold emphasis in his rewrite of Israel's history.

First, the Chronicler's portrayal of the Judahite kings is driven by his cult-retribution ideology. Retribution ideology can be summarized as the belief in the existence of a moral order whereby there is exact correspondence between one's conduct and one's destiny. Further, for

---

[7] Scanty internal and external evidence makes the precise dating of Chronicles difficult. However, modern scholarship's consensus view tilts towards assigning the composition of the book within the 4th century BCE.

[8] J.A. Thompson, *1, 2 Chronicles*, NAC 9 (Nashville: Boardman and Holman, 1994), 31–3.

the Chronicler, the paradigm for the outworking of retribution in the Judah's history is provided by the cultus. So significant is the cultus for the Chronicler that the Judahite kings are approved or rejected on the basis of his cultic fidelity or infidelity, with the dynasty promise itself being conditional to cultic faithfulness.[9] Thus the Chronistic representation of the Judahite history displays a deliberate interweaving of the cult and retribution ideologies. This can be illustrated by taking as an example the Chronicler's account of king Asa (2 Chron. 14–16) as distinct from the Deuteronomistic History's (DtrH) account (1 Kgs. 15.9–24). In 1 Kings, Asa is commended with the conventional Deuteronomistic positive appraisal of doing 'what is right in the eyes of the LORD' (15.10) since he carried out religious reforms (15.12–13) and his heart was fully committed to the Lord all his life (15.14). However, throughout his reign he had war with Baasha of Israel (15.16–17) and he died diseased (15.23–24). As can be observed, the DtrH's account of Asa is devoid of immediate cause-effect arrangement—there is no explanation for why a good king's reign is marked by misfortune.

The Chronicler however brings in the cultic element as an explanation for events. He rearranges the source account with a substantial interpolation of new material so that Asa's reign is divided into years of cultic fidelity (14.2–15.18) and apostasy (16.1–12). The later years are a perfect mirror image of the early years in terms of both Asa's behavior and consequences:

A Prosperity and military victory through seeking God (14.2–15)
  B Obedience to prophetic oracle (15–18)
    C Covenant with God (15.9–18)
    C' Covenant with man (16.1–6)
  B' Rejection of prophetic oracle (16.7–10)
A' Incurable disease through not seeking God (16.11–12)[10]

Consider the contrasts: When Asa faces a war threat from Zerah the Cushite in the first period of his reign; his response is to

---

[9] See William Riley, *King and the Cultus in Chronicles: Worship and the Reinterpretation of History*, JSOT Suppl. Series 160 (Sheffield: JSOT Press, 1993), 58ff, 72–3, 202–3.

[10] Adapted from Martin J. Selman, *2 Chronicles*, TOTC (Leicester: IVP, 1994), 385.

seek YHWH (14.11).[11] As a result, although he is overwhelmingly outnumbered, God delivers Zerah's army into his hands (14.12). In the second period, however, in the face of aggression from Baasha of Israel, Asa seeks alliance with Ben-Hadad of Syria. This is an expression of lack of faith in God, a grave error in the Chronistic evaluation,[12] and a breach of covenant made with God earlier (15.12). Second, he pays heed to the prophetic oracle in the first period, resulting in further reforms. But in the second period he disregards it and persecutes the prophet instead.[13] Thus his reliance on men rather than seeking God and rejection of the prophetic oracle become his nemesis. Third, there are other elements of contrast, such as, the covenant with God which marks the high point of the first period and the covenant with Ben-Hadad which marks the beginning of his straying away from God; the votive gifts which are presented to the temple in the first period are later used for paying tribute to Syria; further, peace is replaced by war and prosperity turns into sickness. Thus the Chronicler demonstrates that Asa is evaluated in terms of his guardianship of the cultus, a pattern he follows for all Judahite monarchs.

Secondly, the Chronicler reworks his DtrH source in democratizing[14] the king-cult relationship—he significantly increases the participation of the people in the cultus, the term 'all Israel'

---

[11] The significance of this motif of 'seeking the LORD' can be better appreciated when it is perceived that the term *dārash* ('to seek') has a strong cultic connotation. Thompson explains that the phrase was a summary description of the right response to God, involving not just the mere act of seeking God's help and guidance but 'stood for one's whole duty towards God'. Moreover, seen in conjunction with 1 Chron. 28.9, it can be understood as equivalent to 'knowing God and serving him with whole hearted devotion'. Thompson, *1, 2 Chronicles*, 226; Wagner states that it denotes 'the Chronicler's typical ideal of piety'. He further notes that the concept is 'so complex that very important consequences are causally connected with it': success (2 Chron. 17.5), peace (2 Chron. 14.5–6), life (1 Chron. 10.13–14; 2 Chron. 15.13) and even Saul's downfall (1 Chron. 10.14). S. Wagner, '*dārash*', in G. Johannes Botterwick and Helmer Ringgren (eds.) *TDOT*, vol. 3, (Grand Rapids: Eerdmans, 1978), 300–301. Thus this motif of seeking the LORD, or the failure to do so, captures the essence of a monarch's cultic devotion and resurfaces in the evaluation of other Judahite monarchs.

[12] Roddy Braun, *1 Chronicles*, WBC 14 (Waco: Word, 1986), xxxvii.

[13] Selman, *2 Chronicles*, 400.

[14] Sara Japhet, *I and II Chronicles*, OTL (Louisville: WJK, 1993), 47.

occurring far more frequently than in the DtrH. Such democratization surfaces especially in the formative and defining moments of history such as temple-building and king-making.[15] By doing this, the Chronicler communicates that once monarchy fails as guardian-of-the-cult and is punished by extinction, the inheritors of the privilege are the people. This has a significant implication for the Chronicler's post-monarchic audience. By demonstrating that the constant is the cultus rather than the monarchy, the Chronicler posits that the dissolution of geo-political integrity does not strip the people of the essence of their identity. The past gains a new relevance and the present its legitimacy.[16] Fidelity to the cultus becomes the mark of a true Israelite.

Such a conception of identity strongly influenced the self-understanding of the Jewish community of the STP.[17] Following the fall of Jerusalem in 586 BCE, whether Jews lived in Palestine or in the wide-flung diaspora, foreign domination exposed them to complex external influences in every aspect of their life—political, religious and cultural—particularly as Alexander the Great set in motion the Hellenization of his empire. It was during this time that Jewish cultural identity was both most powerfully challenged and best demonstrated, as witnessed to by the Jewish literature of this period. Take for example, the books of *Tobit, Wisdom of Solomon* and *4 Maccabees*. The book of *Tobit* (Eastern Diaspora;[18] 225–175 BCE[19]) encourages strict adherence to the Torah even in the face of severe misfortunes and persecution through the narration of the

---

[15] For example, David's enthronement is portrayed as confirmed by national recognition, supported by all Israel, 1 Chron. 10.14b–11.1 (contra 2 Sam. 1–4); the capture of Jerusalem—the dynastic seat and the future site of the temple—is portrayed as accomplished by David and 'all Israel' 1 Chron. 11.4 (contra 2 Sam. 5.6); Along with Solomon the temple-building is entrusted to 'all the leaders of Israel' (1 Chron. 22.17–19); all Israel participates in the restoration of temple initiated by Joash (2 Chron. 24.10).

[16] Japhet, *1 and 2 Chronicles*, 49.

[17] STP usually designates the period between 516 BCE, when the second temple was finally completed, to 70 CE, when it was destroyed by the Romans.

[18] Benedict Ozten, *Tobit and Judith* (Sheffield: Sheffield Academic Press, 2002), 58.

[19] R.H. Charles (ed.), *The Apocrypha and Pseudepigrapha of the Old Testament in English*, vol. 1 (Oxford: Clarendon Press, 1976), 174.

story of Tobit, a model of cultic faithfulness. The motivating factor and the teaching underpinning this story is the belief in earthly retribution vis-à-vis the cult. *Wisdom of Solomon* (Alexandria; 50 BCE–30 CE[20]) on the other hand enunciates a doctrine of retribution (and rewards?) that extends into the after-life—a direct extrapolation of Chronistic ideology necessitated by the puzzling fact that life in the diaspora often entailed suffering *despite* cultic faithfulness. The author addressed this by positing that there is more than meets the eye, especially in the case of the righteous. While in the case of the unrighteous suffering and death is purely retributive, in the case of the righteous these are interpreted as tests of their goodness (3.5ff),[21] with immortality as their destiny. *4 Maccabees* (Syrian Antioch[22] or Asia Minor;[23] first century CE[24]) is an exhortation to remain loyal to the Torah even in the most extreme of cases. It presents martyrdom as preferable to renouncement of one's religious beliefs through a dramatic narration of a confrontation between the martyrs and Antiochus IV, where the martyrs choose death over apostasy and loss of identity. The author seeks to demonstrate that through their steadfast adherence to the Torah they bring about the defeat of the tyrant and attain immortality.[25]

It seems then, that the STP Jewish community appropriated the Chronistic cult-retribution ideology, albeit with radical adaptation to their historical context. This theological reworking not only pushed the frontiers of the cult-retribution principle but also affected history-in-the-making. It can be argued from literature such as *2 Maccabees* (first century BCE[26]), that the first Jewish struggle for religious liberty—the Maccabean Revolt which culminated in the capture of Jerusalem in

[20] Daniel J. Harrington, *Invitation to the Apocrypha* (Grand Rapids: Eerdmans, 1999), 55.

[21] Charles (ed.), *The Apocrypha and Pseudepigrapha*, 530.

[22] Nickelsburg, *Jewish Literature*, 258.

[23] Jan Willem van Henten, *The Maccabean Martyrs as Saviours of the Jewish People: A Study of 2 and 4 Maccabees*, vol. 8 (Leiden: Brill, 1997), 73–8.

[24] David A. deSilva, *4 Maccabees* (Sheffield: Sheffield Academic Press, 1998), 18.

[25] Jan Willem van Henten and Friedrich Avemarie, *Martyrdom and Noble Death: Selected Texts from Graeco-Roman, Jewish, and Christian Antiquity* (London: Routledge, 2002), 48.

[26] Van Henten, *The Maccabean Martyrs*, 41.

164 BCE — was informed by the understanding that there is retribution for cultic fidelity/infidelity. Whether in the diaspora or in Palestine, whether in times of peace or persecution, whether through pacifist or military resistance, pious Jews of the STP seem to have viewed as their *primary identity marker*, cultic loyalty and the adherence to the Torah ordinances. Thus it is reasonable to say that were it not for the formation of an identity so strongly reflective of its historiography, the course of Jewish history could have turned out very different.

2. History and History Books in India

The nature of historiography and the socio-historical context aside, it is methodologically permissible to import into the present discussion on Indian group identities the basic premise established in the section above, that history books *do* influence cultural identity by their function as a reservoir of group 'memories'.

A starting point for this discussion would be a brief survey of Indian historiography in the modern period. Here, history writing has passed through four distinct paradigms:[27] the colonial, the secular-nationalist, the Marxist and the subaltern. Common to all four is that they address the making of India as a nation. Their reasons for this enterprise vary vastly, and stem from 'different intellectual persuasions, theoretical assumptions, political perspectives and social commitments'.[28] *Colonial* history characteristically demarcated the history of India into the ancient Hindu period, the medieval Muslim period and the modern British period, presenting the medieval period as one in which Hindus suffered Muslim tyranny.[29] In this sense, embedded in colonial historiography was a distinctive vein of the *religious-communalist* perspective. As commonly held, this construct served to project the British as emancipators of the Hindus; legitimized and even glorified the colonial administrative institutions as having

---

[27] See for an overview Shireen Moosvi, '"Open Door" in Indian Historiography', Address to the Andhra Pradesh History Congress, http://ahsaligarh.tripod.com (accessed 20 October 2010).

[28] K.N. Panikkar, 'History as a Site of Struggle', *The Hindu*, 15 August 2007.

[29] First articulated by James Mill (1818) and then among others, by J.R. Seeley and T.B. Macaulay.

unified (supposedly) traditionally conflicting communities; and, pre-empted a unified resistance to the British rule.[30]

The post-colonial period saw a reaction to colonial historiography by way of *secular-nationalist* and *marxist* approaches, both fired by Nehruvian socialist ideals. While the nationalists[31] depicted India as a homogeneity, the Marxists (1970s onwards)[32] pictured India as an aggregate of internally differentiated classes. Both, however, insisted on the secular nature of the post-colonial Indian nation. The *subaltern* school,[33] which took a collective shape since 1982, developed the marxist approach to its logical end narrating Indian history from below — as experienced by peasants, tribal groups, women and dalits — persuaded that even subjugated communities maintained a 'cultural autonomy'.[34] Meanwhile, the *religious-communalist* perspective that was so distinctive of colonial historiography established a formal presence soon after Independence in two series on either side of the new Indo-Pakistan border — R.C. Majumdar's *History and Culture of the Indian People* (1951–1977) and I.H. Qureshi's *Freedom Struggle of the Muslims in the Indo-Pakistan Sub-continent.* Both assume an irreconcilable hostility between Hindus and Muslims ever since Islam's entry into India. This communalist perspective gained official sanction in the period 1999–2004 when the religious- fundamentalist Bharatiya Janata Party (BJP)-led National Democratic Alliance (NDA) came to power at

---

[30] See Mridula Mukherjee and Aditya Mukherjee, 'Communalization of Education: The History Textbook Controversy: An Overview', in The Delhi Historians' Group, *Communalization of Education: The History Textbooks Controversy* (New Delhi: Jawaharlal Nehru University, 2001), http://www.sacw.net/India_History/DelHistorians.pdf (accessed 15 October 2010).

[31] Among them, Tara Chand, Mohammad Habib, Nilakant Shastri, D.V. Poddar and S. Gopal.

[32] Among them, D.D. Kosambi, R.S. Sharma, Susobhan Sarkar, A.R. Desai, K.M. Ashraf, Satish Chandra, Irfan Habib, Bipan Chandra, B.B. Chaudhuri, Romila Thapar and Sumit Sarkar.

[33] Among them Ranjit Guha, Shahid Amin, David Arnold, Partha Chatterjee, David Hardiman, Gyanendra Pandey and B.R. Ambedkar.

[34] Irfan Habib, 'History and Interpretation: Communalism and Problems of Historiography in India', http://www.sacw.net/India_History/IHabibCommunalHistory.html (accessed 15 Oct 2010); P. Kesava Kumar, 'Indian Historiography and Ambedkar: Reading History from Dalit Perspective', *Indian Journal for South Asian Studies* 1.1 (2008), http://www.pondiuni.edu.in/journals/ssas/6_keasavakumar.pdf (accessed 17 October 2010).

the centre. Being the political face of the Sangh Parivar, their ideology moved them towards mobilizing a 'minority complex of the majority'[35] so as to deal with a perceived Muslim threat. The 'crisis' demanded, *inter alia*, communalist revision of history books.

The reason for school level history textbooks being a major ground for ideological battles is that education, especially school level education is, as Lall puts it, 'the most logical entry point for the process of change in the society',[36] or as Merriam states, the system of formal history education is 'most consciously contrived for the purpose of influencing the next generation'.[37] Adolescence (12–20 years approximately) is the period when the quest of identity provides the guiding orientation for the child's interaction with the world. It is here that children develop a sense of self.[38]

We may turn now to making the link between history, history books and cultural identity mobilization. We will do this by studying a sample speech each from the Hindu and Muslim fundamentalist blocs. We will demonstrate how these voices draw from the formal reservoirs of 'memories' (that is, history books), as they mobilize a specific group identity.

3. Hindu Cultural Identity

Sadhvi Rithambra's speech below was delivered in April 1991, and is representative of the ones she regularly delivers as spokesperson for the Sangh Parivar.[39] At this time, the general elections had been announced, and the BJP was making its bid for power at the centre. Five months earlier police firing in Ayodhya had killed kar-sevaks agitating to demolish the Babri Masjid, setting off communal riots across the

---

[35] Aminah Mohammad Arif, 'Textbooks and Nationalism in India and Pakistan', in Veronique Benei (ed.), *Manufacturing Citizenship: Education and Nationalism in Europe, South Asia and China* (New York: Routledge, 2005), 157.

[36] Marie Lall, 'Introduction', in Marie-Carine Lall and Edward Vickers (eds), *Education as a Political Tool in Asia* (Oxon: Routledge, 2009), 1.

[37] Charles Merriam cited in Dorschner and Sherlock, 'The Role of History Textbooks', 276.

[38] Child Development Institute, 'Stages of Social-Emotional Development in Children and Teenagers', http://childdevelopmentinfo.com/development/erickson. html (accessed 5th October 2010).

[39] The speech is taken form Kakar, *The Colours of Violence*, 199–213.

country. As Kakar points out, Rithambra simultaneously functions as a manipulator of Hindu cultural symbols and as an articulator of the unexpressed thoughts of the Hindu community. The primordialist and instrumentalist paradigms operate simultaneously — 'Rithambra appeals to a group identity [*even*] while creating it.'[40]

> Hail mother Sita! Hail brave Hanuman! Hail Mother India! Hail the birthplace of Rama! Hail Lord Vishwanath (Shiva) of Kashi (Benares)! Hail Lord Krishna! Hail the eternal religion [dharma]! Hail the religion of the Vedas! Hail Lord Mahavira! Hail Lord Buddha! Hail Banda Bairagi! Hail Guru Gobind Singh! Hail the great sage Dayananda! Hail the great sage Valmiki! Hail the martyred kar-sevaks! Hail Mother India!

In Rithambra's opening salvo of salutations, first, we note that the persons hailed segue smoothly from the religio-mythological to the religio-historical[41] to current news. Mythology, history and today's news flow as one. Obstacles to this flow are not tolerated, and even history is doctored to suit. Thus, when the BJP government undertook the revision of school history books, the inconvenient fact supported by archaeology that the Vedic Aryans ate beef, was deleted.[42] What with the taboo on cow-slaughter having become one of the markers of Hinduism,[43] the great stream of millennial continuity was retrojectively purified at the fountainhead.

Secondly, Jainism, Buddhism, Sikhism and the reformist Arya Samaj are swept back into the fold of the mother religion. Mughal-resisters and would-be demolishers of masjids suggest that Muslims are excluded. Thirdly, the land is tied to Hinduism by association recalling Aurobindo Ghosh's famous assertion (in 1909) of the *sanatana dharma*: 'This is the Dharma that for the salvation of humanity was cherished in the seclusion of this peninsula from of old . . . It is for the

---

[40] Kakar, *The Colours of Violence*, 198.

[41] All found in history textbooks over Standards 6–10.

[42] *Shatapatha Brahmana* 3.4.1.2; *Vasistha Dharmasuthra* 4.8; *Brihadaranyaka Upanishad* 6.4.18 cited in The Delhi Historians' Group, 'Section 4: Text of the Deletions made from the NCERT Books', in *Communalization of Education: The History Textbooks Controversy* (New Delhi: Jawaharlal Nehru University, 2001), http://www.sacw.net/India_History/DelHistorians.pdf (accessed 15 October 2010).

[43] Koenraad Elst, *Who is a Hindu?: Hindu Revivalist Views of Animism, Buddhism, Sikhism and Other Offshoots of Hinduism* (New Delhi: Voice of India), http://www.voi.org (accessed 14 October 2010).

Dharma and by the Dharma that India exists.'[44] Lastly, 'this peninsula' itself is presented and positioned possibly as a demi-goddess in this abbreviated Hindu pantheon (Mother India), which personification would restrict access to her by non-Hindus.

The net effect, as Kakar rightly points out, is that Rithambra begins the construction of Hindu identity by demarcating the boundaries of this group[45] — in terms of heroes ancient and present, mythological and historical; sacred books; religion; sacred places. The last encompasses India itself. By a highly selective appeal to history, the boundaries of the Hindu community have been made coterminous with the boundaries of India. This collapsing of religious and geo-political boundaries becomes explicit as Rithambra conflates Ayodhya and India:

> As far as the construction of the Rama temple is concerned, some people say Hindus should not . . . quarrel over a small piece of land. I want to ask these people, 'If someone burns the national flag, will you say "Oh it doesn't matter. It is only two metres of cloth which is not a great national loss."' The question is not of two metres of cloth but of an insult to the nation. Rama's birthplace is not a quarrel about a small piece of land. *It is a question of national integrity.* The Hindu is not fighting for a temple of brick and stone. He is fighting for the *preservation of a civilization*, for his *Indianness, for the national consciousness* . . . We shall build the temple![46]

The group's stake on the *land* is contingent on the claim to a *civilization* in it — that of the Indo-Aryans. As historian Romila Thapar observes: 'The insistence on the indigenous origin of the Aryans allows [Hindutva ideologues] to maintain that the present-day Hindus are the lineal descendants of the Aryans and the inheritors of the land since the beginning of history.'[47] Where the claim falters is that though the early Indo-Aryans generated a great corpus of literature from the *Vedas* to the epics *Mahabharata* and *Ramayana,* it is disappointing (especially to Hindutva ideologues) that no material culture can be associated with the early Vedic period. A convenient way to fill this lacuna is to appropriate the Indus (or Harappan) Civilization.

---

[44] Aurobindo Ghosh, 'Uttarpara Speech', *SABCL* 2 (1972), http://intyoga.online. fr (accessed 29 October 2010).

[45] Kakar, *The Colours of Violence*, 200.

[46] Rithambra in Kakar, *The Colours of Violence*, 201-2 (emphases added).

[47] Romila Thapar, 'Hindutva and History', *Frontline,* 13 October 2000, 15–6.

ICSE and CBSE textbooks regularly present either the Aryan Invasion Theory (AIT) or the more current Aryan Migration Theory (AMT).[48] In this narrative, the Indus Valley (or Harappan) Civilization (2600–1900 BCE) is understood to *predate* the Aryan entry into the subcontinent (1500–1000 BCE). While the Harrapans had a sophisticated urban culture alongside an agrarian population, the Indo-Aryan immigrants from Central Asia were a largely nomadic-pastoralist society.

Conversely, the BJP's revisionist endeavour (2001 onwards) identifies the river Saraswati of the *Vedas* with a river in the Indus region.[49] This move marries the Aryans to Harappa, and allows the desired 'Indus-Saraswati civilization'. [50] More recently (2006), this revisionist wave washed ashore in California with the history textbook agitation moved by diaspora Hindutva activists.[51] Meanwhile, Saraswati Sishu Mandirs and the Vivekananda Vidyalayas, run on the basis of the 'Hindu Philosophy of Life', submit as historical fact a competing narrative called the Out-of-India Theory (OIT)[52] postulating an Aryan *emigration* from India, claiming that the Indians/Aryans were the first settlers in Iran.[53]

This rewriting of official 'memories' involves manipulating history on two fronts— linguistics and archaeology.[54] For a quick example, the revisionist linguists must ignore that the Sanskrit of the Vedas contains

---

[48] K.C. Khanna, *Discover History*, no. 6, Middle School History and Civics for ICSE Schools, rev. edn (New Delhi: Orient Blackswan, 2007), 42–8, and 66–72.

[49] Thapar, 'The Aryan Question Revisited', Transcript of lecture delivered 11 October 1999, Jawaharlal Nehru University, New Delhi, http://ascjnu.tripod.com/aryan.html (accessed 12 October 2010).

[50] Saba Naqvi Bhaumik, 'History, Vacuum-Cleaned', in The Delhi Historians' Group, *Communalization of Education: The History Textbooks Controversy* (New Delhi: Jawaharlal Nehru University, 2001), http://www.sacw.net/India_History/DelHistorians.pdf (accessed 15 October 2010).

[51] Ashfaque Swapan, 'Compromise Reached on California Textbook Controversy About Hinduism', *India West*, 03 March 2006, http://news.pacificnews.org/news/view_article.html (accessed 12 October 2010).

[52] Among its better known publishing proponents are Shrikant G. Talageri, *The Aryan Invasion Theory: A Reappraisal* (New Delhi: Aditya Prakashan), 1993; *The Rigveda: A Historical Analysis* (New Delhi: Aditya Prakashan), 2000; *The Rigveda and the Avesta: The Final Evidence* (New Delhi: Aditya Prakashan), 2008. For Koenraad Elst's prolific publications in *Voice of India*, see http://www.voi.org.

[53] Anjali Mody, 'History as Told by Non-Historians', *The Hindu*, 16 December 2001.

[54] See http://www.eastwestcultural.org for a helpful selection of articles on the Aryan Migration Theory debate, representing both camps.

loanwords from sub-continental languages for words such as 'plough', 'furrow' and 'threshing floor', and (more tellingly) 'mortar' since these lead to the inference that Vedic Aryans were nomadic pastoralists rather than agriculturist urban settlers, and were thus migratory groups from outside India rather than synchronous with the Harappan civilization.[55] Similarly, revisionist archaeologists attempt to Aryanize the Indus Civilization[56] by 'discovering' the Vedic distinctive of the horse—in the *Rigveda* even the storm clouds 'gallop' across the heavens, their thunder like the neigh of a stallion[57]—in Indus seals thus far distinctively devoid of horses. [58] Summing up, the coordinates of Hindu group identity are so emphatically geographic that Sadhvi Rithambra bewails the current 'mutilated India . . . An India with its arms cut off'[59]—a reference to the loss of territory that is now Bangladesh and Pakistan. Rithambra has thus far demarcated Hindu communal identity vis-à-vis the sub-continent's 'civilization'. She now excludes those outside these boundaries:

> Intellectuals and scholars of the world, wherever you come upon broken monuments, you will find the signature of Islam. Wherever you find creation, you will discover the signature of the Hindu. We have never believed in breaking but in constructing . . . Scholars, turn the pages of history and tell us whether the Hindu, riding a horse and swinging a bloody sword, has ever trampled on anyone's human dignity? We cannot respect those who have trod upon humanity . . . If you want to behave like the son of Babar, then the Hindu youth will deal with you as Rana Pratap and Chatrapati Shivaji dealt with your forefathers . . . Hindus, if you do not awaken, cows will be slaughtered everywhere. In the retreats of our sages you will hear the chants 'Allah is great.' You will be responsible for these catastrophes for history will say Hindus were cowards. Accept the challenge, change the history of our era.[60]

Through a return to the colonial historiographical paradigm, the medieval period becomes an 800-year period of oppression by Muslim tyrants, over the course of which the glories of ancient Hindu India are

---

[55] John Keay, *India: A History* (London: Harper Perennial, 2000), 24.

[56] N.S. Rajaram and Natwar Jha, *The Deciphered Indus Script: Methodology, Readings, Interpretations* (New Delhi: Aditya Prakashan, 2000).

[57] Keay, *India*, 25.

[58] See the detailed response of Michael Witzel and Steve Farmer, 'Horseplay in Harappa: The Indus Valley Decipherment Hoax', *Frontline* 17.20 (2000), http://www.safarmer.com/frontline/horseplay.pdf (accessed 15 October 2010).

[59] Kakar, *The Colours of Violence*, 207.

[60] Rithambra in Kakar, *The Colours of Violence*, 204, 205, 211.

extinguished. Rithambra's allusions resonate with the history textbook verbs describing the exploits of the Turks of Ghazni and Ghor — 'invaded' and 'plundered' and 'conquered'[61] — casting the Muslim as a permanent and hostile alien who must be resisted violently, in the tradition of the Rajputs (Rana Pratap) and Marathas (Shivaji) who conflicted with the Mughal empire.

Rithambra omits the inconvenient truth that Shivaji was a pluralist,[62] and throws into eclipse the economic, philosophical, technological, literary and architectural achievements of the medieval Muslims.[63] Indeed, revisionist history even appropriates their accomplishments — thus, for example, the Qutub Minar was built by Samudragupta![64]

Thus, Rithambra's strategy for mobilizing Hindu identity has been a selective retrieval of 'memories' from school-book history. These 'memories' lead the Hindu to recognize that his *primary marker of cultural identity* is land, the *'bhoomi'*, the geo-political entity 'from the Indus to the seas'.[65] It generates both his citizenship and his faith. Excluded is the Muslim, the historical invader whose rights of residence remain quasi-legitimate. Thus she concludes, 'Say with pride, we are Hindus! Hindustan is ours!'

4. Muslim Communal Identity

Maulana Obaidullah Khan Azmi is a Congress MP in the Rajya Sabha. Considered a powerful orator, he is a moderate fundamentalist — one who opts to work with the existing socio-political structures while recognizing that the ideal Islamic society existed at the dawn of Islam and the Islamic Caliphate. The extracts below are from a speech he delivered in 1985 in the event of a petition filed in a district court in Rajasthan seeking a ban on the Qur'an. As in the case of Rithambra's speech, we study it for the strategy by which communal identity is simultaneously appealed to,

---

[61] Jayanti Sengupta, *The Trail: History and Civics for the Middle School*, Book 2 (New Delhi: Oxford University Press, 2004), 36–9.
[62] Rafiq Zakaria, *Communal Rage in Secular India* (Mumbai: Popular Prakashan, 2002), 159.
[63] Sengupta, *The Trail*, 59–63, 80–115.
[64] Mukherjee and Mukherjee, 'Communalization of Education'.
[65] V.D. Savarkar cited in Elst, *Who is a Hindu?*

and created.[66] In the earlier part of the address, Azmi sketches the Indian Muslim as Mother India's *suput* ('good son'), giving graphic examples of Muslim military heroism in the conflicts post-Partition. In contrast, the Hindu is pictured as the *kuput* ('bad son') using an appropriate selection of anti-heroes—the assassins of Mahatma Gandhi and Indira Gandhi.[67] However, this identity in terms of a filial relationship with India begins to show some interesting cracks as he recalls the history of Muslims in the sub-continent:

> And you who . . . talk of a ban on the Qur'an . . . [i]t was the believers in the Qur'an who taught you the graces of life, taught you how to eat and drink. All you had before us were tomatoes and potatoes. What did you have? We brought you jasmine, we brought frangipani. We gave the Taj Mahal, we gave the Red Fort. India was made India by us. We lived here for eight hundred years and we made India shine. In thirty five years you have dimmed its light and ruined the country . . . Do not force us to speak out. Do not force us to come in front of you as an enemy.[68]

First, the Muslim is implicitly led to the recognition that he is, relatively speaking, an 'outsider'. Secondly, the Muslim is explicitly urged towards identification with superiority. This is what Samuel Huntington's oft-invoked *Clash of Civilizations* sets out: 'The underlying problem for the West is not Islamic fundamentalism. It is Islam, a different civilization whose people are convinced of the superiority of their culture.'[69] While some—notably, Amartya Sen—would dispute there is a clash at all,[70] instruments of identity mobilization regularly invoke superiority. Thus, Abu Philips, responding to Huntington, agrees: 'Most Muslims openly claim that Islam is better than all other religions and philosophies, a claim that is a natural consequence of their belief that the religion of Islam was revealed from God. Logically, Muslims assume the culture created by practicing God's religion must be superior to any other culture resulting from human experiment.'[71]

---

[66] The excerpts are taken from Kakar, *The Colours of Violence*, 223–37.

[67] Kakar, *The Colours of Violence*, 231–3.

[68] Azmi in Kakar, *The Colours of Violence*, 200.

[69] Samuel P. Huntington, *The Clash of Civilizations and the Remaking of World Order* (New York: Simon and Schuster, 1996), 217–18.

[70] Sen, *Violence and Identity*, 10–12, 40–58.

[71] Abu Ameenah Bilal Philips, *Clash of Civilizations: An Islamic View* (Qatar: n. pub., 2004), 8.

Thirdly, it is an interesting contrast with Rithambra that Azmi does not have to demarcate identity boundaries for his group. The reason for this becomes apparent:

> This is not a challenge to the two hundred and twenty million Muslims of India but to the over a billion Muslims of the world . . . Do you think the Qur'an can be finished off by merely banning it? We have lived with the Qur'an for fourteen hundred years. We have passed under arches of swords. We have come through the battlefields of Karbala. We have passed through the valleys of Spain, through the hills of Gibraltar, through the plains of India. We can say with pride that in spite of thousands of ordeals it has undergone, the Muslim nation remains incomparable.[72]

Mother India's *suput* speaks of another familial fealty which transcends the borders and history of the sub-continent. First, as Kakar observes: '[I]n fundamentalist discourse it is the wider, Arab-centred history of Islam rather than the history of Indian Muslims through which a collective Muslim identity is sought to be shaped.'[73] This is so even for a Muslim state. A Pakistani counterpart to Azmi would be Barkat Ali, who emigrated to Faisalabad at the Partition in 1947. His mobilization of Muslim identity carries the same appeal to Islamic history: 'O conquerors of the wonderful kingdoms of Caesar and Byzantine! You made the Call to the Prayer in the valleys of Europe. You tore the strength and sovereignty of Rome to pieces. You touched the borders of France and China. You broke down the iron fort of Constantinople. You alone introduced the Islamic rule of Law in Spain.' The heroes he invokes belong to Islam's golden past when the Islamic Empire stretched from Spain to Sindh: 'Is there any Jamal-ud-Din Afghani? Is there any Salah-ud-Din Ayyubi? Is there any Muhammad-bin-Qasim?'[74] Indeed, few groups, if any, accord so central a role to history in the mobilization of identity—'in its education, in its awareness of itself, in the common language of everyday talk'[75]—as Islam does with its exhortation, 'Recognize your history (*tarikh*)!'[76]

---

[72] Azmi in Kakar, *The Colours of Violence*, 234, 236-7.

[73] Kakar, *The Colours of Violence*, 222.

[74] Respectively, the 19th century political activist, the 12th century warrior against the Crusaders, and the 8th century Ummayid who pushed the frontiers of the Caliphate beyond the Indus. Abu Anees Muhammad Barkat Ali, *Unity of Muslims* (Faisalabad: Dar-ul-Ehsan, n.d.), 2.

[75] Bernard Lewis, *The Political Language of Islam* (Chicago: University of Chicago Press, 1988), 9.

[76] Kakar, *The Colours of Violence*, 221.

The reservoir for these 'memories' of Islamic history is created either formally (through the *madrasa*) or informally (within families). With the fall of the Mughal empire in India, the Muslim elite saw the traditional centres of Islamic education — the *madrasa* — as the route to the revitalization of the Muslim population. The only *madrasa* to experiment with the western-scientific paradigm of education (founded 1875) eventually became Aligarh Muslim University (1920).[77] The others of the post-1857 'Madrasa Movement', were reactionary, seeking to preserve their Arabic-Persian legacy through traditional education.[78] Estimated currently at thirty to forty thousand,[79] the curriculum of the Indian *madrasa* remains constructed around 'the protection and promotion of the *deen* [religion]'.[80] It thus favours the 'revealed sciences' over the 'rational sciences',[81] a component of the former being Islamic History.[82] With the method of education being rote-learning and most of the textbooks dating back some 700 years,[83] reservoirs of 'memories' are readily filled — at least, for the several lakh Muslims for whom this is the only education they receive.[84] For the majority that are schooled in secular institutions, 'memories' of Islamic history are garnered from world history taught in school[85] and/or — as is more often — informally learned within the familial environment, either by word-of-mouth or through recommended reading.[86]

[77] S. Farooq, 'Madrasa Education in India — A Need for Reorientation' (Aligarh: Aligarh Muslim University), http://cps-amu.org/reorient.htm (accessed 25 October 2010).

[78] David Emmanuel Singh, 'The Independent Madrasas of India: Dar al-'Ulum, Deoband and Nadvat al-'Ulama, Lucknow', http://www.ocms.ac.uk/docs/madrasas_deoband.pdf (accessed 24 October 2010).

[79] Farooq, 'Madrasa Education in India'.

[80] Akhtarul Wasey, 'Reforming Indian Madrasas', http://madrasareforms. blogspot.com (accessed 25 October 2010), translated by Yoginder Sikand from 'Dini Madaris Ka Nisab Wa Nizam Aur Asr-e Hazir Ke Taqaze', *Islam Aur Asr-e Jadid*, April 2010.

[81] Wasey, 'Reforming Indian Madrasas'.

[82] Singh, 'The Independent Madrasas of India'.

[83] Wasey, 'Reforming Indian Madrasas'.

[84] Farooq, 'Madrasa Education in India'.

[85] Sengupta, The Trail, 3–5; D.E. Sequeira, Total History and Civics, Book 9, rev. and enlarged (New Delhi: Morning Star, 2007), 112–5.

[86] Informal interviews with two Muslims (one Bangalorean and the other Lucknowi, identity withheld), 26 October, 2010.

Azmi harnesses this memory-bank of Islamic history towards the formation of a specific group identity:

> We need to maintain relationships with Muslims all over the world. We have tried and succeeded in developing these relationships. We can then deal with any challenge that comes from either inside or outside the country.[87]

The group identity being invoked is that of the *ummah*, a term generally understood to refer to the worldwide community of Muslims. In most Muslim countries, Islam remains the 'ultimate criterion of group identity', the one that subsumes all others especially during crises.[88] Barkat Ali is explicit in his invocation of this identity: '1000 million are bound together by the bond of brotherhood . . . set up by the Prophet Muhammad . . . In face of this bondage, all other relations, such as father and son, sister and brother, are like a weak thread.' The umbilical cord of this *ummah* is attached to 'not Istanbul, Cairo, Damascus, Islamabad or Jjakarta', but Mecca. Thus, it is grave error that 'You are Pakistanis or Iranians, Afghanis or Bengalis, Arabs or non-Arabs *first* and *then* you are Muslims, and even that, only in slumber!'[89]

Significantly, mobilization of an *ummah*-contoured identity is not restricted to fundamentalist discourse. For example, Datin Mansor, the wife of the Malaysian Prime Minister appealed to this identity when recently addressing a gathering of converts to Islam. She explained the *ummah* as 'not founded on race, nationality, occupation, kinship . . . but transcend[ing] national borders and political boundaries'.[90] This 'international brotherhood' demands that the individual Muslim pay attention to the facts that: 'The Palestinian refugees have no rest. The general massacre of the Muslims is underway in India. The whole Muslim world is on fire.'[91] Such a solidarity of the *ummah* is governed by the principle of *al-wilayah* which endorses mutual protection, based on the Prophet's dictat that '[t]he whole of a Muslim for another Muslim is inviolable:

---

[87] Azmi in Kakar, The Colours of Violence, 237.

[88] Lewis, The Political Language of Islam, 4.

[89] Barkat Ali, 'The Unity of Muslims', 2 (emphasis added).

[90] 'Muslims Have Role to Play in Strengthening Spirit of Ummah', Bernama, 26 October, 2010, http://www.bernama.com/bernama/v5/newsgeneral.php?id=538328 (accessed 30 October 2010).

[91] Barkat Ali, 'The Unity of Muslims', 2.

his blood, his property, and his honour'.[92] This allegiance demarcates group boundaries to include the believer; meanwhile, '[f]rom the time of the Prophet to the present day, the ultimate definition of the Other, the alien outsider and presumptive enemy, has been the *kafir*, the unbeliever.'[93]

It becomes clear then, that for the Indian Muslim—as for most others—the invoking of 'memories' establishes the *primary marker of cultural identity* as the global community—the *ummah*.

5. Conclusion

We conclude that narratives of a group's past as passed on through formal (history books) and informal (oral) re-telling are invariably ideological. These narratives, when self-applied by individuals or when wielded by a mobilizer of identity, can press into shape the cultural identity of that group. Thus, the identity of the Indian Hindu is seen to be inseparable from the land of his fathers and his faith; the identity of the Indian Muslim is incorporated into the identity of the universal *ummah*. What identity-shaping narratives of the past fill the Indian Christian's reservoir of 'memories'? In most regions of India—Kerala being among the few exceptions—it seems the Indian Christian has unwittingly fallen into the indigo vat of periodized colonial historiography. The period he most owns as his past is, thus, that of the British occupation. In addition, the stories he hears through religious education—in the most formative years, this is Church-sponsored curriculum such as Sunday Schools—mostly gravitate his group identity towards a skewed, Eurocentric 'universal' church. The issue before the Indian Christian, then, is to retell his history more carefully than he has in the past—carefulness in terms of loyalty to both land and faith—so that it will mobilize his identity in the context of the 21st century. What identity markers will the recalling of these 'memories' lead him to? That is an answer Indian Christian historians need to provide.

---

[92] Mahmoud Abu-Saud, Concept of Islam (Indianapolis: American Trust Publications, 1983), 130–31.

[93] Lewis, The Political Language of Islam, 5.

References

Abu-Saud, Mahmoud. *Concept of Islam*. Indianapolis: American Trust Publications, 1983.

Ali, Abu Anees Muhammad Barkat. *Unity of Muslims*. Faisalabad: Dar-ul-Ehsan, n.d.

Arif, Aminah Mohammad. 'Textbooks and Nationalism in India and Pakistan'. Pp. 143–69 in *Manufacturing Citizenship: Education and Nationalism in Europe, South Asia and China*. Edited by Veronique Benei. New York: Routledge, 2005.

Bhaumik, Saba Naqvi. 'History, Vacuum-Cleaned'. In The Delhi Historians' Group, *Communalization of Education: The History Textbooks Controversy*. New Delhi: Jawaharlal Nehru University, 2001. http://www.sacw.net/India_History/DelHistorians.pdf (accessed 15 October 2010).

Braun, Roddy. *1 Chronicles*. WBC 14. Waco: Word, 1986.

Charles, R.H. (ed.). *The Apocrypha and Pseudepigrapha of the Old Testament in English*. Vol. 1. Oxford: Clarendon Press, 1976.

Child Development Institute. 'Stages of Social-Emotional Development in Children and Teenagers'. http://childdevelopmentinfo.com/development/erickson.html (accessed 5th October 2010).

DeSilva, David A. *4 Maccabees*. Sheffield: Sheffield Academic Press, 1998.

Dorschner, Jon and Thomas Sherlock. 'The Role of History textbooks in Shaping Collective Identities in India and Pakistan'. Pp. 275–316 in *Teaching the Violent Past: History Education and Reconciliation*. Edited by Elizabeth A. Cole. Maryland: Rowman and Littlefield, 2007.

Elst, Koenraad. *Who is a Hindu?: Hindu Revivalist Views of Animism, Buddhism, Sikhism and Other Offshoots of Hinduism*. New Delhi: Voice of India. http://www.voi.org (accessed 14 October 2010).

Farooq, S. 'Madrasa Education in India—A Need for Reorientation'. Aligarh: Aligarh Muslim University. http://cps-amu.org/reorient.htm (accessed 25 October 2010).

Ghosh, Aurobindo. 'Uttarpara Speech'. *SABCL* 2 (1972). http://intyoga.online.fr (accessed 29 October 2010).

Habib, Irfan. 'History and Interpretation: Communalism and Problems of Historiography in India'. http://www.sacw.net/India_History/IHabibCommunalHistory.html (accessed 15 Oct 2010)

Harrington, Daniel J. *Invitation to the Apocrypha*. Grand Rapids: Eerdmans, 1999.

Huntington, Samuel P. *The Clash of Civilizations and the Remaking of World Order*. New York: Simon and Schuster, 1996.

Japhet, Sara. *I and II Chronicles*. OTL. Louisville: WJK, 1993.

Kakar, Sudhir. *The Colours of Violence*. New Delhi: Penguin, 1995.

Keay, John. *India: A History*. London: Harper Perennial, 2000.

Kesava Kumar, P. 'Indian Historiography and Ambedkar: Reading History from Dalit Perspective'. *Indian Journal for South Asian Studies* 1.1 (2008). http://www.pondiuni.edu.in/journals/ssas/6_keasavakumar. pdf (accessed 17 October 2010).

Khanna, K.C. *Discover History*. Vol. 6. Rev. edn. Middle School History and Civics for ICSE Schools. New Delhi: Orient Blackswan, 2007.

Lall, Marie. 'Introduction'. Pp. 1–9 in *Education as a Political Tool in Asia*. Edited by Marie-Carine Lall and Edward Vickers. Oxon: Routledge, 2009.

Lewis, Bernard. *The Political Language of Islam*. Chicago: University of Chicago Press, 1988.

Michael Witzel and Steve Farmer, 'Horseplay in Harappa: The Indus Valley Decipherment Hoax'. *Frontline* 17.20 (2000). http://www. safarmer.com/frontline/horseplay.pdf (accessed 15 October 2010).

Mody, Anjali. 'History as Told by Non-Historians'. *The Hindu*, 16 December 2001.

Moosvi, Shireen. '"Open Door" in Indian Historiography'. Address to the Andhra Pradesh History Congress. http://ahsaligarh.tripod.com (accessed 20 October 2010).

Mukherjee, Mridula and Aditya Mukherjee. 'Communalization of Education: The History Textbook Controversy: An Overview'. In The Delhi Historians' Group, *Communalization of Education: The History Textbooks Controversy*. New Delhi: Jawaharlal Nehru University, 2001. http://www.sacw.net/India_History/DelHistorians.pdf (accessed 15 October 2010).

[n.a.]. 'Muslims Have Role to Play in Strengthening Spirit of Ummah'. *Bernama*, 26 October, 2010, http://www.bernama.com/bernama/v5/ newsgeneral.php?id=538328 (accessed 30 October 2010).

Ozten, Benedict. *Tobit and Judith*. Sheffield: Sheffield Academic Press, 2002.

Panikkar, K.N. 'History as a Site of Struggle'. *The Hindu*, 15 August 2007.

Philips, Abu Ameenah Bilal. *Clash of Civilizations: An Islamic View*. Qatar: n. pub., 2004.

Rajaram, N.S. and Natwar Jha. *The Deciphered Indus Script: Methodology, Readings, Interpretations.* New Delhi: Aditya Prakashan, 2000.

Riley, William. *King and the Cultus in Chronicles: Worship and the Reinterpretation of History.* JSOT Suppl. Series 160. Sheffield: JSOT Press, 1993.

Selman, Martin J. *2 Chronicles.* TOTC. Leicester: IVP, 1994.

Sen, Amartya. *Identity and Violence: The Illusion of Destiny.* London: Allen Lane, 2006.

Sengupta, Jayanti. *The Trail: History and Civics for the Middle School.* Book 2. New Delhi: Oxford University Press, 2004.

Sequeira, D.E. *Total History and Civics.* Book 9. Rev. and enlarged. New Delhi: Morning Star, 2007.

Singh, David Emmanuel. 'The Independent Madrasas of India: Dar al-'Ulum, Deoband and Nadvat al-'Ulama, Lucknow'. http://www. ocms.ac.uk/docs/madrasas_deoband.pdf (accessed 24 October 2010).

Swapan, Ashfaque. 'Compromise Reached on California Textbook Controversy About Hinduism'. *India West,* 3 March 2006. http://news. pacificnews.org/news/view_article.html (accessed 12 October 2010).

Talageri, Shrikant G. *The Aryan Invasion Theory: A Reappraisal.* New Delhi: Aditya Prakashan, 1993.

Thapar, Romila. 'Hindutva and History'. Pp. 15–6 in *Frontline,* 13 October 2000.

———. 'The Aryan Question Revisited'. Transcript of lecture delivered 11 October 1999, Jawaharlal Nehru University, New Delhi. http://ascjnu. tripod.com/aryan.html (accessed 12 October 2010).

The Delhi Historians' Group. 'Section 4: Text of the Deletions made from the NCERT Books'. In *Communalization of Education: The History Textbooks Controversy.* New Delhi: Jawaharlal Nehru University, 2001. http://www.sacw.net/India_History/DelHistorians.pdf (accessed 15 October 2010.

Thompson, J.A. *1, 2 Chronicles.* NAC 9. Nashville: Boardman and Holman, 1994.

Van Henten, Jan Willem. *The Maccabean Martyrs as Saviours of the Jewish People: A Study of 2 and 4 Maccabees.* Vol. 8. Leiden: Brill, 1997.

Van Henten, Jan Willem and Friedrich Avemarie, *Martyrdom and Noble Death: Selected Texts from Graeco-Roman, Jewish, and Christian Antiquity.* London: Routledge, 2002.

Wagner, S. *'dārash'.* Pp. 300–301 in *TDOT.* Vol. 3. Edited by G. Johannes

Botterwick and Helmer Ringgren. Grand Rapids: Eerdmans, 1978.

Wasey, Akhtarul. 'Reforming Indian Madrasas'. http://madrasareforms. blogspot.com (accessed 25 October 2010). translated by Yoginder Sikand from 'Dini Madaris Ka Nisab Wa Nizam Aur Asr-e Hazir Ke Taqaze,' *Islam Aur Asr-e Jadid*, April 2010.

Zakaria, Rafiq. *Communal Rage in Secular India.* Mumbai: Popular Prakashan, 2002.

The Poetics and Politics of Pauline Identity: Wrestling with an Ancestor to Articulate Our Identity as 'Indians' and 'Christians'

Simon Samuel*

1. Introduction

The choice of the topic 'Indian and Christian: Changing Identities in Modern India' in SAC2010 is indicative of the fact that we, Evangelical and Charismatic Christians, too are now keen to engage in a socio-political and cultural discourse on our subcultural religious (Christian) and national (Indian) identities. Generally the debate on identity within a nation occurs in the context of a crisis, uncertainty or even disorientation of its citizens (or at least a segment of them), concerning their identity. Such a crisis, if not disorientation, is taking place in India now. This is mainly due to the emergence and dominance of Hindutva nationalism and politics, which alienates minority religious communities and other people groups such as the Dalits, Adivasis, etc.[1] The crisis has been intensified by the invasive economic imperialism of national and multinational corporations on subaltern peoples and their homes and resources, and the neo-colonial agenda of global markets. These are causing wrinkles and ruptures in the socio-cultural, political and economic fabric of the nation, and many feel disillusioned, dislocated and disoriented in their psyche (if not from their own land), wondering whether they belong at all to this sovereign, socialist, secular, democratic republic called India.[2]

These uncertainties, wrinkles and ruptures are leading to a search for certainties. Some find them in an imagined monolithic communal

---

* Simon Samuel, PhD, is Professor of New Testament Studies and Christian Origins and Principal of New Theological College, Dehradun, Uttarakhand, India.

[1] One needs only to observe the way the legislative and judiciary resolve swung in favour of the right wing agenda in the recent Allahabad High Court verdict in the case of the title deed of the Babri Masjid. See V. Ramakrishnan, 'In the name of Faith', A.G. Noorani, 'Muslims Wronged', D.N. Jha, 'History has Taken a Back Seat', in *Frontline* (22 October 2010): 4–11, 125–9, 132–3.

[2] Arundhati Roy, *Broken Republic: Three Essays* (New Delhi: Penguin, 2011).

identity (offered by Savarkar and others);[3] others in the creation of a new inclusive imagined national identity (Gandhi-Nehru model);[4] and yet others in their own racial, caste, linguistic and ethnic identities (the subaltern, subcultural model)[5]

In this paper I propose that these uncertainties must be mended through consciously sustaining a strategic national mould in which the various cultural entities and collectivities may locate their specific identities, and where they are assured economic justice, political participation and cultural plurality. In this model, the very idea of creating a unified Indian 'self' must be erased. In its place we must cast an authentic Indian cultural identity which is dynamic, polyglotic and pluriform in nature.[6] This paper makes a strong plea for this model and finds support for it in early Christian discourses, especially the Pauline letters.

1.1. Why Wrestle with an Ancestor?

The theme of SAC 2010 invites us to wrestle with our specific and intersecting (two/more-in-one) identities as 'Christians' and 'Indians' *of* modern India.[7] Wrestling of any kind requires some kind of training from an expert, experienced wrestler. The wrestling we intend to engage in here involves the kind of cultural politics that someone practised and professed quite well in the past—the apostle Paul.

---

[3] V.D. Savarkar, *Hindutva,* 6th edn (Mumbai: Savarkar Prakashan, 1989). For a critique of the agenda of Savarkar, Golwalkar, Hedgewar and the RSS, see Jyotirmaya Sharma, *Terrifying Vision: MS Golwalkar, the RSS and India* (New Delhi: Viking, 2007).

[4] See *The Collected Works of Mahatma Gandhi* (New Delhi: Publication Division, Govt. of India, 1978) and J. Nehru, *Discovery of India* (New Delhi: JNM Fund, 1946).

[5] The advocates of this model have been inspired by B.R. Ambedkar and others. Manifestations of this ideology may be seen in Dalit/Tribal/Adivasi theologies, subaltern studies, etc.

[6] See T.K. Oommen, 'Insiders and Outsiders in India: Primordial Collectivism and Cultural Pluralism in Nation-building', in Bidyut Chakrabarty (ed.), *Communal Identity in India: Its Construction and Articulation in the Twentieth Century* (New Delhi: OUP, 2003), 231–55; Amartya Sen, *The Argumentative Indian: Writings on Indian History, Culture and Identity* (New Delhi: Penguin, 2005); Amartya Sen, *Identity and Violence: The Illusion of Destiny* (New Delhi: Penguin, 2006), 149ff.

[7] I use 'of' to emphasize our belonging to this country from the very beginning of Christianity.

Through his poetics, piety, preaching and practice, Paul wrestled with the complex politics of culture in between three or four distinct and intersecting cultures (worlds) of his time, to lead his community rather successfully in a much more complex and difficult world than ours.[8]

1.2. Hermeneutics and Method

In this paper, I assume a 'correspondence of relationship'[9] between the first century subcultural and multicultural milieu of Paul and our present subcultural, multicultural milieu in India. Therefore I wish to engage in a common cultural critical hermeneutics across the centuries.[10] This would help us learn from Paul, who maintained a distinct ethnic identity as a Pharisaic Jew, a liminal, hyphenated identity as an Asiatic Syrian-Greco-Roman Jew in terms of his culture and political citizenship, and as a Jewish Christian and Roman citizen, all at the same time.[11] In the same vein we may perceive and project ourselves (whether we like it or not) as 'Dalit', 'Adivasi', 'Naga', 'Mizo', 'Syrian', 'Goan', etc. Christians, and as 'Malayali', 'Madrasi', 'Chattisgarhi', 'Oriya', 'Naga', 'southern', 'northern', etc. Indians, all at the same time (ethno-linguistic-regional-communal-national

---

[8] 'Wrestling with Paul' is something that Daniel Boyarin does as a postmodern Talmudist Jew and Jewish cultural critic to locate his identity as a Jew and as a world citizen, in his book *A Radical Jew: Paul and Politics of Identity* (Berkeley: University of California Press, 1997), 1–12. He says: 'I am indeed wrestling here with Paul—a metaphor that I think he would have appreciated—in two senses: I am wrestling alongside of him with the cultural issues with which he was wrestling, and I am also wrestling against him in protest against some of the answers he came up with.'

[9] Clodovis Boff, *Theology and Practice: Epistemological Foundations*, trans. R.R. Barr (Maryknoll: Orbis, 1987), 63ff.

[10] This model in hermeneutics may be seen in A. Thiselton, *The Two Horizons: New Testament Hermeneutics and Philosophical Description* (Grand Rapids: Eerdmans, 1980), 3–23; Dale Martin, *Pedagogy of the Bible: An Analysis and Proposal* (Louisville: WJK, 2008).

[11] R. Wallace and W. Wynne, *The Three Worlds of Paul of Tarsus* (London: Routledge, 1998); N.T. Wright, *Paul In Fresh Perspective* (Minneapolis: Fortress, 2005) 3–12; J. Zangenberg and M. Labahn (eds), *Christians as a Religious Minority in a Multicultural City: Modes of Interaction and Identity Formation in Early Imperial Rome* (London: T&T Clark, 2004).

identities).[12] The essential and mixed hyphenated identities of Paul and of ours are such that we may see a correspondence between them. Therefore, there may be something that we may learn from Paul in relation to living with our distinct and mixed identities.[13]

Methodologically, I wish to explore this issue (the particularities and commonalities of our identities as 'Indians' and 'Christians' and of Paul's as a Greco-Roman-Pharisaic-Jewish-Syrian-Christian) from the Postcolonial Studies perspective.[14]

2. Postcolonialism

The field of Postcolonial Studies gained currency in literary and cultural studies, and much later in biblical studies, after the publication of Edward Said's influential critique of the western constructions and representations of the Orient, including the works of a few modern western biblical critics, in his book *Orientalism*.[15] In this book Said

---

[12] Since the emergence of Dalit/Adivasi/Tribal theologies (and subaltern/ postcolonial historiography), there is an increased sense that Dalit/Adivasi Christians (and Buddhists and others) need not necessarily silence or forget their ethnic and caste identities. Rather, they may use these as platforms to launch a dynamic (dialogic, affiliative-antagonistic) liberative discourse. These are slippery slopes but could be used for a very shrewd identification. According to Sathinathan Clarke and Philip Peacock, 'For Dalits, the predicament to live out of the human dialogic nature involves mediating between the hegemonic realities that seek to constitute identities and the liberative privilege that wills to somewhat deliberately construct authentic identifications.' See 'Dalit and Religious Conversion: Slippery Identities and Shrewd Identifications', in *Dalit Theology in the Twenty-first Century* (New Delhi: OUP, 2010), 178–95, especially 190ff. in F. Hrangkhuma (ed.), *Christianity in India: Search for Liberation and Identity* (New Delhi: ISPCK, 1998). Also see Partha Chatterjee, 'Communities and the Nation' and Gyanendra Pandey, 'Disciplining Difference', in S. Dube (ed.), *Postcolonial Passages: Contemporary History-writing in India* (New Delhi: OUP, 2004), 115–31, 159–76. Pandey thinks of 'people of India' as an empty signifier to be filled in by political contingency ('Difference', 167).

[13] I am of the view that an objective, disinterested history or exegesis is neither possible nor desirable. We can be better historians and exegetes if we understand our own interests, and our perceptual and epistemological limitations and contingencies (cf. Dale Martin, *Pedagogy*).

[14] For an introductory reading, see Ania Loomba, *Colonialism/Postcolonialism* (London: Routledge, 1998); Leela Gandhi, *Postcolonial Theory: A Critical Introduction* (Edinburgh: Edinburgh University Press, 1998).

[15] Edward Said, *Orientalism: Western Conceptions of the Orient* (London: Penguin Books, 1978).

unravels the western colonial discourses' conscious or unconscious construction of Europe as the dominant 'self' and the colonized as the 'others'.[16] After *Orientalism* Postcolonial Studies, as an investigative discipline in literary, cultural and biblical studies, gained credence through the publication of *The Empire Writes Back*.[17] Ever since, a daunting number of studies on postcolonial theory and practice have appeared. Most of them theorize or engage the political, economic, cultural and discursive practices of the imperial/colonial nations of Europe, in light of the emerging and influential postcolonial literature from the former colonies. European colonialism and its impact on the perceptual sphere of colonized cultures and peoples, and the latter's decolonization strategies via postcolonial novelistic, creative, etc. discourses, constitute the main resource for the theory and practice of Postcolonial Studies.

Though the sphere of Postcolonial Studies is primarily focused on modern European colonialisms and their aftermath in Latin American, African and Asian countries, attempts have also been made to apply its critical tool to unravel the cultural politics in ancient colonial contexts such as the Greco-Roman-Jewish worlds.[18] Such initiatives have helped biblical scholars to examine biblical discourses as discursive responses (poetics and politics of culture) that originated in the ancient world of the Jews and Jewish-Christians, living under colonial domination and engaged in their own anti-colonial struggle.[19]

---

[16] For more on the origin and development of Postcolonial Studies, see Simon Samuel, *A Postcolonial Reading of Mark's Story of Jesus* (New York: T&T Clark, 2007), 7ff.

[17] B. Ashcroft, G. Griffiths and H. Tiffin, *The Empire Writes Back: Theory and Practice in Postcolonial Literatures* (London: Routledge, 1989).

[18] D.J. Mattingly (ed.), *Dialogues in Roman Imperialism: Power, Discourse, and Discrepant Experience in the Roman Empire,* JRA Supp. Series 23 (Portsmouth: JRA, 1997); Jane Webster and N. Cooper (eds), *Roman Imperialism: Post-Colonial Perspectives* (Leicester: The University of Leicester, 1996); Simon Swain, *Hellenism and Empire: Language, Classicism, and Power in the Greek World AD 50–250* (Oxford: Clarendon, 1998).

[19] Jon Berquist, *Judaism in Persia's Shadow: A Social and Historical Approach* (Minneapolis: Fortress, 1995); Laura Donaldson (ed.), *Postcolonialism and Scriptural Reading, Semeia* 75 (1998); Stephen Moore and F.F. Segovia (eds), *Postcolonial Biblical Criticism: Interdisciplinary Intersections* (London: T&T Clark, 2005); Sugirtharajah (ed.), *Postcolonial Bible* (Sheffield: SAP, 1998); Samuel, *A Postcolonial Reading;* Elizabeth Schüssler Fiorenza, *The Power of the Word: Scripture and the Rhetoric of Empire* (Minneapolis: Fortress, 2007).

Postcolonialism is now used as a critical discursive strategy to explore the cultural complexities of people who live with or in the aftermath of displacement and colonialism. It assumes that intersecting identities and overlapping histories and cultures do occur when people of two cultures come into contact with each other.[20] Such contacts may either be due to migration or displacement (exile) of people from one geographical location to another[21] for one reason or another (which is the focus of diaspora and displacement studies[22]) or due to imperial, colonial expansion and domination of one country/people by another country/people.[23]

Postcolonialism explores the discursive spaces constructed by the colonist and colonized peoples which can either be a *pro-* or *anti-* or a *post*colonial space. The first two spaces celebrate polarity. The pro-colonial celebrates cultural collaboration with the colonial masters. The anti-colonial attempts total detachment, and romanticizes and retrieves into an imagined past cultural purity (difference). The anti-colonial invokes the cultural past as a resistance tool to use in the present. But the postcolonial resorts to a hyphenated, in-between, liminal space—neither here nor there, yet at the same time here and there—from where s/he affiliates and distances, accommodates and disrupts, mimics and mocks both the native and alien discourses of power, almost simultaneously. This postcolonial spacing and posturing is a mimetic, ambivalent, hybrid posturing, which is a strategically essentialist and transcultural hybrid and cannot be put in an 'either-or' category.

[20] Virgilio Elizondo, 'Transformation of Borders—Border Separation or a New Identity' and Regina A. Quinn 'Crossing Borders: Cultures, Identities and the Ginkgo Tree', in P. Gnanapragasam and Elizabeth Schüssler Fiorenza (eds), *Negotiating Borders: Theological Explorations in the Global Era Essays in Honour of Prof. Felix Wilfred* (New Delhi: ISPCK, 2008), 19–32, 33–43.

[21] Bhabha, *The Location of Culture* (London: Routledge, 1994).

[22] See Satendra Nandan, 'The Diasporic Consciousness: From Biswas to Biswasghat' and C. Vijayasree, 'The Politics and Poetics of Expatriation: The Indian Version(s)', in Harish Trivedi and Meenakshi Mukherjee (eds), *Interrogating Post-colonialism: Theory, Text and Context* (Shimla: IIADS, 1996), 49–66, 221–9; E. Boehmer, *Colonial and Postcolonial Literature: Migrant Metaphors* (Oxford: OUP, 1995); F.F. Segovia, 'Toward Interculturalism: Reading Strategy from the Diaspora', in Segovia and Tolbert (eds), *Reading from this Place: Social Location and Biblical Interpretation in Global Perspective,* vol. 2 (Minneapolis: Fortress, 1995), 303–30.

[23] Edward Said, *Culture and Imperialism* (London: Vintage, 1993), 1ff.; B. Chakrabarty, 'Introduction', in Bidyut Chakrabarty (ed.), *Communal Identity in India*, 3.

Thus 'post' in postcolonialism is a spatial category (not referring to sequence—'after', or polarity—'against') suggestive of an interstitial cultural space (trope) between the colonists and the colonized. It is a critical discursive strategy for delineating the discourses that originate from colonial contexts and contacts. This would entail a potential for its trans-historical application. For postcolonial literary, cultural and biblical critics, this would mean a critical examination of at least some of the literary, cultural and biblical discourses that emanate from modern or ancient colonial contexts, as interstitial discourses that accommodate and disrupt both the native and the alien colonial discourses of power. 'Post' in postcolonialism, as a marker of the 'beyond', may be understood in terms of consensual-conflictual hybridity or in terms of an ambivalent affiliative-antagonistic cultural engagement in between the colonist and colonized cultures. This would open the door for a critical scrutiny of at least some of the biblical discourses as postcolonial discourses, as strategic essentialist and transcultural hybrid discourses, that accommodate and disrupt both the native and the alien colonial discourses of power.

In Postcolonial Studies, there is recognition now that we can talk about colonialism and postcolonialism as universal concepts only by means of specific manifestations in particular times and places. And it is only in those particular discussions, grounded in particular discourses and their contexts, that strategic postcolonial moves can take place.[24] So Postcolonial Studies need not necessarily be confined to dealing exclusively with the economic, political and cultural issues emanating from modern European colonialism in 'other' parts of the world. One can expand the horizon of Postcolonial Studies by undertaking a trans-historical view of colonial histories within the framework of postcolonialism. This can be done by considering modern colonialism to be in some measure similar to, say for instance, the Hellenistic or Roman colonialism, and the discursive responses to modern colonialism to be similar to the discursive responses of the colonised communities (Jews and Christians) in biblical and post-biblical times.[25]

---

[24] Susan VanZanten Gallagher, 'Mapping the Hybrid World: Three Postcolonial Motifs', *Semeia* 75 (1998): 229–40.

[25] F.F. Segovia, 'Notes Toward Refining the Postcolonial Optic', *JSNT* 75 (1999): 103–14.

On the basis of this we may assume a 'correspondence of relation' with Paul. In an analysis of Paul's identity as a diaspora Syrian Jew with Greco-Roman colonial cultural and political influences and Christian beliefs, we may take seriously his colonial and diasporic contexts and his subjective positions and experiences. So also in understanding our identity and nationality we cannot overlook the colonial context of India and its influence in our identity, nationalism and nation formation. Paul reveals his static and shifting identities in his epistles (poetics) which we may interrogate in this paper in order to understand and appreciate our static and shifting identity concerns.

3. Intersecting Identities as 'Indians' and 'Christians' of India

The creation of 'India' and our identity as 'Indians' is the result of Indian nationalism, which again is a by-product of our western colonial experience.[26] 'India', 'Indian' and 'Indian-ness' are colonial and postcolonial political nationalistic constructs, expressing our common national identity, that need not necessarily repress our primordial collectivities, histories and pluriform (ethnic and cultural) identities.[27]

3.1. Discourses on 'Indian National' Identity

Historians writing the 'history of India' generally tend to portray regional histories, localized cultures and primordial collectivities as the history of the whole of India. For example, the history of the Indus people or the Aryan immigrants/conquerors and the origination of the *Janapadas* or *Mahajanapadas* (*gana sanghas* or republics) in the Sindhu-Ganga belt, or the eventual formation of Magadhan, Mauryan, Kushan,

---

[26] Ashish Nandy, *The Illegitimacy of Nationalism* (New Delhi: OUP, 1994). For nationalism as a 'derivative discourse', see Benedict Anderson, *Imagined Communities: Reflections on the Origin and Spread of Nationalism* (London: Verso, 1991). A challenge against this view is posed by P. Chatterjee in *Nationalist Thought and the Colonial World: A Derivative Discourse?* (London: Zed Books, 1986) and *The Nation and Its Fragments: Colonial and Postcolonial Histories* (Princeton: Princeton University Press, 1993).

[27] See Rowena Robinson, 'Fluid Boundaries: Christian "Communities" in India' and T.K. Oommen, 'Insiders and Outsiders in India: Primordial Collectivism and Cultural Pluralism in Nation-building', in B. Chakrabarty (ed.), *Communal Identity in India*, 231–55, 287–305.

Vardhana, Gupta, etc. empires in the northern Indo-Gangetic belt. While this gives a kind of coherent, continuous conception of Indian history,[28] it ignores the fact that these events/groupings/collectivities/ cultural and political formations/histories are only regional or local in nature. The image of India as a single coherent geo-political entity and 'Indian' as a monolithic entity has been constructed and projected by western Orientalist, Indic and national historians of the right (Hindutva historians), left (Marxist historians) and middle (Gandhian-Nehruvian historians) wing persuasions.[29]

But it may not be wrong to suggest that India has never been one nation or polity, despite the unifying geographical boundaries, civilizational forces, political configurations, imperial unifications, post-independent (voluntary and, at times, forcible) political integration, the current majoritarian democracy (in practice, a dictatorship) and the apparent 'rule of law'.[30] This is the emerging and increasingly accepted understanding of social, subaltern and postcolonial histories, historians, sociologists and creative writers (Ranajit Guha and the Subaltern Studies Group, sociologists like Kancha Ilaiah and T.K. Oommen, Ashish Nandy and creative writers like Mohan Rakesh,

---

[28] While studying for my Master's degree in History, the glories of Indian art, architecture, etc. were taught as though I am a rightful heir of these cultures and heritages, and should be proud of them. Now, as I read these history books and locate myself in my context and experiences, I find the centers of some of those arts, architecture and cultures so far away from my context and culture. History is taught in post-independent times primarily to inject a zealous nationalist feeling into the mind of the students. No wonder we are now facing the rise of nationalist fundamentalism (cocktailed into a religio-cultural framework, even among the educated Indians) and political polarizations of a violent kind in India today.

[29] See David Kopf, *British Orientalism and the Bengal Renaissance* (California: University of California Press, 1969); P. Spear, *A History of India*, vols. 1–2 (New Delhi: Penguin, 1965); A.L. Basham, *The Wonder that was India* (New Delhi: OUP, 1986); R.C. Majumdar (ed.), *The History and Culture of the Indian People*, vols. 1–11 (Bombay: Bhartiya Vidya Bhavan, 1951–1977); D.D. Kosambi, *An Introduction to the Study of Indian History* (Bombay: Popular Prakashan, 1975); Romila Thapar, *Cultural Pasts: Essays in Early Indian History* (New Delhi: OUP, 1999); Sunil Khilnani, *The Idea of India* (New Delhi: Penguin, 1997). For a brief survey see Rowena Robinson, *Christians of India* (New Delhi: Sage, 2003), 11–7.

[30] The various insurgency movements, the Maoist rebellion, and regional/ caste/ethnic-based political configurations and revolts are the best examples to prove this.

Salman Rushdie, Arundhati Roy and many others).[31] These historians, sociologists and creative writers acknowledge and give expression to difference, diversity, plurality and hybridity of histories, cultures and identities of the 'ruled' and 'un-ruled' peoples who live in this geographical landscape.[32]

This approach to identity, culture and history must be the way forward to understand, acknowledge and appreciate the communities and their histories, cultures and identities in India, including that of the Christians of India. In this approach of spacing ourselves and our strategic essentialist and transcultural hybrid identities, we are not alone. We may solicit the support of others like the subalterns (Dalits, Tribals, Adivasis and other minority communities, both religious and ethnic) and the strong voices of those who promote pluriformity and multiculturalism in India today, in this endeavour to assert our 'sameness' and 'difference' in the body polity and cultural politics of India. This would ensure that the violent tendencies to mutate, assimilate and erase or the eulogistic tendencies to alienate, polarize and ghettoize our complex identities into an 'either-or' category, can be refused and rejected with a greater level of success.[33]

3.2. *Discourses on 'Indian Christian' Identity*

Similarly, the construct of our 'Christian' identity has its own fluidity. The advent of Christianity in India through a series of west-Asian-Syrian-Christian immigrants, its spread through conversion of natives, western

---

[31] See R. Guha (ed.), *Subaltern Studies: Writings on South Asian History and Society*, vols. 1–2 (New Delhi: OUP, 1982, 1983); Guha and Spivak (eds), *Selected Subaltern Studies* (New Delhi: OUP, 1988); K. Illiah, *Why I am not a Hindu* (Calcutta: Samya, 1996); Arundhati Roy, *The God of Small Things* (London: Flemingo, 1997); Salman Rushdie, *Midnight's Children* (New York: Avon, 1980); Mohan Rakesh, *Na Aane Wala Kal* (Delhi: Hindi Pocket Books, 1987 [orig. 1968]).

[32] Edward Said, 'Foreword', in Guha and Spivak (eds), *Selected Subaltern Studies*, viii; James C. Scott, *The Art of Not Being Governed: An Anarchist History of Upland Southeast Asia* (New Delhi: Orient Blackswan, 2010). Also see S. Dube (ed.), *Postcolonial Passages*; B. Chakrabarty (ed.), *Communal Identity in India*.

[33] See Jaidev, 'Na Aane Wala Post-colonialism?', in Trivedi and Mukherjee (eds), *Interrogating Post-colonialism*, 177–86; Bhikshu Parekh, 'Discourses on National Identity', in B. Chakrabarty (ed.), *Communal Identity in India*, 110–27; Dipesh Chakrabarty, 'Minority Histories, Subaltern Pasts', in S. Dube (ed.), *Postcolonial Passages*, 229–42.

Christian missionary movements and colonialism, and its long history of adaptations and missional expansions over two millennia, have given it an identity both as a native (self) and an alien (other) religion, just like any of the other religions of India.[34]

The identity of Indian Christians cannot be viewed without recognizing the diverse self-definitions we hold due to our regional affiliations, denominational persuasions, ecclesiastical traditions, doctrinal preferences and the unfortunate but prevailing ethnic, caste, tribal and linguistic specificities.[35] Indian Christians are Syrian, Dalit, Adivasi/Tribal, Anglo-Indian, Ao, Angami, Thangkul Naga, Kuki, Mizo, etc. Christians.[36] These identities are apparently entrenched in our ethnic consciousness, giving us an essentialist identity of which we often boast. This identity difference is sometimes taken up as a tool to fight for justice and liberation[37], and at other times it is used with annihilative effect.[38] The pretentious sameness that is maintained at the superficial level in the past (that we are Christians) has in fact adversely affected the Christian segments from the lower caste and outcaste background. Christians of high caste origin or of Syrian Christian background maintained caste barriers in all realms of life. The inter-tribal conflict in north-east Christianity again affirms the fact that

---

[34] F. Hrangkhuma (ed.), *Christianity in India*; Robinson, *Christians of India*. For history of Christianity in India, see A.M. Mundadan, *History of Christianity in India: From the Beginning up to the Middle of the Sixteenth Century*, vol. 1 (Bangalore: CHAI, 1984); Jacob Kollaparambil, *The Babylonian Origin of the Southist among the St. Thomas Christians* (Roma: Pont. Institutum Studiorum Orientalium, 1992); M.S. Renick, *Christian Missionary Movement in Northern India with Special Reference to Uttar Pradesh 1562 A.D. to 1947 — update 1999* (New Delhi: ISPCK, 2004).

[35] Robinson, 'Fluid Boundaries', in B. Chakrabarty (ed.), *Communal Identity in India*, 287–305.

[36] I view the emergence of Dalit/Adivasi/Tribal theologies as affirmations and assertions of their respective, specific particularities and identities even while having a common 'Christian' identity. See, for a latest work on Dalit theology by a member of the younger generation of Dalit theologians, S. Clarke et al (eds), *Dalit Theology* (New Delhi: OUP, 2010); James Massey (ed.), *Deciphering the subaltern Terrain* (Bangalore: BTESSC/SATHRE, 2009); Shimray (ed.), *Tribal Theology: A Reader* (Jorhat: ETC, 2003).

[37] I think of Dalit/Adivasi Christian struggles for liberation here.

[38] Here, I am thinking of the Naga versus Kuki tribal conflicts, the Dalit Christian conflict in Kandhamal and the Syrian Christian versus Dalit Christian power struggles in our seminaries and churches. For details of the Khandas (tribe) and Panas (Dalit community) conflict in Kandhamal, see Clarke and Peacock in *Dalit Theology*, 178–95.

ethnic, tribal and cultural essentialist elements lurk just beneath our skin despite the cosmetic conversional make-up through a title change, 'Christians'. This is the scene in our local and regional situations, where we affirm and uphold our ethnic specificity and difference, even when we have an overarching 'Christian' community identity. Our Christian identity insufficiently permeates and transforms our other identities.

But when it comes to the national political scene, or in an oppositional discursive context, or in the context of a Hindu cultural nationalist polemical rhetoric, we uphold our overarching Christian identity. In such contexts, we transcend our ethnic, ecclesiastical, doctrinal boundaries and project ourselves as a united Christian community. Only in a polemical context, when threatened by 'outsiders', or in a national context where we see ourselves as a tiny powerless minority, we appear to have a strong community consciousness and rhetoric. But on all other occasions and situations, such as of marriage, ecclesiastical office appointments, etc., our ethnic essentialist identity takes precedence and supremacy over our community consciousness and identity as Christians.

So one is a Syrian-Malayali-Christian-Indian or a Dalit-Punjabi-Christian-Indian, or an Ao-Naga-Christian-Indian in an intra-communal context. As the situation demands, we resort to the essentialist ethnic, linguistic and cultural elements of our identity within our 'Christian' frame of reference, and to our common identity within a 'national' or a polemical frame of reference. At times we claim our ethnic identity strongly, and at other times we opt for our ecclesiastical or regional identity.

The crucial question, therefore, is: are the specificities of our identity, the differences (ethnic, ecclesiastical, regional and communal), erasable? Are these specificities of value or are they only an obstacle in the striving for justice and liberation? Paul has something to teach us on this issue.

4. The Poetics and Politics of Pauline Identity

4.1. *Paul Among the Enlightened European Scholars*

The Pauline studies since European Enlightenment have been plagued by questions relating to Paul's Hellenistic and Jewish identities. Scholars of liberal Protestant persuasions, especially in Germany, sought the origin of early Christianity from a polarity that was created between

Judaism and Hellenism (F.C. Baur, D.F. Strauss, A. von Harnack and the old History-of-Religions School).[39] From Alexander to Constantine, anything remotely related to Greek language and culture in the eastern Mediterranean was classified as Hellenistic,. Anything a Jew said, did or believed was taken as a form of Judaism. All these scholars give credit to Paul for Hellenizing and universalizing Christianity from a Jewish particularity.

However, there was a counter voice that spoke of Hellenism as essentially foreign to Paul (from Schweitzer, Schoeps, Stendhal, W.D. Davis, to EP Sanders and the new perspective on Paul [new History-of-Religions] school). For Schweitzer, Paul's thought derived completely from Judaism and the Hellenization of Christianity began only in the post-Pauline phase. He thinks that Pauline thought emerged from the seedbed of Judaism, and was based on OT, Hellenistic Judaism, rabbinic Judaism and apocalypticism. Schweitzer was, to a large extent, influenced by a debate on Hebraism versus Judaism in Europe.

This debate in Europe—Hebraism and Hellenism as universal and Judaism as particularistic and, therefore, inferior—has an ideological base in Europe. In the modern period, when the European nation states were forming strong national identities, the Jews were constructed as the 'other'. That is, it was claimed that the Indo-European Aryan race, language, etc, was superior to Semitic language and race. This debate on Judaism versus Hellenism was maintained in European scholarship due to the nationalistic, ecclesiastical and cultural needs of Europe.

Today, most scholars of antiquity admit that both Hellenism and Judaism in the ancient world present important irreducible complexities. There is an increasing recognition that Judaism was not devoid of Hellenism and Hellenism was not devoid of oriental cultures such as Jewish, Syrian, and other Asiatic cultures.[40]

---

[39]   See Ben Witherington III, *The Paul Quest: The Renewed Search for the Jew of Tarsus* (Downers Grove: IVP, 1998), 9ff.

[40]   For a brief but enlightening survey and analysis, see Dale B. Martin, 'Paul and the Judaism/Hellenism Dichotomy: Toward a Social History of the Question' and Philip Alexander, 'Hellenism and Hellenization as Problematic Historiographical Categories', in T. Engberg-Pedersen (ed.), *Paul Beyond the Judaism/ Hellenism Divide* (Louisville: WJK, 2001), 29–80. Also see John M.G. Barclay, *Jews in the Mediterranean Diaspora: From Alexander to Trajan (323 BCE–117 CE)* (Berkeley: University of California Press, 1996).

4.2. The Location of Paul's Culture and Identity

The poetics of Paul are his epistles to the churches which he and his circle of disciples founded in Asia Minor, Greek peninsula, Macedonia and elsewhere, and also to individuals with whom he had intimate pastoral ties. These letters show the ease with which he could use the Koine Greek (a hybrid language originated out of a mixture of Attic Greek with Asiatic languages) prevalent in Asia Minor, Macedonia, and also his familiarity with Greco-Roman-Asiatic rhetoric.[41] Linguistically Paul belonged to at least four worlds: Hebrew, Aramaic, Greek, (Latin?) and Asiatic (Syrian).[42]

From the short autobiographical glimpses in Paul's letters and Lukan biographical highlights in the Acts of the Apostles, we learn of Paul's initial identity as that of a Syrian-(Cilician-Tarsisian)-Jew[43] who was zealous for the traditions of his fathers (Gal. 1.13ff; 2 Cor. 11.22ff; Phil. 3.4ff). While he inherited and held a strong Jewish ethnic and religio-cultural identity (as a zealous, faultless, blue-blooded Pharisaic Jew), he was also a Roman citizen (Acts 22.25). He was well-versed in Hebrew, Aramaic, Greek and, perhaps also, Latin and Syriac. Despite these extensions in his identity, he often boasted of his ethnic essentialist Jewish, racial identity and credentials—circumcised on the eighth day, of the tribe of Benjamin, a zealous Pharisee and a blameless practising Jew (when measured on observing Jewish ritual purity laws and of months, days, seasons and festivals of the Jewish calendar). As regard to the zeal, he was a persecutor of the radical wing of the early Christian sect (the Hellenistai Stephenites[44]) due their gentile mission initiatives and inclusion of Gentiles into the Nazarene sect of Judaism. Thus, though he was living away from the homeland of the Jews, he was an orthodox Jew through his practice of Jewish cultural nationalism.

---

[41] Ben Witherington has recently highlighted Paul's Asiatic rhetoric in Colossians in his latest commentary on Colossians.

[42] Witherington, 'Paul the Writer and Rhetor', in *The Paul Quest*, ch. 3.

[43] This aspect of Paul's identity is emphasized by Martin in Pedersen (ed.), *Paul*, 29–61.

[44] For Stephenite Hellenistai, see Simon Samuel, 'The Acts of Philip and the Certain Men of Cyprus and Cyrene: A Remapping of Early Christian Mission Frontiers', in *Remapping Mission Discourse* (Dehradun: NTC/Delhi: ISPCK, 2008), 42–71.

The discrepancies between the Lukan record of Paul in Acts (biographical portraits of Paul) and Paul's own records in his epistles (autobiographical portraits) are matters for endless scholarly debate.[45] But it appears that though Paul was a diaspora Jew, he held some strong ties (at least at the emotional level) with the heartland of Judaism (Jerusalem). He can best be described as a zealous diaspora Jewish cultural nationalist with strong Jerusalem ties. However, at the same time, he was comfortably living with his Roman citizenship in Tarsus (the Oxford of the time) in the Roman-Syrian province of Cilicia (just like the many Hindutva or Jihadi zealots of Indian and Pakistani origin, who are comfortable with their US or European citizenship). So in Paul, we see a plural person living in three or four worlds with changing (intertwining and overlapping) identities, despite his zealous Jewish ethnic essentialism and cultural nationalism.

Later, as a result of the Jesus revelation in his life, Paul became a zealous Jewish-Christian transcultural missionary. Apparently through this revelation (which was most probably mystical and apocalyptic in nature[46]), he found in Judaism a theological and cultural contradiction, that is, its narrow ethnocentrism and universal monotheism. His shift into the emerging Nazarene sect of the time was to resolve this question: how can one be culturally Jewish and be different, when there is only one God for both Jews and Gentiles? In other words, how can there be one God and two different peoples: Jews and Gentiles?

Within early Christianity, prior to Paul's entry, there were some Jews who practised their faith in Jesus as the Messiah within framework of zealous Jewish cultural nationalism (the right wing conservative Jewish-Christians, who were known as the circumcision party or the party of the Pharisees—Acts 15; Gal. 2.14ff). They tried to resolve this contradiction and answer Paul's question by attempting to Judaize the Gentile believers in Christ, through imposing circumcision, purity laws and the Jewish calendar on them (a kind of Jewish cultural nationalism), so that the difference may be erased and that there be one people.

---

[45]   See John Knox, *Chapters in a Life of Paul* (Macon: Mercer University Press, 1987).

[46]   Alan Segal, *Paul the Convert: The Apostolate and Apostasy of Saul the Pharisee* (New Haven: Yale University Press, 2001).

Apparently Paul's transition was not into this conservative early Jewish-Christian segment which affirmed Jewish difference. In fact he considered their approach as not resolving the contradiction: erasure of the cultural diversity of the Gentiles and the Jews was not Paul's agenda in preaching the Gospel. His transition was into that early Christian segment which maintained a strategic, ambivalent relation with Judaism, affiliating and distancing from it almost simultaneously (the so-called middle wing)[47]. Hence we see him with the same tongue boasting of his essentialist ethnic identity and Jewish cultural practices (shaving of his hair, paying for ritual purity, observing festivals, allowing circumcision of Timothy) while also counting all those as rubbish (e.g., upset at the circumcision of Titus). He is prepared to be cut off from the salvation of Christ for the sake of his countrymen if they would turn to Christ (Rom. 9), yet he tells the Gentile believers in Galatia, 'remain as I am for I have become as you are' (Gal. 4.12). It appears that Paul is a Jew and Gentile both at the same time. He is a strategic essentialist, who retains traits of Jewish cultural practices, and a transculturalist, who crosses beyond the cultural bounds of Judaism to the Gentiles. He has no quarrel with those Jews who believe in Christ and yet follow certain Jewish cultural practices. He has huge difficulty with those Jewish Christians who tried to impose their cultural practices on Gentile believers, in order to first convert them to Judaism to convert them to Christianity, as though only a good Jew can be a good Christian. He wished the Gentiles to remain culturally different, though they believed in Christ now. So Paul appears to have been an advocate for strategic difference. He may best be described as a particularist-universalist[48], who advocated that people with diverse cultural and regional identity backgrounds may believe in Christ, without erasing their cultural and regional particularities.

As a follower of Christ, Paul preached Christ as the *Kurios*, but at the same time he appeals to Caesar, in order to be safe from the hands

---

[47] For various self-definitions within early Christianity see Ben Meyer, *The Early Christians: Their World Mission and Self-Discovery* (Wilmington: Michael Glazier, 1986).

[48] See John M.G. Barclay, 'Universalism and Particularism: Twin Components of Both Judaism and Early Christianity', in Bockmuehl and Thompson (eds), *A Vision for the Church: Studies in Earliest Christian Ecclesiology* (Edinburgh: T&T Clark, 1997), 207–24.

of his native Jewish persecutors. He lived as a Roman citizen, practised Jewish rituals whenever necessary (shaving his hair), preached Christ (not Caesar) as the *Kurios* of both Jews and Gentiles, and identified increasingly and passionately with the Gentile believers.

Here we see the strategic postcoloniality (not universalism or imperialism) of Paul. He is affiliated to his native Jewish religio-cultural traditions, while distancing himself from them at the same time. Similarly he is affiliated to Rome, while distancing himself from her and her imperialist agenda for the world. He advocated 'peace, victory and salvation of Jesus Christ' in the context where Rome propagated 'Pax Romana', and Roman victory and salvation.[49] Pauline identity may thus best be descried as an ambivalent 'affiliative-alterity' identity, attached and detached almost simultaneously with/from his native Jewish cultural traditions and the Roman colonial rule. He is an ethnic essentialist (particularist) and universalist at the same time.[50]

Daniel Boyarin, in his book *A Radical Jew: Paul and the Politics of Identity* argues that Paul, as a first century Jewish Christian, was a zealous advocate of a universal identity for himself and for his Gentile and Jewish converts. His agenda was to create 'one new humanity' in Christ without any cultural and ethnic boundaries and barriers. Boyarin thinks that Paul believed in the erasure of difference in Galatians 3.26–28, under the pretext of making a Universal Human Body (one new humanity). By advocating this, he has become an archetypal universalist and imperialist. The politics of culture employed by Paul, according to Boyarin, was that of a Christian imperialist, and in the Christian churches that he founded, in the 'new Israel of God', there is no room for 'difference'.

But a closer reading of Paul would reveal that it is not Paul but the conservative, rival Jewish Christian missionaries who challenged his version of the Gospel in Galatia, Corinth and all other Pauline congregations. They attempted to create a Universal Jew in order that such a Jew can become a good Christian. By preaching and imposing

---

[49] K. Wengst, *Pax Romana and the Peace of Christ* (Philadelphia: Fortress, 1987); N. Elliot, *Liberating Paul: Justice of God and the Politics of the Apostle* (New York: Orbis, 1994).

[50] Alan Segal, in his reading of Paul, comes close to saying something like this. See his *Paul the Convert*.

the practice of circumcision, food laws and the Jewish calendar, it is the rival conservative Jewish Christians who tried to erase the cultural difference of the Gentile believers in Galatia and elsewhere. It is this erasure of difference and the freedom that they have in Christ, which the Jewish cultural nationalist Christians tried to steal from the Galatians and other Gentile believers, that Paul objected to so vehemently in his letter. For doing this, Boyarin accuses Paul of being a Christian universalist and imperialist.

Paul advocated a politics of identity for himself and his believers, both Jews and Gentiles, which can best be seen as a strategic essentialist and transculturally hybrid identity. It is strategically essentialist, that is, a Jew who becomes a believer in Christ may continue following Jewish cultural particularities. Paul's words to an insincere hypocritical Peter is pertinent here: 'If you, though a Jew, live like a Gentile and not like a Jew, how can you compel the Gentiles to live like Jews?' (Gal. 2:14b). Paul's politics of identity and culture is also transcultural in nature, for Paul tends to live like a Jew among the Jews, and as a Gentile among the Gentiles, for the sake of Christ. Here too his intent is evangelism, not erasure of cultural difference. He believed that people with cultural diversities can believe in and follow Christ within their cultural diversities. Though he says, for instance, that in Christ there is no male or female, he did not mean that maleness of the male or the femaleness of the female must be erased in order to become a new human in Christ. He did not mean erasure of particularity and difference.

Thus Pauline identity and his advocacy of identity may be located in the in-between third space (postcolonial space). This space may best be described as the Ecclesial Space of Emancipation, affiliative and abrogative to any polar opposite identification or erasure of identification. In the Ecclesial Space of Emancipation that Paul envisaged, anyone from any cultural space may enter and be ensured of an affiliative-alterity cultural dynamic. Paul did not advocate complete cultural adherence but, at the same time, he did not advocate complete antagonism. In his mission praxis, he adhered to certain Jewish cultural practices, while outrightly rejecting any attempt to erase the cultural difference of his Gentile believers.

Paul's evangelistic mission paved the way to form communities of faith toward the west coast of the ancient Mediterranean. These were mixed communities. There were Jews, Greeks, possibly Romans, and other native pagans, as members of his communities. Paul's westward mission, in the first century context, needs to be understood as an attempt to undertake the hardest of mission tasks in the darkest of mission fields of his time. The areas west of Rome—Spanish, Gaul, Germanic and Anglo-Saxon tribal areas in Europe were the most uncivilized warring tribal areas (akin to the Afghan and Pakistani tribal areas of today) which the Romans too found difficult to control. It is to these parts, and not to the east where lay perhaps was the most civilized and richest parts of the ancient world, that Paul desired to take the Gospel. He was perhaps aware of the missionaries moving into the relatively prosperous east. But as an Asiatic Syrian Jew, he preferred to move into the uncivilized warring western tribal parts of the Roman Empire, the hardest mission fields of the day, in order that the east and the west be hyphenated through the good news of Christ.

5. Conclusion

It is this task of hyphenation that should take place through the Gospel of Christ. This should not only be an intra-communal hyphenation within the Christian community, but also a subcultural, transcultural, national and trans-national hyphenation. One can therefore be a Syrian-Charismatic-Christian-Indian and a world citizen, all at the same time.

References

Banerjee-Dube, Ishita and S. Dube (eds). *Ancient and Modern: Religion, Power, and Community in India*. New Delhi: OUP, 2009.

Barclay, John M.G. *Jews in the Mediterranean Diaspora: From Alexander to Trajan, 323 BCE–117 CE*. Berkeley: University of California Press, 1996.

Barrett, C.K. *On Paul: Essays on his Life, Work and Influence in the Early Church*. New York: T&T Clark, 2003.

Becker, J. *Paul: Apostle to the Gentiles*. Louisville: WJK, 1993.

Bhabha, Homi. *The Location of Culture*. London: Routledge, 2004.

Bockmuehl, M. and Thompson (eds). *A Vision for the Church: Studies in Earliest Christian Ecclesiology*. Edinburgh: T&T Clark, 1997.

Boyarin, Daniel. *A Radical Jew: Paul and the Politics of Identity.* Berkeley: University of California Press, 1994.

Castelli, Elizabeth. *Imitating Paul: A Discourse of Power.* Louisville: WJK, 1991.

Chakrabarty, B. (ed.). *Communal Identity in India: Its Construction and Articulation in the Twentieth Century.* New Delhi: OUP, 2003.

Chilton, Bruce and C. Evans (eds). *The Missions of James, Peter and Paul: Tensions in Early Christianity.* Leiden: Brill, 2005.

Clarke, Sathinathan et al (eds). *Dalit Theology in the Twenty-first Century.* New Delhi: OUP, 2010.

Dube, Saurabh (ed.). *Postcolonial Passages: Contemporary History-writing on India.* New Delhi: OUP, 2004.

Dunn, J.D.G. *The Theology of Paul, the Apostle.* Grand Rapids: Eerdmans, 1998.

Elliott, Neil. *Liberating Paul: The Justice of God and the Politics of the Apostle.* New York: Orbis, 1994.

Engberg-Pedersen, Troels (ed.). *Paul Beyond the Judaism/ Hellenism Divide.* Louisville: WJK, 2001.

Gandhi, Leela. *Postcolonial Theory: A Critical Introduction.* Edinburgh: Edinburgh University Press, 1998.

Gnanapragasam, P and E. Schüssler Fiorenza (eds). *Negotiating Borders: Theological Explorations in the Global Era. Essays in Honour of Prof. Felix Wilfred.* New Delhi: ISPCK, 2008.

Guha, Ranajit and G.C. Spivak (eds). *Selected Subaltern Studies.* New York: OUP, 1988.

Joseph, Teresa. *Family of Truth: The Liminal Context of Inter-Religious Dialogue: An Anthropological and Pedagogical Enquiry.* New Delhi: ISPCK, 2009.

Khilnani, Sunil. *The Idea of India.* New Delhi: Penguin, 1997.

Lentz Jr. and John Elayton. *Luke's Portrait of Paul.* Cambridge: CUP, 1993.

Loomba, Ania. *Colonialism/ Postcolonialism.* London: Routledge, 1998.

Meyers, Ben. *The Early Christians: Their World Mission and Self-Discovery.* Wilmington: Michael Glazier, 1986.

Reisner, R. *Paul's Early Period: Chronology, Mission Strategy, Theology.* Grand Rapids: Eerdmans, 1998.

Roy, Arundhati. *Broken Republic: Three Essays.* New Delhi: Penguin, 2011.

Said, Edward. *Culture and Imperialism.* London: Vintage, 1993.

Samuel, Simon. *A Postcolonial Reading of Mark's Story of Jesus.* New York: T&T Clark, 2007.

——. 'Remapping Mission Discourse: Mission Amidst Affluence and Affliction'. Pp. 160–84 in Simon Samuel and P.V. Joseph (eds), *Remapping Mission Discourse: A Festschrift in Honor of the Rev. George Kuruvila Chavanikamannil.* Dehradun: NTC/Delhi: ISPCK, 2008.

Sanders, E.P. *Paul and Palestinian Judaism: A Comparison of Patterns of Religion.* Philadelphia: Fortress, 1983.

Segal, Alan. *Paul the Convert: The Apostolate and Apostasy of Saul the Pharisee.* New Haven: Yale University Press, 2001.

Sharma, Jyotirmaya. *Terrifying Vision: M.S. Golwalkar, The RSS and India.* New Delhi: Penguin, 2007.

Sen, Amartya. *The Argumentative Indian: Writings on Indian History, Culture and Identity.* New Delhi: Penguin, 2005.

——. *Identity and Violence: The Illusion of Destiny.* London: Penguin, 2006.

Thapar, Romila. *Cultural Pasts.* New Delhi: OUP, 2000.

Varma, Pavan, K. *Becoming Indian: The Unfinished Revolution of Culture and Identity.* New Delhi: Penguin, 2010.

Volf, Miroslav. *Exclusion and Embrace: A Theological Exploration of Identity, Otherness, and Reconciliation.* Nashville: Abingdon Press, 1996.

Wallace, R. and W. Wynne. *The Three Worlds of Paul of Tarsus.* London: Routledge, 1998.

Watson, F. *Paul, Judaism and the Gentiles: A Sociological Approach.* Cambridge: CUP, 1986.

Witherington, Ben, III. *The Paul Quest: The Renewed Search for the Jew of Tarsus.* Downers Grove: IVP, 1998.

Wright, N.T. *Paul in Fresh Perspective.* Minneapolis: Fortress, 2005.

Zangenberg, Jurgen and Michael Labahn (eds). *Christians as a Religious Minority in a Multicultural City.* London: T&T Clark, 2004.

Early Christian Identity Formation and Its Relevance for Modern India

Cornelis Bennema[*]

1. Introduction

'I am a Christian' is a statement of identity that multitudes of Jesus-followers from various cultures, nationalities and ethnicities have made for over two millennia. But what does it mean to say, 'I am a Christian'? The term 'Christian' occurs only thrice in the New Testament (Acts 11.26; 26.28; 1 Pet. 4.16), so when and how did Jesus-followers receive or adopt this term as part of their identity? Christian identity is also inextricably related to conflict and persecution—both the New Testament and world history testify to this. I recount, for example, the story of Polycarp, bishop of Smyrna, who died a martyr about 155 CE:

> Now, as Polycarp was entering the stadium, a voice from heaven came to him, saying, 'Be strong and courageous, O Polycarp!' No one saw who spoke to him but those of our brothers who were present heard the voice. And as he was brought forward, there was a great uproar when they heard that Polycarp had been arrested. When he came near, the proconsul asked him whether he was Polycarp. On his confessing that he was, the proconsul tried to persuade him to deny [Christ], saying, 'Have respect for your old age', and other similar things according to their custom, such as, 'Swear by the fortune of Caesar; repent and say, Away with the Atheists.'[1] But Polycarp gazed with a stern face on the entire multitude of wicked heathen in the stadium and held out his hand towards them. With groans he looked up to heaven and said, 'Away with the Atheists.' Then, as the proconsul urged him, saying, 'Swear, and I will release you; insult Christ', Polycarp declared, 'I have served him eighty-six years and he never mistreated me. How then can I blaspheme my King and my Savior?' And when the proconsul continued to press him, saying, 'Swear by the fortune of Caesar', he answered, 'Since you vainly urge that, as you say, I should swear by the fortune of Caesar, and pretend not to know who and what I am, hear me boldly declare, *I am a Christian*. And if you wish to learn the teachings of Christianity, appoint me a day, and you shall hear it' (*Martyrdom of Polycarp* 9.1–10.1).

[*] Cornelis Bennema is Associate Professor of New Testament at South Asia Institute of Advanced Christian Studies (SAIACS) in Bangalore. For his publications, see www.saiacs.org/Faculty-Publications-Bennema.html.

[1] Christians were called 'atheists' because they did not participate in the veneration of Graeco-Roman gods.

Today, there are over two billion Jesus-followers or 'Christians' —
many of whom face religious violence or social persecution, including
Christians in India.[2]

Modern India is a nation with multiple religions, ethnicities
and cultures. Having become a global economic, military and
technological power, India is rethinking issues of national, ethnic
and religious identity. There is much debate on what it means to
be 'Indian', and who has the legitimacy to define it. The political-
nationalist Hindutva movement, for example, desires India to be a
Hindu *rashtra* and uses religious-cultural identity to polarize Indian
society, viewing non-Hindu Indians, such as Muslims, Christians
and Tribals, as the excluded 'other'.[3] Nobel laureate Amartya Sen,
however, vehemently argues that Indian and Hindu identity should
not be equated. He argues that people should have considerable
freedom to choose their identity, or combination of identities, and the
significance they attach to these identities.[4] Differently again, Pavan
Varma claims that a new pan-Indian identity has emerged, which
is supranational, cosmopolitan, accommodating and increasingly
homogeneous, despite regional or subcultural parochialisms.[5] This
ongoing identity debate is very relevant to the Indian church. What
does it mean, for example, to say, 'I am an Indian Christian' or 'I
am a Tamil or Naga Christian'? Is there scope for the categories
'Hindu Christian' or 'Muslim Christian' — a follower of Christ within
Hinduism or Islam? Can a 'Hindu Christian' perform *puja* to Jesus in
a Hindu temple, or a 'Muslim Christian' offer *salah* or *namaz* to Jesus
in a mosque? And how has the religious persecution experienced by
various Indian Christians over the last two decades affected Christian
identity formation?

---

[2] T.M. Johnson and K.R. Ross (eds), *Atlas of Global Christianity 1910–2010*
(Edinburgh: Edinburgh University Press, 2009), 9, 42–3.

[3] C. Bennema, 'Religious Violence in the Gospel of John: A Response to the
Hindutva Culture in Modern India', in F. Fox (ed.), *Violence and Peace: Creating a
Culture of Peace in the Contemporary Context of Violence* (Bangalore: CMS/ATC, 2010),
131–5.

[4] A. Sen, *The Argumentative Indian: Writings on Indian Culture, History and
Identity* (New Delhi: Penguin, 2005), ch. 16.

[5] P.K. Varma, *Being Indian: The Truth about Why the 21ˢᵗ Century Will Be India's*
(New Delhi: Penguin, 2004), ch. 5 (esp. 149–53).

In this study, I will sketch the historical development and nature of early Christian identity in the first two centuries CE to show that it evolved from being a Jewish ethno-religious identity into a Christian identity unattached to a particular geopolitical and ethno-cultural identity. This development occurred in a context of internal and external conflicts with Judaism and the Roman Empire. I will also argue that the Christian identity transcended, included, relativized, transformed but did not abrogate existing identities. I contend that understanding how the early Christians viewed themselves and were perceived by others could help us to comprehend how Christian identity is shaped in modern India. The first-century Graeco-Roman world and modern Indian society share significant features. Both environments are characterized by (religious) pluralism in which Christianity's truth claim has to compete with many other truth claims, so that Christian identity formation often occurs in a context of conflict.[6] Religion was an important identity marker in the first-century Mediterranean world, just as it is in contemporary India. Besides, many conflicts in India are related to religious identities. Furthermore, the hellenization of the Roman Empire (i.e., the permeation of the Mediterranean world by Greek culture, thought and language) is comparable to the anglicization (even westernization) of India. Finally, in both worlds, identity was predominantly group- rather than individual-oriented.[7] In view of these similarities, I will apply my findings on early Christian identity formation to the debate on Christian identity in contemporary India.

2. Early Christian Identity Formation in Contexts of Conflict

'Christianity' developed from a messianic sect within the milieu of late Second Temple Judaism to a religion distinct from Judaism in

---

[6] In the first century, Christianity's truth claim had to compete with claims made by the imperial cult and the Graeco-Roman pantheon, the mystery religions, various philosophies and Judaism. In modern India, Christianity's truth claim is up against claims made by, for example, Hinduism and its pantheon, Hindutva ideology, Islam, Buddhism, western-driven (economic) globalization and even atheism.

[7] Nevertheless, modern India is witnessing an increasingly individualized identity, especially among the urban middle class.

the second century. This development was not without difficulties. There were conflicts both with Second Temple Judaism and the Roman Empire, and within the emerging movement itself. I will trace the development of early Christianity from its inception to Paul (keeping to the emphasis of Acts) and then to 'mainstream' Christianity.[8] I will examine the biblical witness and that of the Apostolic Fathers, following the spread of the Christ-movement in the first two centuries CE through the then-known world—the Roman empire—rather than to, for example, Africa, Central Asia and India.[9]

2.1. Christian Identity and Judaism

'Christianity' started as a Jewish messianic renewal movement in about 30 CE. Its first members were Jews (and perhaps proselytes), who continued to visit the temple and synagogue and, most probably, observed the Torah. Yet, from its inception, infant Christianity was in conflict with its mother Judaism. In fact, already in his own time, Jesus had been in conflict with fellow Jews, especially the religio-political leaders in Jerusalem, regarding the Torah and other central issues. Peter and the other apostles clashed with the Sanhedrin authorities over their proclamation of the crucified Jesus as God's messianic agent of Israel's renewal (Acts 3–5). The Jews and the Sanhedrin were upset when they assumed Stephen was attacking the temple and the Torah; Stephen was killed for his criticism and alleged blasphemy (Acts 6–7).

Paul often clashed with fellow Jews over his proclamation of Jesus as the Messiah and his 'law-free' (i.e., not Torah-based) Gospel, both in

---

[8] Early Christianity was much more diverse than I can sketch here. For the diversity of early Christianity, see especially J.D.G. Dunn, *Unity and Diversity in the New Testament: An Inquiry into the Character of Earliest Christianity* (2nd edn; London: SCM, 1990).

[9] This should not devalue, of course, the study of early Indian Christian identity based on the apostle Thomas's mission to South India in the first century, which resulted in a church that was Hindu in culture, Christian in religion and Judeo-Syro-Oriental in terms of origin and worship—the *Mar Thoma* church. For the historical plausibility of Thomas's mission to South India, see E.J. Schnabel, *Early Christian Mission* (2 vols; Downers Grove: IVP, 2004), 1:880–95. See also S. Neill, *A History of Christianity in India: The Beginnings to AD 1707* (Cambridge: CUP, 1984); R.E. Frykenburg, *Christianity in India: From Beginnings to the Present* (Oxford: OUP, 2008).

the Diaspora (9.22–23; 13–14; 17.1–13; 18.1–17) and in Jerusalem (9.29; 21.27–24.23). When Paul was arrested in Jerusalem, the Jews levelled these charges against him: 'This is the man who is teaching everyone everywhere against our people, our law, and this place [the temple]' (21.28; cf. 21.21), and '[w]e have found this man a pestilent fellow, an dissenter among all the Jews throughout the world, and a ringleader of the sect of the Nazarenes' (24.5). Thus, fellow Jews felt that Paul was un-Jewish, a non-conformist who was disloyal to his people and traditions.

Nevertheless, such clashes between the early Christian movement and Second Temple Judaism were an *intra-Jewish* conflict. Evidently Jews perceived 'Christians' as a sect *within* Second Temple Judaism (Acts 24.5, 14; 28.22), much like the Sadducees (Acts 5.17) and the Pharisees (Acts 15.5; 26.5). Further, the leaders of the early Christian movement (Peter, James, Stephen, Paul) were all Jews. Eventually though, the implications of the crucified Jewish Messiah Jesus and his teachings caused the movement to burst out of its Jewish matrix. By the early second century, Graeco-Roman writers perceived Christians as distinct from Jews (see further section 2.3), and for Ignatius, Christianity and Judaism had already parted (*Magnesians* 8.1; 10.3; *Philadelphians* 6.1).[10]

2.2. Christian Identity and Christianity

Christianity did not develop within the Jewish identity as a homogeneous movement. Almost from its inception, disagreements occurred. The dispute in Acts 6.1–6, just a few months after Pentecost, reveals a tension in the early Christian community between the 'Hebrews' (Aramaic-speaking Jewish believers) and the 'Hellenists' (Greek-speaking Diaspora Jews who had settled in Jerusalem and become believers).[11] Besides, the 'Hellenist' Stephen's critique of the temple, rooted in Jesus' teaching, may not have been directed only

---

[10] J.D.G. Dunn explains that 'the parting of the ways' between Christianity and Judaism was a complex drawn-out process (*The Partings of the Ways: Between Christianity and Judaism and their Significance for the Character of Christianity* [London: SCM, 1991], 230–43).

[11] Schnabel, *Mission*, 1:653–5; J.D.G. Dunn, *Beginning from Jerusalem* (Vol. 2 of Christianity in the Making; Grand Rapids: Eerdmans, 2009), 246–51.

at his fellow non-Christian Greek-speaking Jews (Acts 6.9–14), but also at the Aramaic-speaking Jewish Christians (the 'Hebrews' of 6.1), whose regular temple attendance possibly betrayed a displaced loyalty towards the temple cult.[12] The most significant dispute in early Christianity, however, ran along ethnic lines.[13]

Ethnic expansion or Gentile inclusion caused early Christianity to become a missionary, trans-ethnic movement.[14] The seeds were sown by Philip in his mission to the Samaritans and the Ethiopian eunuch (Acts 8), and by Peter in the incident with the God-fearer Cornelius (Acts 10). More substantially, the church in Antioch saw a large influx of Gentile believers in the mid-30s (Acts 8.1, 4; 11.19–26). But it was primarily Paul's programmatic mission to the Gentiles that abolished the Jewish ethnic boundary.[15] A critical re-evaluation of the soteriological and sociological dimensions of the law, caused Paul to question its salvific efficacy and its ethnic disposition to separate Jews from Gentiles (Gal. 2–5; Rom. 2–7; cf. Eph. 2.11–21). Consequently, he envisaged a life of freedom in Christ, led by the Spirit and apart from the law (Gal. 5; Rom. 8), and redefined the categories 'Jew' (Rom. 2.28–29) and 'Israel' (Rom. 9.6) in non-ethno-national terms. While Judaism allowed Gentiles to join *as Jews* through proselytizing (i.e., adopting the Jewish ethno-cultural identity), for Paul, Christianity is equally open to Gentile and Jew alike—a Gentile can (even should) join Christianity *as a Gentile* rather than a proselyte.

In 48–49 CE, the Jerusalem council settled the ethnic dispute about the admission of Gentiles. The importance of the Jerusalem decree was that Christianity was no longer attached to a particular ethno-religious identity. Gentiles could be part of the people of God without exchanging their Gentile identity for a Jewish one. Faith in Christ, evidenced by the reception of the Spirit to signal God's acceptance, was the only requirement for membership into the true people of God—for Jew

---

[12] Dunn, *Beginning*, 260–263. Cf. Schnabel, *Mission*, 1:661–5.

[13] False teachings often threatened early Christianity too (e.g., Acts 20.30; 2 Cor. 11.1–15; 1 Tim. 1.6–7; 4.1–5; 2 Tim. 4.3–4; 2 Pet. 2; 1 John 2.18–28; Rev. 2.6, 14–15, 20).

[14] A trans-ethnic Christianity means that ethnicity is irrelevant for Christian membership—one does not need to reject an existing ethnic identity or adopt a specific other identity in order to join.

[15] For the chronology of Paul's life and mission, see Schnabel, *Mission*, 1:45–52; Dunn, *Beginning*, 497–512.

and Gentile alike (Acts 15.8–9). The Jerusalem council thus provided authoritative direction for the entire Christian mission.[16] With the backing of the Jerusalem decree, Paul carried through this programme of trans-ethnic Christianity effectively (Acts 16–20; Rom. 15.18–19).

2.3. Christian Identity and the Roman Empire

In the first century, there were no major confrontations between Christianity and the Roman Empire. The earliest conflict was (obviously) the crucifixion of Jesus as a messianic pretender under Pilate about 30 CE. Then, Acts records a few conflicts between Paul and Roman city authorities, but these were incidental in nature (Acts 16.19–24; 18.12–17; 19.23–41; 23–25). The Roman historian Tacitus narrates Nero's erratic persecution of Roman Christians in 64 CE (*Annals* 15.44.2–5). In 1 Peter 4.16, probably written during the reign of Domitian, we meet a new phenomenon: to suffer '*as a Christian*', i.e., for the name itself (cf. 1 Pet. 4.14). Revelation, probably written during the latter part of Domitian's reign, reflects the sporadic, incidental persecution Christians experienced in Asia Minor, while anticipating more systematic and widespread persecution. In general, however, Christianity had not yet attracted the attention of Rome because it was still viewed as a Jewish sect (Acts 16.19–20; 18.15) and hence shared in the protection and privileges that the Jews had under Roman rule.[17]

The second century, however, was marked by conflict, and systematic persecution of Christians by Rome gradually developed. The major reason for this progressive conflict was the gradual emergence of Christianity from Second Temple Judaism as a distinct religion.[18] In the early part of the second century, the Romans started noticing the Christians. Tacitus, writing around 110 CE about Nero's scapegoating

---

[16] See especially R. Bauckham 'James and the Jerusalem Church', in *idem* (ed.), *The Book of Acts in Its Palestinian Setting* (Vol. 4 of B.W. Winter [ed.], *The Book of Acts in Its First Century Setting*; Grand Rapids: Eerdmans, 1995), 415-80.

[17] Cf. K. Bediako, *Theology and Identity: The Impact of Culture upon Christian Thought in the Second Century and Modern Africa* (Oxford: Regnum; 1992), 18–9; B.W. Winter, 'Gallio's Ruling on the Legal Status of Early Christianity (Acts 18:14–15)', *Tyndale Bulletin* 50 (1999): 213–24.

[18] A. Tripolitis, *Religions of the Hellenistic-Roman Age* (Grand Rapids: Eerdmans, 2002), 98–9; P.A. Harland, *Dynamics of Identity in the World of the Early Christians: Associations, Judeans, and Cultural Minorities* (New York: T&T Clark, 2009), 172–6.

Roman Christians in 64 CE, viewed Christianity as a 'pernicious superstition' (*Annals* 15.44.3). Pliny the Younger, governor of Bithynia and Pontus in northern Asia Minor, wrote to emperor Trajan about 111–112 CE to inquire how to handle the Christian 'superstition':

> I have never been present at an examination of Christians, so I do not know what punishment is required or how far it is to be carried out. Nor do I understand the legal grounds for a prosecution, or how stringently it is to be prosecuted . . . Is it *the name* ['Christian'] *itself* which is prosecutable, even if not involved in crimes, or only those crimes associated with the name? In the meantime, I now handle it this way with those who are turned over to me as Christians. I ask them directly, in person, if they are Christian, I ask a second and third time to be sure, and indicate to them the danger of their situation. If they persist, I order them to be executed . . . An anonymous list has been brought out which contains the names of a great many persons. I decided to dismiss charges against any on this list who stated that they were now not, nor had ever been Christians, if they repeated after me a prayer of invocation to the Gods, and made an offering of wine and incense to your statue, which I had brought in to the court along with the statues of the Gods, for this purpose. And in addition they were to formally curse Christ, which I understand true Christians will never do . . . I found nothing worthy of blame other than a *depraved and excessive superstition* (*Epistle to Trajan* 10.96).

By the mid-second century, the actions against Christians had become more systematic and established — they were persecuted simply for the name 'Christian'. As we saw in the introduction, when Polycarp was urged by the Roman proconsul to deny his beliefs, he proudly proclaimed, 'I am a Christian', and was burnt alive (*Martyrdom of Polycarp* 10.1; 12.1–3). Around the same time, Justin Martyr wrote that 'if any of the accused deny the name, and say that he is not a Christian, you acquit him, as having no evidence against him as a wrong-doer; but if any one acknowledge that he is a Christian, you punish him on account of this acknowledgment' (*1 Apology* 4.5). Martyrdom, persecution and the construction of early Christian identity, expressed by the claim 'I am a Christian', were inextricably linked in the second century. Thus, the experience of martyrdom and the confession 'I am a Christian' articulated (perhaps even constituted) Christian identity.[19] The Christian martyrs did not die *for* Christianity but *as* Christians — the

---

[19] J.M. Lieu, '"I am a Christian": Martyrdom and the Beginning of "Christian" Identity', in *idem, Neither Jew nor Greek: Constructing Early Christianity* (Edinburgh: T&T Clark, 2002), 211–5.

individual confession 'I am a Christian' itself determined death and was the martyr's existential statement of identification with the suffering Christ.[20] While the label 'Christian' was initially a denigrating and accusatory term used by outsiders (Acts 11.26; 26.28; Tacitus, *Annals* 15.44.2; Pliny, *Epistle to Trajan* 10.96), Christians soon adopted and reversed it, till it became a mark of honour and self-identity, and a direct cause of suffering (1 Pet. 4.16; cf. Ignatius, *Magnesians* 4.1; *Romans* 3.2).[21]

In the course of the second century, various Roman writers provided better-informed and more sympathetic critiques of Christianity.[22] A parallel development was that educated Christians, such as Justin Martyr and other Christian apologists, learned to present and defend their faith in categories of Graeco-Roman philosophies.[23] The efforts of the Christian apologists were successful because, towards the end of the second century, Christianity had gained increasing social and intellectual acceptance, as we can see, for example, in Tertullian's *Apology*:

> [Ch. 1] [T]hose who once hated Christianity because they knew nothing about it, no sooner come to know it than they all lay down at once their enmity. From being its haters they become its disciples. By simply getting acquainted with it, they begin now to hate what they had formerly been, and to profess what they had formerly hated; and their numbers are as great as are laid to our charge. The outcry is that the State is filled with Christians—that they are in the fields, in the citadels, in the islands: they make lamentation, as for some calamity, that both sexes, every age and condition, even high rank, are passing over to the profession of the Christian faith.[24]

2.4. Christian Identity and Other Identities

We have seen that Christianity developed as a religion that is unattached to a particular geopolitical, ethno-cultural identity. The *Epistle to*

---

[20] Cf. Lieu, 'Martyrdom', 213, 222, 225.

[21] Lieu, 'Martyrdom', 212; *idem, Christian Identity in the Jewish and Graeco-Roman World* (Oxford: OUP, 2004), 250–254; D.G. Horrell, 'The Label Χριστιανός: 1 Peter 4:16 and the Formation of Christian Identity', *Journal of Biblical Literature* 126 (2007): 361–81. Horrell argues that while 1 Pet. 4.14 indicates insiders' ways to describe their identity (suffering for the name of Christ), Peter's use of the label 'Christian' in 1 Pet. 4.16 (suffering as a Christian) indicates the transition from a negative description by outsiders to a proud self-designation.

[22] T. Barnes, 'Pagan Perceptions of Christianity', in I. Hazlett (ed.), *Early Christianity: Origins and Evolution to AD 600* (Nashville: Abingdon Press, 1991), 234–6.

[23] Bediako, *Theology*, 30–31, 42–3. Cf. Tripolitis, *Religions*, 101–4.

[24] Barnes, 'Perceptions', 236.

Diognetus, from the late second century, provides a good example of this:

> For the Christians are distinguished from other men neither by country, nor language, nor the customs which they observe. For they neither inhabit cities of their own, nor employ a peculiar form of speech, nor lead a life which is marked out by any singularity. The course of conduct which they follow has not been devised by any speculation or deliberation of inquisitive men; nor do they, like some, proclaim themselves the advocates of any merely human doctrines. But, inhabiting Greek as well as barbarian cities, according as the lot of each of them has determined, and following the customs of the natives in respect to clothing, food, and the rest of their ordinary conduct, they display to us their wonderful and confessedly striking method of life. They dwell in their own countries, but simply as sojourners. As citizens, they share in all things with others, and yet endure all things as if foreigners. Every foreign land is to them as their native country, and every land of their birth as a land of strangers. They marry, as do all others; they beget children; but they do not destroy their offspring. They have a common table, but not a common bed. They are in the flesh, but they do not live after the flesh. They pass their days on earth, but *they are citizens of heaven*. They obey the prescribed laws, and at the same time surpass the laws by their lives. They love all men, and are persecuted by all . . . To sum up all in one word—what the soul is in the body, that are Christians in the world (*Epistle to Diognetus* 5.1–6.1).

The Christian's heavenly citizenship, resulting in an other-worldliness or foreignness in this world, is a distinct aspect of the Christian identity.[25] Paul had already spoken of Christians as heavenly citizens (Php. 3.20; cf. Eph. 2.6, 19), and John had stressed the Christian's distinctiveness of being 'in yet not of the world' (John 17.14–16). It is not surprising, therefore, that Christians were presented or perceived by some as a new or third 'race', in contrast to Jews and Greeks (e.g., 1 Pet. 2.9–10; *Epistle to Diognetus* 1.1; Aristides, *Apology* 2; Clement of Alexandria, *Stromata* 6.5.41; cf. Tertullian, *Ad Nationes* 8, 20).[26]

The New Testament, however, does not speak of Christians being a *new* ethnic group *distinct* from Jews and Greeks. Instead, it portrays them as the *renewed* people of God *incorporating* both Jews and Greeks. Paul stressed that 'in Christ', people are a new creation (2 Cor. 5.17; Gal. 6.15), and that in this renewal there is no longer scope for (discriminating)

---

[25] J.M. Lieu, 'The Forging of Christian Identity and the *Letter to Diognetus'*, in *idem, Neither Jew nor Greek: Constructing Early Christianity* (Edinburgh: T&T Clark, 2002), 178–9, 188–9.

[26] See further Lieu, *Identity*, 259–66; Bediako, *Theology*, 34–41.

distinctions between Jew and Greek, slave and free, male and female (Gal. 3.28; Rom. 10.12; cf. Col. 3.10–11; Eph. 2.11–16). From Paul's credo 'in Christ, no Jew or Greek', I infer three principles. First, the Christian identity transcends and takes priority over other identities. At the same time, 'in Christ', no particular ethnicity has priority over the others. Second, the Christian identity subsumes the Jewish and Greek identity (and other identities), not by obliterating them but by accommodating them. Aspects of the Jewish and Gentile identities can be retained as long as they do not clash with the Christian identity or each other. Third, the Christian identity infuses and transforms existing identities by directing them to Christ. A Jewish Christian, for example, could no longer be ethnocentric or boast in the law. 'In Christ', Paul regarded his own ethno-religious identities worthless (Php. 3.5–8), could easily switch between cultural identities (1 Cor. 9.20–23), and was relaxed about cultural issues such as food and special days (Rom. 14; 1 Cor. 8; 10.25–32).[27]

In conclusion, the Christian identity is a religious identity, irrespective of ethnicity, nationality or culture. At the same time, the Christian identity includes and affirms rather than abrogates existing identities. Regarding ethnicity, the Christian identity is a trans-ethnic identity. As such, the Christian identity surpasses, absorbs, affirms, relativizes and transforms but does not abrogate existing geopolitical and ethno-cultural identities. The Christian identity is therefore also a *unifying* identity — it incorporates diverse identities in terms of ethnicity, nationality, culture, status and role, and converges them towards Christ in terms of beliefs, practices and ethos.

3. Christian Identity Formation in Modern India

I must now substantiate the claim that understanding the process of early Christian identity formation informs the modern debate about identity in India. I shall summarize my findings and relate them to three areas, focusing on *what* can be done rather than *how* this should be done — further research must deal with the latter.

---

[27] Paul's assertion, 'to the Jews I became as a Jew, in order to win Jews' (1 Cor. 9.20), is remarkable. Did he no longer regard himself a Jew? He certainly no longer ascribed to a Torah-based Jewish ethnocentric identity.

3.1. Christian Identity and Conflict

Early Christian identity developed in contexts of conflict. The main contention with Judaism was the religious issue that Jesus is the Messiah; within the movement itself it was the ethnic issue; and with the Roman Empire it was the religio-political issue that Jesus is Lord. It is remarkable that the internal conflicts experienced by early Christians (especially the ethnic issue) did not lead to an implosion or schism. Similarly, the Indian church must learn to solve internal conflicts while preserving unity. Too often, Indian Christians are divided on issues of ethnicity, caste, doctrine or on the more trivial issues of property and politics. The extent to which the Indian church can unite determines the credibility and effectiveness of her witness in society (cf. John 17.20–23).

Indian Christian identity formation also occurs in contexts of external conflict, often related to political, ethnic, religious and economic issues. For example, with Hinduism the contentious issue is the uniqueness of Christ, and with the Hindutva movement it also is the foreignness or non-Hindu quality of the Christian identity. While the Christian identity is a religious identity that is not attached to a particular ethno-cultural and geopolitical identity, the Hindu identity is religious-cultural with the Hindutva identity adding an ethno-geopolitical dimension to it (like the Jewish identity). Just as Jews and Jewish ethnocentric believers required Gentiles and Gentile believers to 'judaize' to be accepted, so Hindutva proponents insist that 'foreigners' (whether Muslims, Christians or Tribals) 'hinduize' in order to be part of a homogeneous Hindu fold. While Indian Christians should resist any homogenization that threatens diversity or equality, they themselves must not 'christianize' others into a uniform melting pot but must preserve the rich diversity in unity.

Another example of external conflict is the violent persecution of Christians in Kandhamal, Orissa, during August–September 2008. This was similar to what early Christians experienced during the Roman Empire. Just as Nero scapegoated the Christians for the great fire in Rome, so the Sangh Parivar preferred to believe that tribal Christians in Kandhamal had murdered Swami Laxmanananda, even though Maoists had claimed responsibility for the act. The following account recalls that of Polycarp:

'I was conducting a prayer meeting in Orissa's Makandapur village when more than 300 Vishwa Hindu Parishad activists arrived with lathis, swords, guns, spears and trishuls. They said they would kill us *because we were Christians,*' said Father Ashish Missale who fled the murderous mob to spend two days in the wilderness. Recounting the ordeal to the media on Tuesday, Father Missale said how one of the devotees was done to death right in front of his eyes. 'They hit Mukund Bardhan on his head. They then flung him in the air and stabbed him. His cry still pierces my ears' (*Times of India*, 3 September 2008).

Two years later, the National People's Tribunal on Kandhamal, held in New Delhi on 22–24 August 2010, reported on this religious-ethnic-economic conflict as follows:

The jury observes that a majority of victim-survivors and their families are from marginalized groups, particularly from the *dalit* and *adivasi* (SC and ST) Christian community, and that most live in abject poverty and on the brink of despair . . . They have faced persecution in all its forms — such as social and economic boycott as well as religious, caste-based and cultural discrimination . . . The jury observes that communal forces have used religious conversions as an issue for political mobilisation and to incite horrific forms of violence and discrimination against the Christians of SC origin and their supporters in Kandhamal. The object is to dominate them and ensure that they never rise above their low caste status and remain subservient to the upper castes. The jury observes, with deep concern, that a range of coercive tactics have been used by the communal forces for conversion or re-conversion of a person into the Hindu fold, including threat, intimidation, social and economic boycott and coercion, as well as the institutionalization of humiliating rituals. The state and district administrations have, on no occasion, intervened to protect the freedom of religion and freedom of expression.[28]

The formation of Christian identity in contexts of conflict is a present reality in India. For the early Christian martyrs, persecution was the defining moment in which their true identity surfaced. Similarly, in many parts of India today, religious persecution is a harsh reality, forcing people to work out and disclose their identity. Besides, just as second-century Christian apologists learned to present and defend their faith against various accusations and other truth claims, so Indian Christians should engage their critics and competing ideologies *in writing* in order to inform and participate in the larger debate. This very book *Indian and Christian: Changing Identities in Modern India* is meant to aid the Indian church to be a more meaningful player in the larger debate on the subject.

---

[28] http://christianpersecutionindia.blogspot.com/2010/08/national-peoples-tribunal-on-kandhamal.html has the full report (accessed 3 October 2011).

3.2. Christian Identity and Other Identities

We discovered three characteristics of the Christian identity. First, the Christian identity is a *religious* identity that is not attached to a particular geopolitical entity (a nation), ethnicity or culture. Second, it is an *inclusive transformational* identity that transcends, absorbs, affirms, relativizes, pervades, rather than abrogates, existing identities. Third, it is a *unifying* identity that directs the various identities towards Christ. This has important ramifications for today. For example, the Christian identity should superintend all identities that one brings into Christianity. When one becomes a Christian, any prior identities are not lost; rather, these are re-evaluated in view of the new Christian identity. So, a Naga Christian must re-evaluate a possible nationalistic identity, and perhaps let go of the desire for an independent geopolitical Nagaland. A Christian cannot be ethnocentric either. Although one's own ethnic identity need not be rejected, neither can one boast about or gloat in it at the expense of appreciating and celebrating the other's ethnicity. Christians should not use their ethnic, tribal, national or even religious identities to erect dividing walls that Paul was so keen to take down. In Christ, there is no Angami or Ao, Tangkhul or Kuki, Tamilian or Marathi, Indian or Pakistani, Pentecostal or Baptist. How then shall we evaluate the existence of mono-ethnic churches in India's multi-ethnic cities? When it comes to caste identity, Christians must reject the Hindu *apartheid* or social system of *varna* or caste because of its inherent inequality — in Christ, there is no Brahmin or Dalit (cf. articles 15 and 17 of the Constitution of India).

Then what about a religious identity one has prior to taking on a Christian identity — is there scope for a 'Muslim Christian' or a 'Hindu Christian'? Perhaps. But just as early Christianity burst out of its Jewish jacket, another religious identity probably cannot contain the Christian identity. Vice versa, it seems impossible to retain another religious identity within the Christian identity. Thus, when a Hindu or Muslim becomes a Christian, the religious aspect of one's identity has to be relinquished, while keeping the cultural aspect. However, since Hindu and Muslim are religio-cultural identities, in practice it will be difficult to distinguish between the religious and cultural aspects. I suggest that when a Hindu turns to Christ, one should not try to be a 'Christian Hindu' or 'Hindu Christian', holding on to a Hindu religious-(ethno-)cultural identity. Instead, perhaps one should view oneself as an 'Indian Christian', adopting a trans-ethno-cultural identity. The new Christian should no longer worship the gods of one's ethnos but the one true, universal God, who accepts everyone *in Christ*, irrespective of ethnicity, nationality and culture. Y.D. Tiwari, a well-known Brahmin convert to Christianity, remarks:

> When I decided to be baptized, I did not think that I was 'leaving' Hindu society. I thought I was adding something new, something glorious to my Hindu heritage. I wanted to continue to live with my parents to co-operate with other Hindus in social work, to visit the temple, etc. I was like early Christians who met daily at Solomon's porch in the temple. Soon I discovered that this was not possible.[29]

Thus, while the Christian identity transcends other identities, it also permeates and transforms them, thereby 'emptying' existing identities of specific religious contents. This may be a gradual process over time.[30] Those who claim allegiance to Jesus cannot remain where they are and as they are. Every believer is called out of some prior environment—whether this be Hinduism, Islam, secularism, atheism or otherwise.[31] Those who allow a Christian to remain part of his or her prior environment in an unqualified sense, for example as a 'secret' or 'anonymous' believer, must grapple with the historical reality that the Christian identity, despite its Jewish roots, could *not* be contained within the Jewish identity.

3.3. Christian Identity and Culture

Paul often relativized the importance of culture and reconsidered aspects of it in the light of the Gospel (section 2.4). Flemming explains that Paul was at home within overlapping Jewish and Graeco-Roman environments, and could therefore contextualize the Gospel for both

---

[29] Cited in P.S. Jacob, 'Religious Climate in India Today: An Introspective Analysis', in M.T.B. Laing (ed.), *Nationalism and Hinduism* (New Delhi: CMS/ISPCK, 2005), 79.

[30] Cf. Bennema, 'Violence', 153–5.

[31] Cf. C. Bennema, 'Spirit and Mission in the Bible: Toward a Dialogue between Biblical Studies and Missiology', *Trinity Journal* 32 (2011): 249–50, 255–6.

Jews and Gentiles *as a cultural insider*. For Paul, the Gospel could affirm, relativize, confront and transform culture.[32] Flemming also suggests that since '[t]he gospel is both at home in every culture and alien to every culture', both particular and universal, the church must address this dynamic interaction between the local and the global, by engaging in *intercultural* conversation (local Christians being part of a global interpretative community) and *transcontextual* theology (local theologizing in the context of the global church).[33] Thus, rather than pursuing a 'pure' or abstract Christianity, Indian Christians must produce a Christianity that expresses itself in and through *Indian* culture, i.e., localized, inculturated, contextualized forms of Christianity.

At the same time, we have observed that what survived historically was a Christianity that was not contingent on a particular ethnic, cultural and national identity. Instead, it was adaptable to a particular context, namely the Hellenistic culture of the Roman Empire. Paul's Christianity survived, partly because it was not geopolitical, ethnic or cultural in nature, and could therefore translate itself for the Graeco-Roman world. This was what Jewish ethnocentric Christianity was unable to do. Paul's Christianity adjusted to, articulated itself for, and was in conversation with, Graeco-Roman culture. Paul devalued his ethno-religious identities (Php. 3.5–8) and was willing to 'translate' himself for the sake of the Gospel (1 Cor. 9.19–23). Thus, Christianity can never be static but should always be dynamic, translating itself for the challenges of new contexts. The trans-ethno-cultural nature of the Christian identity causes Christianity to be uniquely 'survivable' and 'translatable' for any context in any time. Yet, whenever Christianity enters a new context, it will encounter conflict because of the Gospel's radical and transformative nature. As Paul observed, 'we proclaim Christ crucified, an insult to Jews and nonsense to Gentiles' (1 Cor. 1.23).

---

[32] D. Flemming, *Contextualization in the New Testament: Patterns for Theology and Mission* (Leicester: Apollos, 2005), 125–50.

[33] Flemming, *Contextualization*, 306–15 (quotation from p. 306).

References

Bauckham, R. 'James and the Jerusalem Church'. Pp. 415-80 in *The Book of Acts in Its Palestinian Setting*. Edited by R. Bauckham. Vol. 4 of *The Book of Acts in Its First Century Setting*. Edited by B.W. Winter. Grand Rapids: Eerdmans, 1995.

Barnes, T. 'Pagan Perceptions of Christianity'. Pp. 231–43 in *Early Christianity: Origins and Evolution to AD 600*. Edited by I. Hazlett. Nashville: Abingdon Press, 1991.

Bediako, K. *Theology and Identity: The Impact of Culture upon Christian Thought in the Second Century and Modern Africa*. Oxford: Regnum, 1992.

Bennema, C. 'Religious Violence in the Gospel of John: A Response to the Hindutva Culture in Modern India'. Pp. 129–61 in *Violence and Peace: Creating a Culture of Peace in the Contemporary Context of Violence*. Edited by F. Fox. Bangalore: CMS/ATC, 2010.

————. 'Spirit and Mission in the Bible: Toward a Dialogue between Biblical Studies and Missiology'. *Trinity Journal* 32 (2011): 237–58.

Dunn, J.D.G. *Beginning from Jerusalem*. Vol. 2 of Christianity in the Making. Grand Rapids: Eerdmans, 2009.

————. *The Partings of the Ways: Between Christianity and Judaism and their Significance for the Character of Christianity*. London: SCM, 1991.

————. *Unity and Diversity in the New Testament: An Inquiry into the Character of Earliest Christianity*. 2nd edn. London: SCM, 1990.

Flemming, D. *Contextualization in the New Testament: Patterns for Theology and Mission*. Leicester: Apollos, 2005.

Frykenburg, R.E. *Christianity in India: From Beginnings to the Present*. Oxford: OUP, 2008.

Harland, P.A. *Dynamics of Identity in the World of the Early Christians: Associations, Judeans, and Cultural Minorities*. New York: T&T Clark, 2009.

Horrell, D.G. 'The Label Χριστιανός: 1 Peter 4:16 and the Formation of Christian Identity'. *Journal of Biblical Literature* 126 (2007): 361–81.

Jacob, P.S. 'Religious Climate in India Today: An Introspective Analysis'. Pp. 70–87 in *Nationalism and Hinduism*. Edited by M.T.B. Laing. New Delhi: CMS/ISPCK, 2005.

Johnson, T.M. and K.R. Ross (eds). *Atlas of Global Christianity 1910–2010*.

Edinburgh: Edinburgh University Press, 2009.

Lieu, J.M. *Christian Identity in the Jewish and Graeco-Roman World.* Oxford: OUP, 2004.

———. 'The Forging of Christian Identity and the *Letter to Diognetus*'. Pp. 171–89 in *Neither Jew nor Greek: Constructing Early Christianity.* Edinburgh: T&T Clark, 2002.

———. '"I am a Christian": Martyrdom and the Beginning of "Christian" Identity'. Pp. 211–31 in *Neither Jew nor Greek: Constructing Early Christianity.* Edinburgh: T&T Clark, 2002.

Neill, S. *A History of Christianity in India: The Beginnings to AD 1707.* Cambridge: CUP, 1984.

Schnabel, E.J. *Early Christian Mission.* 2 Vols. Downers Grove: IVP, 2004.

Sen, A. *The Argumentative Indian: Writings on Indian Culture, History and Identity.* New Delhi: Penguin, 2005.

Tripolitis, A. *Religions of the Hellenistic-Roman Age.* Grand Rapids: Eerdmans, 2002.

Varma, P.K. *Being Indian: The Truth about Why the 21st Century Will Be India's.* New Delhi: Penguin, 2004.

Winter, B.W. 'Gallio's Ruling on the Legal Status of Early Christianity (Acts 18:14–15)'. *Tyndale Bulletin* 50 (1999): 213–24.

THEOLOGY and PHILOSOPHY

Indian _____ Christian: Filling the Blank Theologically

Kethoser (Aniu) Kevichusa*

1. Introduction

The theme of the Consultation, 'Indian and Christian: Changing Identities in Modern India', is pregnant with possible meanings and implications. Some will, no doubt, object that it is a loaded theme, and that some of its basic assumptions are themselves open to contestation. For instance, one might contest whether 'modern' is a term that is wholly applicable to India. The term can also be problematic if it is being used with political, historical, and sociological naïveté: Are terms such as 'pre-modern', 'modern', and 'post-modern' (along with other cognates such as, say, 'modernity') applicable to India? It might also be said that *'changing* identities' betrays a fundamental assumption about the notion of identity that not everyone will accept. The debate on whether identities *really* change is, after all, far from over. Then there may be those who take issue with both the terms 'Indian' and 'Christian', arguing that they are not only false, but also hegemonic constructs. 'India', 'Indian', 'Christian', or 'Christianity', they might say, are constructions that have very little to do with 'reality'.

To be sure, these are not issues that I personally have. I have neither the competence nor the interest for such historical and philosophical investigations: 'I do not involve myself in great matters or in things too difficult for me' (Ps. 131.1). In any case, I think these issues can be fairly easily clarified for our purposes. I take it, for instance, that the term 'modern' is being used here in the fairly innocuous and uncontroversial sense; that is, 'as relating to the present or recent times'. I also take it that no one has one single identity. Everyone has

* Kethoser (Aniu) Kevichusa is a lecturer in Shalom Bible Seminary, Nagaland. He has a BA(Hons) from Nagaland University (Patkai Christian College), a BD from the Senate of Serampore (Union Biblical Seminary), an MTh from the University of Oxford (Wycliffe Hall), and is currently pursuing his PhD from the University of Wales (Oxford Centre for Mission Studies). He is married to Ono and they have three sons.

multiple identities—some created others constructed, some conceived others conditioned, some chosen others compelled, some constant others changing. I also take it that the terms 'Indian' and 'Christian' can be fairly easily defined and delimited.

The problematic issue I want to investigate in this paper lies elsewhere, and stems from the little word 'and'. I want to delete it for a moment, and explore whether there might be other ways of filling the blank left in its place. Thus, 'Indian _____ Christian: Filling the Blank Theologically'. Though the title says that the exploration is 'theological', the questions I ask and the implications that I draw will be essentially 'political' in nature and form. To that extent, this may be called an exercise in (some sort of) 'political theology'—or 'theological politics'.

Inevitably, I conduct this exploration from the background and perspective—indeed, *bias*—of my own overlapping and perhaps conflicting identities: a *Christian Naga Indian*. I am a Christian by faith and confession, a Naga by ethnicity, and an Indian by citizenship. I come from a family that has served both the Indian state and the Naga nationalist cause. I grew up, as is not uncommon among most Nagas, believing in Naga nationalism and detesting Indian rule over the Nagas. Yet, I have also experienced firsthand how Naga nationalism has brought about untold suffering both to Nagas and Indians for too long. I know the dark side of violent nationalist zealotry and the attendant state atrocity. As an Indian citizen, I enjoy the numerous benefits that come along with it. I am also proud of my Naga identity, for what it is worth. Yet, as a Christian, in the muddle of my ethnic affinities, political leanings, and social duties, I often wonder what it means to give my primary allegiance to the God revealed in Jesus Christ of whom the claim *'Jesus is Lord!'* is made.

This paper is merely a part of that wondering, and will proceed as follows. In the first part, I will highlight possible ways of filling the blank. These are not exhaustive, but samplers, so more creative permutations and combinations are certainly possible. In the second part, I will argue that the New Testament presents a gospel that, on the one hand, relativizes and downsizes imperialism, and yet, on the other, subverts parochial nationalism. I will then, in the third part, draw the political implications of this two-pronged challenge, exploring how it might be appropriated today, and what it might mean for negotiating

'Indian' and 'Christian'. I will finally conclude by mentioning briefly how *I* would want to fill the blank, and what that might demand of me.

2. Indian _____ Christian: Some Possibilities

One way of configuring 'Indian' and 'Christian' would be to say 'Christian, *not* Indian'. Such a configuration may, at first glance, appear ridiculously outlandish. But such language and thinking, as we will explore soon, could very easily have been found on the lips and minds of the Apostles themselves. The Gospels present the Apostles as being preoccupied — both before the resurrection and for a short while after — with the restoration of the Jewish nation. They seemed to view the overthrow of the Roman yoke as a necessary corollary of their following the Messiah (Matt. 16.13–23; Matt. 20.20–28; Acts 1.6). To that extent, their view may have been — to put it anachronistically in our Consultation's parlance — 'Christian, *not* Roman'.[1]

Even today, there are many ethnic and political conflicts that have their roots in or are fuelled by religious differences — Northern Ireland, the Balkans, Nigeria, Kashmir, to name a few. In an insightful study, Naga historian K. Linyü shows that it was during the most turbulent years of the Indo-Naga conflict (the 1950s and '60s) that Nagas turned in their tens of thousands to Christianity: '[T]he strangest thing was this revival movement happened when the Nagas were literally fighting.'[2] The question that he then asks is, 'How do we understand this phenomenal growth?'[3] Linyü's answer is quite remarkable. He

---

[1] It could be objected here that the analogy between 'Christian, not Indian' and 'Christian, not Roman' is improper. During the Consultation, the official respondent to the paper said, 'I do not think this [the analogy] works because Jews were obviously never considered to be Roman or perceived themselves to be Roman in the first place.' In response, it can be said (a) that I am aware, as recorded, that the analogy is anachronistic, and that I am using the analogy merely for (I suppose) stylistic reasons; but (b) that, even if the Jews were not considered or considered themselves Roman, the fact was that they were under the Roman imperialistic rule; and (c) that there were indeed Jews who were also Roman citizens (e.g., the apostle Paul).

[2] Keviyiekielie Linyü, *Christian Movements in Nagaland* (Kohima: N.V. Press, 2004), 134.

[3] Linyü, *Christian Movements in Nagaland*, 132.

says that with the Naga nationalist leaders using the slogan 'Nagaland for Christ' to galvanize the Nagas to stand united against the 'Hindu' Indian Army, and with the Government of India, represented by the Indian Army expelling the foreign missionaries in Naga areas, desecrating Naga churches, killing church leaders, and raping Naga women, India came to be viewed as, at the same time and in the same sense, *anti-Naga* and *anti-Christian*. Christianity thus became a rallying point for Naga nationalism during these most turbulent years.[4] This led to the mass conversions commonly known as the 'Naga revivals'. To sharpen Linyü's point: For a Naga, then, to say that he or she was religiously a Christian was equivalent to making the statement that he or she was politically *not* an Indian—'Christian, *not* Indian'.[5]

A second way of filling the blank would be to say 'Indian, *not* Christian'. This is the mirror image of the first, and, it seems to me, is part of the reasoning behind some of the *Hindutva* movements. For them, 'Indian' and 'Christian' are diametrically opposite, mutually exclusive identities, which call for an *either/or*. If one is Indian, one cannot be Christian, and vice versa. If one is Indian, one *must* be Hindu, which is the flip side of 'Indian, not Christian': 'Indian, *therefore* Hindu'. This assumes an almost one-to-one correspondence between one's religious identity and one's political, ethnic, and geographical identity. We find this elsewhere too, sometimes explicitly and in other instances in subtler forms. Many of the Islamic nations would fit this configuration in one way or another. Some churches and nations in the post-Christendom West, even after the not-very-pleasant 'Bible and Flag' colonial experience, continue to reflect and endorse a close alignment between Christianity and country. Even Christians in Western nations that do not historically carry the colonial baggage can reflect this alignment. For example, I sometimes wonder what message is really being believed and conveyed when many churches in America position The Star Spangled Banner right next to the pulpit, or when churches in Northern Ireland boldly inscribe on their walls words like 'For God and Ulster'.

---

[4] Linyü, *Christian Movements in Nagaland*, 142–3.

[5] Linyü's thesis, along with my point, is potentially controversial and open to debate. I should also add that not all Naga nationalists would use or endorse religious arguments and not all Naga Christians would harbour or endorse nationalist sentiments.

It is in the explicitly stated theme of our Consultation that we find the third and perhaps commonest way of configuring 'Indian' and 'Christian': 'Indian *and* Christian'. I also assume that this is a configuration most Indian Christians would accept with little hesitation. It deals with the two identities—'Indian' and 'Christian'—in a fairly straightforward manner by dichotomizing and compartmentalizing the two identities into different spheres—the 'political' and the 'religious' respectively. The two spheres are kept separate from each other in some sort of 'non-overlapping magisteria' (NOMA, *à la* Gould), then political and religious activities are put in their respective boxes. These boxes are never opened to each other.

Certainly this way of laying out the identities simplifies matters to a great extent and may also be realistic. It correctly recognizes that there is such a thing as a 'sacred' polity which must be distinguished from a 'secular' polity, and that it is perilous to confer all religious, legal, social, and political authority on a few, select individuals.

That notwithstanding, there are a number of problems with this configuration, especially if there is an insistence that the spheres—religious/sacred and political/secular—be watertight and foolproof. Let me briefly spell out a few. First, such a strict separation is a typically modern phenomenon that has very little analogy in the ancient world, not least the biblical world. Second, if one uncritically accepts this dissociation, one unwittingly plays an other-worldly religious game that, in turn, effectively plays into the hands of not-so-benign forces that are more than willing to monopolize the political realm and the public domain. Third, for many people even today, their religious convictions have serious public and political implications, and they would simply refuse to keep their faith in the ghettoes of the world. Fourth, separation of church and state is one thing; separation of faith and politics is quite another. Unless this subtle distinction is maintained, the configuration inevitably leads to the sidelining and privatization of religion. In other words, the separation of politics and religion is good for politics but bad for religion. Fifth, no matter how much we try to maintain the separation, in reality, people's political and religious identities continually trespass, overlap, mix, and conflict. This is being seen the world over—and in India itself—in the increasing *politicization of religion* and *religionization of politics*.

Sixth, and most importantly, from a Christian theological standpoint, such a view stems from, and results in, an implicit denial of the lordship of Christ *over all*.

3. The New Testament, the Gospel, and Politics

In recent years, one of the most exciting developments in New Testament studies is the exploration of how the gospel that Jesus, and subsequently Paul and the Apostles, proclaimed related to the politics of the day. Though I am not an expert in the New Testament, in what follows, I risk venturing into that world and text. In particular, I want to examine the interface of the gospel with two aspects of politics — namely, imperialism and nationalism — simultaneously offering two propositions: (a) the gospel undercuts imperialism; (b) the gospel subverts nationalism.

3.1. *The Gospel and the Undercutting of Imperialism*

Right from the beginning, there has been a political dimension to the gospel. Unfortunately, this dimension is so heavily overlaid with more politically innocuous interpretations of the gospel that Christians today are, almost by default, set to miss it. The other attributes of Jesus — such as his divine nature, or his *personal* relationship with the individual, which are undeniably true — have been so emphasized (especially within evangelical circles) that the *political* Christ is either forgotten altogether or viewed with suspicion, if remembered. But we need reminding that the world that Jesus entered was *ipso facto* a world of politics. Jesus entered a political arena, and a volatile one at that. Moreover, the earliest and simplest Christian confession and proclamation — *'Jesus is Lord!'* — was a claim with serious political overtones that implied at least two things. First, in their affirmation that Jesus is Lord, the earliest believers were appropriating the Old Testament belief of the lordship and kingship of YHWH over Israel, the nations, and the whole of creation itself, and ascribing that status and role to Jesus himself. This in turn meant, secondly, that the confession served to downsize all other earthly authorities, kingships, and lordships, not least the Roman Empire and Caesar himself, who made claims to divinity: 'Their claims to divine status, to some kind of ultimacy, dissolve before him.'[6]

This proclamation of the kingship of Jesus and the simultaneous undercutting of earthly political powers is found throughout the Gospels, especially in the key moments of Jesus' life. In the birth narrative, we find the Magnificat declaring that God 'has brought down the rulers from their thrones' (Luke 1.52). The Sermon on the Mount too is pregnant with political overtones. According to Wright, 'The popular image of the sermon is of a gentle, quietly romantic view of the religious life, somewhat detached from the world . . . [But] he was staging something that would look to us much more like a political rally. He was like someone drumming up support for a new movement, a new great cause.'[7] Jesus himself declares after the resurrection, 'All authority in heaven and on earth has been given to me' (Matt. 28.18). But the lordship of Christ over all is found most starkly at the Crucifixion. At the cross, Jesus himself becomes a direct victim of imperial violence. But his suffering under the imperial forces of Rome, far from attesting to their victory over him, actually revealed God's victory over them, exposing their shame, absorbing and exhausting their evil.[8] Here, I find the words of the journalist Malcolm Muggeridge more insightful and powerful than any theologian or biblical scholar I have read. And it is worth citing *in extenso:*

> What, then, does the Crucifixion signify in an age like ours? I see it in the first place as a sublime mockery of all earthly authority and power. The crown of thorns, the purple robe, the ironical title 'King of the Jews', were intended to mock or parody Christ's pretensions to be the Messiah; in fact, they rather hold up to ridicule and contempt all crowns, all robes, all kings that ever were. It was a sick joke that back-fired. No one it seems to me, who has fully grasped the Crucifixion can ever again take seriously any expression or instrument of worldly power, however venerable, glittering or seemingly formidable.
>
> When Christ was tempted in the wilderness he declined the Devil's offer to give him sway over the kingdoms of the earth (a refusal which must be intensely

[6] Duncan B. Forrester, *Theology and Politics*, Signposts in Theology (Oxford: Basil Blackwell, 1988), 107.

[7] N.T. Wright, *The Original Jesus: The Life and Vision of a Revolutionary* (Oxford: Lion Publishing, 1996), 48.

[8] On the Cross and empire, see Neil Elliot, 'The Anti-Imperial Message of the Cross', in Richard A. Horsley (ed.), *Paul and Empire: Religion and Power in Roman Imperial Society* (Harrisburg: Trinity Press, 1997).

irritating to those who believe that it is possible through Christian good-will to set up a kingdom of heaven on earth); the Crucifixion demonstrated why — because the Devil's offer was bogus. There are no kingdoms for him to bestow; only pseudo or notional ones presided over by mountebanks masquerading as emperors and kings and governments.

Look under the crown and you see the thorns beneath; pull aside the purple robe, and lo! nakedness; look into the grandiloquent titles and they are seen to be no more substantial than Christ's ribald one of King of the Jews scrawled above his cross. In Christ's day the Roman emperors claimed to be gods and induced their subjects to pay them divine honours. He, a man, exposed the hollowness of their claim by dying, thereby becoming God in the eyes of successive generations of men, who went on worshipping him long after the Roman Empire had ceased to exist.

In this sense, Christ's death on the cross may be seen as the exact converse of the next most famous death as far as our civilization is concerned — that of Socrates. Socrates obediently drank hemlock and died to support and enhance the State: Christ died on the cross in derisive defiance of all States, whether Roman, Judaic, or any other.[9]

3.2. The Gospel and the Subversion of Nationalism

If the gospel, on the one hand, undercuts imperialism, it also, on the other, subverts parochial, politico-, religio-, and ethno-nationalism. Jewish nationalist sentiments were strong during the time of Jesus. Storkey says, 'Whatever the name, *nationalists* were around throughout the hundred years from the time of Herod the Great's accession until the sack of Jerusalem.'[10] He goes on to say, '[I]n Jesus' time the nationalist perspective was strong and burned in the hatreds and hopes of ordinary people. The tax burden, Roman and Herodian soldiers, Herod's viciousness, and the disrespect of Roman culture for the Jewish God — all these rankled the Jews.'[11] The Jewish nationalistic ideology, combined with a fanatical zeal for the Law, contained three fundamental propositions:[12] First, God was to be their only ruler and Lord, which, in turn, meant that they were to be free from human

[9] Malcolm Muggeridge, *Jesus Rediscovered* (London: Fontana, 1969), 47–8.

[10] Alan Storkey, *Jesus and Politics: Confronting the Powers* (Grand Rapids: Baker, 2005), 52.

[11] Storkey, *Jesus and Politics*, 55.

[12] See Mark B. Poe, 'Was Jesus a Political Revolutionary?' http://www.scribd.com/doc/31488546/The-Cooley-Center-Articles-Was-Jesus-a-Political-Revolutionary (accessed on 18 September 2010.)

rulers and kings; second, taxes were to be rejected, for paying them was tantamount to idolatry, apostasy, and self-imposed slavery; third, humans were to participate in bringing about God's reign. 'The coming of God's reign depended on human "revolutionary activity", and could not simply be awaited quietisticly and passively. It was realized only in active cooperation with God.'[13] The question, then, is: Does the New Testament portray Jesus as part of the Jewish nationalist movement?

There is a sense in which the Gospels, by detailing, *inter alia*, Jesus' lineage to David, his personal links to the Zealots, his calling of the Twelve, and his popularity among the common people, lend themselves to being understood as portraying Jesus as the long-awaited Jewish nationalistic (political and military) messiah. There is little doubt that the followers of Jesus too perceived him as such, and sought to co-opt him to their nationalist cause—indeed, 'to take him by force and make him king' (John 6.15), for they 'were hoping that it was he who was going to redeem Israel' (Luke 24.21). The Romans also viewed him as a political threat and had him crucified, charging him for claims to be the 'King of the Jews'.

And yet, as one looks beneath this veneer, one discovers Jesus' refusal to endorse or be party to the narrow and violent nationalism of his day. Consider, for instance, Jesus' call for repentance.[14] In his magisterial work, *Jesus and the Victory of God*, Wright argues convincingly that 'repentance' carried with it not just the spiritual dimension as commonly understood, but also the political call of Jesus to Israel to abandon their nationalistic, revolutionary zeal: 'Eschatological repentance, and national repentance from violent rebel activity, were joined together in Jesus' proclamation and summons.'[15] This call to repentance was a call to Israel to pursue their national life and vocation following the way of Jesus, not the way of the nationalist revolutionaries. Like Jeremiah, Jesus saw that Israel's tendency to violent nationalism was precisely where the danger

[13] Martin Hengel, *Victory over Violence*, trans. David E. Green (London: SPCK, 1975), 57.

[14] Other examples can be given: Jesus' response to Pilate (John 18.36); Jesus' understanding of the kingdom of God as fundamentally against Satan's kingdom (Luke10.18–19); Jesus' response to the high priest and officials (Matt. 26.64; Mark 14.62; Luke 22.69); Jesus' words about how the kingdom of heaven has suffered under violent men (Matt. 11.12). On these, see Poe, 'Was Jesus a Political Revolutionary?'

[15] N.T. Wright, *Jesus and the Victory of God* (London: SPCK, 1996; repr. 2004), 253.

of her imminent destruction lay. And again, like Jeremiah, Jesus was perceived to be anti-Jewish and a threat to Jewish national survival: 'For if we let him go on like this, everyone will believe in him, and the Romans will come and take away both our place and nation' (John 11.48), so 'it is expedient for us that one man should die for the people and not that the whole nation should perish' (John 11.50), the Jewish leaders reasoned. In the end, it is Barabbas, 'who was in chains with his fellow rebels because they had committed murder in the rebellion' (Mark 15.7), who the crowd demand 'should rather be released to them' (Mark 15.11). This is not an incidental detail, but a significant theological point: Jesus stood outside the nationalistic position—and the people themselves recognized this. *Jesus rejects, and is rejected by, nationalism.*

But Jesus did not reject Jewish nationalism with imperious condemnation or spiteful denigration. Rather, he wept over Jerusalem, the city that did not know 'the things which make for peace', as he foresaw how, with the Jewish people continuing to pursue the way of violent nationalism, the great city itself would be sacked by imperial Rome (Luke 19.40–44). It is even possible that Jesus sought to heal the wounds of nationalism. Given how much the Jews of his day had suffered under Roman imperial atrocity, Storkey surmises that many of the healings and exorcisms Jesus undertook may have had to do with what is now called Post-traumatic stress disorder (PTSD)—cases of madness, trauma, or deep depression common among people who witness great violence and atrocities.[16] Take, for instance, the Gerasene demoniac in Mark 5.1–13 (cf. Luke 8.26–39). It is likely that this man was suffering from PTSD. Living among the tombs, mutilating himself, he calls himself 'Legion', a unit of 3,000–6,000 men in the ancient Roman army. He asks Jesus why he has come and begs him not to *torture*—perhaps like the Roman soldiers did— him. Jesus casts 'Legion' out, has the man clothed, and returns him to his family. Was Jesus healing the wounds of war caused by revolutionary zealotry and concomitant imperial atrocity? I think so.

3.3. *Three Key Passages*

The gospel's downsizing of imperialism, on the one hand, and the subversion of nationalism, on the other, is found in three key New

---

[16] Storkey, *Jesus and Politics*, 53–4.

Testament passages. In what follows, I want to examine them briefly to see what sense we might finally make of Jesus, the gospel, and politics. The first passage is found in the argument over the payment of taxes to Caesar (Matt. 22.15–22), in particular, Jesus' injunction, 'Render to Caesar the things that are Caesar's and to God the things that are God's' (v. 21); the second, Jesus' trial before Pilate (John 18.28–38), where he says, 'My kingdom is not of this world' (v. 36); and the third in Romans 13.1–7, where Paul says, 'Let every one be subject to the governing authorities. For there is no authority except from God, and the authorities that exist are appointed by God' (v. 1). These verses have probably been most responsible for blunting Christianity's political edge and deepening the wedge between Christianity and politics.

Consider, first, Jesus' statement regarding the payment of taxes. The principle usually drawn is that people, including Christians, are to give to political authorities, usually the state, whatever is asked of them. On the face of it, Jesus appears to be siding with the imperial power and opposed to the nationalist revolutionaries who would rather not pay taxes. And this would be true. Jesus refuses to be co-opted to the nationalist cause. He *does* say that what is owed Caesar *should* be given to Caesar. Yet, that is only one side of the truth. There is a tradition of interpreting the verse that would result in a very different understanding and lead to a very different conclusion.[17] As the passage tells us, Jesus first asks for a coin and queries, 'Whose image and inscription is this?' (Matt. 22.20). The answer is, 'Caesar's'. Jesus' explicit answer is that what bears Caesar's image properly belongs to Caesar and can be properly given to him. But beneath Jesus' dramatic actions and words is an implicit question, its answer, and its corollary: 'What bears the image of God?' 'Humans.' 'Then give to God what rightfully belongs to God.' According to Hinchcliff, 'The implication of this interpretation is that there is no separation of spheres. The whole of man bears God's image, therefore all of himself is owing to God, including his political life. What he owes to Caesar is a small part of what he is worth. God claims the whole, and therefore reigns supreme even over the political sphere.'[18] To do otherwise is to ascribe

---

[17] The ancestry of this interpretation goes back to Tertullian (c. 160–225).
[18] Peter Hinchliff, *Holiness and Politics* (London: Darton, Longman and Todd, 1982), 4.

to temporal things an ultimacy that does not belong to them: 'He who surrenders himself without reservation to the temporal claims of a nation, or a party, or a class is rendering to Caesar that which, of all things, most emphatically belongs to God: himself.'[19]This quite simply means that the Christian's duty to God is all-encompassing and all-surpassing—a duty that effectively relativizes all other duties and renders all other allegiances negotiable.

Consider, second, Jesus' trial before Pilate. His words, 'My kingdom is not of this world', are often taken to mean that his kingdom is an other-worldly, spiritual, inward, and privatized kingdom that has little or nothing to do with earthly kingdoms; a kingdom that has no political purchase or implications whatsoever. This view, it seems to me, is also mistaken. The point is not so much that Jesus' kingdom has a different *sphere* as it is that his kingdom has a different *source* and a different *strategy*. 'My kingdom,' Jesus says, 'is not *from here*' (v. 36b). His kingdom is the kingdom *of God*; it finds its origin in God, not the world. And because its origin is different, its strategy is too: 'If my kingdom were of this world, *my followers would fight*,' Jesus says. As Wright says, 'Jesus' kingdom has a different *modus operandi*.'[20] Jesus' words, thus, undercut the prevalent ways in which the different political players of the day ought to fulfil their personal, religious, nationalist, or imperial agendas through strategies that were 'of this world': cheating, scheming, bribing, struggling, threatening, fighting, killing. Moreover, Jesus later says to Pilate, 'You have no power at all against me *unless it had been given you from above*' (John 19.11). In so saying, Jesus effectively downsizes the imperial power of Rome that harboured pretensions of sovereignty, deluding themselves and others that their authority was self-derived and their power self-sufficient.

Consider, third, the passage where Paul commands 'everyone to be subject to the governing authorities'. It is possible that Paul is here trying to curb the revolutionary instinct of the early Christians, not least because of their confession of the lordship of Christ, and simultaneously allaying Roman suspicion. Christ's lordship, for Paul, does not condone revolution and anarchy. But, again, that is only one

---

[19] C.S. Lewis, *The Weight of Glory* (New York: Harper Collins, 1980), 53.
[20] N.T. Wright, 'The New Testament and the "State"', *Themelios* 16.1 (1990): 13.

side of the truth. Paul's injunction is two-edged. When one remembers that it is to the Christians in *Rome* that Paul is writing, his words take a highly subversive turn: 'There is no authority', Paul says, '*except from God* and the authorities that exist are *appointed by God*.' Paul's point is that, however much the rulers and authorities of this world believe in their own sovereignty and behave as such they ultimately remain accountable to the one true God. 'Reminding the emperor's subjects that the emperor is responsible to the true God is a diminution of, not a subjection to, imperial arrogance.'[21]

4. Some Implications for Today

So what would the implications of all this exploration be? Let me tentatively suggest four, summarised as: (a) the cultivation of distance; (b) the politics of forgiveness; (c) the remembrance of temporality; and (d) the ministry of reconciliation. The first has to do with the need for Christians to cultivate what might be called 'critical distance' both from the state and from narrower allegiances such as clans, tribes, castes, races, or nations. By 'critical distance', I do not suggest they be cynically critical of or apathetically distant from their state, their national identities, or other identities and traditions they might be a part of. Instead I mean a settled, deliberate, steady conviction and resolution to maintain a certain distance from their other identities and traditions—a distance critical for ensuring that Christians do not capitulate to or collude with what can only be called 'the idols of the nations', not least among them being 'the idol of nationalism'.[22] How this actually plays out will differ from context to context, and, indeed, from individual to individual. I can only speak for myself. As one who has lived with a history of Naga nationalism and opposition to against

---

[21] N.T. Wright, 'Paul's Gospel and Caesar's Empire', in Richard A. Horsley (ed.), *Paul and Politics* (Harrisburg: Trinity Press, 2000), 172. On this passage, see also Neil Elliot, 'Romans 13:1–7 in the Context of Imperial Propaganda', in Richard A. Horsley (ed.), *Paul and Empire: Religion and Power in Imperial Society* (Harrisburg: Trinity Press, 1997).

[22] It should also be added here that this distancing, far from resulting in a denigration of our other identities and cultures, is, in fact, critical for ensuring a more sober and truer—hence, greater—appreciation of them.

the Indian state, and continues to live in a region that experiences systematic state-promulgated violence (enforced through such state instruments as the Armed Forces Special Powers Act), it is relatively easy for me to distance myself from my Indian identity. I may not, to that extent, be in danger of becoming an Indian nationalist. But my temptation—not unlike Luther's drunken peasant who falls off his horse to the right, then gets back on only to fall off to the left—is to fall prey to racial hatred of mainland Indians; to Naga nationalistic zeal and jingoism; and indeed, to revolutionary violence itself. For others who are comfortable with and even proud of being Indian, it might mean reflecting on how far they would be willing to go to express their allegiance and loyalty to the Indian state. It might mean saying that because of their loyalty to the state they would take part in the processes that contribute to a well-functioning society, such as paying taxes, participating in elections, and the like. But while they would contribute to and pray for the welfare of the state, they would not regard the state as having the final say or being the absolute authority—as 'sacred'—over them. It might mean, in other words, approaching their relationship with the state and its systems as negotiable, insisting that their values and priorities will not, in the final analysis, be determined or dictated by the voice of the state alone.[23]

Second, Christians, in considering their relationship with politics, must practise what can only be called a politics of forgiveness.[24] Since I have neither the time nor the space to elaborate this thesis, let me give you the gist of what I mean. As a people who are issued the dominical command to embody and practise forgiveness, I believe that 'forgiveness' must be a critical and central concept in understanding and negotiating the Christian relationship with existing political 'realities'. Christian theology affirms and empirical reality confirms that everything in the world is imperfect or less than

---

[23] See also Rowan Williams, 'Early Christianity and Today: Some Shared Questions', http://www.gresham.ac.uk/event.asp?PageId=45&EventId=744 (accessed on 18 September 2010).

[24] On the politics of forgiveness, see Haddon Willmer, 'The Politics of Forgiveness: A New Dynamic', *The Furrow* 30.4 (1979); Haddon Willmer, *Forgiveness and Politics* (Belfast: Centre for Contemporary Christianity in Ireland, 2003).

ideal. The 'less-than-ideal' includes all existing political arrangements. And yet, because Christians accept that there are no alternatives to the 'given' political reality, they will engage with the existing structures. This requires a politics of forgiveness—a politics that acknowledges that things are not ideal or perfect, and still chooses to work with the imperfect and less-than-ideal. I do not know how this will play out in other contexts, but for Naga Christians, a politics of forgiveness might even mean that they continue to work and engage with—indeed, learn to accept—life under the governance of the Indian state, even if such a life is not the ideal that they desire.

The motivation for cultivating a critical distance and engaging in a politics of forgiveness lies partially in the Christian belief that all existing political systems and arrangements are temporal. Inasmuch as all existing political arrangements are less than ideal, they are also less than eternal. The Indian state, like all other kingdoms of this world, will not last forever; it too will 'pass away'. That is also why Christians cannot pledge ultimate allegiance to it. Similarly, the Naga nationalistic cause is not a 'holy cause' that should be pursued 'at any cost'. The Naga 'homeland' is also temporal and contingent. It was neither divinely ordained from eternity nor are its borders celestially marked out for perpetuity. 'No political arrangement can presume on being ordained by God . . . No borders are inscribed in heaven.'[25] This means that Naga Christians, no matter how genuine their grievances against Indian aggression or strong their desire for an independent homeland, must not presume that a 'sovereign', 'independent', 'united' Nagaland is ordained by God. If it happens, it happens. If it does not, so be it. Naga Christians must place a greater premium on *peaceful co-existence and tranquil community* than on *political independence and territorial unity*.

This leads to the final implication: the ministry of reconciliation. For Paul, reconciliation across social, political, gender, and ethnic divides is not just a horizontal by-product of the vertical reconciliation between God and humanity. The coming together of peoples who were once enemies is at the heart of and the manifest proof of the reconciliation that Christ brings about between God and the world (Eph. 2.14–18).What

---

[25] Nigel Biggar, 'Forgiving Enemies in Ireland', *Journal of Religious Ethics* 36.4 (2008): 567.

is more, Paul says that it is to us Christians that God has entrusted the ministry of reconciliation (2 Cor. 5.16–19). We are the ones who are to bring the word of reconciliation to those caught in the vortex of hatred, hostility, and violence, reconciling ourselves with our own enemies, and pleading with enemies to learn to live together and to love one another. We cannot disregard this task and leave the work of reconciliation to politicians, institutions, and governments, who may have concern but nevertheless lack the internal resources for such a divinely-ordained task. Neither can we afford to relinquish the language and vocabulary of reconciliation to those who simply do not know how to use them.

5. Conclusion

It is also almost certain that Christians, if they seek to take the route I am suggesting, will risk being misunderstood and labelled. Again, speaking for myself, in taking seriously the gospel's challenge to undercut imperialism, and applying that challenge to my relationship with the Indian state, I run the risk—and perhaps even put Indian Christianity at risk—of being misunderstood and labelled as 'unpatriotic', 'anti-state', 'anti-national', 'anti-Indian', and the like. But this is who I am: 'Indian, *but* Christian'. At the same time, in taking Jesus' rejection of Jewish nationalism seriously, and transposing that to my position on Naga nationalism, I run the risk—and perhaps even put Naga Christianity at risk—of being understood and labelled as 'pro-Indian', 'anti-Naga', 'compromiser/ compromised', 'traitor', and the like. But this too is who I am: 'Naga, *but* Christian'.[26] Ironically, that puts the likes of me, however much we wish to avoid that place, in an unenviable position: *the place of the 'peacemakers'.* Peacemakers, often caught in the middle, misunderstood, misinterpreted, and labelled by conflicting parties, do not usually have an identity that they can truly call their own. Thanks be to God that it is to such that God himself gives *his* identity and *his* label: For 'Blessed are the peacemakers, they shall be called *the children of God*' (Matt. 5.9).

---

[26] To say that I am 'Indian, but Christian' or 'Naga, but Christian', I simply mean to say that I look at, and engage with, my Indian or Naga identities within the larger framework of my Christian identity.

References

Biggar, Nigel. 'Forgiving Enemies in Ireland'. *Journal of Religious Ethics* 36 (2008): 559–79.

Elliot, Neil. 'The Anti-Imperial Message of the Cross'. Pp. 167–83 in *Paul and Empire: Religion and Power in Roman Imperial Society*. Edited by Richard A. Horsley. Harrisburg: Trinity Press, 1997.

———. 'Romans 13:1–7 in the Context of Imperial Propaganda'. Pp. 184–204 in *Paul and Empire: Religion and Power in Imperial Society*. Edited by Richard A. Horsley. Harrisburg: Trinity Press, 1997.

Forrester, Duncan B. *Theology and Politics*. Signposts in Theology. Oxford: Basil Blackwell, 1988.

Hengel, Martin. *Victory over Violence*. Translated by David E. Green. London: SPCK, 1975.

Hinchliff, Peter. *Holiness and Politics*. London: Darton, Longman and Todd, 1982.

Lewis, C.S. *The Weight of Glory*. New York: Harper Collins, 1980.

Linyü, Keviyiekielie. *Christian Movements in Nagaland*. Kohima: N.V. Press, 2004.

Muggeridge, Malcolm. *Jesus Rediscovered*. London: Fontana, 1969.

Poe, Mark B. 'Was Jesus a Political Revolutionary?' http://www.scribd. com/doc/31488546/The-Cooley-Center-Articles-Was-Jesus-a-Political-Revolutionary. Accessed on 18 September 2010.

Storkey, Alan. *Jesus and Politics: Confronting the Powers*. Grand Rapids: Baker, 2005.

Williams, Rowan. 'Early Christianity and Today: Some Shared Questions'. http://www.gresham.ac.uk/event.asp?PageId=45&EventId=744. Accessed on 18 September 2010.

Willmer, Haddon. *Forgiveness and Politics*. Belfast: Centre for Contemporary Christianity in Ireland, 2003.

———. 'The Politics of Forgiveness: A New Dynamic'. *The Furrow* 30.4 (1979): 207–18.

Wright, N.T. *Jesus and the Victory of God*. London: SPCK, 1996. Reprint, 2004.

———. 'The New Testament and the "State"'. *Themelios* 16.1 (1990): 11–7.

———. *The Original Jesus: The Life and Vision of a Revolutionary*. Oxford: Lion Publishing, 1996.

———. 'Paul's Gospel and Caesar's Empire'. Pp. 160–83 in *Paul and Politics*. Edited by Richard A. Horsley. Harrisburg: Trinity Press, 2000.

Being Indian, Becoming Christian: Toward a Theological Vision for Identity Formation

Paul Joshua Bhakiaraj*

1. Introduction

From the first century, when the gospel of Jesus Christ was introduced, to the twenty-first century, when Christianity plays an important part in national life, questions of being Indian and being Christian have occupied scholars, leaders and laypeople alike. One central issue in such enquiries has been the ambiguity and perhaps the problematic that resides in the Indian Christian identity, which is alluded to in its very epithet. Just sitting as they do incongruously next to each other, the two terms 'Indian' and 'Christian' seem to raise knotty dilemmas and pose serious questions.[1] One example is: do they necessarily stand in conflict with each other or could they potentially complement each other? If the former is the case, why is that so? If the latter is the case, how can that be so? Understandably therefore, this issue has had a complex and long history, both in terms of its study and in terms of the forces that have shaped its perception and reception. While numerous attempts have shed light on the matter, many recognize that, weighty as it is, it will continue to invite critical and scholarly attention. Clearly as they are not static but dynamic entities, concepts and realities like nation, culture, society and religion require ongoing study and analysis.

2. Theology as Resource

One discipline, and by no means the only one, that has and continues to shed light on the identity of Indian Christians has been formal

---

* The author teaches in the Theology Department of the South Asia Institute of Advanced Christian Studies (SAIACS).

[1] For a helpful discussion on this issue, see Christopher Duraisingh, 'Indian Hyphenated Christians and Theological Reflections: A New Expression of Identity', *Religion and Society* 26.4 (1979): 95–101 and Jayakiran Sebastian, 'Pressure on the Hyphen: Aspects of the Search for Identity Today in Indian Christian Theology', *Religion and Society* 44.4 (1997): 27–41.

theology. Formal theology could be understood, at least minimally in this instance, as an articulation of who we are, by focusing on what we believe and how we act. If so, it offers us ways and means by which Christian identity in India can be conceived, formed and even communicated to the wider world. The varied attempts at explicating who we are, conversing as it did with Indian religious systems and engaging with Indian socio-economic issues, to name just a few conversation partners, have clearly assisted us in stressing the complexities of identity perception, construction and maintenance.

Yet for all its profundity and value, those who are acquainted with the inner workings of formal theology will realize the lack of salience of some attempts in some particular contexts. For example Classical Indian theology, while it was expressive of Indian reality and creatively knit Christian theology with Indian culture,[2] did not necessarily speak to and for the millions of non-Brahmins of our land. In fact many of them felt that it only accentuated the alienation that they felt, even within the church, for it continued to stress the hegemony of a Brahminical worldview. To address such a major lacuna, the development of Dalit Theology was mooted as an exercise pursued for, by and about Dalits.[3] While this was a promising development, over time the lack of clear ecological concern within Dalit Theology was identified. In its place Green Liberation was advocated, whereby our connectedness with the earth was emphasized, as was the consequent responsibility of caring for it.[4] Indian Christian Theology has therefore helpfully underlined the importance of our variegated cultural base as well as our common ecological base for the project of identity creation.

Similarly, another knotty dilemma is the clear disjoint that exists between the formal theology produced and the everyday experience of the vast number of ordinary Christians. The former, for the most part, speaks the language of academia and refers to theories that arguably have little resemblance to everyday life as seen by the people. On the other hand, people have little time for and see little value in pursuing or

---

[2] See, e.g., Robin Boyd, *An Introduction to Indian Christian Theology* (Delhi: ISPCK, 1974 [rev. edn]).

[3] See, e.g., Arvind P. Nirmal, *A Reader in Dalit Theology* (Chennai: GLTCRI, 1990).

[4] See, e.g., George Mathew Nalunnakkal, *Green Liberation: Toward an Integral Eco-theology* (Delhi: ISPCK, 1999).

even evincing interest in formal theology. Even though there have been concerted efforts to address the issue, common perceptions suggest that the two have little in common. Furthermore, common people work outside the orbit of formal theology to forge an identity for themselves, and use resources that are often far removed from the objects that the formal theological enterprise works with. And sometimes it is not just the modus operandi that differs; there could also be more profound differences in other areas as well.

Nevertheless formal Indian theology has been true to its name. It has been Indian, in that the local context is the base from which the theological enterprise has been pursued. It has engaged with a range of issues that the region throws at us. The multiplicity of approaches to formal theology is an expression of the importance of culture and context. It is the negation of the idea that a neutral and value-free interpretation is possible. However, it does seem to raise a fundamental issue of the salience of such interpretations and constructions of theology. If all theologies are equal and valid (they are just different ways of looking at scripture and faith), what then of normative criteria when two interpretations clash? If Brahmanical theology and Dalit Theology are posed in a particular manner, a clash is inevitable. Is political correctness the only arbiter? If not, who then determines what is right and proper? Why is a particular judgement valid over another judgment? In a world of competing ideologies and perspectives this predicament, which really amounts to a legitimation crisis, appears acute.

3. Quest for a Comprehensive Vision

Recognizing the pertinence and persistence of this dilemma, it occurs to me that perhaps conceptually, prior to the project of identity creation, there exists a real need to articulate a comprehensive vision for such a project. Whether it is through the vehicle of formal theology, a more activist approach or through any of the other options before us, the project of identity perception, construction and maintenance seems to be propelled by a set of assumptions of what is ideal, good, and, conversely, what represents the opposite. However it may be pursued and achieved, it is this set of assumptions that provides identity creation its proper conceptual schema and its appropriate framework. I submit that since this set of assumptions pertains to conceptions of being and becoming, conceptions of well-being, of flourishing and of overall good, it is in essence a theological framework. That is to say, who we are and who we want to become is guided by a prior framework of desired, even ideal, good, which is in the final reckoning a theological matter. This is perhaps not recognized as widely as it ought to be.

Hence could it be that the ongoing quest for comprehensive clarity and salience in the theological debate is in effect an implicit yearning for such a vision? Could it be that in the cacophony of these multiple attempts at identity creation, this need for a larger vision is not being recognized? If this is the case perhaps an appropriate theological vision is required to provide a framework within which identity may be constructed, maintained and shared. Perhaps this could furnish us with an agenda that could situate and even fire the imagination of those who are involved in the varied attempts at identity creation. I believe that this vision could possibly supply us with an epistemological framework within which we pursue the project of identity creation. Insofar as it supplies the necessary groundwork and/or conditions for the pursuit of knowledge that yields to an identity, it could represent in part a theological epistemology. Yet, given that the term 'theology' may not be looked on with unanimous enthusiasm by all, perhaps its use here may not be ideal. Nevertheless, since one aim of this paper is to urge that Indian Christians see their life, presence and witness, which includes identity creation, as a theological project, in the broad sense (and not necessarily in the narrow one that 'theologians' work at), perhaps the reader will indulge and work with me. What I am therefore implying is that we envision identity creation as a theological project and hence go to the scriptures as our first port of call, for an infusion with its plot and dynamic.

In this paper, I propose to lay out one dimension of a basic theological vision of how we can conceive of who we are and how we ought to live. This I will attempt to do by delineating some fundamental theological principles and then seek to demonstrate how that could fit us for the significant task of finding and expressing ourselves through a wholesome identity that is at once Indian and Christian. Clearly in a short piece such as this it will be impossible to be as detailed as one would like. Let me say at the outset therefore that this is only a précis of one part of a larger argument that I am working on, and hence this paper remains limited in scope. Yet I trust, it will be helpful for thinking through and acting upon the project of identity construction and maintenance.

4. Creation

Let us begin at the beginning, Genesis 1–2. If we are honest, many of us are accustomed to approaching this passage armed with a defensive posture at worst and cautious posture at best. This is probably because it has become a battleground for the raging debate on creationism vs. evolution. Clearly while Genesis 1–2 is about the origins of the universe, theologically speaking there is much more in the passage. When viewed from this broader perspective, the first point we find is God. 'In the beginning God', suggests that before anything (that is anything non-God) existed, God existed. The fundamental reality of God as the ground, being and possibility of all other reality is underlined in that very first statement. Indeed God is Being itself. This is a profound theological assertion that the Bible begins with: God is. This assertion then serves as the context in which what follows is to be understood and interpreted.

The first word that was said, is to be said and will be said, is and will always be 'God'. This theological point of the sovereignty and supremacy of God in and over creation is not negated even when Christ's role in creation is explicated in the New Testament (e.g., John 1.1–4, 10; Col. 1.15–17; Heb. 1.1–2). In fact, in asserting that Christ, the second person of the trinity, is the agent of creation and for whom all creation exists, there is a process of ontologically equating Christ with God and thereby asserting the primacy of the Triune God.

Next, we find that the scriptures stress that God created everything that there is (Gen. 1.1). He is the one responsible for the fact that something rather than nothing exists, for he is the one who brought everything into being. The reality and being of creation depends conceptually and ontologically on the reality and being of God; if there was no God, there would have been no universe. How exactly that creation was brought into being is not within the remit of this paper, but that it happened at the instigation and prerogative of God is what is crucial. If God is sovereign creator, the universe is a contingent creature. The universe has no independent existence of its own; its dependence on God is thus emphasized. This theological point has been a rule of faith for Christians.[5] For that matter other Semitic religions, like Judaism and Islam, also take their cue from such a theology.

Another major issue in the early chapters of Genesis is sin. Strangely enough, sin has been an attractive proposition for Christian theologians. The focus on the sin of Adam and through him the total depravity of humankind has guided our deliberations. Though we find ample evidence for the corporate nature of sin in the scriptures,[6] the individual nature of sin has been at the forefront of much theological discussion, and hence salvation tends to be conceived of in an individualistic sense. Consequently, this individualistic conception of sin and its solution have been at the centre of understanding the gospel. Now, clearly the fall and individual human culpability are part of the teaching of Genesis, and one cannot avoid or minimize that. However, after creation and before sin found its way into the world, much transpired between God and created order. Perhaps the focus on sin has forced us to neglect these other important aspects of the narrative. This may have led to a lopsided understanding of God's intention for creation, human society and culture.

God's intention for created order is that it would, in being true to itself and fulfilling the design it was created for, worship him, the Triune creator. That created order fulfilled the design to which it was brought into being was clearly noticed by God. Not only did he notice it, he cherished it. He took pleasure in it. He called it 'Good!' That pronouncement by God himself occurs no less than seven times in Genesis 1. The seventh time it occurs, referring to the creation of humankind, the adjective 'very' is added to the 'good'. When God called His creation good, it is an indication that God delighted in His creation. Besides being good by virtue of the one who created it, creation was also good as a result of its value and beauty. As a result, God took pleasure in His creation. He saw beauty in it. He saw value in it. He observed that it fulfilled the purpose for which it was made. While different from each other in character and role, the various

---

[5] So, e.g., the Apostles' Creed asserts that God is the maker of heaven and earth.

[6] E.g., see Paul's argument in Romans 5–8.

components of creation nevertheless accomplished their purpose and in so doing, individually and corporately, fulfilled their destiny. This was their response to their creator, their worship of God. The divinely desired life for creation is a full and fulfilling life for creatures. In living this life, two results accrue: God is glorified and we are satisfied and fulfilled. The creator is given His due and creation achieves its destiny.

In addition to the implicit stress of the biblical record, this idea of course found expression in the writings of the Early Church Fathers. Irenaeus, for example, who served as a Bishop of Lyons toward the end of the second century, famously spoke of God creating the world with His two hands, the Son and the Spirit.[7] He went on to posit that the, 'glory of God is a living human person'.[8] What he meant was that human beings living as they were meant to be, as God intended them to do, was in truth expressive of the glory of God. Being fully human was, in effect, accomplishing divine desire. God's creation fulfilling its purpose brought glory to God by accomplishing His overall purpose. Goodness, that was true of God alone, was now expressed in creation as well. Not that creation possessed a self generated goodness, moral or otherwise, but by virtue of God's creative activity, His good character was revealed in His creation. Having said that though, I would not want to relate this exclusively to the human person alone. Doubtless human beings play an important role in creation. Yet an anthropocentrism, which may be part of the cause of much of the problems we see in the world, needs to be avoided. It would therefore be legitimate to extend that idea to equally say, that the glory of God is revealed in a creation that is fully alive; creation fulfilling its purpose and in so doing accomplishing God's purpose. The Psalmist voices this sentiment eloquently: 'The heavens declare the glory of God; the skies proclaim the work of his hands. Day after day they pour forth speech; night after night they display knowledge. There is no speech or language where their voice is not heard' (Ps. 19.1–3).

If creation voices God's praise, sings and preaches His glory by being itself, by performing its God-intended role, then we seem to find a development of that idea when God invites Adam to tend and care

---

[7] *Against All Heresies*, Book IV, Ch. 20.1. The entire text is available at http://www.newadvent.org/fathers/0103420.htm (accessed 5 Oct 2010).

[8] *Against All Heresies*, Book IV, Ch. 20.7.

for this creation (Gen. 2.15). Further nuance and/or complexity is added when the narrative goes on to describe how God brings the animals that he has made to Adam and allots him the task of assigning names to these creatures (Gen. 2.19). What is rather striking in the narrative is that God, who created the universe, now looks to human beings to tend and take care of His handiwork. Seen from a human perspective it seems rather overwhelming, to say the least. It is no less than God Almighty who invites His creatures—humankind—to assist him in what he has done, and potentially is still doing. How is that possible? Does the clear ontological and qualitative gulf that exists between creator and creature, as emphasized earlier, not preclude such an arrangement? Should not that deter God from seeking the co-operation of humankind to help him in tending His creation?

It is in Genesis 1.26–27 that we perhaps find an answer: the concept of the image of God. This concept seems to provide the bridge on which one may cross this gulf. After carefully sculpting human beings into existence, God endows them not only with the breath of life but also with a special quality of life that is akin to the divine quality of life. A little bit of God, as it were, was placed in human life. Humans are therefore not just living beings; they are living beings who bear the image of God. They are clearly created beings, yet they bear an indelible stamp of the creator, unlike any other created being. Much ink has been spilt on this topic so I will not rehearse the debate here, but suffice to say that by virtue of being made in the image of God, seen as constitutively being in relation with God and created order,[9] human beings are now invited to partner with God in tending and caring for creation, including naming the animals. The creative act of God that brought into existence the universe is followed with this gracious invitation to partnership, to continue that process of creation: to cultivate it, to care for it, to employ language creatively and incorporate animal and plant life into an inclusive ecological system. Care is to be provided; nature is to be cultivated; creativity is to be employed; creation is to be enhanced. Having fitted Adam and Eve with spiritual, physical, emotional and intellectual capabilities, in inviting them to such a calling, God now

---

[9] For example, the discussion in Stanley Grenz, *The Social God and the Relational Self: A Trinitarian Theology of the Imago Dei* (Louisville: Westminster John Knox Press, 2001).

provides them with a vocation, which possesses both economic and cultural dimensions.

Unless these gifts can be used however, they remain useless. Therefore, in the calling issued to humans, these faculties are to be used to add value to creation, to enhance creation. In tending and caring for creation, which had the in-built potential to grow and develop further, humankind served as co-labourers with God. Creation had to live its own life, and under the care of human beings, grow into what it could potentially become in its full-blown form. So in that sense, it appears that 'good' can potentially be further accentuated, clarified, and enhanced. In organizing their own lives, caring for created order and creatively employing their God-given skills to do so, human beings are as a matter of fact partnering with God in the ongoing process of creation. In establishing their own human culture, a place for themselves, and providing space for animal and plant life in that culture, humankind was fulfilling their divine calling. In other words, by creating a wholesome and integral identity for themselves in the midst of the larger created order, humankind were in truth being themselves, being true to their divine calling and, hence, worshipping God.

When seen from this perspective, identity creation is a theological project. It is the process of establishing, under God's overall providence and in response to God's calling, a place for humans—a culture; a place for animals and plants—an ecology; and, in general, a place for created order. This theological vision that we find in Genesis enables one to situate humans and created order on a larger canvas; it allows us to envision human value, roles and vocation in its proper light. It provides divine blessing and sanction on the pursuit of life, in all its multi-coloured variety. Equally the earthiness of life is stressed; its worldly quality is underlined. We do not find here any rationale or warrant for an escape from created reality, for the yearning of the spiritual, as understood in opposition to the worldly. To be true to God-given gifts and calling, the human project is necessarily a worldly project. It is in pursuing such a worldly vision that we are most truly ourselves, most fulfilled, and most true to the reason we were created: worship of the triune God.

5. Incarnation

The theology of the incarnation is the next dimension of this vision that I am constructing, or to put it more accurately, I am pointing to. Here again a deck-clearing exercise may be necessary, for the incarnation is often seen merely as a necessary prelude to the crucifixion. As a result, some of its deeper dimensions are lost on some of us. One of those deeper dimensions relates to the clear indwelling of the human body by Jesus Christ; a notion that is starkly portrayed by the employ of flesh (σάρξ) in John 1.14. God took on human flesh. If God was the author of creation, we now find that the author enters the story in His own person, the second person of the trinity. He does not just remain as an outsider, as a deist view would have us hold. Rather, after having created the universe and then actively taken part in its ongoing life, he now becomes part of creation, one of the human race. The God-human encounter is henceforth played out in the flesh, in a human form. As a result, it is in this Jesus Christ that humanity and the created order is redeemed (2 Cor. 5.19). Indeed as Gregory of Nazianzus (325–390 CE), one time the Archbishop of Constantinople, pointed out: 'That which was not assumed is not healed; but that which is united to God is saved.'[10] The incarnation is therefore the vindication of the value of created order, though a created order marred by sin. This value that God places on the created order is affirmed when Jesus Christ takes on 'flesh'. In order to demonstrate who God really was and who humankind could really become, human flesh was the 'stuff' that was employed. It was through the particularity of humankind that God decided to demonstrate the universality of the God-human relationship. The identity of human life, and particularly human life that follows Jesus Christ, is now suffused with a divine quality, which is nonetheless fully human.

If the stuff of this world is 'good' enough for God to indwell, sufficient for His redemptive purpose, then the attitude of disdain that some of us have to the world and society stands judged. If human culture is the means by which no less than God chooses to reveal himself, and does so conclusively (Heb. 1.1–2), then the warp and woof of life as we know it can and does remain the sacrament of grace through which God continues

---

[10] *Epistle 51 to Cledonius, (Contra Appolinarius).* For more on St Gregory of Nazianzus, see John McGuckin, *St. Gregory of Nazianzus: An Intellectual Biography* (New York: St Vladimir's Seminary Press, 2001).

to work, to accomplish His redemptive work in the world. One ought to be mindful that this sanctification of nature by God when he takes on human flesh does not adopt an instrumentalist approach, a utilitarian employ of nature. In the early church, Docetism (which taught that Jesus did not really take on flesh and that it only seemed so) was pronounced as a heresy. Sadly remnants of that teaching are perhaps evident in a modified form today, in our aversion for worldliness. In effect, the Jesus that we profess to follow seems far removed from the pain and pathos of life, from the joys and highlights of contemporary experience. The Jesus we follow tends to be a docetic Christ, living in flesh but only apparently. Or if we do proclaim a Christ involved in life as we know it, does it really speak to all? Or is he a sectarian Christ?

The identity that followers of Christ establish for themselves will necessarily be one that is entwined with the affairs of the world. This is because it is the cosmos and not just humans, as we find alluded to in Romans 8, that is to be redeemed by His grace. Such an identity will therefore be a sign or symbol of the potential redemption of the world through Christ and of the sanctification of the world through him. But while it affirms the world, it will also be a judgement of the world, because God in His love also judges the world (John 3.16–18). An identity that simply affirms the world devoid of a prophetic core will eventually die a natural death, and not many will recognize its absence nor be cognizant of its contribution. Our engagement in the world will therefore be a 'no' and a 'yes'. To paraphrase Karl Barth: Jesus is God's 'no' to sin, yet he is also God's 'yes' to the world![11] Consequently the church, as the body of Christ, will also adopt a similar schema in its relationship with the world. It will confidently proclaim a 'yes' when appropriate, and boldly pronounce a 'no' when necessary. Both affirmation and critique will characterize our engagement.

6. Eschaton

The third dimension in the theological vision is the eschaton, or the doctrine of the last things. Here again a measure of deck-clearing seems necessary. Much like creation, the last things has been the site of a

---

[11] Karl Barth, *Church Dogmatics IV/1* (Edinburgh: T&T Clark, 1956), 347.

heated debate on when and how Jesus will return. This has diverted from some significant insights on the nature of created reality and its place in the larger scheme of things that God has envisioned. An insight into the role of nature including human society and its place in the scheme of the last things is given for us in Revelation 7.9–10. The great multitude that we find worshiping God, has been identified as belonging to 'every nation, tribe, people and language'. Additional description is provided when it says they were 'standing before the throne and in front of the Lamb. They were wearing white robes and were holding palm branches in their hands. And they cried out in a loud voice: "Salvation belongs to our God, who sits on the throne, and to the Lamb".' Clearly the created order plays a creative and significant role in the worship of God. If, as noticed above, ever since creation there has been a process of employing created order itself, including the cultural production of humans, as gifts in the worship of God, we find that process being brought to its completion here. What we find stressed here is that our cultural specificity, expressed in linguistic, ethnic and national particularity, along with items borrowed from nature, is the stuff that is used to worship God. This is probably what is meant when we read of the *pleroma* of Christ being enriched by multiple appropriations of him in Ephesians 4.13. Indeed Andrew Walls has made the point that as mission translated the significance of Christ to the many cultures, that significance grew greater. It was as if Christ himself actually grew with each new act of translation.[12] We may say that human identity, in all its particularity, is not obliterated in the final analysis. Rather, it finds its fulfilment and destiny as it is used in the worship of God, who sits on the throne. If cultural products are the gifts we bring to worship of the Triune God, it means that our expressions of identity, made new by and in Christ yet simultaneously constructed by the cultural artefacts that we produce, is in this scheme not considered an interim project meant merely for, and possessing salience only, for our existence in the world. That is to say identity creation, that employs the building blocks of culture, is a project with eternal relevance. Its goal is not merely asserting one's culture here

---

[12] Andrew Walls, *The Missionary Process in Christian History: Studies in the Transmission of the Faith* (New York: Orbis, 1996).

and now, a temporary project with a limited shelf life. Rather identity creation in this scheme is a project with eternity as our time frame; its goal is the worship of God that will last for eternity. Worship that will last into eternity will be expressed through an identity that we create, with natural and cultural artefacts, in the here and now.

7. 'Mark Out' or 'Mark In'

Having briefly sketched out a theological vision for identity creation, I now move to discuss its significance and salience in our context. In most discussions of identity one will come across the notion of an identity marker. This could be a certain practice, belief or characteristic that is accorded the privilege of signalling people out from the larger populace and affirming that they belong to a particular group. This particular element serves as a sign or symbol of the identity of that particular group. Identity markers are those features that make evident the identity of the person in question. It helps to create boundaries, so that those who are in and those who are out may be clearly perceived. So when one speaks of nationality, it could for example mean that holding or not holding a particular passport or citizenship certificate will either qualify that person as being a national of that particular country or not. The passport or certificate, in this case, serves as an identity marker. As far as some religions go, it could mean wearing particular attire or adorning particular religious paraphernalia. An identity marker therefore could be a visible sign or an invisible belief on which the person acts, which serves as a symbol of identity.

Now while this practice does have its merits in various situations and needs, there is a sense in which such identity markers can also and equally essentialise the individual in question. When people are seen solely through the lens of the identity marker, whether that is internally prescribed or externally imposed, people tend to be known and judged on the basis of that particular identity they assign for themselves or are assigned. Some of these markers have a tendency to slot persons into a predetermined box whether or not they actually fit into that box. Sadly, the worst stereotypes are often the ideas/images that come to the fore when such an approach is followed, and hence lock identity into those negative schemas.

While dress, belief and practices can mark out a person from others, the question that I would like to raise is: does it necessarily define a person exhaustively? So while a woman may be identified as a Muslim because she wears a burqa, does that mean the observer knows all that there is to that person by such identification? Does that identity marker describe her conclusively? Amartya Sen has alerted us to the dangers of such a move. In his *Identity and Violence: The Illusion of Destiny*[13] he has drawn our attention to the ease with which a stress on identities, singularly perceived, have led to mindless violence for example. In contrast he points to the importance of the multiple identities that a person may possess and argues against essentialising identity.[14] To the question, is there only one dimension to the burqa-clad woman's identity, Sen will argue a categorical 'no'. Laying undue emphasis on specific identity markers, which in turn determine a person's identity, does not seem as helpful as it has been perceived to be. And this is true for the observer as much as it is for the authorities of a particular group who prescribe it.

What does an identity marker have to do with the theological vision that I have been constructing and the larger issue at hand? Clearly the discussion of identity creation and maintenance cannot escape the point about identity markers. However what I would like to do is to revisit the role of an identity marker for our particular purpose. When we look at our efforts at identity creation, for too long some Christians have focused almost exclusively on marking themselves out from society, stressing our particular distinctiveness, and our uniqueness. We have even found biblical warrant for such a strategy. We have seen identity markers, whatever they may be, and often singularly conceived, as that which marks us out from society,

[13] (Delhi: Penguin, 2006).

[14] Sen explains: 'A person's citizenship, residence, geographic origin, class, politics, profession, employment, food habits, sports interests, taste in music, social commitments, etc., make us members of a variety of groups. Each of these collectivities . . . gives her a particular identity.' If that is the case, 'Should they be categorized in terms of inherited traditions, particularly the inherited religion, of the community in which they happen to be born, taking that unchosen identity to have automatic priority over other affiliations involving politics, profession, class, gender, language, literature, social involvements, and many other connections?' (*Identity and Violence*, 5, 150).

sets us apart from others. While that may be a helpful to a certain extent, deeper scrutiny will reveal that this has sadly and often been at the cost of a spirituality that ties us integrally with history and life in society, which is equally what this theological vision engenders. We have unfortunately pitted a 'creation-centred orientation' against a 'redemption-centred orientation', as if they were mutually exclusive.[15] We have created a dichotomy between what the Bible clearly sees as being of one piece. Indeed our specific distinctiveness (and often they were redemption-centred as opposed to being creation-centred) is the sole criteria upon which we have sought to identify ourselves, sought to set ourselves apart from our context. Difference is valued and sameness with our surroundings frowned upon.

By way of departure from such a practice I submit that the theological vision, the creation-incarnation-eschaton schema I have been articulating, has the merit of 'marking us in' into the larger scheme of created order, rather than 'marking out' our identity from created order. By equally emphasizing Creation, Incarnation (Redemption) and Eschaton, I have sought to be true to the biblical story that urges Christians to simultaneously adopt an affirmation and critique of the world. This biblical framework, within which we can conceive of ourselves and our role in God's larger scheme of things, has the potential to subvert the lopsided Christianity that many of us have been inhabiting. By either stressing creation at the cost of redemption, or underlining redemption at the cost of creation, we have unwittingly fallen prey to certain cultural and philosophical compulsions rather than allowing the scriptures to shape and direct us. The dichotomy thus created not only distorts the integral relationship that exists between creation and redemption, but also does not provide space for the eschaton in its schema. An integral element in the theological vision of the scriptures is thus not accorded its due place. In that sense therefore, we unfortunately have a conception of the biblical story that has been distorted thrice over and an equally famished spirituality. Consequently a poor strategy for identity creation is what we follow.

Now just so that one is clear, in encouraging sameness with the world, I do not intend to promote a facile pluralism that values

---

[15] Stephan Bevans, *Models of Contextual Theology* (New York: Orbis, 1999), 16.

sameness and frowns upon difference. Surely such uniformity, as we have seen in more recent times advocated by some sections of our society, plays havoc, at the least, to the founding idea of India, which is unity in diversity. Clearly difference is necessarily ours by virtue of the unique components of our faith. But what I would like to underline equally is that stressing difference cannot come at the expense of sameness with the world. For the theological vision that I have sought to articulate blatantly invites us to an intentional and deliberate attempt at creating an identity that is at once Indian and Christian. It calls us to be as worldly as we are spiritual. It calls us to be faith-filled citizens, just as it calls us to be faithful Christians.

This then leads to the point that when speaking of identity, the language of 'primary, secondary and tertiary' is not very helpful. Following Amartya Sen, I tend to think that this practice may not be the most helpful in actually reflecting the ambiguous and sometimes conflicting nature of identity and action. The hard reality of life as we know it is far more complex and layered than this linguistic tool affords us. However, while Sen is helpful here, a significant lacuna in his work is the fact that he fails to accord religion as significant a role in his discussion as it deserves. This is rather surprising, for how may one conceive of India, which is one region he concentrates on, without its religious dimension? Even conceptions of secular India do not remove religion from the discussion but rather accord all of them equal rights and privileges. Moving beyond Sen, I would like to suggest that religion can and should play a significant role in discussions of identity and hence it ought not to embarrass us. But the question of how we describe the role that religion plays still remains.

Rather than grading identities as primary, secondary and so on, I would like to submit that we conceive of this theological vision as the integrating factor for our life and presence, and hence in our project of identity creation. This story that we are part of, this mission of God that we are privileged to participate in, supplies us with a dynamic and structure that not only includes us but also, and more particularly, invites others, including creation itself, into that story. The creation-incarnation-eschaton narrative is one that is scripted by divine authority and purpose, and therefore its scope is not restricted to one community or one ethnic group. It is a vision that is as expansive as

God is; it is as gracious as its creator is; it is as creative as its redeemer is. While it may not be an identity in itself, it clearly represents an implicit identity marker with which we may conceive of the project of identity creation and maintenance. This theological vision provides for us a grid, if you like, through which we see reality, perceive our role, and engage critically yet constructively with the world. Yet it is a grid that does not promote a 'marking out' exclusively but indeed facilitates a 'marking in' holistically. It is this theological vision that will facilitate a 'marking out' by a 'marking in'.

8. Conclusion

The theological vision that I have been articulating possesses the potential to subvert some of the erroneous and misdirected approaches that have kept us at bay from the world, and has promoted to some extent a secluded and perhaps inconsequential life. When we have engaged with the world, the ambiguity with which we have done so may be embarrassing for some, while for others the depth of their activity may be obvious. Whatever the case, the questions of how we relate to culture in its variety, and how we deal with multiplicity and pluralism, continue to invite answers. As we continue to face those questions, this theological vision could potentially enable us to understand and constructively engage with the twin tasks of affirmation and critique. It could help set us apart by setting us together with the world. Inviting us to such a unique stance are the early Christians, who were described as follows:

> For the Christians are distinguished from other men neither by country, nor language, nor the customs which they observe. For they neither inhabit cities of their own, nor employ a peculiar form of speech, nor lead a life which is marked out by any singularity. The course of conduct which they follow has not been devised by any speculation or deliberation of inquisitive men; nor do they, like some, proclaim themselves the advocates of any merely human doctrines. But, inhabiting Greek as well as barbarian cities, according as the lot of each of them has determined, and following the customs of the natives in respect to clothing, food, and the rest of their ordinary conduct, they display to us their wonderful and confessedly striking method of life. They dwell in their own countries, but simply as sojourners. As citizens, they share in all things with others, and yet endure all things as if foreigners. Every foreign land is to them as their native country, and every land of their birth as a land of strangers. They marry, as do all [others]; they beget children; but they do

not destroy their offspring. They have a common table, but not a common bed. They are in the flesh, but they do not live after the flesh. They pass their days on earth, but they are citizens of heaven. They obey the prescribed laws, and at the same time surpass the laws by their lives. They love all men, and are persecuted by all. They are unknown and condemned; they are put to death, and restored to life. They are poor, yet make many rich.[16]

For the project of identity creation and maintenance in our contemporary context, this theological vision and its outworking in history is a promising and salutary lesson. When adopted and followed seriously, this vision could potentially form a creative and constructive framework within which we could stand and operate. For as you will recognize, it does not supply us with a list of do's and don'ts, a schooling in how to be an Indian and Christian, as if there was only one way of being so. Rather as we imbibe its dynamic, this framework has the potential to educate us to become the Christians we are meant to be. It liberates us from the dangers of a ghettoisation of the mind, a conceptually narrow base on which one builds identity. Since it is divinely authored and scripturally sanctioned, it gives us further confidence that indeed ours is a faith that roots us into the context just as it fastens us to transcendental reality–God of the universe. When it is said that, 'People are not changed by moral exhortations but by transformed imaginations',[17] it seems to me that this is a vision that could potentially transform our imaginations. And in doing so, enable us to become more Christian as we become more Indian by engaging with life in the world, for the glory of the Triune God.

References

Barth, Karl. *Church Dogmatics IV/1*. Edinburgh: T&T Clark, 1956.

Bevans, Stephan. *Models of Contextual Theology*. New York: Orbis, 1999.

Boyd, Robin. *An Introduction to Indian Christian Theology*. Rev edn. Delhi: ISPCK, 1974.

Brueggemann, Walter. *Hopeful Imagination*. Philadelphia: Fortress Press, 1986.

---

[16] *Epistle to Diognetes*, ch. V. http://www.ccel.org/ccel/schaff/anf01.iii.ii.v.html (accessed 12 May 2011).

[17] Walter Brueggemann, *Hopeful Imagination* (Philadelphia: Fortress Press, 1986), 25.

Duraisingh, Christopher. 'Indian Hyphenated Christians and Theological Reflections: A New Expression of Identity'. *Religion and Society* 26.4 (1979): 95–101.

Grenz, Stanley. *The Social God and the Relational Self: A Trinitarian Theology of the Imago Dei*. Louisville: Westminster John Knox Press, 2001.

Irenaeus. *Against All Heresies*. Book IV. Http://www.newadvent.org/fathers/0103420.htm.

McGuckin, John. *St. Gregory of Nazianzus: An Intellectual Biography*. New York: St Vladimir's Seminary Press, 2001.

Nalunnakkal, George Mathew. *Green Liberation: Toward an Integral Eco-theology*. Delhi: ISPCK, 1999.

Nirmal, Arvind P. *A Reader in Dalit Theology*. Chennai: GLTCRI, 1990.

Sebastian, Jayakiran. 'Pressure on the Hyphen: Aspects of the Search for Identity Today in Indian Christian Theology'. *Religion and Society* 44.4 (1997): 27–41.

Sen, Amartya. *Identity and Violence: The Illusion of Destiny*. Delhi: Penguin, 2006.

Walls, Andrew. *The Missionary Process in Christian History: Studies in the Transmission of the Faith*. New York: Orbis, 1996.

Identity beyond Violence and the Politics of Friendship

Brainerd Prince[*]

The violence between Hutus and Tutsis, between Croats and Četniks, and closer home, between Sikhs and others in Delhi in 1984, and in our present times, between Christians in Khandamal, Orissa and others, and between Nagas and others, for being themselves, for not wearing masks, is real. But why this violence for being 'who' you are? While one can perhaps expect a violent response for being named as the 'other' in derogatory terms, why does violence erupt when you are called by one's own name? It seems that one's own *ipseity* has become derogatory. In the South Asian context, not just 'Christian', but equally other religious identity-marking terms such as 'Muslim', 'Hindu' and 'Sikh' have contributed to and have been the recipients of hostility. Equally, terms denoting national-identity such as 'Indian' have become contentious. Can these terms be emancipated from this stranglehold of violence?

1. Introduction

The terms 'Indian' and 'Christian' within the South Asian context have gained enormous semantic weight not just because they are political and religious identity — markers respectively, but more so because of the animus relationship between them. If Christians in India have been accused of not being patriotic Indians, Indians are equally advised not to convert to the foreign religion of Christianity. Thus, at face value 'Indian' and 'Christian' species of the genera 'national' and 'religious' identities, appear incompatible and irreconcilable. If it were merely a case of conceptual animosity, probably these terms, 'Indian and Christian', would not have captured a central place in the imagination of contemporary commentators on modern India. Rather, I believe, it is their power to perpetuate enmity resulting in acts of violence that have brought them to the centre-stage of our deliberations.

[*] Brainerd Prince is a PhD candidate at OCMS, Oxford and is working on Sri Aurobindo's Integral Philosophy with implications for Religious Studies.

In the engagement between religious and political identities in the South Asian context three kinds of conflicts and violence, in a variety of forms, have resulted: firstly, the clash between different religions has resulted in communalism; secondly, the clash between conflicting national identities has resulted in insurgency or ethno-nationalism depending on 'who' is narrating the story[1] and finally the engagement between religion and nationalism has resulted in a variety of religious nationalisms.[2]

However, the title of our consultation, in joining these two terms 'Christian', 'Indian' with the conjunction 'and' not only presupposes this 'distance' but also foresees a teleological crossing, and it is this latter state being sought as desirable that has invited our current discussion. Thus, we are faced directly with the question of 'how'— 'how' can this 'exclusion' be turned into an 'embrace'. My attempt at answering this 'how' encompasses three steps, which will flow into the three parts of this paper.

Firstly, for the 'how' to be answered we must begin with the 'why' in order to understand the mechanism that causes this 'exclusion', resulting in violence between identities. Here I argue that it is a politics based on identity that is the culprit. But before I argue for the conflicting nature of identity, I present a brief survey of the historical development of identity-politics.

Secondly, I argue that identity-politics is both shaped and sustained by a faulty theory of identity. As Miroslav Volf argues, 'the problem of ethnic and cultural (*and we can add religious and national*) conflicts is part of a larger problem of identity and otherness.'[3] Thus, the theory of identity that underlies the politics of identity takes on immediate concern as to understanding why identities, through identity-politics, cause conflict and violence. Though 'modern' South Asia is full of instances of identity-politics, the last three decades, especially with the rise of the BJP with its explicit communal politics, have witnessed an

---

[1] Patricia Mukhim, 'Negotiating Ethnic Identity in a Democracy', in B.B. Kumar (ed.), *Problems of Ethnicity in North-East India* (New Delhi: Astha Bharati, 2007), 103.

[2] T.K. Oommen, 'Religious Nationalism and Democratic Polity: The Indian Case', *Sociology of Religion* 55.4 (1994): 455–72.

[3] Miroslav Volf, *Exclusion and Embrace: A Theological Exploration of Identity, Otherness and Reconciliation* (Nashville: Abingdon Press, 1996), 16.

exponential rise in identity based violence. *Hindutva* has been argued to be the governing ideology behind this politics of violence. The title of its founding text *Hindutva: Who is a Hindu* by Vinayak Damodar Savarkar, betrays an explicit connection between that ideology and Hindu identity. Much scholarly work has been done on *Hindutva* as part of the discourse on communalism and religious nationalism within the South Asian context. However, to my knowledge, no work has been specifically done on Savarkar's 'theory of identity' that birthed the political ideology of *Hindutva*. Therefore, our critique of the 'theory of identity' governing identity-politics will be done through the critique of the 'theory of identity' presupposed by Savarkar in articulating the *Hindutva* ideology.

Finally, building on the critique of Savarkar's theory of identity, I would like to propose an alternative theory of identity based on the works of Paul Ricoeur which will aim at conceptually liberating 'identity' from the clutches of identity-politics. His exploration of identity began towards the end of his three-part volume *Time and Narrative* and finds its complete expression in his 1985/86 Gifford lectures published in 1992 as *Oneself as Another*. After having looked at identity *before* identity-politics, we will end this study by looking at its significance for politics *beyond* identity-politics.

I would like to make three preliminary clarifications as we begin: firstly, I use the term 'South Asia' in place of 'India', not only because the latter is one of the terms under this analytical scrutiny, but also as the former represents the spatio-temporal locale prior to independence in which the politics of identity originated; secondly, this paper is not theorizing the consequence of identity-politics, namely, conflict and violence but, focuses narrowly on the conceptual prehistory of the idea of identity-politics thus looking at 'identity before identity politics' echoing the words that frame the title of Linda Nicholson's work;[4] finally, with regard to the use of the term 'politics', I use the term in both its formal and informal sense—formal in the sense of governance through constitution, laws and the exercise of power and authority, and informal in the sense of a 'master-science', as the Prussian statesman Bismarck would say 'a craft'—an activity or practice

---

[4] Linda Nicholson, *Identity before Identity Politics* (Cambridge: CUP, 2008), 5.

in both interpersonal relationships and the diverse civil institutions through which a community is held together, and a *consensus juris* reached.[5]

2. Identity-Politics: A Theoretical Exploration

What is identity-politics? Linda Nicholson defines identity-politics as 'identical to the turn any national, ethnic, or religious group takes when it defines the needs of its own group as paramount over the needs of society as a whole.'[6] She, in her genealogical trace, argues that historically it originated in the late 1960s in America, when Civil, Women and Gay rights movements became 'Black Power' and Women's and Gay liberation movements with slogans such as 'black is beautiful' and 'sisterhood is powerful'. This development shifted society's focus to identity issues.[7] Finally she argues that by the late eighties, identity politics was 'largely dead, or, at minimum'.[8]

This account fails to take into consideration identity-politics prior to the sixties in other parts of the world such as South Asia, and, more importantly, by tracing the origins of identity-politics to 'informal' politics and 'civil' challenges to formal political structures it overlooks the initial enshrining of 'discriminations' within formal politics, which, I argue, to be the authentic origin of identity politics. For example, in the *Indian Councils Act 1909* which regulated the election of legislative council members in South Asia, the qualifications for being a member as mentioned in Regulations IV states that 'No person shall be eligible for election as a member of the Council if such person (b) is a female.'[9] Thus, identity-politics can be argued to have begun with the framing of this *Act* on the basis of identity differences—in this case differentiation

[5] Bernard Crick, *In Defence of Politics* (London: Continuum, 2005 [orig. 1962]), 9; Andrew Haywood, *Political Theory: An Introduction* (Basingstoke: Palgrave, 1994), 52.

[6] Nicholson, *Identity*, 4.

[7] Nicholson, *Identity*, 1–2.

[8] Nicholson, *Identity*, 4.

[9] Courtenay Ilbert, 'The Indian Councils Act, 1909', *Journal of the Society of Comparative Legislation* 11.2 (1911): 248. However this is not to claim that there are no references to different social identities before this time. Examples can be of *varna* identities that go all the way back to ancient India to Manu and also the way the term '*mleccha*' used by Indians for outsiders, especially Muslims in medieval India.

on the basis of gender, which can be argued to have both began and set in motion the cycle of identity-politics.

This brings us to the question of the conflicting nature of Identity-politics. Our argument is that politics based on identity begets violence. Nancy Fraser argues that there was a shift from an earlier politics of redistribution to a politics of recognition which reconfigured political claims on the basis of group-specific cultural identity thus birthing identity-politics.[10] The 'bare fact' of ethnic violence in the eighties and nineties, the period when identity-politics was at its highest, is sure evidence to the reality of identity based conflicts.[11] But the question is—is identity-politics intrinsically conflicting? Broadly two arguments have been presented in support of an affirmative answer. On the one hand it has been argued that identity politics' shifting *away* from a politics of 'equal dignity and rights' concerning the whole society and drawing *towards* a politics based on difference focussing on rights on the basis of specific interest groups, has resulted in a focus on 'difference' which is the source of conflict.[12] This has resulted in two opposing modes of politics—liberal politics of equal dignity and the communitarian politics of difference. It is the clash between these two modes of politics that causes the conflict. The former is Universalist in nature and seeks to give equal rights to all by treating people in a 'difference-blind' manner, while the latter acknowledges and even fosters particularity.[13] On the latter it has been argued that identity-politics informally brings the notion of 'recognition' to centre-stage and the denial of 'equal recognition' through the processes of *misrecognition* and *nonrecognition* have led to contestation of identities amongst people resulting in conflicts, not only between the elites and the marginalised but also among those 'engaged in different recognition struggles'.[14] The former challenges formal political arrangements based on difference

---

[10] Nancy Fraser, 'Rethinking Recognition: Overcoming Displacement and Reification in Cultural Politics', in Barbara Hobson (ed.), *Recognition Struggles and Social Movements: Contested Identities, Agency and Power* (Cambridge: CUP, 2003), 22.

[11] Fraser, 'Rethinking Recognition', 21.

[12] Volf, *Exclusion and Embrace*, 18.

[13] Charles Taylor, 'The Politics of Recognition', in Amy Gutmann (ed.), *Multiculturalism: Examining the Politics of Recognition*, (Princeton: Princeton University Press, 1994), 42–3.

[14] Barbara Hobson, 'Introduction,' in Hobson (ed.), *Recognition Struggles*, 5.

while the latter the dynamics of informal personal politics based on *mis-* or *non-* recognition.

However, the notions of *difference* and *recognition* within the domain of human identities are directly related to one's theory of identity or the philosophical pre-suppositions one holds on the nature of 'identity'. Therefore, while accepting these above explanations, I would like to shift our analytical focus from 'politics' to 'identity' and would like to argue that all politics of identity (both formal and informal) are shaped by the *theory of identity* presupposed by it. As we will see, this detour into identity studies will naturally lead us back into politics, and enable us to envision politics beyond identity-politics, which will nevertheless not forsake the importance of identity.

3. Theory of Identity: A Critique *Via* Savarkar

The philosophical discussion on *identity* begins literally with the origin of the 'western philosophical tradition' with Plato's 'one over many' and his 'theory of forms'[15] and has a complex historical trajectory. But, can there really be anything problematic about identity? As Wittgenstein said, 'to say of two things that they are identical is nonsense, and to say of one thing that it is identical with itself is to say nothing at all.'[16] So, could one ever go wrong with identity? Or as David Lewis said 'identity is utterly simple and unproblematic. Everything is identical to itself . . . two things can never be identical.'[17] So then, if there is nothing problematic with identity, how can it be a source of violence? Are we barking up the wrong tree? Or, maybe human identities are of a different sense and more complex than what Wittgenstein and Lewis make of the idea of identity. Then, what does a study of human identity entail? There are three elements, as conceptualised by Paul Ricoeur, upon which the theory of human identity is built, namely, episteme of identity, conception of self and dialectic of self-other. Using this framework we critique the theory of identity underlying

---

[15] Tim Crane and Katalin Farkas, *Metaphysics: A Guide and Anthology* (Oxford: OUP, 2004), 217.

[16] Ludwig Wittgenstein, *Tractatus Logico-Philosophicus* (New York: Cosimp, 2009 [orig. 1922]), 89.

[17] David Lewis, *On the Plurality of Worlds* (Oxford: Blackwell, 1986), 192–3.

identity-politics in the context of South Asia by particularly evaluating Savarkar's theory of identity.

Though the personal identity of Savarkar himself can be of much interest, especially as he has been both demonized and deified, evoking either respect or hate respectively,[18] our interest is in the theory of identity that he presupposed in his writings, even as he authored *Hindutva* ideology. Savarkar, the father of *Hindutva*, is simultaneously considered as one of the founding fathers of Hindu nationalism.[19] My critique of Savarkar consists of two parts: firstly, I would like to establish that his work was a response to both existing as well as anticipative of formal identity-politics; secondly, I will analyse his contribution to identity-politics by teasing out the theory of identity presupposed by his work in terms of the three components I posited above: episteme of identity, conception of self and dialectic of self and other.

3.1. Savarkar's Response to South Asian Identity-Politics

In the South Asian context, identity politics can be argued to have clearly begun with the formal politics of the colonial government. Its origin can be traced back to the first Census in India in 1872. Bhagat argues for the defining role played by the census with its questions on 'religion, caste and race' 'in the construction of mutually exclusive religious communities and their particular demographic and geographical features' resulting in 'furthering the communal consciousness in colonial India'.[20] *The Indian Councils Act 1909* which introduced the system of election by replacing nomination for the legislative councils further cemented this politics of difference by reserving seats for Muhammadans irrespective of their population and by introducing separate electorates on the basis of religion.[21] This politics of difference reached a crescendo in the 'recognition of

---

[18] Jyotirmaya Sharma, *Hindutva: Exploring the Idea of Hindu Nationalism* (New Delhi: Penguin, 2003), 172.

[19] A. Copley, 'Introduction: Debating Indian Nationalism and Hindu Religious Belief', in Antony Copley (ed.), *Hinduism in Public and Private: Reform, Hindutva, Gender and Sampraday* (Delhi: OUP, 2003), 7.

[20] R.B. Bhagat, 'Census and the Construction of Communalism in India', *Economic and Political Weekly* 36.46/47 (2001): 4352.

[21] Ilbert, 'The Indian Councils Act, 1909', 251.

religion as a basis for the establishment of a state' through the creation of Pakistan.[22] Thus, in the modern South Asian context all the ensuing *informal* politics of identity have to be seen against this background of formal political arrangement based on difference and as a response to it. I argue that Savarkar was primarily reacting to this formal politics of difference that gave differential treatment on the basis of religion and ethnicity.

On the one hand, he was reacting to the differential electoral structure which he refers to as 'communal electoral role': 'a truly Indian National electorate must be only an 'Indian' electorate pure and simple without the least mention of the unnational and unreasonable differences of race or religion' he argued.[23] On the other hand, he reacted to the preferential treatment guaranteed by the constitution to the minorities, which can be termed as *minority politics*. He argues that the Hindus though majority in number were being cheated by the communal constitution that favoured minorities. He argues, 'but the Hindus will never tolerate the absurd and the unheard of claim of the minorities to have any preferential treatment, weight age or special favours over and above what the major community obtains.'[24] Furthermore, not only was Savarkar challenging the communal formal politics of colonial India but he was arguing for it to be de-communalised. He states:

> Let the Indian State be purely Indian. Let it not recognise any invidious distinctions whatsoever as regards the franchise, public services, offices, taxation on the grounds of religion and race. Let no cognizance be taken whatsoever of man's being Hindu or Mohammedan, Christian or Jew.[25] We, though we form the overwhelming majority in the land, do not want any special privileges for our Hindudom[26]

Finally, foreseeing the political division of Pakistan on the basis of difference, we find Savarkar opposing it in his presidential speech in Akhil Bharatiya Hindu Mahasabha's nineteenth session at Karnavati in 1937.

---

[22] John E. Brush, 'The Distribution of Religious Communities in India', *Annals of the Association of American Geographers* 39.2 (1949): 81.
[23] Vinayak Damodar Savarkar, *Hindu Rashtra Darshan* (Bombay: Laxman Ganesh Khare, 1949), 34.
[24] Savarkar, *Hindu Rashtra Darshan*, 31.
[25] Savarkar, *Hindu Rashtra Darshan*, 10.
[26] Savarkar, *Hindu Rashtra Darshan*, 12.

> It is only enough to remind you of the audacious proposal openly debated in the League regarding the Moslem demand to cut up the body politic of our Motherland right in two parts—the Mohammedan India and the Hindu India—aiming to form a separate Moslem country—Pakistan—comprising of the provinces of Kashmir, Punjab, Peshawar and Sind![27]

Thus, Savarkar's critique of the communal nature of formal politics is definitely a critique of identity-politics. However, what this hides is his contribution to identity-politics. For example, with regard to Savarkar's critique of the Muslim demand for a separate state, Nandy argues that 'when Savarkar propounded his two-nation theory—the first to explicitly do so in South Asia—it was a clear sixteen years before the Muslim League embraced the idea of the Hindus and the Muslims as two distinctive nations and demanded the division of India.'[28] Thus, implicit in his critique is a 'theory of identity' which I argue continued the politics of identity, and it is to its analysis that we now turn.

3.2. *Episteme of Identity*

This refers to the nature of identity. With what horizon are we addressing it? Is it a natural essence intrinsic to the 'thing' or 'person' named and hence directly posited or is it constructed? But first, how did Savarkar understand the nature of identity? Savarkar's understanding of identity is intertwined with his coining of *Hindutva*, a neo-Sanskrit term, as an identity marker and 'constitutive' of Hindu identity.[29] Lipner argues

---

[27] Savarkar, *Hindu Rashtra Darshan*, 12.

[28] Ashis Nandy, 'The Demonic and the Seductive in Religious Nationalism: Vinayak Damodar Savarkar and the Rites of Exorcism in Secularizing South Asia', in *Heidelberg Papers in South Asian and Comparative Politics* (Heidelberg: Heidelberg University, 2009), 3.

[29] Probably used for the first time by Bankimchandra Chatterji in his revolutionary novel *Anandamath* in 1882 and though it was 'popularized in Bengal during the 1890s by Chandranath Basu and used by national figures such as Tilak, its contemporary usage derives largely from Vinayak Damodar Savarkar'. Julius Lipner, 'On Hinduism and Hinduisms: The Way of the Banyan,' in Sushil Mittal and Gene Thursby (eds), *The Hindu World* (New York: Routledge, 2004), 18. Chetan Bhatt, *Hindu Nationalism: Origins, Ideologies and Modern Myths* (Oxford: Berg, 2001), 77.

that the term 'Hindutva', on the basis of its linguistic construction[30], is an abstract noun which simply denotes a property or condition which is identified by the root-stem 'Hindu' and that the term in itself does not refer to the content of the property whatsoever. Thus, grammatically 'Hindutva' is without value and must get its content from the dominant characteristic of the term 'Hindu'. This interpretation of *Hindutva* however betrays Lipner's constructivist epistemological position, one which was not subscribed by Savarkar. On the contrary Savarkar gives the 'name' *Hindutva* a metaphysical ontological status:

> the association of the word with the thing it signifies grows stronger and lasts long, so does the channel which connects the two states of consciousness tend to allow an easy flow of thoughts from one to the other, till at last it seems almost impossible to separate them. And when in addition to this a number of secondary thoughts or feelings that are generally roused by the thing get mystically entwined with the word that signifies it, the name seems to matter as much as the thing itself . . . there are words which imply an idea in itself extremely complex or an ideal or a vast and abstract generalization and which seem to take, as it were, a being unto themselves or live and grow as an organism would do. Such names . . . are the very soul of man.[31]

Savarkar lived prior to the linguistic and postmodern turn of the sixties that challenged realist assumptions and problematized language; therefore, one would expect him to have an uncritical and essential view of identity, similar to what Moya calls the essentialist tendencies of the cultural nationalist movements of the sixties and seventies.[32] An essentialist view of identity promotes the view that members of a group are all the *same* as they all possess the same

---

[30] *Hindutva* or *hinduta* is a perfectly regular construction formed by the application of a well known grammatical rule in Sanskrit, i.e. rule 5.1.119 in the grammarian Panini's magisterial work, the *Astadhyayi*. Introducing the (*taddhita*) suffixes –*tva* and –*ta*, Panini comments: *tasya bhavas tvatalau.* This may be construed as follows: 'The abstract noun formed when either the suffix –*tva* or the suffix –*ta* is added to a nominal stem denotes a state or condition as identified by that nominal stem'. Julius Lipner, 'Ancient Banyan: An Inquiry into the Meaning of "Hinduness"', *Religious Studies* 32 (1996): 112.

[31] Vinayak Damodar Savarkar, *Essentials of Hindutva* (1922), 3.

[32] Paula M.L. Moya, 'Introduction: Reclaiming Identity', in Paula M.L. Moya and Michael R. Hames-Garcia (eds), *Reclaiming Identity: Realist Theory and the Predicament of Postmodernism* (New Delhi: Orient Longman, 2000), 2.

'essence' both in characteristics and experiences.[33] However, Savarkar is aware of the distinction between the word and the thing represented — the signifier and the signified — but conjoins them on the basis of a 'mystical entwining' into an essential whole which can be termed as *linguistic essentialism*. A postmodern critique would precisely argue against this 'presumed identity of linguistic and objective structures' advocating a 'naive "mirrorlike" or "picturelike" relationship between language and reality'.[34] It reduces identities to mere 'fabrications' and 'constructions'[35] and overlooks the 'reality' of linguistic frameworks containing 'identities' that are intrinsic to how people make sense of their lives. Moya argues that the essentialist theory of identity 'overestimates' while the postmodernist theory 'underestimates' the 'political salience of actual identities'[36] and therefore the question is — is there an alternative third view of conceiving identity?

3.3. Conception of Self

Human identity is directly related to how the human 'self' is understood as Taylor argues, an exploration of identity is necessarily a tracing of the various notions of what it is to be a 'human agent, a person or a self'.[37] Even though the term 'self' for a human being is historically conditioned and used in a variety of ways, in modern western thought, there are two dominant and opposing ways of looking at it — the Cartesian *cogito* which is absolute, transcendental and universal and the Nietzschean shattered *cogito*, which denies any universal validity to the self. What view did Savarkar have of the self or who is a Hindu? He argues:

> A Hindu, therefore, to sum up the conclusions arrived at, is he who looks upon the land that extends from Sindhu to Sindhu . . . (as) his Fatherland (Pitribhu), who inherits the blood of that race whose first discernible source

[33] Brent R. Henze, 'Who Says Who Says? The Epistemological Grounds for Agency in Liberatory Political Projects', in Moya and Hames-Garcia (eds), *Reclaiming Identity*, 232.

[34] Caroline S. Hau, 'On Representing Others', in Moya and Hames-Garcia (eds), *Reclaiming Identity*, 155.

[35] Satya P. Mohanty, 'The Epistemic Status of Cultural Identity', in Moya and Hames-Garcia (eds), *Reclaiming Identity*, 32.

[36] Moya, 'Introduction', 8.

[37] Charles Taylor, *Sources of the Self* (Cambridge: CUP, 1989), 3.

could be traced to the Vedic Saptasindhus . . . who has inherited and claims as his own the culture of that race as expressed chiefly in their common classical language Sanskrit and represented by a common history, a common literature, art and architecture, law and jurisprudence, rites and rituals, ceremonies and sacraments, fairs and festivals; and who above all, addresses this land, this Sindhusthan as his Holyland (Punyabhu), as the land of his prophets and seers, of his godmen and gurus, the land of piety and pilgrimage. These are the essentials of Hindutva—a common nation (Rashtra) a common race (Jati) and a common civilisation (Sanskriti).[38]

Huntington argues that to the question 'who are we?' people define themselves in terms of 'ancestry, religion, language, history, values, customs and institutions'.[39] Thus, one could argue that Savarkar has his own version of Huntington's civilizational theory[40], which views the uniqueness of the Hindu self in terms of its civilizational essence. Savarkar argues 'the story of the civilization of a nation is the story of its thoughts, its actions and its achievements. Literature and art tell us of its thoughts; history and social institutions of its actions and achievements'[41] and that the Hindu self exclusively appropriates the Hindu story to itself. Thus, he has set forth a universal criterion for the Hindu self. Even though his view of identity has elements of a narrative understanding, he fails to recognise 'difference' either between diverse Hindu selves or the changing nature of the self over time. Thus, the philosophical question that Savarkar is posed with is—does the Hindu self change over time or does it remain the same? Even though he is aware of this problem, he ultimately holds on to an essential view of the self.

A postmodern critique based on Nietzschean *cogito* argues against this substantialist claims hidden within essentialism and gets rid of the self altogether through its genealogical deconstruction. So yet again the question is—is there a mediating position between Cartesian essentialist self and Nietzschean vacuous self?

---

[38] Vinayak Damodar Savarkar, *Hindutva: Who Is a Hindu?* (Mumbai: Pandit Bakhle, 1923), 72.

[39] Samuel P. Huntington, *The Clash of Civilizations: And the Remaking of World Order* (London: Simon & Schuster, 1996), 21.

[40] Huntington's civilizational theory has been extensively critiqued even in the South Asian context by Vinoth Ramachandra (*Faiths in Conflict* [Secunderabad: OM Books, 1999], 13) and Amartya Sen (*Identity and Violence: The Illusion of Destiny* [London: Penguin, 2006], 10–11).

[41] Savarkar, *Essentials of Hindutva*, 34.

3.4. Dialectic of Self-Other

In the words of Taylor, 'one is a self only among other selves' and that a self can never be described without reference to the 'others' around it, thus it is always situated within 'webs of interlocution'.[42] Here again there are two opposing positions. On one hand we have the Hegelian dialectic between self-other, as illustrated in his famous Master-Slave dialectic—always opposing and situated within internal hierarchies. On the other there is Husserl's transcendental self for which there is no 'other' independent of it. The 'other' seems to disappear and become an object of one's own consciousness. What did Savarkar have to say about the dialectic between the Hindu self and the other? He writes:

> Self is known to itself immutable and without a name or even without a form. But when it comes in contact or conflict with a non-self then alone it stands in need of a name . . . added to the circumstances which brought us first into contact and then into a fierce conflict with the world at large, soon enabled the epithet *Hindu* to assert itself once more and so vigorously as to push into the background even the well beloved name of Bharatakhanda itself.[43] Nothing makes self conscious of itself so much as a conflict with non-self. Nothing can weld peoples into a nation and nations into a state as the pressure of a common foe. Hatred separates as well as unites.[44]

Three strands of ideas can be detected from this compilation of quotes from Savarkar's *Essentials*: first, the other is a non-self, or a contrary self. The non-self is a foe and one that is both separated and excluded from the self—thus an *excluded other*. Secondly, the values or goods that govern the relationship between the self and the other are hatred, conflict and assertion—thus a *distancing morality*. However, Nandy argues that Savarkar's hatred for the other did not originate in 'ideas of ritual purity and impurity or caste hierarchy but from his prognosis of communities that could or could not be integrated— assimilated or dissolved—within the framework of a modern Indian state'—one defined by him on the basis of an essential Hindu identity. Therefore, it was modernist notions of nationalism that fuelled this rhetoric of hatred for the other. Thus, Savarkar's *Hindutva* was fuelled by nationalist sentiments, whose high values were inspired by Mazzini,

---

[42] Taylor, *Sources of the Self*, 35–6.
[43] Savarkar, *Essentials of Hindutva*, 8.
[44] Savarkar, *Essentials of Hindutva*, 19.

the Italian nationalist and German Romanticism and less from any strands of Hindu thought. Finally, that, this hatred of the common non-self will in turn enable a diverse people to become a common self which will become the national and state self—thus *a politics based on violence*. Thus, as anticipated, our detour into identity studies has naturally brought us back to politics. Here the question for us is if there is an alternative way of understanding the relationship between self and other and if a different set of goods will govern the self which will result in a politics not based on violence?

Now, to summarise this critique of Savarkar's theory of identity: firstly, the *episteme of identity* for him was mediated through a linguistic essentialism that not only vitalized identities but also gave an ontological status to the linguistic signifier. Secondly, his *conception of self* is in line with Huntington's civilizational essentialism, which on one hand homogenised the Hindu self through un-recognition of internal diversities, while on the other it conceived it as unchanging and essential thus resembling the Cartesian *cogito*. Finally, the *dialectic between self-other* based on his notion of the excluded other, embracing a distancing morality, revealed an identity-politics that perpetuated violence. This leads us to the question—how can this politics of violence be overturned? Therefore, if Savarkar's theory of identity continued politics based on identity and a postmodern response does injustice to identity and therefore is unacceptable then could an alternative theory of identity overturn violence and yet retain identity? It is with this hope that we look for a theory of identity based on the works of Paul Ricoeur.

4. Identity and the Politics of Friendship

This section has two tasks that will have to be simultaneously done: firstly, to address the three questions raised by the above analysis of Savarkar's theory of identity; secondly, to propose an alternative coherent theory of human identity that will conquer the politics of violence. I will be primarily depending on Ricoeur's *Oneself as Another* to guide us through this final study.

We begin with *episteme of identity*—how can we overcome the limitations that come with both the essentialist and the postmodernist models of identity? There have been several ways offered: Spivak's *strategic essentialism* combines an antirealist account of necessity with the pragmatic acceptance of identity categories[45] and Mohanty's *postpositive realism* built on a fallible yet real epistemic agent[46], are two such ways. Yet, we need a proposal that will overcome the critiques of both realist and constructivist accounts. Ricoeur argues for an adequate grounding of identity in narrative in the following manner: firstly, identity is always a response to 'who' which is mostly in the form of 'naming'; secondly, that the basis that justifies our taking a single *name* of the subject throughout a life from birth to death is 'narrative'. In other words the answer to the question 'who' is always 'to tell the story of a life'. Therefore the identity of this 'who' must be a narrative identity.[47] Thus, he concludes, understood in narrative terms, 'identity can be called, by linguistic convention, the identity of the character' — a character in a narrative.[48] 'Narrative identity' he further argues overcomes the antinomy between essentialism and postmodernism. By considering identity as a narrative, we overcome the dilemma of having to either posit an unchanging subject 'through the diversity of its states' or following Hume and Nietzsche and along with the postmodernists dismiss the 'identical subject' as 'nothing more than a substantialist illusion'.[49]

If identity is a narrative identity then how should the *conception of the self* be? As human identity is closely related to the human self, the same framework of questions posed to the nature of identity is posed to the self. How can the *cogito* mediate between Cartesian transcendentalism and Nietzschean deconstructionism? Ricoeur posits that the identity of a subject has two dimensions: identity as sameness (*idem*) and identity as selfhood (*ipse*) and it is the dialectic between *idem* and *Ipse* that contains the identity of the subject.[50] He argues that *Ipseity*

---

[45] Gayatri Spivak, *In Other Worlds: Essays in Cultural Politics* (New York: Routledge, 1988), 205.

[46] Satya P. Mohanty, *Literary Theory and the Claims of History* (Ithaca: Cornell University Press, 1997), 114.

[47] Paul Ricoeur, *Time and Narrative*, trans. Kathleen Blamey and David Pellauer, vol. 3 (Chicago: University of Chicago Press, 1988), 246.

[48] Paul Ricoeur, *Oneself as Another*, trans. Kathleen Blamey (Chicago: University of Chicago Press, 1992), 141.

[49] Ricoeur, *Time and Narrative*, 246.

[50] Ricoeur, *Oneself*, 116.

is not *Sameness* and that the many difficulties related with identity is a failure to distinguish between these two distinct usages of the term 'identity'.[51] The philosophical question here has to do with the status of the subject's *permanence in time* which is the bone of contention between Descartes and Nietzsche. If Descartes argued for permanence based on a substantial self, Nietzsche counter-argued that there is no substantial self over time. Ricoeur proposes an alternative—he argues that while *Idem*-identity as sameness is what is permanent over time in the sense of a numerical identity, *Ipse*-identity constitutes the changes over time. But, we have already established that within a narrative view, identity of a subject is the identity of the 'character' within a narrative. Therefore, he concludes that in the narrative character, there is an overlap of *Ipse* and *Idem*. To summarise his multilayered complex argument, he argues that if *character* 'designates the set of lasting dispositions by which a person is recognised' then the *disposition* is to be seen as both a *habit* as well as *acquired identifications* which are both being formed and already acquired. There is a dialectic between *innovation* (acquiring identifications) and *sedimentation* (becoming habits) which, while conferring on character a sense of permanence also contains an openness for change. Translating this philosophy into the social context he writes, 'the identity of a person or a community is made up of these identifications with values, norms, ideals, models, and heroes, *in* which the person or the community recognizes itself' while equally, identification with these models and heroes displays 'otherness assumed as one's own' through *Ipseity* [52] In other words, identity is redeemed as it has validity as a shorthand for legitimate identifications due to its *Idem* nature. However, its *ipse* nature presents a genuine openness for change leading to an unfixed and unessential identity. Thus, Amartya Sen would argue that every individual possesses a plurality of identifications, and therefore none of them should be privileged over the others.[53]

The *dialectic between self-other* is firmly situated within the domain of *ethics* and *politics* thus bringing us back to the question of identity based politics with which we began this inquiry. In the above analysis

[51] Paul Ricoeur, 'Narrative Identity', *Philosophy Today* 35.1 (1991): 73.
[52] Ricoeur, *Oneself*, 121.
[53] Sen, *Identity and Violence*.

of Savarkar we observed that the exclusion of the other (non-self) from self produced values of 'hatred' and 'conflict' which was then argued to form the basis of the political institution of the nation-state. It is in countering this explicit identity-politics that we offer a proposal. Our position has already been betrayed in the above section with espousing *Ipseity's* openness to the other in the formation of the self. If there be no ontological exclusion, then must not there be embrace? Ricoeur argues that 'otherness is not added on to selfhood from outside . . . but that it belongs instead to the tenor of meaning and to the ontological constitution of selfhood.'[54] In a rather reverential tone Ricoeur writes, 'to keep the self from occupying the place of foundation . . . that (it) will neither be exalted . . . nor be humiliated . . . I spoke of this work of the broken cogito' — a self that is defined by the other.[55]

5. Implications for Politics beyond Identity-Politics

I conclude by drawing the implication of this view of identity for the two forms of politics that has been of concern to this work — informal and formal politics. We saw how the formal politics of identity evoked a response of an informal politics of violence and hatred, which in turn has resulted in and continues a formal politics based on identity through the numerous differential bills and laws continually being proposed and passed even till this day in India, for example, the *Communal Violence Bill, 2009*. And this cycle of *Identity and Violence*, to echo Amartya Sen's classic work, continues. I argue that this cycle can be broken through a 'politics of friendship' beginning in the domain of informal inter-personal relationships which will consequentially dethrone the formal identity based politics.

Ricoeur argues that the ethical aim of the self with its focus on the 'good life' is self-esteem, whose dialogical structure requires it to be defined as *'aiming at the good life with and for others in just institutions'*. The self's aim for the 'good life' is argued to make sense only in reference to the other and furthermore it is incomplete outside of reference to just institutions.[56]

[54] Ricoeur, *Oneself*, 317.
[55] Ricoeur, *Oneself*, 318.
[56] Ricoeur, *Oneself*, 172.

The self's life-plans and practices are unified under the idea of the 'good life'. The practices have 'standards of excellence' which are termed in MacIntyrean language as 'internal goods'. The self's reflection on its authorship of these internal goods is a source of its *self-esteem*. Furthermore, this reflection is also accompanied by a constant back and forth interpretation of the teleology of the internal goods, which is the aim of the good life in light of the self's particular actions in the search for adequation between the life ideals and the practical decisions. This is called self-interpretation which in turn is nothing but self-esteem. However, there are two lacks in the self's pursuit of the good life: first, this self-interpretation needs verification, for an 'other' to evaluate and assess one's actions; secondly and more importantly there is an intrinsic lack between the self's capacities and realization of the good life. Ricoeur argues that this *lack* creates space, for the mediation of lack, through the other—for the friend who exercises the virtue of friendship. Hence, '*lack dwells at the heart of the most solid friendship*'. Thus, a self knows itself through the eyes of the other and also is able to flourish through the friendship of the other. This is the *friendship of the good* as opposed to the other two kinds of Aristotelian friendship—of utility and pleasure. Ricoeur argues that it is this intrinsic *mechanism of friendship* between the self and other which breaks the bonds of exclusion.

Though friendship is primarily at work within interpersonal relationships between the self and the other, it is also the gateway for formal politics through the idea of *mutuality*. Friendship is a mutual relationship with *reciprocity* as its most basic definition. In the idea of mutuality each loves the other *as being the man he is*. It is this mutuality, Ricoeur argues, which loves the other *equally* as oneself, and borders on the notion of *justice*, which being the first virtue of social institutions, shifts the terrain of relationship from inter-personal to institutional thus to formal politics. Thus, politics based on justice and equality is primarily a politics of friendship. Thus, friendship not only loves the other as oneself in personal relationship but also ensures institutional justice not on the basis of difference which underlies the politics of identity but on the basis of equality. However, the working out of formal politics on the basis of friendship needs to be explicated.

I can anticipate two immediate critiques to this proposal: first, is it after all a going back to the all-familiar liberal politics of 'equal rights and dignity' on whose critique the politics of identity originated? Ricoeur answers a vehement NO! He argues for a move beyond the 'principle of justice' of deontological ethics based on Kantian morality which governs liberal politics to an Aristotelian teleological ethics that has a *sense* of justice. The second critique, echoing MacIntyre, would inquire—'*Whose Justice? Which Rationality?*' should govern politics in South Asia? This maybe a simplistic response but could also be a truism that—it has to be a justice and a rationality founded on a friendship of the 'good'. The demands of friendship are high—a broken cogito, embracing the other and a sense for justice are its costs.

Nietzsche's radical demand of friendship, 'one ought still to honour the enemy in one's friend' is only surpassed by Christ's demands, which is worthy to be our 'internal (super) good'—*You have heard that it was said, 'Love your neighbour and hate your enemy.' But I tell you: Love your enemies and pray for those who persecute you*—a high aim whose realization cannot be even envisioned except through the eyes of the 'good' friend.

References

Bhagat, R.B. 'Census and the Construction of Communalism in India'. *Economic and Political Weekly* 36.46/47 (2001): 4352–6.

Bhatt, Chetan. *Hindu Nationalism: Origins, Ideologies and Modern Myths*. Oxford: Berg, 2001.

Brush, John E. 'The Distribution of Religious Communities in India'. *Annals of the Association of American Geographers* 39.2 (1949): 81–98.

Copley, A. 'Introduction: Debating Indian Nationalism and Hindu Religious Belief'. Pp. 1–30 in *Hinduism in Public and Private: Reform, Hindutva, Gender and Sampraday*. Edited by Antony Copley. Delhi: Oxford University Press, 2003.

Crane, Tim and Katalin Farkas. *Metaphysics: A Guide and Anthology*. Oxford: Oxford University Press, 2004.

Crick, Bernard. *In Defence of Politics*. London: Continuum, 2005 [orig. 1962].

Fraser, Nancy. 'Rethinking Recognition: Overcoming Displacement and Reification in Cultural Politics'. Pp. 21–32 in *Recognition Struggles and Social Movements: Contested Identities, Agency and Power*. Edited by Barbara Hobson. Cambridge: Cambridge University Press, 2003.

Hau, Caroline S. 'On Representing Others'. Pp. 133–70 in *Reclaiming*

Identity: Realist Theory and the Predicament of Postmodernism. Edited by Paula M.L. Moya and Michael R. Hames-Garcia. New Delhi: Orient Longman, 2000.

Haywood, Andrew. *Political Theory: An Introduction.* Basingstoke: Palgrave, 1994.

Henze, Brent R. 'Who Says Who Says? The Epistemological Grounds for Agency in Liberatory Political Projects'. Pp. 229–50 in *Reclaiming Identity: Realist Theory and the Predicament of Postmodernism.* Edited by Paula M.L. Moya and Michael R. Hames-Garcia. New Delhi: Orient Longman, 2000.

Hobson, Barbara. 'Introduction'. Pp. 1–17 in *Recognition Struggles and Social Movements: Contested Identities, Agency and Power.* Edited by Barbara Hobson. Cambridge: Cambridge University Press, 2003.

Huntington, Samuel P. *The Clash of Civilizations: And the Remaking of World Order.* London: Simon & Schuster, 1996.

Ilbert, Courtenay. 'The Indian Councils Act, 1909'. *Journal of the Society of Comparative Legislation* 11.2 (1911): 243–54.

Lewis, David. *On the Plurality of Worlds.* Oxford: Blackwell, 1986.

Lipner, Julius. 'Ancient Banyan: An Inquiry into the Meaning of "Hinduness"'. *Religious Studies* 32 (1996): 109–26.

———. 'On Hinduism and Hinduisms: The Way of the Banyan'. Pp. 9-34 in *The Hindu World.* Edited by Sushil Mittal and Gene Thursby. New York: Routledge, 2004.

Mohanty, Satya P. 'The Epistemic Status of Cultural Identity'. Pp. 29–66 in *Reclaiming Identity: Realist Theory and the Predicament of Postmodernism.* Edited by Paula M.L. Moya and Michael R. Hames-Garcia. New Delhi: Orient Longman, 2000.

———. *Literary Theory and the Claims of History.* Ithaca: Cornell University Press, 1997.

Moya, Paula M.L. 'Introduction: Reclaiming Identity'. Pp. 1–26 in *Reclaiming Identity: Realist Theory and the Predicament of Postmodernism* Edited by Paula M.L. Moya and Michael R. Hames-Garcia. New Delhi: Orient Longman, 2000.

Mukhim, Patricia. 'Negotiating Ethnic Identity in a Democracy'. In *Problems of Ethnicity in North-East India.* Edited by B.B. Kumar. New Delhi: Astha Bharati, 2007.

Nandy, Ashis. 'The Demonic and the Seductive in Religious Nationalism: Vinayak Damodar Savarkar and the Rites of Exorcism in Secularizing South Asia'. Pp. 1–10 in *Heidelberg Papers in South Asian and Comparative Politics*. Heidelberg: Heidelberg University, 2009.

Nicholson, Linda. *Identity before Identity Politics*. Cambridge: Cambridge University Press, 2008.

Oommen, T.K. 'Religious Nationalism and Democratic Polity: The Indian Case'. *Sociology of Religion* 55.4 (1994): 455–72.

Ramachandra, Vinoth. *Faiths in Conflict*. Secunderabad: OM Books, 1999.

Ricoeur, Paul. 'Narrative Identity'. *Philosophy Today* 35.1 (1991): 73–81.

———. *Oneself as Another*. Translated by Kathleen Blamey. Chicago: University of Chicago Press, 1992.

———. *Time and Narrative*. Translated by Kathleen Blamey and David Pellauer. Vol. 3. Chicago: University of Chicago Press, 1988.

Savarkar, Vinayak Damodar. *Essentials of Hindutva*. [n.p.], 1922.

———. *Hindu Rashtra Darshan*. Bombay: Laxman Ganesh Khare, 1949.

———. *Hindutva: Who Is a Hindu?* Mumbai: Pandit Bakhle, 1923.

Sen, Amartya. *Identity and Violence: The Illusion of Destiny*. London: Penguin Books, 2006.

Shani, Ornit. *Communalism, Caste and Hindu Nationalism: The Violence in Gujarat*. New Delhi: Cambridge University Press, 2007.

Sharma, Jyotirmaya. *Hindutva: Exploring the Idea of Hindu Nationalism*. New Delhi: Penguin, 2003.

Spivak, Gayatri. *In Other Worlds: Essays in Cultural Politics*. New York: Routledge, 1988.

Taylor, Charles. 'The Politics of Recognition'. Pp. 25–73 in *Multiculturalism: Examining the Politics of Recognition*. Edited by Amy Gutmann. Princeton: Princeton University Press, 1994.

———. *Sources of the Self*. Cambridge: Cambridge University Press, 1989.

Volf, Miroslav. *Exclusion and Embrace: A Theological Exploration of Identity, Otherness and Reconciliation*. Nashville: Abingdon Press, 1996.

Wittgenstein, Ludwig. *Tractatus Logico-Philosophicus*. New York: Cosimp, 2009 [orig. 1922].

Hindu and Christian: Conflict or Challenge?

Michael Amaladoss, S.J.[*]

Indian and Christian. To put these two words together and say 'Indian Christian' would be problematic today. There are at least some Indians— mainly under the Hindutva umbrella—who think that Christians are not Indians. What is surprising is that some Christians would agree with this. While there is still talk of the need to indigenize Christianity in India, implying that it is not fully Indian, others say that there is nothing that can be called 'Indian'. Successive invasions and migrations over the centuries have left India a multi-cultural country, with some cultures in conflict. So there is little that is 'Indian' with which Christians can identify, especially if they belong to subaltern groups. Many scholars today hold that 'India' is the creation of the colonial powers that once ruled the region and what is said to be 'Indian' is really the dominant culture, thus marginalizing or subordinating the subaltern cultures. So a Dalit or a Tribal, for instance, will revisit the dominant 'Indian' culture. In a culturally pluralistic situation, Christians add one more culture to the mix. I propose that it is possible to be Indian politically, without being so culturally and/or religiously. Today, personal and social identities seem to be shifting under the influence of globalisation—thanks to large scale migration, the homogeneity of the global markets and the media. Increased incomes, the liberation and earning capacity of women, inter-cultural and inter-religious marriages all serve to blur social identities.

If being an 'Indian Christian' is problematic, being a 'Hindu-Christian' is more so. Today we come across people of other religions who call themselves 'devotees of Christ' or *Christu Bhaktas,* across different classes in society. There are people living in Christian and other ashrams who claim to be Hindu-Christians. Raimon Panikkar famously said: 'I left Europe as a Christian, I discovered I was a Hindu and returned as a Buddhist without ever having ceased to be Christian.' It is not merely a problem of personal and social identity. Given the present conflict, sometimes violent, between fundamentalist religious

[*] Professor Michael Amaladoss is Director of the Institute of Dialogue with Cultures and Religions in Chennai.

groups, it is a religious question. In the face of seemingly incompatible views about God, humanity, the world and the project of salvation/ liberation among the different religions, it becomes also a theological question.[1]

Ultimately, as adults, we construct our own identities and being a Hindu-Christian is primarily a personal issue. A person like Panikkar has constructed a special religious identity for himself. While being a Christian, he has integrated Hindu and Buddhist elements in his spiritual way so that he can call himself a Hindu-Buddhist-Christian. He did not live this as a conflicting experience, but it must certainly have been a challenge. Panikkar explained himself in an interview which he gave in 2000. Let me quote it because it is keeping with the orientation of my paper:

> I was brought up in the Catholic religion by my Spanish mother, but I never stopped trying to be united with the tolerant and generous religion of my father and of my Hindu ancestors. This does not make me a cultural or religious 'half-caste', however. Christ was not half man and half God, but fully man and fully God. In the same way, I consider myself 100 percent Hindu and Indian, and 100 percent Catholic and Spanish. How is that possible? By living religion as an experience rather than as an ideology.[2]

To the casual observer this may seem not merely a challenge, but as conflicting. Being a Christian or a Hindu is not just about personal identity. It has a social and also an institutional dimension. Being a disciple of Christ personally is different from being a Christian socially and institutionally. It ceases then to be a merely personal problem and becomes a social and institutional problem and a theological question: Is it possible to be a Hindu-Christian or, for that matter, a Christian-Hindu? How do we define religious identity? Is double or multiple-religious identity possible? If yes, then under what conditions?

These questions may require some explanation. For the purposes of this reflection I shall distinguish between identity and belonging. I understand 'identity' as something personal. I am a disciple of Christ. I know many 'Hindus' who claim to be disciples of Christ. This is not

---

[1] I have discussed this problem earlier in two of my articles. See Michael Amaladoss, 'Double Religious Belonging and Liminality', *Vidyajyoti Journal of Theological Reflection* 66 (2001): 21–34; *idem*, 'Double Religious Identity: Is It Possible? Is It Necessary?' *Vidyajyoti Journal of Theological Reflection* 73 (2009): 519–32.

[2] *The Christian Century*, 16–23 August 2000, 834–6.

a sociological, but a religious (spiritual?, faith?) claim. But they do not belong to the Christian community as a social and institutional group. To belong to it one has to undergo a 'rite of passage' (e.g. Baptism) and accept certain obligations. In the passage from Panikkar, quoted above, he distinguishes between experience and ideology. I am not raising these questions academically and in the abstract. I am trying to understand people who claim to have a certain experience — partly because I share their experience. The question, then, is whether it is possible for someone to belong to one community but share the religious experience of another community. Such experience may involve beliefs, worldviews, methods of *sadhana*, etc., while excluding official creeds (i.e. doctrinal formulas), rituals, social belonging, etc.

So, let me say at the outset that I am approaching this question not purely objectively, but as a partisan. More than fifteen years ago I wrote a small book *Towards Fullness. Searching for an Integral Spirituality.* I wrote in the Preface: 'I am obviously searching as an Indian. I can specify this identity further as *Hindu-Christian.*'[3] Theology is faith seeking transformation through understanding and faith itself involves a commitment. As a believer, one cannot and need not claim to be neutral. Let me also say that I am not identifying 'Hinduism' with 'Brahminism' as some (Dalit) Christians tend to do today. My argument will be that there are, as a matter of fact, people who claim to be Hindu-Christians and I think that their claim should not be dismissed as absurd if it refers to personal identity and experience and not to creed, community/institution and ideology. Some people may not make the shift formally but may still live as Christians. Socially they would be in the margins of both communities, because neither religious community may accept this. Theology can only seek to understand it. For the purposes of this paper, however, I am not going to analyse myself, but others. I shall start with some examples and then go on to present my theological arguments. While my examples are taken from different Christian traditions, my theological argument will be influenced by my own Roman Catholic tradition.

---

[3] Michael Amaladoss, *Towards Fullness: Searching for an Integral Spirituality* (Bangalore: NBCLC, 1994), Preface, 2. See also *The Dancing Cosmos: A Way to Harmony* (Anand: Gujarat Sahitya Prakash, 2003).

1. Some Examples

All through the history of Christianity in India there have been people who have been on the borders between Hinduism and Christianity. One could call them *liminal* persons. I shall just introduce a few of them here. It is significant that they all tend to be intellectuals who did not simply join a community or an institution, sometimes for non-religious reasons, but sought to understand and personalize their Christian faith and practice.

Brahmabandab Upadyaya (1861–1907) became, first an Anglican and then a Catholic.[4] He became a *sannyasi*, but was forbidden by religious authorities to start an ashram. He was also an ardent nationalist and co-founded, with Rabindranath Tagore, Shantiniketan. He declared that he was socially a Hindu but religiously a Christian. He distinguished between socio-cultural and religious identity.

> Our *dharma* has two branches: *samaj dharma* and *sadhan dharma* . . . We are Hindus. Our Hinduism is preserved by the strength of *samaj dharma*. While the *sadhan dharma* is of the individual its object is *sadhan* and *muktee* (salvation). It is a hidden thing and one to be meditated upon. It has no connection whatever with society. It is a matter known to the *guru* and *shisya* only. A Hindu, so far as *sadhan* goes, can belong to any religion.[5]

Upadhyaya's hymns to Jesus Christ and the Trinity contain 'Hindu' terminology.[6] In his school he allowed the Hindu children to sing the praises of *Saraswati*, the Hindu goddess of learning. He himself underwent rituals of purification after his voyage to Europe according to the Hindu social tradition. He also suggested that Krishna could have been God's avatar or manifestation for the Hindus, even though Jesus is the only incarnation of God. At this stage he was suspected of having reverted to Hinduism in some way. When he died both his Hindu and Christian friends had disputes over his body, with the Hindus finally cremating it.

Sadhu Sundar Singh (1889–1929) became a Christian after a personal vision of Jesus Christ. He refused to be associated with any

---

[4] Cf. B. Animananda, *The Blade: Life and Work of Brahmabandab Upadhyaya* (Calcutta: Roy & Son, ca 1947).

[5] Animananda, *Blade*, 200.

[6] See an English translation of the hymns in Robin H.S. Boyd, *An Introduction to Indian Christian Theology* (Chennai: CLS, 1969), 70, 77–8.

church, even surrendering a preacher's licence that he had secured in the
Anglican Church. Instead, he travelled widely, preaching the good news
of Jesus and probably died a martyr in Tibet. His way of life and manner
of teaching had Indian, if not Hindu, overtones.[7] He was guided by the
Yoga and the *Bhakti* traditions of Hinduism and had a deep influence
on disciples like A.J. Appasamy, who wrote a book on Christianity as a
Bhakti Marga (way of devotion).[8] Sundar Singh declared:

> I belong to the Body of Christ, that is, to the true Church, which is no material
> building, but the whole corporate body of true Christians . . . We Indians do not
> want a doctrine not even a religious doctrine . . . We need the Living Christ . . . It
> is quite natural that no form of Church service can ever satisfy deeply spiritual
> people, because such persons already have direct fellowship with God in
> meditation, and they are always conscious of His blessed presence in their souls.[9]

Sundar Singh did not belong to any Christian denomination, but he
did not belong to Hindu institutions either. He tried to integrate Hindu
traditions into his Christian spirituality.

Pandita Ramabai (1858–1922) was an accomplished Sanskrit
pandit well versed in the Hindu *shastras*. She became a Christian,
translated the Bible into Marathi and engaged in social work for the
liberation of women.[10] She refused allegiance to any established church.

> I believe in Christ and His God, and as one of His disciples—though least—am
> bound to do and believe in his teaching, as I have promised in my Baptism.
> But at the same time I shall not bind myself to believe in and accept everything
> that is taught by the Church.[11]

In her lectures in England and in the United States of America she
introduced herself as a Hindu. For her, it was more than a national
identity, as her friends tried to make out. She says:

> My parents were Hindus. I have thoroughly imbibed within me all the good
> Hindu lessons of morality they taught me. More than half of my life has
> been spent in the study of the Hindu religion and philosophy, *Smriti* and the
> *Puranas*, etc. and although there is much that may not be fully acceptable, yet,
> there are many good things about them.[12]

---

[7] Cf. A.J. Appasamy, *Sundar Singh: A Biography* (London: n.p., 1958).

[8] Cf. A.J. Appasamy, *Christianity as Bhakti Marga* (Chennai: CLS, 1928).

[9] See Boyd, *Introduction*, 105–6.

[10] Cf. Shamsundar Manohar Adhav, *Pandita Ramabai* (Chennai: CLS, 1979).

[11] Adhav, *Pandita Ramabai*, 137.

[12] Adhav, *Pandita Ramabai*, 189.

Panditha Ramabai was neither a Hindu nor a Christian institutionally. Spiritually she was a Christian who followed Christ, but she integrated it with a Hindu way of life.

Pandipeddi Chenchiah (1886–1959) sought to find the 'raw fact of Christ' behind the doctrinal statements of the Churches.[13] He was deeply influenced by two Hindu masters—Kanchupati Venkata Rao Venkatasami Rao, known popularly as Master CVV, and Aurobindo—in his understanding the 'raw fact of Christ' in a secular and evolutionary perspective.

> The fact of Christ is the birth of a new order in creation. It is the emergence of life—not bound by Karma; of man, not tainted by sin nor humbled by death; of man triumphant, glorious, partaking the immortal nature of God; of a new race in creation—sons of God.[14]

> Let it be clearly understood that we accept nothing as obligatory save Christ. Church doctrine and dogma, whether from the West or from the past, whether from the Apostles or from modern critics, are to be tested before they are accepted.[15]

Chenchiah too declared a certain independence from the institution of the Church and felt free to dialogue with and integrate 'Hindu' theological perspectives in understanding Christ.

Swami Abhishiktananda (Henri Le Saux) was a French Benedictine monk who was influenced by Ramana Maharishi and sought all his life to have the *advaitic* or non-dual experience according to the Hindu tradition. He claims to have had it. He struggled all his life to reconcile intellectually his Christian and this Hindu experience without success. A few months before his death, however, he had a heart attack and seems to have transcended the tensions. According to Abhishiktananda, the Absolute transcends all that is relative, including its relative manifestations. He writes:

> People are converted—they receive an initiation [*diksha*], they become Christian, Muslim, Sufi, Vedantin, etc. All those are superimposed forms. Whereas the essential thing is to strip oneself of all that is superfluously added, to recover one's proper form [*svarupa*] that was lost.[16]

---

[13] See Boyd, *Introduction,* 144–64.

[14] Adhav, *Pandita Ramabai,* 148.

[15] Adhav, *Pandita Ramabai,* 147.

[16] Swami Abhishiktananda, *Ascent to the Depth of the Heart* (Delhi: ISPCK, 1998), 379.

For the Christian point of view, of course, Christ is the Unique — it is through him that we see all the theophanies. He is the End of them, their Pleroma . . . Wonderful, but from the standpoint of eternity . . . The brilliance of the *paramartha* overcasts [overthrows] all scale of values on the level of *vyavahara*! Our Cosmic Christ, the all embracing *Isvara*, the *Purusha* of the Veda/Upanishads . . . we cannot escape to give him such a full dimension, expansion . . . Yet, why then call him only Jesus of Nazareth? Why say that it is Jesus of Nazareth whom others unknowingly call Shiva or Krishna? and not rather say that Jesus is the theophany for *us*, the Bible-believers, of that unnameable mystery of the Manifestation, always tending beyond itself, since Brahman transcends all its/his manifestations?[17]

Raimon Panikkar (1918–2010), born to a Spanish Catholic mother and an Indian Hindu father, was brought up a Catholic and came to India only at the age of 35. He spent at least one semester every year in Varanasi and visited the Hindu holy places in the Himalayas. His book *The Unknown Christ of Hinduism* is well known. His spiritual experience as a Hindu-Christian can be gauged from *Mantramanjari*, a collection of texts from the Hindu scriptures, selected, translated and commented by him. I had begun this paper with a couple of quotations from him. Here is one more.

In the West identity is established through difference. Catholics find their identity in not being Protestant or Hindu or Buddhist. But other cultures have another way of thinking about one's identity. Identity is not based on the degree to which one is different from others. In the Abrahamic traditions (Judaism, Islam, Christianity), people seek God in difference — in superiority or transcendence. Being divine means not being human. For Hindus, however, the divine mystery is in man, in what is so profound and real in him that he cannot be separated from it, and it cannot be discharged into transcendence. This is the domain of immanence, of that spiritual archetype that is called *brahman*. In the Hindu system, people are not afraid of losing their identity. They can be afraid of losing what they have, but not of losing what they are.

I am not such a relativist as to believe that the truth is cut up in slices like a cake. But I am convinced that each of us participates in the truth. Inevitably, my truth is the truth that I perceive from my window. And the value of dialogue between the various religions is precisely to help me perceive that there are other windows, other perspectives. Therefore I need the other in order to know and verify my own perspective of the truth. Truth is a genuine and authentic participation in the dynamism of reality. When Jesus says 'I am the truth,' he is not asking me to absolutize my doctrinal system but to enter upon the way that leads to life.[18]

---

[17] James Stuart, *Swami Abhishiktananda: His Life told through his Letters* (Delhi: ISPCK,1989), 273.

[18] See Pannikar's interview in *The Christian Century*, 16–23 August 2000, 834–6.

This small galaxy of intellectuals who attempted/forged a spiritual encounter between Hinduism and Christianity can serve as a background to my theological reflections on the problems of identity involved in such encounters.

2. The Problem

From the official Catholic point of view, such an encounter and exchange is itself problematic. A recent Roman document, *Dominus Iesus*, said that while the Church has the fullness of the means of salvation, the other religions were inadequate for the purpose. I shall just quote a text without any comments:

> With the coming of the Saviour Jesus Christ, God has willed that the Church founded by him be the instrument for the salvation of *all* humanity (cf. Acts 17.30–31). This truth of faith does not lessen the sincere respect which the Church has for the religions of the world, but at the same time, it rules out, in a radical way, that mentality of indifferentism 'characterized by a religious relativism which leads to the belief that "one religion is as good as another"'. If it is true that the followers of other religions can receive divine grace, it is also certain that *objectively speaking* they are in a gravely deficient situation in comparison with those who, in the Church, have the fullness of the means of salvation. (original emphasis).[19]

The question then is: why should anyone be interested in encountering Hinduism at all? Must a Hindu who has become a Christian abandon Hinduism? The Church has the fullness of the revealed truth about God and the assured means to reach God. That is why the people in my list would be tolerated as liminal people, or even condemned as dangerous examples to the faithful.

But before I address this problem I have to clear the ground by addressing another one that concerns the relationship between Gospel and culture. We saw above how some like Brahmabandab Upadhyaya distinguished between culture and religion. The possibility of such a distinction, however, has been challenged in recent times. If Christianity is necessarily linked to a particular culture, then we cannot talk about Indian Christians, and certainly not Hindu-Christians. That is why we must discuss the question of Gospel-culture relations before we can talk about inter-religious encounters.

---

[19] The Congregation of the Doctrine of the Faith, *Dominus Iesus* (2000), No. 22. See http://www.vatican.va/roman_curia/congregations/cfaith/documents/ rc_con_cfaith_doc_20000806_dominus-iesus_en.html.

3. Gospel and Culture

The Church is officially open to the various cultures of the world. It affirms that the Gospel transcends all cultures and has to become incarnate in every culture in order to transform it from within. The very term 'in-culturation', patterned on the word 'in-carnation' suggests this. Paul VI said: 'The gospel must impregnate the culture and the whole way of life of man . . . [It is] above all cultures.'[20] More recently, however, such openness has been restricted. John Paul II, for instance, seems to speak in two voices.

> Simply because the mission of preaching the Gospel came first upon Greek philosophy in its journey, this is not taken to mean that other approaches are excluded . . . When the Church deals for the first time with cultures of great importance, but previously unexamined, it must even so never place them before the Greek and Latin inculturation already acquired. Were this inheritance to be repudiated the providential plan of God would be opposed, who guides his Church down the paths of time and history.[21]

Benedict XVI has said that the Judaic culture in which Jesus communicated the gospel and the Greco-Roman culture in which it took an intellectual shape are normative to all Christians. He told a university audience at Regensburg:

I must briefly refer to the third stage of dehellenization, which is now in progress. In the light of our experience with cultural pluralism, it is often said nowadays that the synthesis with Hellenism achieved in the early Church was an initial inculturation which ought not to be binding on other cultures. The latter are said to have the right to return to the simple message of the New Testament prior to that inculturation, in order to inculturate it anew in their own particular milieux. This thesis is not simply false, but it is coarse and lacking in precision. The New Testament was written in Greek and bears the imprint of the Greek spirit, which had already come to maturity as the Old Testament developed. True, there are elements in the evolution of the early Church which do not have to be integrated into all cultures. Nonetheless, the fundamental decisions made about the relationship between faith and the use of human reason are part of the faith itself; they are developments consonant with the nature of faith itself.[22]

---

[20] Paul VI, *Evangelization in the Modern World*, 20.
[21] John Paul II, *Faith and Reason*, 72.
[22] Benedict XVI, *Faith, Reason and theUniversity* (address at Regensburg University).

I find this statement and its implications insulting. It pretends that the Greeks have a monopoly on reason and all that others can do is to adopt it. We can imagine the complexity of an identity which demands that an African Christian should be 'a little Semitic, a little Greek, fully Roman and authentically African', as a French-Roman Cardinal phrased it once.[23] In this way, the official Church protects its existing creedal, ritual, cultural and organizational structures. No wonder that converts like Sadhu Sundar Singh and Pandita Ramabai who became Christians after a serious intellectual and spiritual search distanced themselves from the official structures both of Hinduism and Christianity. In fact, Ramabai said:

> I have just with great efforts freed myself from the yoke of the Indian priestly tribe, so I am not at present willing to place myself under another similar yoke by accepting everything which comes from the priests as authorized command of the Most High.[24]

Resistance to ecclesial structures may already be due to the influence of a certain free spirit of searching and experiencing in Hinduism. Such freedom may also be available in the Protestant tradition, though not in the institutional structures of various confessional churches. When, in addition, the ecclesial structures are seen as European and therefore rejected, an Indian identity asserts itself.

4. Cosmic and Metacosmic Religions

The discussion on gospel-culture encounter supposes that one can make a neat distinction between culture and religion. But culture and religion are closely related. Both deal with the question of meaning. Religion focuses on 'ultimate meaning' while supposing the other levels of meaning given by a culture. The different levels of meanings are integrated. When we seek to re-express the gospel in Indian culture we may not be able to do away completely with Hindu influences. The question then arises whether such Hindu influences can be integrated if they are not in conflict with Christian meanings.

---

[23] I am quoting from memory of newspaper reports. It was Cardinal Paul Poupard, who was at that time the head of the Pontifical Council of Culture. I was living in Rome at that time.

[24] Adhav, *Pandita Ramabai,* 131.

We can look at this question from two different points of view. When God reveals Godself, God does so in a given social, cultural and religious context of a people. The influences of this context are inevitable. While not considering them normative, we will have to dialogue with them. On the other hand, we also have to look at the possibility of an unconscious inter-religious encounter.

Aloysius Pieris distinguished between cosmic and metacosmic religions.[25] While cosmic religions try to find the meaning of life within the cosmos, which includes the spirit world, the metacosmic religions invoke a 'Transcendent Principle'. A metacosmic religion takes on board the local cosmic religiosity with its heavens and hells, angels and demons, agricultural and seasonal rituals and festivals. Some incompatible elements in the cosmic religions may be eliminated and the others reinterpreted to make a new whole. When a metacosmic religion spreads to other areas, it finds new roots in the local cosmic religions. This is inevitable for its survival and growth. This was true of Christianity till the colonial period. After that, rather than spread in the above pattern, it began to be 'imported' from Europe and imposed on other cultures. The consequence at a popular level is the phenomenon of double or parallel religiosity, quite prevalent in Asia, Africa and Latin America. During the celebration of the 'rites of passage' and festivals, alongside the official rituals, there are other local rituals that seem to speak more directly to the people. These rituals are 'Christianized' by adding a sign of the cross or a prayer. This is an unacknowledged, perhaps unconscious, sometimes hidden phenomenon of double religious identity.[26]

All the people I have listed above confess to being believers in Jesus Christ, to whom they have surrendered themselves. However, while they no longer 'belong' to Hindu institutional structures and despite the differences among them, they all felt rooted in and tried to integrate the Hindu spiritual tradition as understood by them into their Christian experience. Brahmabandab Upadyaya did not fault Hindu students worshiping Krishna and Saraswati and he himself underwent the rituals of purification—*prayascitta*—after a foreign trip,

---

[25] See Aloysius Pieris, *An Asian Theology of Liberation* (Maryknoll: Orbis, 1988).
[26] See Thomas Bamat and Jean-Paul Wiest (eds), *Popular Catholicism in a World Church: Seven Case Studies in Inculturation* (Maryknoll: Orbis, 1999).

viewing it as a social ritual. Abhshiktananda and Panikkar undertook pilgrimages to Gangotri and Kailash, sacred to worshippers of Shiva. Abhishiktananda, performed the initiation rites of his disciple Marc, in the Ganges, inviting Swami Chidananda, a Hindu *sannyasi*, to be a co-initiator, because *sanyasa* is a Hindu religious practice. He was also attached to *Arunachala*, the mountain on which Shiva is believed to manifest himself as a column of fire. Abhishiktananda's own guru, Swami Gnanananda, initiated him into the *advaitic* tradition. At no time, however, was there any question about his loyalty to Jesus Christ and Christian rituals like the Eucharist.

5. Interreligious Encounter

Abhishiktananda's *sadhana* or spiritual pursuit was not limited to pilgrimages to Hindu sacred places. His was a search to experience his non-dual oneness with the Absolute. Jesus became both the model and the mediation of that encounter with the Absolute. Here is a sample of Abhishiktananda's vision taken from one of his last writings.

> The absoluteness of the ultimate mystery is discovered in the absoluteness of the self itself, of oneself seen in its full truth. The Self is then seen in the self. In the light of pure consciousness, Being shines with its own light. Then the eternity, the aseity, the absoluteness, the sovereignty of God are no longer notions which man tries desperately to understand by way of analogy or negations. They are realized in their own truth in the discovery that oneself *is*, beyond all conditioning. Then God is no longer a HE about whom men dare to speak among themselves, nor even only a THOU whose presence man realizes as facing him. Rather, necessarily starting from oneself, God is discovered and experienced as I, the '*aham asmi*' of the Upanishads, the '*ehieh asher ehieh*' of the Burning Bush. It is not an I which I abstract or conclude from the Thou that I say to him, but an I of which I am aware in the very depth of my own I.[27]

Here we have an encounter between two metacosmic religious traditions. How is this possible theologically?

After the Second Vatican Council in the Catholic Church, there has been a growing appreciation of other religions. While the council itself spoke of 'good and holy elements' in other religions and the need for dialogue with them, further reflection has led some to see in other

---

[27] Swami Abhishiktananda, 'The Upanishads and Advaitic Experience', in *The Further Shore* (Delhi: ISPCK, 1975), 116.

religions the possibility of divine-human encounter. Having no space here to trace this theological development, I shall be satisfied with two quotations. A Document on *Dialogue and Proclamation* said:

> Concretely it will be in the sincere practice of what is good in their own religious traditions and by following the dictates of their conscience that the members of other religions respond positively to God's invitation and receive salvation in Jesus Christ, even while they do not recognize or acknowledge him as their Saviour.[28]

John Paul II acknowledged the presence and action of the Holy Spirit in other cultures and religions.

> The Spirit manifests himself in a special way in the Church and in her members. Nevertheless, his presence and activity are universal, limited neither by space nor time (DEV 53) . . . The Spirit's presence and activity affect not only individuals but also society and history, peoples, cultures and religions . . . Thus the Spirit, who 'blows where he wills' (cf. Jn 3.8), who 'was already at work in the world before Christ was glorified' (AG 4), and who 'has filled the world . . . holds all things together (and) knows what is said (Wis. 1.7), leads us to broaden our vision in order to ponder his activity in every time and place (DEV 53) . . . The Church's relationship with other religions is dictated by a twofold respect: 'Respect for man in his quest for answers to the deepest questions of his life, and respect for the action of the Spirit in man.'[29]

Today many theologians believe that every religion can facilitate a salvific divine-human encounter. A seminar on *Sharing Worship* took this seriously. It said that, if worship in different religions are different symbolic ways to one and the same Absolute, there is no difficulty to participate in them.[30] What then is religious identity?

6. Religious Identity

Why does one have a religious identity? There are two possible reasons. The first is that a person is born and raised in a religious community

---

[28] Congregation for the Evangelization of Peoples and The Pontifical Council for Interreligious Dialogue, *Dialogue and Proclamation* (1991), No. 29. For the document see www.vatican.va/.../interelg/documents/rc_pc_interelg_doc_19051991_dialogue-and-proclamatio_en.html -88k -1999-07-14.

[29] John Paul II, *The Mission of the Redeemer* (1990), Nos. 28–29. For the Document see http://www.vatican.va/holy_father/john_paul_ii/encyclicals/documents/hf_jp-ii_enc_07121990_redemptoris-missio_en.html.

[30] Paul Puthanangady (ed), *Sharing Worship* (Bangalore: NBCLC, 1988).

and therefore belongs to it. While such a person may have no problem participating occasionally in the worship of other religions the person's identity is defined by the community he/she belongs to. For example, Ramakrishna Paramahamsa claims to have had the experience of other religions[31] although he was a Hindu and a *Shaivite* with a special devotion to the goddess Kali. He says:

> I have practised all religions—Hinduism, Islam, Christianity—and I have also followed the paths of the different Hindu sects . . . I have found that it is the same God towards whom all are directing their steps, though along different paths.[32]

A second reason is that a person has experienced God in a particular religious tradition. The experience is reciprocal: it is not only his/her choice; s/he has the experience of a special manifestation of God. There is a sense of a 'vocation'—a call. This experience constitutes his/her personal religious identity. While s/he is open to the possibility that God may manifest Godself to others through other symbols, his/her relationship with God is something unique. It is not exclusive, but special. Sadhu Sundar Singh and Pandita Ramabai became Christians through special encounters with Jesus Christ—they were not members of a Christian community. Such membership then becomes secondary.

Such a special relationship can also develop with a second religion that one relates to. For example, Swami Abhishiktananda wanted to have an *advaitic* or non-dual experience of the Absolute. He recognized it was 'Hindu', and yet transcending Hinduism as a religious tradition. He did not belong to any Hindu community. As a *sannyasi* he was beyond all such communities.

So we contend that while a person may belong to a particular religious community, both sociologically and experientially, s/he can be open to other religious experiences. There is no antagonism towards other religions and the person may encounter and be enriched by them while still being rooted in one religion. This rootedness could also be in a community different from the one in which one is born, because it is based on a personal religious experience. This was the case of Sadhu Sundar Singh and Pandita Ramabai. In the case of

---

[31] See Ramakrishna Paramahamsa, *Cultural Heritage of India* (Calcutta: Belur Math), Vol. II, 494, cited in Boyd, *Introduction,* 58.

[32] Paramahamsa, *Heritage,* 518, cited in Boyd, *Introduction,* 59.

Abhishiktananda and Panikkar, they are rooted in the community they were born in, confirmed also by their personal experience of Jesus, but are open to experience the Absolute through other symbols. Ramakrishna Paramahamsa and Mahatma Gandhi are corresponding examples from the Hindu tradition. In all these cases there is a realization that the Absolute is one, though experienced through different mediations.[33] One's own religious experience, however, is special and privileged, without being exclusive or inclusive. Panikkar, despite claiming to be 100% Christian and 100% Hindu, wrote about *The Unknown Christ of Hinduism*, not about *The Unknown Krishna of Christianity*.

Identity is always personal, though it is in the context of a community. A person born and raised in a community usually identifies with it. While growing up or because of a particular encounter one may reconfirm one's identity or change it. The change may not be as much against one's former religion as in favour of a new religion. One could also choose an ideology instead of a religion. Even so, one would likely need a community or group of people who think along similar lines.

7. Multi-Religious Families

We also have the phenomenon of people born in a multi-religious family where the parents belong to different religions. The children, then, grow up, not always as members of a religious community, but in a more neutral situation, open to different influences. I know of a few such multi-religious families. In some families one or other parent is firm that the children are brought up in his or her religious tradition. In countries like the United States the prevailing situation for many is Christian and that affects the children too. In other cases, one or other parent may not be practicing his/her religion. But what happens if the

---

[33] This is a theological, not a biblical affirmation., though theologians would claim to be rooted in the biblical faith. For elaborate theological explanations of such a perspective on religious pluralism, which is not possible within the short space of this paper, see S.J. Samartha, *One Christ, Many Religions: Towards a Revised Christology* (Maryknoll: Orbis, 1991) and Jacques Dupuis, *Towards a Christian Theology of Religious Pluralism* (Maryknoll: Orbis, 2002).

parents encourage their children to be open and make their own choice of religious identity? I contacted one such family with three young adult children living in Mumbai. The father is a modern Hindu and the mother is an active Catholic. The youngest, Ashutosh (17) says: 'I do not have a religious identity. I have a spiritual identity . . . I detest all religions. I believe in a higher power, God, if you like.' Nivedita (19) affirms:

> I love my double identity because it makes me different. I've been given the power of choice, the ability to think for myself and the gift of being introduced to different faces of God. Why would I say 'No' to any? I believe in a higher power but I also believe that people have to make their own God. Religion is just a social construct that people have made up to please themselves.

Gayatri (21) declares that she likes stories and festivals, nature and sacred places, but not idols and ritual. In her words:

> I don't have a religious identity at all. I have a spiritual identity. I have a moral identity. I have an ethical identity. I have a code of conduct by which I believe I should live my life, which is not religion because what works for me may not work for someone else. It is not universal. It leaves me more open and understanding and forgiving of others. And yet I chose to get baptized the year I turned 21 . . . I decided to get baptized because being a Catholic is a part of my heritage, a part of my name, and by default, a part of my identity... The feeling of community that belonging to a Church gives me is very important. Growing up in the Sri Aurobindo Ashram also gave me a great sense of community . . . Each one in my Hindu family does their own thing so the sense of community there is missing . . . Even if you are Christian, being Hindu is part of your Indian heritage.

The way that Ashutosh, Nivedita and Gayatri are constructing their religious identities is very interesting and instructive. Their religious self-construction is probably not over yet and may be illustrative of what is happening to many young people in the post-modern world, even some born in orthodox families.

In a way, Swami Abhishiktananda and Raimon Panikkar are post-modern people too. What is significant is their deep sense of personal identity and freedom. They were also seeking a personal experience of God. They related to a community. But they were liminal people, on its borders, though both were ordained presbyters. Their double identity was indeed a challenge for them and for the others who knew them. Swami Abhishiktananda lived in tension much of his life, maybe because Hinduism was new to him. Panikkar does not seem to have had that tension. Some may not have understood them.[34]

8. A Recent Example

Francis Xavier Clooney is an expert in comparative theology and has written many books comparing Hinduism and Christianity.[35] At the conclusion of a book comparing Christian and Hindu *mantras* he explores the possibility of a Christian using the Hindu *mantras*. He says:

> There seems to me to be no reason why a Christian cannot still venture to appropriate the piety, theology, and practice of the three Mantras as well as the insights and theology of Desika's *Essence*, for the sake of a deeply Christocentric manner of prayer.[36]

He suggests that if the Hindus too engage in a similar practice with Christian *mantras* then a new inter-religious community will emerge. Religious identity would then becomes very complex.

9. Conclusion

The problem with Christian identity is that the identity of the individual is subordinated to the identity of the Christian community or the Church — especially in the Roman Catholic Church. The Church claims to be the Body of Christ with a 'divinely-willed' hierarchical structure. It determines what Christian identity is: what a Christian believes, what rituals s/he practices, even what his/her theological reflection should be. So the ordinary Christian feels hemmed in from all directions. But the examples of Abhishiktananda and Panikkar, the tradition of the freedom and primacy of the individual conscience in the face of God fostered by people like

---

[34] For a more contemporary example see S. Painadath, *The Power of Silence: Fifty Meditations to Discover the Divine Space within You* (Delhi: ISPCK, 2009).

[35] Francis X. Clooney, *Hindu God, Christian God: How Reason Helps Break Down the Barriers between Religions* (New York: OUP, 2001); *idem, Divine Mother, Blessed Mother: Hindu Goddesses and the Virgin Mary* (New York: OUP, 2005); *idem, Beyond Compare: St. Francis de Sales and Sri Vedanta Desika on Loving Surrender to God* (Washington: Georgetown University Press, 2008).

[36] Francis X. Clooney, *The Truth, the Way, the Life: Christian Commentary on the Three Holy Mantras of the Srivaishnava Hindus* (Leuven: Peeters, 2008), 191.

St. Ignatius of Loyola and the post-modern praxis of young people are indicators that new models of religious identity are possible. To liberate them from religious control some will call them mystical. I do not think that mysticism is necessarily involved here. Ultimately it is for the individual, responding to God's call, to decide what s/he wants to be. This may involve tensions with the community. At the level of the individual, communal identities like Hinduism and Christianity may already be questioned in the post-modern world. The emphasis today may be on the individual rather than the community, though the community remains important. But a community is built up by a consensus of consenting individuals, especially if they are called by God, not by authoritarian structures.

Once again I would like to make clear that I am not talking about people belonging simultaneously to the social or institutional structures of two religions but about people who seek to integrate in themselves experiential and spiritual traditions which they have inherited from different religious groups they have encountered, though they may be rooted in one particular religious tradition. They may be considered marginal by the institution. This may not have been possible when socio-religious structures were strong and the individuals did not have the freedom. But today people seem to be freer to experience and assert their personal identity. I am not making an abstract argument either, but am trying to understand (and also justify) the religious experience of people whom I have encountered either personally or through their writings. There is a traditional phrase in logic: *contra factum non valet argumentum*—mere arguments are of no value when faced with facts. People with double religious identities, however they may be described, are facts in my experience.

I think that the freedom of God who manifests Godself to whomsoever and in whichever way it pleases God and the freedom of the individual person to respond to God are sacred. The Spirit is God's gift to everyone. In the Catholic tradition we have the tension between the *sensus fidelium*— the consensus of the People of God—and the *Magisterium* or the teaching authority of the hierarchy. Today we may have to add to this the faith experience of the individual. We have also to be clear about the obligation that an individual feels to respond to God in the particular way that God has called him/her, while being open to the reality that God may be calling others through other ways. This means that in building up one's identity an individual must listen not only to one's own desires and to the community to which one is related but also to God who is calling. God's call may be the most basic of the three elements. Whatever problems communities have dealing with multiple identities on the part of individuals, this trend is here to stay. In any case, realizing and living these new identities is more a challenge than a cause for conflict.

References

Adhav, Shamsundar Manohar. *Pandita Ramabai*. Chennai: CLS, 1979.

Amaladoss, Michael. *Towards Fullness: Searching for an Integral Spirituality*. Bangalore: NBCLC, 1994.

———. 'Double Religious Belonging and Liminality'. *Vidyajyoti Journal of Theological Reflection* 66 (2001): 21–34.

———. *The Dancing Cosmos: A Way to Harmony*. Anand: Gujarat Sahitya Prakash, 2003.

———. 'Double Religious Identity: Is It Possible? Is It Necessary?' *Vidyajyoti Journal of Theological Reflection* 73 (2009): 519–32.

Animananda, B. *The Blade: Life and Work of Brahmabandab Upadhyaya*. Calcutta: Roy & Son, ca 1947.

Appasamy, A.J. *Christianity as Bhakti Marga*. Chennai: CLS, 1928.

———. *Sundar Singh: A Biography*. London: n.p., 1958.

Bamat, Thomas and Jean-Paul Wiest (eds). *Popular Catholicism in a World Church: Seven Case Studies in Inculturation*. Maryknoll: Orbis, 1999.

Boyd, Robin H.S. *An Introduction to Indian Christian Theology*. Chennai: CLS, 1969.

Clooney, Francis X. *Hindu God, Christian God: How Reason Helps Break Down the Barriers between Religions*. New York: OUP, 2001.

———. *Divine Mother, Blessed Mother: Hindu Goddesses and the Virgin Mary*. New York: OUP, 2005.

———. *Beyond Compare: St. Francis de Sales and Sri Vedanta Desika on Loving Surrender to God*. Washington: Georgetown University Press, 2008.

———. *The Truth, the Way, the Life: Christian Commentary on the Three Holy Mantras of the Srivaishnava Hindus*. Leuven: Peeters, 2008).

Dupuis, Jacques. *Towards a Christian Theology of Religious Pluralism*. Maryknoll: Orbis, 2002.

[n.a.]. *The Christian Century*, 16–23 August 2000, 834–6.

Painadath, S. *The Power of Silence: Fifty Meditations to Discover the Divine Space within You*. Delhi: ISPCK, 2009.

Pieris, Aloysius. *An Asian Theology of Liberation*. Maryknoll: Orbis, 1988.

Pope Benedict XVI. *Faith, Reason and the University*. Address at the University of Regensburg.

Pope John Paul II. *Faith and Reason*.

Pope Paul VI. *Evangelization in the Modern World*.

Puthanangady, Paul (ed.). *Sharing Worship*. Bangalore: NBCLC, 1988.

Samartha, S.J. *One Christ, Many Religions: Towards a Revised Christology*. Maryknoll: Orbis, 1991.

Stuart, James. *Swami Abhishiktananda: His Life told through his Letters*. Delhi: ISPCK,1989.

Swami Abhishiktananda. 'The Upanishads and Advaitic Experience'. In *The Further Shore*. Delhi: ISPCK, 1975.

———. *Ascent to the Depth of the Heart*. Delhi: ISPCK, 1998.

Communalism *and* Nationalism: Lessons from the Indian Christian Rejection of the 'Communal Award' in 1932

Nigel Ajay Kumar*

1. Introduction

Communalism and nationalism are concepts that use religion and nationality to frame social identity.[1] They are often used as opposites, especially in the context of India, where merging politics with religion is seen to have a horrific past and present. In a post-independent and post-partitioned India, it is popular to uphold secular nationalism and reject communalism. Of course, India's secular nationalism is construed as a unique blend of religious and national identity; with the communal coming in second to the national. Yet communalism, by itself, is associated with divisive (Hindutva) ideologies and practices that alienate minorities and can even lead to violence against other communities. Not surprisingly, communalism is defined as 'politicized religious conflict'.[2]

Christians in India need to be careful about this dismissal of communalism because, if we accept a softer view of communalism (seen when a community defends its interests without the violence that has been associated with religious communalism), Christians are communal too. As Christians, we like to identify ourselves with the ideals of theology and spirituality, yet we also opt for materialist self-definitions when Christian institutions are threatened. We believe in the Trinitarian God's solution for this nation, yet we also resort to minority politics when many Christians still request the state to grant

---

* Nigel Ajay Kumar (PhD candidate) teaches in the Theology Department of SAIACS.
[1] I am accepting the concepts 'nationalism' and 'communalism' *as is*, despite Pandey and others who problematise them. This is largely because I do not have any particular stake in the meaning of these words in this paper. Rather my focus is in the mixing of the categories and thus *imagining* something new.
[2] Peter Heehs, 'Bengali Religious Nationalism and Communalism', *International Journal of Hindu Studies* 1.1 (April 1997): 117.

special rights and protection. Christians often defend their missionary endeavours as spiritual transformations wrought by the Holy Spirit, yet Christian organisations tend to prioritise demographic success, by holding the increasing number of converts and churches in high regard.

Furthermore, scholars have pointed out how a combination of religious and national identities is natural and historically accurate. For instance, Heehs points to how the goals of early Indian nationalism were both cultural and spiritual.[3] Pandey paints a more detailed picture of how in pre-independent India, both communalism and nationalism 'arose together', since they 'were part of the same discourse'.[4] He notes how prior to the 1920s, Hindu and Muslim political involvement was both necessary and inevitable.[5] Gandhi, for instance, saw no contradiction in the Muslim Ali brothers' love for their country even as they were 'Mussulmans first and everything else afterwards'.[6] However, by the mid-1920s, 'communitarian mobilization' began to be termed by nationalists as distorted and unnecessary.[7] Pandey notes the emergence of a secular nationalist rhetoric that strongly urged people to work for the interest of the nation outside community interests. The same Gandhi went on to say that 'Nationalism is greater than sectarianism . . . we are Indians first and Hindus, Mussulmans, Parsis, Christians after.'[8] Eventually 'pure nationalists' aimed to suppress or even discredit community voices and offered that secular nationalism was the only way for unity and progress in India.[9] Nationalism was presented as rational, relevant (to real issues) and progressive, while communalism was projected as pre-modern, irrelevant and regressive.[10]

---

[3] Heehs, 'Bengali Religious Nationalism and Communalism', 132.

[4] Gyanendra Pandey, *The Construction of Communalism in Colonial North India* (New Delhi: OUP, 1992), 236.

[5] Pandey, *The Construction of Communalism*, 235.

[6] M.K. Gandhi, 'To The Mussulmans of India' (24 September 1921) in *Collected Works of Mahatma Gandhi (CWMG)*, Vol. 21, 192.

[7] Pandey, *The Construction of Communalism*, 235.

[8] Gandhi, 'Hindus and Moplahs', *Young India* (26 January 1922) in *CWMG*, Vol. 22, 268. Pandey draws attention to this change in Gandhi in his book *The Construction of Communalism*, 238.

[9] Pandey, *The Construction of Communalism*, 239–42.

[10] Pandey, *The Construction of Communalism*, 241.

Religious and lower caste communities, understandably, reacted fiercely against the notion of secular nation as defined by a 'Hindu elite'.[11] The strongest reaction came from Muslims and other caste and religious minorities, who refused to follow the Congress desire for national integration unless their interests were met. Heehs notes that even the Hindu religious nationalism that emerged after the 1920s, with Savarkar and Golwalkar, was a more extreme communalism than the spiritual cultural nationalism of just a few decades before.[12]

The balance between nationalism and communalism, some scholars suggest, lay in Bipinchandra Pal's 'composite nationalism' — the vision where India's diverse communities would work 'along their respective traditional and historic lines . . . towards one common universal goal'.[13] Pandey explains 'composite nationalism' as being aware of religious communal distinctions; it is not pure nationalism that rejects religious identity over nationality, nor is it pure communalism that constructs national belonging on the basis of a 'hierarchy of cultures'.[14]

It is fair to assume that Indian Christians today are happy to be citizens of both heaven and India, though questions over priority or balance may remain. If we truly want to be considered loyal Indian citizens as well as faithful Christians, we need to find a way to keep intact *both* our communal (Christian) identity and our national (Indian) identity. If we do not, we may be in danger of losing one to the other. This paper is therefore a study of the manner in which Indian Christians negotiated their religious and nationalist identities in pre-independent India. The focus is on how Indian Christians in 1932 rejected the 'Communal Award' using two approaches, namely the political approach and the spiritual approach. Both these approaches are shown to be within the framework of 'composite nationalism', where Indian Christians maintained their communal distinctiveness while aspiring for national integration. The result is a clarification of Christian composite nationalism, with a proposal as to how Christians can reconcile their national and religious identity today.

---

[11] For instance, see Donald Low, *Eclipse of Empire* (Cambridge: CUP, 1993), 86.

[12] Heehs, 'Bengali Religious Nationalism and Communalism', 136.

[13] Bipinchandra Pal, *The New Spirit* (Calcutta: Sinha, Sarvadhikar & Co., 1907), 152–4, cited in Heehs, 'Bengali Religious Nationalism and Communalism', 130.

[14] Pandey, *The Construction of Communalism,* 260–61.

2. The Context: Nationalism Versus Communalism

Nationalism and communalism were important factors in negotiating corporate identity in pre-independent India. Chandra and others remark that for Indians in the early 1900s, communal consciousness was a new way of looking at political involvement in relation to and in opposition to the colonial powers.[15] They also show how these new communal identities and aspirations were in continual conflict with national identity and aspirations, especially when it came to protecting the interests of minority communities.[16] Chandra and others add that economic and social factors 'gave a certain aura of validity to communal politics', such as the intense competition for government jobs, for the business of customers, and for access to education.[17]

Chandra and others are also critical of the rise of communalism and blame the 'Divide and Rule' policy for the growth of communalism in modern India, even as the British government 'used communalism to counter and weaken the growing national movement'.[18] To prove this, they cite how the British Government appealed to the strengthening of communal identity, accepting the Muslim demand for separate electorates in legislative assemblies through the Indian Councils Act of 1909, also known as the Morley-Minto Reforms. [19] The 'Reforms' were a system of separate electorates where Muslims could only vote for Muslim candidates in designated Muslim constituencies. [20] It was reasoned that since Hindus and Muslims had separate political, economic and cultural interests, only Muslims could best represent Muslims.[21]

In 1932, the Morley-Minto Reforms were extended through the Communal Award to include Sikhs, Christians and Scheduled Castes,

---

[15] Bipin Chandra and others, *India's Struggle for Independence: 1857–1947* (New Delhi: Penguin Books, 1989), 401–2. It is not that there was no 'communalism' prior to the 1900s in India, however the concept of communalism as linked to politics was bound to the colonial era. See Pandey, *The Construction of Communalism*, 6–11.

[16] Chandra and others, *India's Struggle for Independence*, 402, 404.

[17] Chandra and others, *India's Struggle for Independence*, 403.

[18] Chandra and others, *India's Struggle for Independence*, 408.

[19] Chandra and others, *India's Struggle for Independence*, 142.

[20] Chandra and others, *India's Struggle for Independence*, 142.

[21] Chandra and others, *India's Struggle for Independence*, 142.

so that for provincial elections 'Muslims, Christians, and Sikhs could only vote for candidates of their own community'.[22] While Congress nationalists and others were apprehensive of this move, most conceded to communal electorates for at least the Muslims.[23] However, Gandhi strongly opposed communal electorates for Scheduled Castes on religious (communal) grounds.[24]

3. The Christian Context

In the 1930s, the Christian community had to face the negative attention that mass conversions generated. With outcastes and lower castes joining Christianity in masses, many Christians promoted mass conversions as the sole focus of mission, suggesting that the goal of Christianity was to increase its numerical strength.[25] The mass conversion movement led to several problems. For instance, there was a politicisation of conversion. Accusations were raised that the Christian community was attempting to gain political clout by increasing their numbers through conversion of backward classes.[26] After all, the Communal Award only made sense for the Christian community after its numbers had increased.[27] The influx of Depressed Castes to the church also led to internal divisions with caste-conscious Christians.[28]

Added to this, in 1931, Gandhi came out strongly against conversion. Influenced largely by his own *swadeshi* ideology of self-reliance, and motivated by an opposition to mass conversions, Gandhi stated, 'Certainly the great faiths held by the people of India are adequate for her people. India is in no need of conversion from one faith

---

[22] Myron Weiner, 'The Struggle for Equality: Caste in Indian Politics', in Atul Kohli (ed), *The Success of India's Democracy* (Cambridge: CUP, 2001), 200.

[23] Weiner, 'The Struggle for Equality', 200.

[24] He feared that the Hindu community would be divided. Weiner, 'The Struggle for Equality', 200.

[25] Duncan B. Forrester, 'Indian Christian Attitudes to Caste in the Twentieth Century', *Indian Church History Review* 9.1 (1975): 8.

[26] J.H. Beaglehole, 'The Indian Christians—A Study of a Minority', *Modern Asia Studies* 1.1 (1967): 63.

[27] Forrester, 'Indian Christian Attitudes to Caste in the Twentieth Century', 8.

[28] Forrester, 'Indian Christian Attitudes to Caste in the Twentieth Century', 7–8.

to another.'[29] He went on to challenge the key institutions of Christianity by rejecting the use of Christian hospitals and Christian schools as a platform for conversion: 'why should I change my religion because a doctor who professes Christianity as his religion has cured me . . . why should the doctor expect or suggest a change whilst I am under his influence?'[30] In fact, Gandhi suggested that he opposed conversion to the extent that if missionaries used humanitarian work as a means for proselytising, he would ask them to withdraw from India.[31]

Albuquerque reveals that Gandhi's views against conversion came as a 'bolt-from-the-blue' for Indian Christians, who had till then largely supported Gandhi.[32] The rise of anti-colonial attitudes had already led to fear concerning their safety after the British left. Gandhi's statements made matters worse. Subsequently, many Christians believed that 'safeguards for religious rights' was a fundamental issue for Indian Christians.[33] Many also asserted that communal representation through separate electorates was the 'only possible safeguard for the community'.[34]

Following the Muslim, Sikh and Schedule Caste communities, many Indian Christians argued that Christians should 'pursue their interests through political mobilization, based on their strength in numbers within any given electorate'.[35] The Indian Catholic Christians, in particular, 'stridently advocated communal electorates in order to secure "Catholic interests"'.[36] Catholic spokesmen provided the further rationale that since 'communal identities constituted the very fabric of Indian society', there was 'the need to retain strong communal

[29] Gandhi, 'Foreign Missionaries', *Young India* (23 April 1931) in *CWMG*, Vol. 46, 28.

[30] Gandhi, 'Foreign Missionaries', 28.

[31] Gandhi, 'Interview to the Press', *The Hindu* (22 March 1931) in *CWMG*, Vol. 45, 320.

[32] Teresa Albuquerque, 'The Role of the Christians in the National Struggle for Freedom', in Asghar Ali Engineer (ed), *They Too Fought for Freedom — The Role of Minorities*, (Gurgaon, Haryana: Hope India Publications, 2006), 202.

[33] Albuquerque, 'The Role of the Christians in the National Struggle for Freedom', 202–3.

[34] Beaglehold, 'The Indian Christians', 65.

[35] Chandra Mallampalli, *Christians and Public Life in Colonial South India, 1863–1937: Contending with Marginality* (New York: RoutledgeCurzon, 2004), 121.

[36] Mallampalli, *Christians and Public Life*, 3.

boundaries' because, by so doing, Catholics were participating in the true fabric and culture of India.[37]

A competing position came from the 'Protestant elites', as Mallampalli calls them. Protestant leaders joined the Congress in their opposition to separate electorates, or at least tempering it with demands for reserved seats in joint electorates.[38] Christian nationalists like K.T. Paul and S.K. Datta opposed separate electorates for Christians. In fact, speaking as the Indian Christian delegate in the Round Table Conference, S.K. Datta stated:

> There are some of us in India who have been brought up with a fierce belief in voluntarism in religion . . . I believe that there is an infringement of my rights when the State says, 'you shall vote in a particular constituency.' What if I say I have got no religion? Does that mean I am going to be disfranchised? I shall have no vote.[39]

Many Protestant Christians objected to the consequent political alienation that Christians would face if the Award was put in place. An editorial in the *National Christian Council Review* gave this strong critique of the communal approach:

> [T]he communal electorates . . . means that an Indian the moment he enters into public life ceases to be an Indian and becomes either a Hindu or a Muslim or a Christian . . . For the growth of the political life of the country, it is clear that the present policy of grouping the followers of each religion as distinct political units should be given up and Indians of all religions, or of no religion . . . should be classified together as one unit for the exercise of their common civic and public rights.[40]

Other Protestants advocated a spiritual approach: Christians were to see themselves as non-political communities, the 'salt of the earth', where Christians could be dissolved in service of the nation. In addition, in their effort to define themselves as non-Western, Indian Christians were not just rejecting a negative missionary legacy but also choosing between either the communal or nationalist rhetoric to define who they were in the Indian political scene. Clearly, Christians were struggling between a unified national identity and their own religious identity. In the 1930s, there was no unanimity on which course to take.

---

[37] Mallampalli, *Christians and Public Life*, 3.

[38] Mallampalli, *Christians and Public Life*, 123.

[39] Editorial, 'Indian Christians and the Communal Award', *The Guardian* (25 August 1932), 349.

[40] Editorial, *National Christian Council Review* 46.10 (October 1926): 580.

4. Indian Christian Responses to the Communal Award

When in August, 1932, the British Government proposed the Communal Award, there was an outcry amongst the 'elite' Christian community. *The Guardian*, the Christian newspaper based in Chennai which largely featured pro-nationalist Christian thinking, unsurprisingly featured several articles against the Communal Award. Of course, there were Christians who rejected the Communal Award on purely nationalist grounds. For instance, B.L. Rallia Ram called the Communal Award a 'subversion of communal to national interest' and urged Indian Christians to 'continue to preach the true Gospel of "nationalism" to the country and prepare it to accept all its implications'.[41] Similarly, an Indian Christian association from the Bombay Presidency argued that if the Communal Award was carried out, it would be a 'national calamity' and give rise to 'unhealthy sectional rivalries'.[42] However it was quite rare to get purely nationalist rhetoric for such a communally charged issue; it was more common to express nationalist opinions within communal concerns.

There were primarily two kinds of concerns raised by Indian Christians against the Communal Award. The more common approach was the political, which rejected the Award for its lack of adequate representation for Christians and/or that it caused problems for the Christian community. The other approach was spiritual, which attempted to combine Christian theology with nationalism so that Christian values would influence how Christians should respond.

4.1. The Political Approach

The political reaction against the Award was represented, for instance, by P.J. Thomas who argued that its 'most serious defect' was that Indian Christians were 'given no representation on the general electorate'.[43] Thomas seemed to be promoting a nationalist approach when he stated, 'The system of separate electorates weakens national solidarity and

---

[41] B.L. Rallia Ram, 'Communal Award', *The Guardian* (September 22, 1932), 392.

[42] Indian Christians from Bombay, 'Christian Opinion on the Communal Award', *The Guardian* (29 September 1932).

[43] P.J. Thomas, 'Indian Christians and the Communal Award', *The Guardian* (6 October 1932), 415.

encourages communal particularism.'[44] However Thomas' concerns were for communal particularism as he stated how after the Communal Award would be put in place, 'Members of the majority community . . . will not have a single Christian constituent and could safely ignore the interests of Christians . . . and the necessity for safeguarding religious interests will diminish.'[45] Thomas argued that the principal 'interests of the Indian Christians' were 'material' and thus 'inextricably connected with their immediate neighbourhood' to the extent that 'such interests can only be properly safeguarded by those who represented territorial constituencies'.[46] Thomas went on to say,

> Whichever system be adopted, it is of the utmost importance that Indian Christians should be given a vote on the general electorate in as large a portion of the Presidency as possible, so that the community may gradually be educated for a thoroughly national system of representation . . . Having given such weightage to Muhammadans and the Depressed Classes, it would be rather unfair to deny it to Christians, who have in the past contributed to the progress of the Presidency more than their numbers indicate, and who are ready to work for the commonweal without grumbling about the cessation of certain advantages.[47]

It is not hard to spot the irony in Thomas' grumblings even as he extols how the Indian Christian community does not grumble! There was in fact substantial anger against the limited Christian representation in the Communal Award. For instance, some Christians in Punjab argued that Christians were short-changed in numerical representation and, instead, those who 'clamoured loudly' got representation that was 'rightly ours'.[48] The Guntur Christians too opposed the Communal Award saying that 'the representation of our community should be much larger'.[49] In an editorial, the *Guardian* undiplomatically complained about how the problematic communities received more representation:

> The worst feature of the weightage system is that it is granted to those minorities which are most powerful and able to defy the majorities and withheld from those communities which need them most . . . the balance between the communities is confined only to those who give the most trouble

---

[44] Thomas, 'Indian Christians and the Communal Award', 415.

[45] Thomas, 'Indian Christians and the Communal Award', 415.

[46] Thomas, 'Indian Christians and the Communal Award', 415.

[47] Thomas, 'Indian Christians and the Communal Award', 415.

[48] [n.a.], 'Punjab Christians and Communal Award', *The Guardian* (22 September 1932), 394.

[49] [n.a.], 'Guntur Christian's Statement', *The Guardian* (27 October 1932), 457.

to the Government and not to those who play a worthy part in the life of the country. This opens out a dangerous prospect and puts a premium on recalcitrancy of the worst form.[50]

Further, an article from the *Catholic Reader* published in the *Guardian* sought a pragmatic approach in rejecting the Communal Award. Noting that the Depressed Classes[51] no longer sought separate electorates, the voice of the Christians had become isolated and the political strength of Catholics was 'considerably weakened'.[52] Thus, the article urged,

> Now that they [Depressed Classes] have definitely decided to merge themselves with the Hindus, the Christian members will be isolated and their voice will be a cry in the wilderness. We shall cut ourselves more and more adrift from the ruling community and the position and prestige hitherto enjoyed by us may be severely impaired. Now that the conditions have changed so radically, would it not be wiser to change our policy and seek to influence the majority community by a system of joint electorates? . . . The cleavage may further be deepened and the result may prove detrimental to our interests, if prompt steps are not taken to find a solution. [53]

There was also a call for a concerted unanimous voice to speak for Indian Christians together, much like the Muslims. Muslims, like Christians, also had a diverse population and yet came across as a united community with a common platform and voice that fought for separate electorates. This unity was attractive and many Indian Christians wanted to achieve the same thing. Again, from the Catholic point of view, the *Guardian* quoted:

> We think the Indian Christians have to blame themselves to a large extent, if their claims have received such scant attention. The Muslims are well united and organised and press their demands repeatedly and emphatically and consequently their voice is heard in the highest Councils of the land as well as in the British Cabinet. But among Indian Christians, Catholics and Protestants, who are from one body for political purposes, there is no recognised organisation which can authoritatively voice their claims, nor are there any accredited leaders, whose views command the general respect and attention of the rank and file of the community.[54]

---

[50] Editorial, 'The Communal Award', *The Guardian* (25 August 1932), 343.

[51] Used interchangeably with Depressed Castes.

[52] From the *Catholic Reader*, 'Indian Christians and the Communal Award', *The Guardian* (6 October 1932), 422.

[53] From the *Catholic Reader*, 'Indian Christians and the Communal Award', 422.

[54] From the *Catholic Reader*, 'Indian Christians and the Communal Award', *The Guardian* (25 August 1932), 349.

There was a similar appeal from some Protestants:

> We, Indian Christian representatives at the Unity Conference, Allahabad, feel the imperative and urgent need of an All-India Organisation of Indian Christians, including both Catholics and Protestants, to bring about solidarity in the community, to voice its feelings and aspirations, and to watch over and advance its interests, the organisation to be of a non-religious character and to deal exclusively with the political and civic interests of the community.[55]

The Communal Award was thus seen as possibly destroying any hope for unity in Indian Christianity. The general belief was:

> The Award will act as a disruptive force within the Christian Church itself. In many electoral revisions the rival candidates will belong to different denominations and to different caste origins and the elections will inevitably lead to the intensifying of denominational differences and to the revival of old caste distinctions which are in process of being forgotten.[56]

Important to note that while the political approach was obviously communal, there was also a non-religious (non-spiritual) character to it, with the belief that political and civic matters need not be confused with matters pertaining to theology.

4.2. The Spiritual Approach

Bishop Azaraiah was one of the more respected and vocal critics of separate electorates and felt it was a serious breach to national life and the Christian church.[57] In no uncertain terms, he argued that 'whatever the followers of other religions may want, we ought not to want separate electorates. We do not want to be treated as strangers in this land.'[58] Azaraiah offered several reasons to reject the Communal Award. He pointed, using an awareness of political communalism, to how the Award could cause divisions among Christians, put a 'serious strain' on the loyalty of the Depressed Classes to the Christian religion, and cause a further separation between the Christian Church and the country in

---

[55] B.L. Rallia Ram, 'Indian Christian Organisation: An Appeal', *The Guardian* (17 November 1932), 488.

[56] [n.a.], 'Christian and the Communal Award', *The Guardian* (13 October 1932), 434.

[57] Bishop Azaraiah, 'Indian Christians and the Communal Award', *The Guardian* (6 October 1932), 415.

[58] Azaraiah, 'Indian Christians and the Communal Award', 415.

general.[59] Angrily he remarked: 'We have permitted ourselves not to be placed on the side of the whole country or the nation, but on the side of a religious sect, a community which seeks self-protection, for the sake of its own loaves and fishes!'[60] However, Azaraiah also offered a theological reason for rejecting the Award:

> The Award stamps the followers of Jesus Christ as a communal entity, with distinct political interests of their own, like Moslems or Sikhs or Europeans . . . [but] the religion of Christ is one of the most dynamic factors in the world. It always bursts its boundaries, however strong and rigid those boundaries may be laid. It refuses to be confined to any one race, class or caste . . . The inclusion of Christians in 'a communal award' is a direct blow to the nature of the Church of Christ.[61]

Related to this, Azaraiah stated that Christians were not a singular socio-political unit defined by their religion. Azaraiah remarked that Christians, despite their religion, often had social and political opinions that were identical to their non-Christian neighbours. Was it right to force these Christians to vote in a Christian constituency, despite having opinions that were similar to the general constituency?[62]

Notice how Azaraiah mixed theological and political reasons. There was a belief in a Christian identity that bound people together and yet the awareness that this in no way impacted the political views of those people insofar as they were united by ethnic or political factors. The Christian community, especially the Indian Christian community, was seen not in terms of how other communities were defined, but as something unique.

Another article in the *Guardian* attempted to draw attention to the theological problems:

> The Award stamps the followers of Jesus Christ as a communal entity, with distinct political interests of their own. But it is of the essence of our whole conception of the Church of Christ that it transcends all differences of community or race or caste in one all-embracive [sic] Brotherhood.[63]

Furthermore, there was an awareness of the political realities alongside the need to bring to bear spiritual principles:

---

[59] Bishop Azaraiah, 'The Communal Award', *The Guardian* (8 September 1932), 368.

[60] Azaraiah, 'The Communal Award', 368.

[61] Azaraiah, 'The Communal Award', 368.

[62] Azaraiah, 'The Communal Award', 368.

[63] [n.a.], 'Christian and the Communal Award', 434.

By the present Award, Christians are cut off from the rest of the country. We are prevented from throwing in our lot with the whole nation and are ranked as a particular sect, seeking for its own position. Now, even if the matter be viewed from the point of view of self-interest, it is surely evident that the interests of Christians would be better preserved by their winning the sympathy and support of the country through a truly national outlook and spirit than by maintaining a very small body of special representation in the Councils, chosen by themselves. But, in fact, we are bound by the principles of our religion to take a higher line than that of self-interest and to set an example of losing our own life to find it.[64]

The principle of religion to take the 'higher line' included self-sacrifice, which was an important religious principle for Indian Christians like D. S. Ramachandra Rao. Rao reiterated,

No sacrifice is too great for the achievement of national unity . . . Leadership comes to those who deny themselves and serve unselfishly. The Christian Indians will never regret throwing their lot with the country. But will they rise to the occasion? Something tells me — "they will."[65]

Chakkarai made another spiritual point by saying that 'there is no such entity as the Christian community nor do we desire to have one.'[66] Chakkarai stated that since Christianity was based on the principle of voluntarism, the bond among Christians was religious.[67] In a significantly more provocative essay, Chakkarai asked rhetorically, 'Should the Indian Christian Community Continue?'[68] Citing the examples of K.T. Paul who asked Indian Christians to be like salt, useful only when dissolved, he sided with those who favoured Christianity 'extinguishing itself *qua* community'.[69] Chakkarai recognised that this was idealistic and for a while India would continue to see 'strongly nationalistic and non-communal' Christians alongside 'strongly conservative and communal' Christians.[70] However Chakkarai urged that Christians 'should renounce separatist claims and take its place

---

[64] [n.a.], 'Christian and the Communal Award', 434.

[65] D.S. Ramachandra Rao, 'Indian Christians and the Communal Award', *The Guardian* (6 October 1932), 422.

[66] V. Chakkarai, 'Indian Christians and Communal Award', *The Guardian* (1 September 1932), 356.

[67] Chakkarai, 'Indian Christians and Communal Award', 356.

[68] V. Chakkarai, 'Should the Indian Christian Community Continue?–I', *The Guardian* (7 April 1932), 100–101.

[69] Chakkarai, 'Should the Indian Christian Community Continue?–I', 100–101.

[70] Chakkarai, 'Should the Indian Christian Community Continue?–I', 101.

within the body politic'.[71] This would naturally lead to a 'weakening' and even a 'wholesale withdrawal of many . . . hall marks [sic] of Christianity' and Christianity 'as ordinarily understood' would be 'relegated to the sphere of the forum of the individual conscience'.[72] The strengthening of Christianity, Chakkarai hinted, would be in the 'highest sense' outside the traditional forms of Christian institutionalism.[73]

4.3. The Spiritual-Political Approach

A pragmatic solution was offered by J.J.M. Nichols Roy, who combined the spiritual and political concerns. Roy suggested Christians must not negatively condemn the Award and instead look at it as a challenge. Roy accepted the spiritual directive:

> Turning to ourselves as Indian Christians we should work for the ideal that there should be no communalism, that the whole of India should be like one nation. Though we are a small community we are willing to lose our individuality in the flow of the national tide, in order to work for the ultimate good of India as a whole. We do not like to see India divided into various communities and form themselves into water-tight compartments. Universalism against Radicalism, and Nationalist against Communalism, are our ideals. Equality in political and social life is our ideal which we have imbibed from our holy universal religion.[74]

Nevertheless, Roy also stated that the ideal can be 'adapted to circumstances for the sake of gaining its object.'[75] Roy argued that while communalism is rooted in 'evil practices, habits and desires', it was possible for Christians with a mind for non-communal thinking to enter the communal political scene with a view of changing the country:

> When communalism has taken the field what should be our attitude? We are ready to be lost in the flow of the national tide for by that we shall gain the ideal of our creed, but when communalism has for the present replaced nationalism, should our voice and influence which are very necessary in the formation of a common national life in India be buried? If we have any virtue as Christians for the up-building of the national life of our country our influence

---

[71] V. Chakkarai, 'Should the Indian Christian Community Continue?–II', *The Guardian* (14 April 1932), 116.

[72] Chakkarai, 'Should the Indian Christian Community Continue?–II', 116.

[73] Chakkarai, 'Should the Indian Christian Community Continue?–II', 116.

[74] J.J.M. Nichols Roy, 'Indian Christians and the Award', *The Guardian* (13 October 1932), 428.

[75] Roy, 'Indian Christians and the Award', 428.

should not be lost to our country. That influence however small it may be, being based on truth, will be like a grain of mustard seed that will grow to be a big tree. Our aim is to serve our God and our country. When we serve our God faithfully we serve our country. Our attitude, therefore, should be to get an opportunity by some legitimate means to promote the spirit of honest and faithful service and the sense of righteousness in our country and to cultivate national brotherhood among all parties and communities. With such a noble object in view we should get a voice in the legislatures of our country for here are the important centres for shaping the ideas of the people.[76]

Thus, for Roy, the Communal Award was not such a bad thing for the present moment. The key factor was that if good Christians were to take high positions, they would make a positive impact. Roy believed that if the Christian community sent members to the Councils who kept 'the noble object of fostering the spirit of peace, justice and goodwill and nationalism against communalism', these Christian representatives would 'rise above communalism' and have 'a very healthy influence in the Councils for the good of our land'.[77] The theological basis: 'Our Lord was born among the Jews but He rose above all races and communities.'[78]

A similar sentiment was reflected by D.A. Chowdhry who urged 'leaders of our community [Indian Christians] who can rise above communal aspects of things' to join the general elections to 'win the love and confidence of the people by their life and service' and gain the popular mandate.[79]

This type of Christian humanism, the belief in the goodness of a Christian, may seem naive today (or even then). However, here was yet another example of how theological reasoning was used within socio-political discussions in a volatile time.

It must be noted that the spiritual approach was not a withdrawal from the national scene, but rather a complete immersion within it. The Christian involvement in the nationalist movement would be indistinguishable from that of any other Indian, except insofar as the *manner* in which the principles of Christ, ethics and self-sacrifice, influenced the Christian's involvement in the nation.

---

[76] Roy, 'Indian Christians and the Award', 428.
[77] Roy, 'Indian Christians and the Award', 429.
[78] Roy, 'Indian Christians and the Award', 428.
[79] D.A. Chowdhry, 'Communal Award', *The Guardian* (22 September 1932), 392.

4.4. The Result: The End of the Communal Award

In 1947, both Protestant and Catholic Christians rallied together during the meeting of the Constitution Advisory Committee on Minority and Fundamental Rights.[80] Abraham Thomas informs that Indian Christians, under the leadership of Mukherjee and Jerome D'Souza, led the community away from the communal line and towards the nationalist line by not only abandoning separate electorates for Christians but also the reservation of seats.[81] This move was praised by Nehru, Patel and other Indian nationalist leaders. It played an important role in influencing the majority community to comply with the Christian request for granting the fundamental right to equality of religion, including the right to propagate it, as well as other rights to conduct private schools that impart religious instruction.[82] Thomas also believes that this was a decisive moment for the formation of the secular Indian state as we have it today.[83]

5. Implications

Mallampalli believes that Protestant Christians were wrong to let go of communal politics, because they failed to recognise the socio-political realities of India. One of his main contentions is that nationalist Christians not only isolated themselves from regional politics and but also remained marginalised in the national scene.[84] Mallampalli does make a fair point on the need to hold on to communal identities in the midst of national-universalist ideologies.

However, in defence of the Indian Christian nationalists, it must be noted that they did not have the benefit of hindsight to judge their

---

[80] Albuquerque, 'The Role of the Christians in the National Struggle for Freedom', 204.

[81] Abraham Vazhayil Thomas, *Christians in Secular India* (Cranbury, New Jersey: Associated University Presses, 1974), 116.

[82] Thomas, *Christians in Secular India,* 116.

[83] Thomas, *Christians in Secular India,* 116. One must avoid an over-zealous interpretation that views this event as an example of Christian purity, when in fact an alternative case could be made that Christian negotiations were influenced by self-interest. However, the official rejection of the Communal Award remains a victory for those Christians who fought against it.

[84] Mallampalli, *Christians and Public Life,* 16.

decision to align with nationalism. Furthermore, Indian (Protestant) Christians did not opt for a secular nationalism; rather they were influenced by their own communal (theological) framework. Surely they interpreted their communal identities differently, looking either for political approaches or spiritual approaches. Nevertheless, they were *both* communal and nationalistic. Even if we were to assume that the nationalist Indian Christians were not relevant to their local communities, they were nevertheless relevant to their 'religious' community as they sought to engage with the nation.

The political approach as expressed by early Indian Christians lacked the theological undergirding that the spiritual approach offered. The spiritual approach rightly looked to apprehend how the Christian faith informed Christian action on the national stage. Out of the two approaches, Roy's combined spiritual-political approach offered the closest parallels with composite nationalism, as well as provided the scope for holding onto specifically Christian ideals and Indian nationalist concerns.

In terms of identity, there are at least three points worth noting. First, many early Indian Christians were willing to identify with the majority people even at the cost of their own privilege. Second, many of these Indian Christians saw no dichotomy in being Indian and Christian; they equated being a Christian as being empowered to be a better Indian. Third, these early Indian Christians were willing to be defined by their actions and their ethics, rather than simply their beliefs or doctrines; their Christian 'Indian-ness' was meant for all to see.

If our goal is to integrate with Indian society, to rid ourselves of a minority complex, to adopt a Christian composite nationalism, then rather than being purely political we could adopt an alternative spiritual-political approach. We can use our faith to determine a clearer understanding of, and develop a more convincing response to, our nationhood; practice our identity as Christians in India. However, what are the principles that should guide our composite nationalism? The *annihilation* of Christian community seems too extreme. Nevertheless, the Indian Christian explorations of communal identity in terms of sacrifice and selflessness, empowered citizenship, as well as predominantly public-ethical behaviour, provide a helpful starting point for negotiating Indian Christian identity today.

I close with this simple case. In the matter concerning the proposed Bill to ban cow slaughter in Karnataka, many Christians took the political approach and decried the Bill as a challenge of our rights. We could have alternatively, informed by New Testament food ethics, joined together to publicly *sacrifice* our freedom to eat beef. We could have, in view of the sensitivity of the cow to the majority Hindu community, apologised for having consumed beef all these years and for hurting their spiritual faith. We could have then committed, as a spiritual community, to reject beef-eating for the future. However, we could *also* express concern about the political motives behind the ban of beef. Thus, we could request the Hindu community to join with us to reject the ban on cow slaughter for the sake of our Muslim brothers and those of the Depressed Castes who still wanted to be free to eat what they want, or even for those who were economically dependent on beef. This, I propose, would have been an effective testimony of Indian Christian self-sacrifice for the betterment of the Indian nation today, as well as potentially shaped how we Christians perceive ourselves and how we are perceived by others.

Certainly, this is idealistic. I am aware of the many difficulties for Indian Christians to agree to this proposal, let alone making a common public statement. Nevertheless, one could also say that such an act cannot be achieved unless the Spirit empowers the Christian community to do so. In effect, by promoting selflessness and a strongly ethical stance, I think it gets us thinking in the right direction about who we are as Indians *and* Christians.

Select References

Albuquerque, Teresa. 'The Role of the Christians in the National Struggle for Freedom'. Pp. 194–210 in *They Too Fought for Freedom—The Role of Minorities*. Edited by Asghar Ali Engineer. Gurgaon, Haryana: Hope India Publications, 2006.

Beaglehole, J.H. 'The Indian Christians — A Study of a Minority'. *Modern Asia Studies* 1.1 (1967): 59–80.

Chandra, Bipan and others. *India's Struggle for Independence: 1857–1947*. New Delhi: Penguin Books, 1989.

Forrester, Duncan B. 'Indian Christian Attitudes to Caste in the

Twentieth Century'. *Indian Church History Review* 9.1 (1975): 3–22.

Gandhi, M.K. *Collected Works of Mahatma Gandhi (CWMG)*, Vols. 21, 22. Ahmedabad: Navajivan Trust, 1966.

————. *Collected Works of Mahatma Gandhi (CWMG)*, Vols. 44, 45. Ahmedabad: Navajivan Trust, 1971.

Heehs, Peter. 'Bengali Religious Nationalism and Communalism'. *International Journal of Hindu Studies* 1.1 (April 1997): 117–39.

Low, Donald. *Eclipse of Empire*. Cambridge: Cambridge University Press, 1993.

Mallampalli, Chandra. *Christians and Public Life in Colonial South India, 1863–1937: Contending with Marginality*. New York: RoutledgeCurzon, 2004.

Pandey, Gyanendra. *The Construction of Communalism in Colonial North India*. New Delhi: Oxford University Press, 1992.

Thomas, Abraham Vazhayil. *Christians in Secular India*. Cranbury, New Jersey: Associated University Presses, 1974.

Weiner, Myron. 'The Struggle for Equality: Caste in Indian Politics'. Pp. 193–225 in *The Success of India's Democracy*. Edited by Atul Kohli. Cambridge: Cambridge University Press, 2001.

RELIGION and CULTURE

Christian Identity and Religious Pluralism in India: Conversion and the Hindutva Challenge to Indian Identity

John Arun Kumar[*]

1. Introduction

Generally ideologies, both religious and others, form an essential element of identity. As elsewhere, Indians choose and possess multiple identities as a continuous process of change. The change in identities could be termed as 'conversion'. Currently, two dominant models of nationalism are evident in multi-religious India—secular and Hindutva, a Hindu nationalist ideology. In the Hindutva discourse and operations, religious conversion is treated as a contentious issue, especially against Christians and Muslims. In the recent past, many from minority castes and tribes chose to embrace other religions, including Christianity. Although they were small in number compared to the Hindu majority, by May 2008 five states in India—Gujarat, Orissa, Madhya Pradesh, Chhattisgarh and Himachal Pradesh—had enacted anti-conversion laws prohibiting Hindus from converting to other religions. The stated purpose of these laws was to prevent and prohibit religious conversions made, allegedly, by 'force', 'fraud' or 'allurement'. On the one hand, some Hindutva fundamentalists claim Christian missionaries forcefully convert Hindus to Christianity. On the other, many among the Christian community have witnessed how some Hindu extremists have been misusing these laws by making false accusations against Christian workers. Throughout the country, violent anti-Christian and anti-conversion campaigns by Hindu extremists continue, following the enforcement of the anti-conversion laws.

My argument here is that Hindutva proponents seem to understand and use the term 'conversion' in a limited and narrow

[*] John Arun Kumar is Head of the Religion Department at SAIACS and teaches Religions.

sense, as referring only to religious conversions of Hindus to another faith. They fail to take into consideration that conversion is a complex multidimensional process and a lived reality; that conversion is integral to the anatomy and life of any ideology, religious and others, including their own. In this sense, conversion results in an identity crisis for all concerned and calls for a resolution. Religion has a crucial role to play in resolving identity-based issues. In light of the above, this paper discusses in order: the understanding of conversion, identity and religion; the challenges to Christian identity in contexts of both religious nationalism and pluralism; and, for Christians, it seeks answers through identification with the early church fathers.

2. Understanding Conversion, Identity and Religion

A list of theoretical orientations from the human sciences in relation to conversions to Islam includes globalization, post-colonial, feminist, cross-cultural, religious/spiritual, intellectualist, narrative, identity, ritual, psychoanalytic, archetypal, attribution, attachment, process/ stage, and Islamization theory.[1] These theories of conversion point to important and interesting dynamics, processes and patterns of religious change.[2]

In sociology of religion, conversion is discussed as a two-way relationship between religion and society. Social reality comprises social facts in their double aspect of being 'things' and subjectively apprehended, and internally meaningful 'collective representations'.[3] In psychology, identity is defined as 'the subjective concept of oneself as an individual. Usage here is often qualified, e.g., *sex-role identity, racial* or *group identity.'*[4] Conventionally identity is couched in the notions of self and other, in-group and out-group, and therefore it is

---

[1] Lewis R. Rambo, 'Theories of Conversion,' *Social Compass* 46.3 (1999): 259.

[2] Rambo, 'Theories', 259–71.

[3] Emile Durkheim, *The Elementary Forms of Religious Life* (New York: Free Press, 1912), 466–72, 482–96.

[4] Arthur S. Reber and Emily S. Reber, *The Penguin Dictionary of Psychology* (London: Penguin, 2001), 318.

inherently dualistic and conceptual.[5] Identification is defined as 'A mental operation whereby one attributes to oneself, either consciously or unconsciously, the characteristics of another person or group.'[6] Identity and identification is the key to locating oneself in a multi-religious social context, and religion becomes an important marker. In the past and in the contemporary multi-religious context, social identities in India had and have been dynamic, and religion is an essential part of them. The processes of identity-forming and the identity-sustaining activities of societies are both forms of conversion. Whether or not people are aware of it, all sorts of ideologies need the agency of conversion to exist, survive and spread among people. According to social scientists, religious conversion marks a transformation of religious identity and is often symbolized by special rituals. Conversions are both intra- and inter-group phenomena, which affect all aspects of the social, religious and political spheres.

As intra-religious activity, conversion is, as Parinitha Shetty notes, 'a process or movement that is never complete, as a break in community and epistemology that never resolves itself within the belief structures sanctioned by a theology or reiterated by the religious practices of a community of believers.'[7] When a social group creates an identity for their newborns and new members, it includes its religious affiliation. In addition, it continuously converts them from being profane to becoming sacred, from being natural or non-religious to religious. Depending on the religious traditions and the kind of change, it has local terms and names. Among Hindus, the practices of *samskaras* (the rites of passage within any caste) or the practice of *ashrama*s (the stations of life) are examples of intra-religious changes in identities. A.D. Nock's term 'adhesion' could relate to this intra-religious experience, where an intrinsic aspect of social organisation of a cultural group, makes no missionary efforts outside its own society, and there are no religious frontiers to cross.[8]

---

[5] Arvin Paul, 'A Grounded Theory Investigation of Awakening/Realization in Direct/Top-down Approach', unpublished Ph.D. dissertation, Institute of Transpersonal Psychology (California: Palo Alto, 2008), 31.

[6] Reber and Reber, *The Penguin Dictionary*, 318.

[7] Parinitha Shetty, 'Missionary Pedagogy and Christianisation of the Heathens', *The Indian Economic and Social History Review* 45.4 (2008): 512.

[8] A.D. Nock quoted in Kwame Bediako, *Theology and Identity* (Oxford: Regnum Books, 1992), 30.

As an inter-religious activity, conversion is, as Shetty notes, 'an act of adopting a new religion, or changing from one to another, and [it] is given a recognisable shape, visibility and legitimacy through the rituals and practices of community and personal life by which that adopted religion authenticates and proclaims membership within its fold.'[9] Nock's use of the term 'conversion' to correspond to 'prophetic religion' could relate to this activity.[10]

Both intra- and inter-religious conversions of an individual or a group is effected either by choice or by force from another individual or group. Generally, in a multi-religious democratic context, the volitional conversion activity of an individual or a group is acceptable, whereas violational use of force, especially physical force, to convert others to their religion is unacceptable.[11]

Society treated as a social structure, and as a complex set of social processes, brings two aspects of religious conversion into discussion. Social conditions influence the rise, spread and institutionalization of ideas and values, including religious ones, that in turn influence the actions of people involved in it.[12]

2.1. Social Structure and Religious Conversion

In the Indian context, trades, conquests, immigrations and emergence of new ideologies (both religious and otherwise) from within and without resulted in the formation of a secular government, which treats all religions as equal.

Drawing from Durkhiem's thesis, Louis Dumont notes that the caste system is the epiphenomenon of Hinduism and both its system and ideology are based on the notions of hegemony of purity over pollution, drawn from the high caste Brahminical understanding of purity.[13] This locates people groups, both those within the system

---

[9] Shetty, 'Missionary', 512.

[10] Nock, *Theology*, 30.

[11] For example, K. Santhanam argued this in the Constituent Assembly Debates, quoted in M.T. Cherian, *Hindutva Agenda and Minority Rights: A Christian Response* (Bangalore: Centre for Contemporary Christianity, 2007), 151.

[12] Thomas F. O'Dea, *The Sociology of Religion* (New Jersey: Prentice-Hall, 1966), 55.

[13] Louis Dumont, *Homo Hierarchicus* (London: Weidenfeld and Nicolson, 1970 [orig. 1966]).

and outside of it, on discriminatory grounds in terms of ideology and physical location.[14] In contrast to Hinduism, other faiths such as Buddhism, Jainism, Christianity, Islam, Sikhism, Zoroastrianism and others are opposed to the caste system and prefer egalitarian values. Therefore, for people belonging to various religions who live side-by-side in cities or villages, their social systems and ideological differences become apparent and problematic. The question about a person or a group's identity becomes significant.[15] A Hindu in 'locating oneself in society' is most often content with expressing his/her identity in terms of his/her city or language, than caste.

2.2. Complex Social Processes and Religious Conversion

The continuous process of change in society results in the breakdown of established social and cultural forms and the emergence of new ones, which affects the different groups in society variously. Durkhiem's term 'anomie' characterizes the state of social disorganisation as a dual process—a loss of solidarity and a loss of consensus, and the two could become disorganised at different speeds.[16] The result is relative isolation, 'normlessness', frustration and aggression against real or imagined difficulties. People then may try various means of escape: pleasure seeking, alcohol, drugs, etc., before finally engaging perhaps in a 'quest for community' and a search for new meaning. This quest paves the way for movements, religious or quasi-religious, which offer new values and solidarities, or less-than-ultimate values and relationships.[17] Overall, this analysis in terms of anomie provides a framework to understand social phenomena such as intra- and inter-religious conversions. The apparent differences among people in India in terms of religious ideologies have resulted in at least three types of reactions among Hindus: two types of intra-religious conversions (a search for egalitarianism within Hinduism, and the formation of Hindutva) and inter-religious conversion (converting from Hinduism to another religion).

---

[14] M.N. Srinivas, *Caste in Modern India and Other Essays* (Bombay: Asia 1962).

[15] Will Herberg, *Protestant, Catholic, Jew* (Garden City, N.Y.: Doubleday, 1955), 12–3.

[16] O'Dea, *Sociology*, 55.

[17] O'Dea, *Sociology*, 55.

2.2.1. Search for Egalitarianism Within

In traditional India, egalitarian notions and aspirations were intra-religious activities in popular Hinduism. This played out in the religious injunctions of annual rituals (e.g., 'there should be no caste differences among the devotees' of Aiyappa).[18] In village festivals, there is the notion that the divine reorders the caste system in ritual contexts for at least a day, when a low caste man officiates as a priest for the high caste.[19] The 10th century Lingayat movement in Karnataka was anti-caste, preferring egalitarian values and forming their own religion based on Saivism. However, some have seen this as an intra-religious conversion, a reformation movement within Hinduism.

Following the colonial rule, organisations such as the Brahmo Samaj and the Arya Samaj were formed, in which Vedic religion was seen as a basis for an egalitarian system. One of the aims of these groups was to combat inter-religious conversions, which were becoming common those days. However, this could not easily translate into bringing in equality among the various caste groups. (This was realised later, as a form of pro-intra-socio-religious conversion based on the Vedas, and anti-inter-religious conversion activity).

Alongside, there was an attempt at egalitarianism based on secularism, where the multi-religious context was acknowledged. In the run–up to Indian Independence, Mahatma Gandhi's secularism was for national unity and not for unity in religious identity. He wanted to preserve the diverse religious identities and disliked the idea of conversion. Gandhi renamed Dalits as Harijans (Children of God) and redefined the caste in terms of vocational roles. Here Gandhi's brand of egalitarianism was of pro-intra-social conversion based on redefinition of caste along traditional vocational lines, and anti-inter-religious conversion, a slight variation of the previous model.

2.2.2. Formation of a Nationalist Movement

The second type of reaction emerged at that phase of the Nationalist Movement where the Hindu religion was sought to be made the basis

---

[18] John Arun Kumar, 'The Idea of the "Family": A Cognitive Model in the Popular Religion of the Hindus of South India', unpublished Ph.D. Dissertation (Leeds: University of Leeds, 2007), 306.

[19] Kumar, 'Idea', 170.

for the emerging identity of India.[20] Sarvakar conceived of the Hindutva ideology.[21] It is suggested that the ideology is patterned after the western fascist ideology.[22] The word 'Hindu' with the Sanskrit suffix '*tva*' meant 'Hindu-ness'. Accordingly, Hindutva was given an identity based on the notion of dharma, the upholding of the caste system, and symbols—both national (such as the lotus, the national flower) and religious (such as the trident or *trishul*, the cow and the colour, saffron). Some scholars note this as a type of postmodernity, where the traditional is married to modernity.[23] As Juergensmeyer explains, when a religious perspective is fused with the political and social destiny of a nation, it is referred to as religious nationalism. Religious nationalists were not just religious fanatics but were political activists who were seriously attempting to create a 'modern' language of politics and provide a new basis for the nation-state.[24] As Rao notes, 'Like in the former Yugoslavia, and Northern Ireland, religion in India has engulfed the politics of identity more so than any other force, including caste, tribe, gender, and class,[25] a sentiment illustrated by Gandhi's assertion that "politics divorced from religion has absolutely no meaning".'[26] Hindutva, by propelling religious-political discord, in part fosters religious in-group bias and out-group derogation, i.e., anti-Muslim and anti-Christian sentiments.[27]

Moreover, Hindutva's programmes of conversions are known popularly as 'saffronisation'. In its manifesto and actions, in creating identity for others, it marks or converts those ideologically opposed to

[20] S.M. Michael, 'Culture and Nationalism: Politics of Identity in India', http://www.sedos.org/english/michael.htm (accessed on 2 June 2010).

[21] V.D. Savarkar, *Samagra Savarkar Wangmaya*, vol. 6 (Poona: Maharashtra Prantik Hindu Sabha, 1964).

[22] Marzia Casolari, 'Hindutva's Foreign Tie-up in the 1930s', *Economic and Political Weekly* (22 January 2000).

[23] Vishal Mangalwadi, *India: The Grand Experiment* (London: Pippa Rann Books, 1997), 270–1.

[24] M. Juergensmeyer, *Religious Nationalism Confronts Secular State* (New Delhi: OUP, 1993).

[25] S. Rao, 'Woman-as-Symbol', *Women's Studies International Forum* 22 (1999): 317–28.

[26] M. Gandhi, 'The Ashram of Soul-Force', in C.F. Andrews (ed.), *Mahatma Gandhi's Ideas* (London: Allen, 1949), 122.

[27] Rao, 'Woman', 317.

it as enemies, especially Christians and Muslims, and ideologies such as secularism that is supportive of those faiths, as Marxism. Increasingly, it wants to turn secular India into a Hindu state by forcing people of other faiths to yield and conform to this dominant group identity. It uses Sanskrit texts, especially the Vedas, to reclaim Hindus within India and abroad into the traditional caste system. 'Sanskritization' is a category M.N. Srinivas coined to note how the low caste imitates the high caste; here it could mean the high caste imposing Sanskritic traditions on the lower castes.

In addition, the Hindutva agenda is to claim the whole world into its fold and ideology.[28] According to this, Hindutva represents the resistance movement against the cultural, religious and economic domination of India by Western powers. It aspires to bring the West to acknowledge the supremacy of Hinduism, as the Original World Faith. Here there is the case of Hindutva embracing globalisation and redefining the concept of dharma as original world faith, the mother of all faiths. I suggest that this is a caste-like hierarchy[29] applied to world religions. This type of movement is anti-intra-religious conversion, anti-inter-religious conversion and anti-secularism.

2.2.3. Inter-Religious Conversions

The third reaction under the discussion on social structure and social processes relates to inter-religious conversions. Among some in the caste groups, there still have been conversions to other religions that accept them. Writing on disorganisation resulting in anomie, Thomas O'Dea notes that,

> People suffering from extreme deprivation and people suffering from anomie (some groups may be experiencing both) display a considerable responsiveness to religions which preach a message of salvation—that is, which present the world as a place of toil and suffering, and offer some means of deliverance from it, Christianity is a religion of this kind. It offers the believer salvation through participation in Christ's victory over evil and death. Other social strata with a more positive stake in society and consequently different kinds of religious needs exhibit other sensitivities.[30]

---

[28] [n.a.], *We or Our Nationhood Defined* (Nagpur: Bharat Publications, 1939), 67.
[29] This could be seen as a type of ethno-centrism.
[30] O'Dea, *Sociology*, 57.

This analysis could be extended to apply to some of the Indian cases of religious conversion. In the 50s, Dr Ambedkar realized the discriminatory aspect of the caste system and chose to convert to Buddhism. Since then, one way or the other, some of those caught in caste struggles have found their peace by changing their religious identity to Buddhism, Islam or Christianity. This showcases the importance of changing one's religious identity, not only for individuals but for groups of subalterns who have come to realize their need for and their freedom to choose their religious identity. Their newly acquired religious identities free them from the clutches of the institutionalized hierarchy of castes, which they found oppressive. Contemporary scholars view these recent social developments and Hindutva as a form of postmodernity (cf. n. 23).

To recap the discussion, interrelationships between social structures, social processes and conversion are important in a multi-religious context. Besides ongoing traditional intra-religious conversions, since the colonial period, Hindu society has been witnessing intra-religious conversions on new bases (such as a fresh search for egalitarianism from within the tradition and within secularism), the rise of an anti-secular national movement, and an increase in inter-religious conversions.

2.3. Challenges Posed to Christians by Hindutva

The Hindutva project is well-orchestrated, using religious identity as a cover for caste ideology and as the basis for its conflict with others. As noted already, it is based on perceptions of the 'self' and 'other' in terms of host and enemy religious identities, where Hindus are attributed the 'host' identity, and others the 'enemy' identity, especially the Muslims and the Christians.

2.3.1. Accusation of Colonial Identity

Although Indian Christians have a traditional historical identity, the Hindutva groups accuse them of having a colonial identity because of the religious affiliations Christians have with the West. In the same way, the Indian Parsis are attributed anglicized identities for their loyalties to the British.[31]

---

[31] Rashna B. Singh, 'Traversing Diacritical Space', *The Journal of Commonwealth Literature* 43 (2008): 29–30.

2.3.2. Accusation of Forced Conversions

Hindutva proponents also accuse Christians of forcing conversions. They define any Christian activity, such as medical work, as conversion activity and use of force. For example, the Australian missionary doctor, Dr Graham Staines, was burnt alive in his jeep on the basis of such reasoning.[32] Discussing the political implications of conversion in contemporary India, Kalyani Menon writes that Hindutva activists have charged Christian missionaries of using trickery and bribery to attract converts, which has led to provocative rhetoric and anti-Christian violence. However, the Hindutva proponents employ nearly identical tactics when converting Christians 'back' to Hinduism.[33] Hindutva thus contradicts itself. With its different valuations and understandings of the relationship between religious affiliation and individual nature, Menon concludes that the conversions and the actions of Christian missionaries are threatening not because they involve any trickery, but because they contradict the assumptions about the particular variant of Hinduism and Indian identity that is central to the Hindutva movement.[34]

By bans on conversions in the states where it is in power, Hindutva limits people's freedom and locks people in the caste-based religious ideology, where those who feel oppressed and suppressed, are left without alternatives. The secular Constitution of India provides favourable conditions for people who live in the country, by guaranteeing its citizens freedom to choose, profess and practice any religion. People could opt out of oppressive ideologies, be it religious or secular, and opt into those that give them dignity and treat them on equal terms. Many high caste and subaltern individuals and groups have been benefiting from this. The State should protect the interests of its subjects.[35]

---

[32] Kalyani Devaki Menon, 'Converted Innocents and their Trickster Heroes', in Andrew Buckser and Stephen D. Glazier (eds), *Anthropology of Conversion* (Lanham: Rowman & Littlefield, 2003), 43.

[33] Menon, 'Converted', 46; I have already established earlier that any ideology (hence also Hindutva) practises conversion.

[34] Menon, 'Converted', 51.

[35] Surely, the current BJP government in Karnataka would deny this.

2.3.3. Accusation of Exclusivism

Besides accusing Christians of colonial identity and of being guilty of forced conversions, Hindutva also accuses Christians of exclusivism. It sees Christianity as a hindrance to its nationalist agenda of uniting India. S. Gurumurthy argues:

> The assimilative Hindu cultural and civilisational ethos is the only basis for any durable personal and social interaction between the Muslims and the rest of our countrymen . . . and only an inclusive Hindutva can assimilate an exclusive Islam by making the Muslims conscious of their Hindu ancestry and heritage. A national effort is called for to break Islamic exclusivism and enshrine the assimilative Hindutva. This alone constitutes true nationalism and true national integration. This is the only way to protect the plurality of thoughts and institutions in this country. To the extent secularism advances Islamic isolation and exclusivism, it damages Hindu inclusiveness and its assimilative qualities. And in this sense secularism as practiced till now conflicts with Indian nationalism. Inclusive and assimilative Hindutva is the socio-cultural nationalism of India. So long as our national leaders ignore this eternal truth, national integration will keep eluding us. [36]

The above quote used elsewhere, calls on Hindutva supporters to make a national effort to break Islamic, Christian and Marxist exclusivism, as well as secularism (for it advances and protects the three former groups) and to enshrine assimilative Hindutva, to ensure true nationalism. The proposition here is to use exclusivism to counter exclusivism, to constitute true nationalism, achieve national integration and, ironically, to protect the plurality of thoughts and institutions in India.

2.3.4. Accusations of Being Enemies of the Nation

Hindutva activists not only make other religious identities 'enemy' identities. They also attack them or their symbols to achieve and maintain a semblance of Hindu unity, which is nothing but maintaining the caste order according to the notions of dharma. Attacks on Muslims in Gujarat and on Christians in Kandhamal district in Orissa ran along communal lines and resulted in loss of many lives and mass dislocation.

According to Julia Eckert's study, appearing to contradict theories of the cause of anomie or alienation, the identity politics of Hindu

---

[36] S. Gurumurthy, 'The Inclusive And The Exclusive', in J. Bajaj (ed.), *Ayodhya and the Future India* (Chennai: Centre for Policy Studies, 1993), 179–80.

nationalism is a proactive project in its enthusiastic embrace of globalization, especially economic liberalization in India since the 1990s, and it uses violence to exclude those who appear to hold India back.[37] It explains that

> The success of Hindu nationalist organizations . . . lies not simply in their nationalist credo but in the specific opportunities of action and participation that are inherent in their mode of operation and form of organization. They reset the terms of inclusion and exclusion . . . offering local possibilities of action . . . that relies on participation and involvement, direct intervention, and localness and accessibility. Violence is organized to create participation and empowerment among the participants. Participatory action achieves an expansion of the space for acting individually and collectively . . . Moreover, the simple friend/foe dichotomization inherent in violence makes possible the integration of different interests and discontents under one banner . . . Hindu nationalism.[38]

Here the power of organized violence to create participation and empower participants to unify becomes a tool Hindutva uses to unite the high caste, the dominant caste,[39] the low caste Hindus, and the outcaste.

To the above challenges posed by Hindutva to Christians in India, add Spohn's brief comparative study on the rise in religious nationalism across the globe in general. He notes on India and Pakistan that the cultural transformation was due to the contact between British Protestantism, particularly the Methodist-evangelical variety,[40] and the Indian elite, the anti-colonial nationalist movement and the ongoing efforts to reconstruct Hinduism and Islam.[41] The result was that after independence, in both states, there evolved a growing pressure on religious nationalism towards religious-national homogenization and, with it, an escalation of the conflicts

---

[37] Julia Eckert, 'The Social Dynamics of Communal Violence in India', *International Journal of Conflict and Violence* 3.2 (2009): 172–87.

[38] Eckert, 'Dynamics', 175.

[39] This term was coined by M.N. Srinivas to refer to a locally dominant caste, which enjoys dominance in a region, or village. M.N. Srinivas, 'The Dominant Caste in Rampura', *American Anthropologist* New Series 61.1 (1959): 1.

[40] Van der Veer and Lehmann, *Nation and Religion* (Princeton: Princeton University Press, 1999), 29.

[41] Willfried Spohn, 'Multiple Modernity, Nationalism and Religion', *Current Sociology* 51.3/4 (2003): 280.

between both nations.[42] Spohn suggests that though secular-pluralist elite nationalism has remained hegemonic in both countries, it is being increasingly challenged, on both sides, by popular religious nationalism.[43] Spohn concludes that

> [This] global intensification of religious and ethnic nationalism cannot be interpreted, as the mainstream modernization paradigm is tempted to assume, as a transitional phase to the western model of civic and secular national identity formation. Nor can it simply be seen as a general defensive reaction of non-western societies to the intensifying forces of western-dominated forms of economic, political and secular-cultural globalization. Rather . . . [it] is part of multiple modernization processes in different world regions, multiple constellations of nation-state formation and democratization as well as religious change and secularization in different civilizations in the present global era.[44]

Here the implication is that Hindutva along with secularism is to be viewed as part of multiple modernization processes in play across the globe, and that these processes in India have been especially caused by contact with British Protestantism.

3. Religion—A Tool for Resolving Identity-Based Conflicts

Renate Ysseldyk, Kimberly Matheson and Hymie Anisman argue for religiosity as identity from a social identity perspective. As posited by Tajfel and Turner[45], 'identification with one's group motivates individuals to distinguish their group from others to preserve positive self-esteem or to attain self enhancement.'[46] They suggest that under distressing circumstances, when an individual's sense of safety and security has been undermined, religious identity may be especially important. They stress that, essentially, identification with one's religious group may provide a sense of unwavering stability and 'solid ground' more than would be gained from other social identities. This could, perhaps, stem from the highly organized support networks or

---

[42] Spohn, 'Multiple', 280.

[43] Spohn, 'Multiple', 280.

[44] Spohn, 'Multiple', 281.

[45] Tajfel and Turner, quoted in Renate Ysseldyk, Kimberly Matheson and Hymie Anisman, 'Religiosity as Identity', *Personality and Social Psychology Review* 14 (2010): 61.

[46] Ysseldyk et al, 'Religiosity', 61.

the shared reliance on faith in a 'higher power'. Therefore, identification with one's religious group to handle issues relating to identity under distressing circumstances is important. Given this, I suggest that, when confronted with a political ideology that wants to impose nationhood by using religion that is built on a hierarchy that discriminates against people (based on purity and pollution notions and practices), we could seek identification within our own religious group and look for answers from its history of handling these issues of identity.

Many attempts have been made in the history of Indian Christianity to attend to identity issues. However, the rise in religious nationalism post-independence, especially over the past three decades, has posed identity issues in relation to safety and security. Given the immense nature of the topic and the size of this paper, I choose to focus only on the earliest attempts documented in world church history, of communities that faced situations similar to the one the Indian church faces today.

Early attempts at handling the forces of religious nationalism and resolving issues of identity can be traced back to the early church, and these could be instructive for us in our times. In this regard, I suggest Kwame Bediako's study on African Christian identity in his work *Theology and Identity*. In this book, he draws upon two seminal studies by A.F. Walls on the dynamics of the encounter in life and thought between Christian Gospel and culture.[47] It especially notes the interplay between two forces which Walls describes as 'making Christianity at home in the life of a people' and 'the conforming of a church's life to standards outside of itself'. He goes on to explore how these forces manifest themselves in the theology of early Hellenistic Christianity and modern African theology.[48] This sort of understanding could be extended to the church in India, located in the multi-religious and Hindutva context.

Bediako's study on 'the problem of Christian identity in the context of Graeco-Roman culture of the early roman empire' notes the fundamental principles governing religion under Roman rule. It quotes Cicero's explicit statement on religion in Roman rule that, 'No-one

---

[47] Kwame Bediako, *Theology and Identity* (Oxford: Regnum Books, 1992), 8.
[48] Bediako, *Theology*, 8.

shall have gods to himself, either new gods or alien gods, unless recognized by the State. Privately they shall worship those gods whose worship they have duly received from their ancestors.'[49] It deduces that under Roman rule, 'Religion, therefore, was not of personal belief and devotion, but of social duty and ancestral practice. By thus tying national (or racial) identity so closely to religion as national cult, the Roman outlook made it impossible for a Roman citizen or a born Roman to hold a "new" foreign or alien religion.'[50]

In addition, the study suggests that Roman works by key figures such as Polybius, Vergil, Augustus and Cicero's Stoic interlocutor, Balbus, in *De Natura Deorum*, all attested to the religious nationalism that underlay Roman governance.[51] It observes that religious nationalism of Roman rule was that 'the religion of tradition' was made the religion of the state; that it was not a missionary religion and religious conversion was not welcome; that conversion to Philosophy, which increasingly used religious language, was acceptable and was in vogue.

The study further suggests that the stories of the early church fathers, confronted with religious nationalism of Roman rule in the Greco-Roman context, serve as models of creating and maintaining Christian identity. It notes that Justin Martyr, being a Greco-Roman convert, made efforts to link Christian faith with Greek philosophy, where conversion to it was acceptable.[52] Justin held to the centrality of 'the Old Testament prediction of incarnation of Saviour, the Word of God, who took human form and was called Jesus Christ and who came, not as the fulfilment of the exclusive, nationalist aspirations of Jews, but supremely as "the expectation of the nations".'[53] This move by Justin, followed by others such as Aristides and Clement of Alexandria, was calculated to eliminate the problem of lack of historical roots and heritage within Greco-Roman world for the Gentile Christians. Tatian was a sustained and serious advocate, an apologist, who established the grounds for Christian self-identity, which was rooted in the history of ancient Israel. He refused to give credence

---

[49] Bediako, *Theology*, 21.
[50] Bediako, *Theology*, 21.
[51] Bediako, *Theology*, 22.
[52] Bediako, *Theology*, 34.
[53] Bediako, *Theology*, 158.

to the cultural and intellectual superiority that Greeks and Romans claimed for themselves.[54] This served the Greco-Roman Christians, mostly the underprivileged and the poor, with a basis for self-identity in their cultural context. Tertullian emphasised the exclusiveness of the truth of the Scriptures, and its embodiment by the separateness of Christian community amidst persecution. He stressed that one was not a Christian by birth, but became a Christian, a radical Christian.[55] Tertullian wrote to Christians held in prison and who were faced with the prospect of martyrdom: 'The Christian outside the prison has renounced the world, but in the prison he has renounced a prison too. It is of no consequence where you are in the world—you who are not of [the world].'[56]

For Christians everywhere, especially for us who face persecution in India, these are relevant lessons from history that we can emulate within our cultural context. Like Justin Martyr, Christians in India need to make serious attempts to look for insights from within Christian historical roots and heritage. Like Titian, we should be apologists who establish the grounds for Christian self-identity rooted in ancient Israel, giving it credence over and above the cultural and intellectual superiority claimed by Hindutva. Like Tertullian, we should be champions of Christian exclusivism, marked by separateness from the world even in the face of persecution and martyrdom. In the current scholarship on religious pluralism, it is commonplace to use the term 'exclusivism' to describe the emphasis evangelicals lay on the professing of the uniqueness of Jesus Christ, which is seen as something to be avoided in a multi-religious society. Here again, in the guise of promoting religious pluralism, this notion that this emphasis must be avoided curtails the freedom of people to profess their faith or choose a faith and celebrate it in its true intentions and forms.

We only need be familiar with the Macedonian call made to the apostle Paul, which was followed by persecutions. For Paul, the Macedonian call was a directive from God to enter the Macedonian region and serve Him there. Paul and his co-workers underwent suffering because the unbelieving Jews throughout the areas of

---

[54] Bediako, *Theology*, 67.
[55] Bediako, *Theology*, 125.
[56] Bediako, *Theology*, 125.

Galatia and Macedonia were fanatical about persecuting both Jews and Gentiles, who had embraced Christianity and were spreading the Gospel of Christ (cf. Acts 13.44–50; 14.1–6; 14.19; 17.1–14). F.F. Bruce writes on Paul in Macedonia,

> He had been virtually expelled as a trouble-maker from one Macedonian city after another. He and his companions had crossed from Asia Minor to Macedonia under what seemed to have been clear divine guidance . . . Had the Macedonian mission proved abortive? In each Macedonian city that he visited Paul had established a community of believers, but he had had to leave them abruptly, quite inadequately equipped with the instruction and encouragement necessary to enable them to stand firm in the face of determined opposition. Would their immature faith prove equal to the challenge? In the event it did, outstandingly so; but Paul could not have foreseen this. His first Macedonian campaign, in the light of the sequel, could be recognized as an illustrious success, but at the time when Paul was forced to leave the province it must have looked like a dismal failure.[57]

Under the Macedonian rule where various religions were tolerated, I suggest that the unbelieving Jews were religious fundamentalists who used the nationalist agenda to counter Paul, his co-workers and believing Jews and Gentiles. We can well imagine the context: Paul and Barnabas' message was to assert Christian self-identity rooted in ancient Israel, in the face of unbelieving Jews and Gentiles. According to Paul, the church at Thessalonica, which he must have planted in the Macedonian region, was exemplary in its Christian faith in the face of persecution. Christians in secular India, faced with the religious nationalism of Hindutva, are up against a context similar to Paul's situation, beginning with his Macedonian call. It is a call, with God's help, to draw many people to Christ in the face of persecution, by following the example of the apostle Paul, the church at Thessalonica and the examples of the early church fathers. In a sense, the present Indian situation is the Macedonian call to the church of Jesus Christ, to incarnate the Christian identity.

What is hindering the people in India from exercising their free will consciously, to choose that religion which could potentially and actually meet their need for identity? It is not inability to exercise free will and choose, consciously, what is right. It is a lack of awareness of

---

[57]   F.F. Bruce, 'St. Paul in Macedonia', a lecture in John Rylands University Library, 1978. http://www.biblicalstudies.org.uk/pdf/bjrl/macedonia_bruce.pdf, 350 (accessed on 19 July, 2011).

their privileges, and the lack of access, means and training to exercise their free will in the face of the persistent effort of forces like Hindutva, which curtail the rights of the people (which is but enforced conversion) and promote a false sense of unity, a pseudo-identity, achieved by the use of violence.[58] Clearly, the ideology of the caste system has taken on a new avatar called Hindutva, fashioned after the ideology of fascism.[59] We must distinguish between the proponents of the ideology and those being enslaved by the proponents of Hindutva. In addition, we must recognise the ex-members of that ideology, who are active in salvaging others caught in the schemes of the ideology.

Empirically, Christian principles of egalitarianism and examples of some genuine practices of it can be evidenced. For example, many Christian institutions working in areas of education, health and community development, have been places that have demonstrated Christian principles. Mother Teresa's love for destitute men and women, irrespective of their religious affiliations, has invoked great respect and admiration the world over and drawn many, both within and outside India, to follow her example. Nevertheless, social systems among some Christians in India have yet to arrive at the full realization of the Christian principle of egalitarianism. It appears that people from various caste groups, now within the Christian fold, have not realized the difference between their positions in their previous social structure of casteism and their present one, in terms of differences in religious identities.

Above all, Jesus Christ serves as the supreme example for us. He constantly faced opposition under the regime of the Romans, from the Jewish and other rulers. Yet, he served and ministered to the needs of the disciples and other people. He taught them both by word of mouth and example, the principles of kingdom of God—to respect those in authority as under God and to love those who hate oneself, even to the

---

[58] Richard Howell (ed.), *Free to Choose* (New Delhi: Evangelical Fellowship of India, 2002), 24.

[59] Sathianathan Clarke, 'Hindutva, Religious and Ethnocultural Minorities, and Indian-Christian Theology', *Religion Online*,

http://www.religiononline.org/showarticle.asp?title=2449 (accessed on 27 April 2010); Vishal Mangalwadi, *Missionary Conspiracy* (St Paul, Minnesota: The MacLaurin Institute, 1996); L. Stanislaus, 'Hindutva and Marginalized—Christian Response,' http://www.sedos.org/english/stanislaus_2.htm (accessed on 27 August 2010).

point of death. That resulted in his crucifixion, and resurrection. Here lies the heart of Christian identity, based on the notions of personhood, respect, honour and value for a fellow being, even if he is a foe. The paradigm of Jesus Christ has served the church by providing it with a distinct Christian identity in the past, and it remains the way forward. According to the belief of the church, this is the work of the Holy Spirit and the person of Jesus Christ, who embodies both ideology and praxis. The Christian church, which is constituted by his followers, is not above its master. At the most, it can become like him.

4. Conclusion

I have argued that social identities are dynamic, and that when their primary and core identity-forming and identity-sustaining processes are rooted in differences (religious or otherwise) and are challenged by changes in social contexts, creating enemy images of 'the other', they lead to identity-based conflicts. In a multi-religious context, religion has become the most important tool for 'locating oneself in society', for identity and identification in a social context. This article has investigated Christian identity with special reference to Hindutva, whose core ideology and praxis lies in the discriminatory caste system. It suggests one way forward in resolving identity conflicts faced by Indian Christians today: to recognize and follow in the footsteps of the early church fathers, who faced situations akin to our own. They chose to affirm and adhere to ideologies, religious or others, that potentially and actually offered an identity rooted in personhood and equality, which is found in the Gospels.

References

Bediako, Kwame. *Theology and Identity*. Oxford: Regnum Books, 1992.

Bruce, F.F. 'St. Paul in Macedonia'. Pp. 337–54 in a lecture in John Rylands University Library (18 October 1978). http://www.biblicalstudies.org.uk/pdf/bjrl/macedonia_bruce.pdf (accessed on 19 July 2011).

Casolari, Marzia. 'Hindutva's Foreign Tie-up in the 1930s'. *Economic and Political Weekly* (22 January 2000).

Clarke, Sathianathan. 'Hindutva, Religious and Ethnocultural

Minorities, and Indian-Christian Theology'. *Religion Online.* http://www.religiononline.org/showarticle.asp?title=2449 (accessed on 27 April 2010).

Despande, Satish. 'Communalising the Nation-Space'. *Economic and Political Weekly* (1995): 3227.

Dumont, Louis. *Homo Hierarchicus.* London: Weidenfeld and Nicolson, 1970 [orig. 1966].

Durkheim, Emile. *The Elementary Forms of Religious Life.* Translated by Karen E. Fields. New York: The Free Press, 1995 [orig. 1912].

Eckert, Julie. 'The Social Dynamics of Communal Violence'. *International Journal of Conflict and Violence* 3.2 (2009): 172–87.

Eriksen, T.H. 'Ethnic Identity, National Identity, and Intergroup Conflict'. Pp. 42–68 in *Social Identity, Intergroup Conflict, and Conflict Resolution.* Edited by R.D. Ashmore, L. Jussim and D. Wilder. Oxford: OUP, 2001.

Gandhi, M. 'The Ashram of Soul-Force'. Pp. 113–29 in *Mahatma Gandhi's Ideas.* Edited by C.F. Andrews. London: Allen, 1949.

Giddens, A. *Modernity and Self-Identity.* Cambridge: Polity Press, 1991.

Gurumurthy, S. 'The Inclusive And The Exclusive'. Pp. 179–80 in *Ayodhya and the Future India.* Edited by J. Bajaj. Chennai: Centre for Policy Studies, 1993.

Herberg, W. *Protestant, Catholic, Jew.* Garden City, N.Y.: Doubleday, 1955.

Howell, Richard (ed.). *Free to Choose.* New Delhi: Evangelical Fellowship of India, 2002.

Juergensmeyer, M. *Religious Nationalism Confronts Secular State.* New Delhi: OUP, 1993.

Kumar, John Arun. 'The Idea of the "Family": A Cognitive Model in the Popular Religion of the Hindus of South India'. Unpublished PhD Dissertation. Leeds: University of Leeds, 2007.

Mangalwadi, Vishal. *Missionary Conspiracy.* St. Paul, Minnesota: The MacLaurin Institute, 1996.

——. *India: The Grand Experiment.* London: Pippa Rann Books, 1997.

Menon, Kalyani Devaki. 'Converted Innocents and their Trickster Heroes'. Pp. 43–55 in *Anthropology of Conversion.* Edited by Andrew Buckser and Stephen D. Glazier. Lanham: Rowman & Littlefield, 2003.

Michael, S.M. 'Culture and Nationalism'. http://www.sedos.org/ english/michael.htm (accessed on 2 June 2010).

O'Dea, Thomas F. *The Sociology of Religion*. New Jersey: Prentice-Hall, 1966.

Paul, Arvin. 'A Grounded Theory Investigation of Awakening/Realization in Direct/Top-down Approach: Implications for a Psychology of Awakening'. Unpublished Ph.D. Dissertation in Clinical Psychology at the Institute of Transpersonal Psychology. California: Palo Alto, 2008.

Rambo, Lewis R. 'Theories of Conversion'. *Social Compass* 46.3 (1999): 259–71.

Rao, S. 'Woman-as-Symbol'. *Women's Studies International Forum* 22 (1999): 317–28.

Reber, Arthur S. and Emily S. Reber. *The Penguin Dictionary of Psychology*. London: Penguin, 2001.

Robinson, Rowena. *Conversion, Continuity and Change*. New Delhi: Sage, 1998.

Robinson, Rowena and Sathianathan Clarke (eds). *Religious Conversions in India*. New Delhi: OUP, 2003.

Savarkar, V.D. *Samagra Savarkar Wangmaya*. Vol. 6. Poona: Maharashtra Prantik Hindu Sabha, 1964.

Shetty, Parinitha. 'Missionary Pedagogy and Christianisation of the Heathens'. *The Indian Economic and Social History Review* 45.4 (2008): 509–51.

Singh, Rashna B. 'Traversing Diacritical Space'. *The Journal of Commonwealth Literature* 43 (2008): 29–30.

Spohn, Willfried. 'Multiple Modernity, Nationalism and Religion'. *Current Sociology* 51.3/4 (May/July 2003): 265–86.

Srinivas. M.N. *Caste in Modern India and Other Essays*. Bombay: Asia, 1962.

Stanislaus, L. 'Hindutva and Marginalized—Christian Response'. http://www.sedos.org/english/stanislaus_2.htm (accessed on 27 August 2010).

Van der Veer and Lehmann. *Nation and Religion*. Princeton: Princeton University Press, 1999.

Ysseldyk, Renate, Kimberly Matheson and Hymie Anisman. 'Religiosity as Identity'. *Personality and Social Psychology Review* 14 (2010): 60–71.

Castes of Mind and the Culture of Conversion: A Study of Indigenous Church Movements in Contemporary Eastern Uttar Pradesh

A. Gangatharan[*]

1. Introduction

The study of the caste system has been attracting a great deal of interest since the beginning of modern times. It has been defined, theorized and delineated by a host of intellectuals, focusing on its pragmatic praxis and problematic ideologies. The ideas of caste assumed functional salience for the first time in the writings of Hegel, Edmund Burke, James Mill, Max Müller, and Marx—who never visited India, but whose prescient prognosis became the *Magna Carta* of company Raj.

The intellectual enquiry into the social history of caste continued during the 19th century, through the process of classification, codification and cataloging. Pertinent data was collected by way of census reports, administrative manual reports, district almanacs, land revenue reports, and anthropological and linguistic surveys. It was an interactive process, in which the required information was elicited in colonial terms and administrative reports were manufactured with the passive consent of the subject. 'Knowledge was both effect and instrument of power,' as Foucault argues. It seems necessary to identify the colonial agenda that went into the making of administrative categories.[1]

Whatever may be its origin, its structure of salience and the capacity for social functioning, caste in colonial India was a modern social phenomenon that emerged as a result of the colonial encounter. To use Nicholas Dirks's words,

> Caste is not in fact some unchanged survival of ancient India, not some single system that reflects a core civilizational value, not a basic expression of Indian

tradition . . . It was under the British that 'caste' became a single term capable of expressing, organizing and above all 'systematizing' India's diverse forms of social identity, community and organization. It was achieved through an identifiable (if contested) ideological canon as the result of a concrete encounter with colonial modernity.[2]

Thus, caste became *omnipresent* in Indian history, by way of governing its everyday socio-political life and effectively articulating its shape in the public sphere.

The caste system as a social *sui generis* has a dynamic history, adapting itself to various socio-cultural-political exigencies arising out of temporal conditions, without losing the essence of its core values of hierarchy, hegemony and dominance. It evolved over a period of time and became the integrative mechanism through which every incoming ethnic group was accommodated with varying degrees of ascribable status into the *Chaturvarna* system. Every nomadic group that ever migrated to the subcontinent was, by and large, brought into the rubric of the encompassing jati ideology.[3]

Jati, with its endogamous features, hereditary occupations and scores of communal norms, has controlled the social history of India for the past few millennia as an agent of hoary Hindu religious tradition. Every effort to undermine its overarching influence has been either repulsed or neutralized by an effective and inclusive policy of syncretic social tradition. From the time of Buddha to the promulgation of the Indian republic's constitution, the caste system managed to retain its ideological supremacy and continues to wield a great deal of influence over socio-political matters, both in the public and the private spheres of life.[4] So to speak, neither indigenous initiatives nor external efforts have been successful in containing its omnipresence, much less effacing it from the Indian social fabric.

Early Christianity, which entered the western coast of India in the beginning of the Common Era, made easy negotiations with the caste ideology to carve out its own sphere of influence. Medieval Islam

[2] Nicholas B. Dirks, *Castes of Mind: Colonialism, and the Making of Modern India* (New Delhi: Permanent Black, 2001), 4.

[3] Romila Thapar, 'Imagined Religious Communities? Ancient History and the Modern Search for a Hindu Identity', *Modern Asian Studies* 23.2 (1989): 209–31.

[4] Pauline Kolenda, *Caste in Contemporary India: Beyond Organic Solidarity* (Jaipur: Rawat Publishers, 1997), 112–4.

came up with an alternative idea—the vision of an egalitarian society. However, it failed to enforce it, eventually succumbing to the invincible power of the graded social structure. Evangelical Christianity, which came in the beginning of the 16th century, was drawn into the battle on the question of caste. However, it could not make a successful breakthrough, in spite of registering initial progress in its proselytizing agenda on the southern coast of India. Ecclesiastical engagement with caste was riven with contentions, contradictions, disjuncture and rupture.[5]

It may be argued on the basis of existing records that no foreign mission seemed to have evolved a uniform mechanism to address the question of social inequality and caste prejudice. The *De Nobilian* model of inculturation in the South, Bengal mission's percolation approach, and the total tolerance of the caste practice adopted by the Leipzig mission, seem to pay initial dividends. However, these dividends faded fast when the cause of proselytization began to be questioned.

The question of conversion has now become an issue of contention, not for its purpose and rationale, but for the means it adopts in executing its enterprise. It is the means and modes that are often criticized, rather than the commitment for religious action. Radical right-wing activists and middle class intelligentsia strongly oppose the idea of conversion, as it entails a great deal of social dislocation, leading to the truncation of individual identity. The question of theology concerning conversion cannot be sustained, at least in the light of Article 25 of Indian Constitution, as it permits the exercise of freedom of conscience by an individual.[6]

Caste as a viable social label provides a sense of security to an individual, a family and a community. As a unifying force, it integrates the members of the community, cutting across geographical location, through meaningful indicators such as nomenclature, commensal ties and social rituals. Whatever the nature and the origin of caste, whether it was invented, constructed or imagined, it continues to offer a sense of social belongingness and comradeship as common stakeholders of social traditions. The loss of identity is in fact a larger issue than the

[5] Duncan B. Forrester, *Caste and Christianity: Attitudes and Policies on Caste of Anglo-Saxon Protestant Missions in India* (London: Curzon Press, 1979), 14–5.

[6] Arun Shourie, *Harvesting Our Souls: Missionaries, Their Design, Their Claims* (New Delhi: ASA Publication, 2000), 25–6.

loss of life. Therefore, the question of conversion, which is as much an issue of caste as it is of religion, becomes an issue of past events, present politics and future economics of an individual.

This paper seeks to study the interrelations between the present performance and past experience of the converts in relation to their everyday lives, delving into how they operate in the public sphere, and whether they mask one identity over another. It raises the following questions: How do they evolve a practical mechanism to cope with their dual or multiple identities? What is the role of the facilitating agencies and what is the reaction of the immediate neighbourhood? These are some of the issues that we focus on to understand the evolution of indigenous church communities in this part of the world.

2. What Is Conversion?

Conversion, as an act of intellectual expression, has been prevalent in the history of human society as a dynamic principle of change. It helps advocates affirm their conviction through public proclamation. As an act of subversion, it unsettles the *status quo* by opening up new vistas of change.[7] The choice to convert has been the catalytic agent for social transformation and political revolutions. Imagination, innovation, introduction of technology and entrepreneurial enterprise, all have come into being as the result of the spirit of conversion. In fact, it represents the human desire for amelioration, advancement and development in the state of existence in as many ways as possible.[8] The idea of progress as an opportunity for change has come to dominate the domain of historical thinking. The culture of conversion has promoted human understanding between communities, cutting across barriers. However, the term 'religious conversion' has increasingly come to refer to the idea of rupture, of sudden shift and the breaking off from the parental religion.

Religious faith and the culture of conversion continue to define the course of human civilization, as competing ideologies. While the latter emphasises the need for free thinking, the former demands from

---

[7] Sunder Raj, *The Confusion Called Conversion* (New Delhi: TRCACI, 1986), 13–6.

[8] Tanika Sarkar, 'Missionaries, Converts and the State in Colonial India', *Studies in History* 18.1 (2002): 121–33.

its followers implicit obedience at all times. Their opposing natures often lead to a point of clash in the life of an individual or a society. Since religion is seen as a discrete entity, hermetically sealed one from the others, conversion entails irreparable damage to social reality. As a matter of fact, every religion (including Brahminical Hinduism and Judaism that do not formally subscribe to the notion of conversion) has evolved through an integrative process, by drawing meanings and inspirations from multiple sites. The idea of conversion was explained and executed depending upon its historical exigency. Belief or the practice of a believer did not need to conform to the pattern of his/her ideological conviction, as long as it did not violate the internal consistency of the religious tradition. For example, the Judaic tradition permits the incorporation of children of cross-cultural marriage into its fold through patriarchal norms.

Conversion is an inevitable social process, bound to take place wherever Christianity exists since it forms the core value of the Christian faith. Historically, Christianity grew rapidly from a marginalized cult to a world religion by enlisting members from across the nations of the world. The conversion of St. Paul, St. Augustine, Constantine and a host of individuals made it a religion of people, by their effective conversions.[9] The performance of conversion is not an individual intellectual commitment; it is very often supported by external agencies. In fact, according to the Christian perspective, it is the act of responding to the divine call, supported by external agencies. The fact that the Church and its associated apparatus is always engaged in the act of facilitating believers to go through the process of conversion is strongly criticized, as it is alleged that it is advanced by 'questionable means'. The problem of conversion becomes a contentious issue in a multicultural society, as it has far-reaching consequences.

3. Problem of Conversion and Mission's Response

Conversion has been the subject of historical and sociological studies aiming to identify the principal motives behind it. Their main concern

---

[9] John Manners (ed.), *The Oxford History of Christianity* (London: OUP, 1993), 1–23.

has been the role of Christianity and that of social, economic and political aspirations in the process of the conversion. The studies primarily focus on the role of missionaries and often view the converts as passive recipients. In their analyses, the modes and methods of conversion are given importance, with the view to explain the causes responsible for the conversions. Conclusions and opinions widely differ; scholars who emphasize the constructive role of the missionaries see a rupture in the process of conversion, since it offers opportunities to converts to improve their social lives.

Geoffrey Oddie argues in his various works that, though the customs and social practices of the converts did not change substantially, conversion still gave them a chance to improve their socio-economic conditions. He emphasizes the importance of the dignity and self-worth resulting from conversion. He further points out that Christian conversion, unlike 'sanskritization', was able to facilitate structural change and that conversion movements represent caste mobility or the realization of a communal identity.[10]

The assimilationists see conversion as a process in which converts acquire new ideas and values, in course of their own progress towards economic prosperity. They note that it does not bring great disruption in their socio-cultural life. Conversion takes place for various socio-economic reasons. Susan Bayly, in her study on the sociological aspect of conversion in Kerala, points out that conversion offers an opportunity to the competing groups to advance their cause through the process of conversion. In the course of time, the contending communities learn to accommodate each other's interest through the process of inculturation and syncretic practice.[11] Anthropologists like David Mosse, Rowena Robinson and Lionel Caplan attempt to view the issue from a convert's point of view, without whose willingness the act can never take place. In their assessment, the role of religion is relegated to the point of

---

[10] G.A. Oddie, 'Christian Conversion among the Non-Brahmans in Andhra Pradesh with Special Reference to Anglican Missions and the Dornakal Diocese, c. 1900–1936', in G.A. Oddie (ed.), *Religion in South Asia: Religious Conversion and Revival Movements in South Asia in Medieval and Modern Times* (New Delhi: OUP, 1977), 95–124. See also G.A. Oddie, *Social Protest in India: British Protestant Missionaries and Social Reforms, 1850–1900* (New Delhi: OUP, 1979).

[11] Susan Bayly, *Saints, Goddesses and Kings: Muslims and Christians in South Indian Society, 1700–1900* (Cambridge: CUP, 1989).

ideology rather than as the prime mover of the action. The question of social dislocation does not arise in this process.[12]

Scholars also assume intellectual motives and a rational outlook to be the cause of conversions, which is perhaps possible in an industrialized society and at an individual level. On the contrary, Humphrey Fisher and Karl Morrison argue for the cause of supernatural influence and chiliastic notion.[13] Conversion as a modern social phenomenon opens up new vistas for the hitherto disaggregated rural masses. In her biographical study of V.S. Azariah, Susan Billington Harper argues that mass conversion in the rural corners of India acted as a social catalyst towards the path of progress to modernity.[14] Conversion has also been treated as religious transformation, which takes place at the instance of religious influence and thus, religion facilitates effective social engineering in the life of converts. Sebastian C.H. Kim attempts to resolve the issue of dislocation of identity, arising out of the process of conversion, through an intellectual enquiry. While it is a matter of socio-political contentions for Hindus; for Christians, it is a matter of theological conviction.[15] Gauri Vishwanathan views conversion as a dislocating experience, causing immense inconvenience to the converts including 'civil death'. She argues that 'conversion is an interpretive act and an index of material and social conflict.'[16]

Conversion as a contentious issue continues to generate a variety of opinions about its pros and cons. Since the debate began during the colonial struggle, it still continues to revolve around the idea

---

[12] David Mosse, 'The Catholic Church and Dalit Christian Activism in Contemporary Tamil Nadu', in Rowena Robinson and Joseph Marianus Kujur (eds.), *Margins of Faith: Dalit and Tribal Christianity in India*, (New Delhi: Sage, 2010), 235–62; Rowena Robinson, *Conversion, Continuity and Change: Lived Christianity in Southern Goa* (New Delhi: Sage, 1998); Lionel Caplan, *Studies in Religious Fundamentalism* (Albany: State University of New York Press, 1987).

[13] Humphrey Fisher, 'Conversion Reconsidered: Some Historical Aspects of Religious Conversion in Black Africa', *Journal of the International African Institute* 43.1 (1973): 27–40; Karl Morrison, *Understanding Conversion* (Charlottesville: University Press of Virginia, 1992).

[14] S. Billington Harper, *In the Shadow of the Mahatma: Bishop V.S. Azariah and the Travails of Christianity in British India* (Richmond: Curzon Press, 2000).

[15] C.H. Kim Sebastian, *In Search of Identity: Debates on Religious Conversion in India* (New Delhi: OUP, 2003).

[16] Gauri Viswanathan, *Outside the Fold* (New Delhi: OUP, 1998), 76.

of national entity, focusing on the question of individual allegiance to the cause of national progress. On the other hand, missionaries and theologians struggle to defend the negative connotations that conversion has acquired, especially in the eyes of the Hindus. The problem of conversion is inextricably linked to the social-cultural aspects of everyday life, and tends to breed communal hatred and suspicion about the agenda of the missionaries, particularly with regard to their work in rural India.

Pondering why conversion has become a vexatious issue in India, Kim notes that 'the problematic nature of conversion is due to communalism'. It is argued that communal tensions in India were exacerbated by 'colonial modernity'. Secondly, conversion becomes an issue of political dominance as it disrupts the clan relationships in a village by uprooting converts from their time-honoured social set-ups. Though economics is the contentious issue, religion provides the ideology for opposition[17] Thirdly, counter-conversion acts undertaken by radical Hindu activists further complicates the matter, by raking up issues concerning national identity and social heritage. In this process, they also attempt to demonstrate their ability to take recourse to violent means in resisting the missionaries' endeavours. Fourthly, conflicting opinions about the nature of conversion between the contending religious groups vitiates the atmosphere. The insistence by missionaries regarding the salvation experience of conversion as opposed to the 'functional worldview' of the Hindus further complicates the issue, by creating no point of convergence.[18]

Some Hindus view conversion as an act of spiritual blackmail, engineered by missionaries to achieve their hidden agenda. Missionaries, on the other hand, persistently emphasize the need to recognize the 'freedom of conscience' as an inalienable right of every human being. Nevertheless, they realize the need to indigenize the mode of worship and other religious activities, by incorporating local elements. Catholic missions have enlarged their scope of 'inculturation' activities by adopting local rituals and customs to expose the 'unknown Christ'

[17] Sebastian, *In Search of Identity*, 4–9.
[18] Sebastian, *In Search of Identity*, 14.

found in Hinduism.[19] However, their overtures of religious syncretism have been lampooned by the right-wing activists as yet another ploy to mislead the 'gullible masses'.[20]

The difference of opinions over the issue of conversion had existed throughout the colonial period as a major source of irritability. Missionaries have endeavoured to convince the Hindu intelligentsia about the uniqueness of the Christian faith through a dialogical process since the beginning of the 19th century. Responding to the call of the Serampore missionaries, Ram Mohan Roy scripted pamphlets problematizing the deity of Jesus Christ. While recognizing the exemplary moral character of Jesus and the social usefulness of Chirstianity, he dismisses the theology of Trinity and the redemptive value of Christ's sacrifice. The Serampore trio—Alexander Duff, Joshua Marshman and John Muir—continued their critical engagement with the pundits of Bengal to find a conciliatory approach. However, they were not as successful as they thought in their exposition of Christian apologetics. Vivekananda advanced his argument in defense of Hinduism to explain the mode of salvation. He also rejected outright the philosophy of grace, the symbol of the cross and the blood of Jesus, as the viable medium to achieve human salvation.[21]

Spiritual realization has its own unique dimension. It emanates from a particular socio-historical experience as the result of an intellectual commitment, and of course, it is not an appendage of external agency. Conversion had thus been seen from a Hindu perspective, as a personal soul-searching experience achieved by individual effort. The debate on conversion reached its nadir by the opening up of a dialogue with M.K. Gandhi in the '30s, when he showed a keen interest in matters of public concern. Hectic parleys were conducted with Gandhi in this regard. Gandhi opined, 'every nation's religion is as good as any other. Certainly India's religions are adequate for her people. We need no converting spiritually . . .

---

[19] W. Richard Taylor, *Christ Acting in Our Society*, in Burke Horst & M.W. Roth Wolfgang (eds.), *Indian Voices in Today's Theological Debate* (Lucknow: [n.p.], 1972), 158–69.

[20] Research Wing, Indian Bibliographic Centre, *Christianity and Conversion in India* (Varanasi: Rishi Publications, 1999), 1–7.

[21] S. Billington Harper, *In the Shadow of the Mahatma*, 293–4.

India stands in no need of conversion from one faith to another.'[22] Further, he asserted in no uncertain terms that the imposition of one's faith on another is a crime against humanity which must be resisted with all means, including legal injunction. Gandhi's remarks had virtually sealed off the fate of the open debate that had been on for about two centuries.

The desire of the missionaries to win over priestly class and caste Hindus seemed to have paid a modicum of dividend and the Indian church was making a steady progress in the hands of hitherto disaggregated subjects of Hindu society. In the meantime, the incipient Indian Christian community was successful in incorporating a clause of freedom of conscience in Article 25 of the Indian Constitution. This was a significant development, as it created a tacit approval for the act of conversion.

The intellectual enquiry into the question of developing indigenous theology began with much fervour; many innovations were introduced in the modes of worship, liturgy and other ecclesiastical affairs. Churches have increasingly realized the need to redefine their function, position and role concerning their commitment to their congregation in particular, and the multi-social fabric of the nation at large.[23]

The creative introspection that went into the theology of evangelism, conversion and Christian identity initiated the evolution of Indian missiology. Thanks to the promotion of liberal theology and the publication of '*Ecclesia in Asia*', these questions have been radically re-interpreted to meet local socio-cultural concerns. Concepts like 'Believing without Belonging', 'Messiah but not *Issai*', 'Devotees of Christ but not Christians' were some of the new concepts through which the theologians attempted to establish bridges to Indian culture. Colonial vocabulary and conventional prescriptions had been replaced to meet local concerns: 'Leading to Jesus', 'Knowing the True God', 'Finding *Jeeva-marga*' were some of the ways through which Gospel was imparted to common people.

[22] M.K. Gandhi, *Young India* (23 April 1931).
[23] J. Neyber, 'Mission Theology After Vatican II', in Kanjamala Augustine (ed.), *Paths of Mission in India Today* (Mumbai: St Paul, 1997), 49–64.

However, the conversion project continues to elude the church as an enigmatic conundrum. Periodically, in times of major persecution such as the recent incidents in Orissa, this matter occupies the central stage through public media. However, as a matter of fact, many of other small and isolated events taking place in rural areas are hardly reported or are otherwise mis-reported. The first information reports (FIRs) always attempt to depict the conflicts as a group or communal clash over a piece of rural litigation.[24]

The recent episode of conversion/re-conversion in Baharaich district is a case in point. Hundreds of families of the *Khanabadosh* community (who are a beef-eating and pig-rearing community) took to Christianity, in defiance against the ill-treatment meted out to them by the caste Hindu and Muslim villages in the Nawabganj block in Baharaich (UP) on 29 July 2010. However, they were re-converted within a week's time, under the leadership of the local BJP MLA Koushlendra Nath Yogi, through a *janeu sanskar*. According to the spokesperson of the VHP, the re-conversion was accomplished in an orderly fashion in the villages[25]. Crucial to our concern are the repercussions as they have far-reaching consequences. The instances of these episodes have not only demonstrated the invincible power of a majoritarian community, but also showed the church in a poor light, as a predator of gullible people.[26] Interestingly, this news was not covered by the national media, but the local press had a field day in recounting the stories for public consumption.

The caste factor has thus been an impediment to the discrimination-free public sphere. The Dalits have to bear the brunt of any consequences that come as a result of their action against the status quo. The sensitivity of the church does not mitigate the misery of the converts, who have to endure innumerable challenges, both physical and mental assaults and tortures, particularly in regard to their religious commitment. Keeping these concerns in the foreground, this study attempts to assess and examine the growth of the Indigenous Church Movement in contemporary Eastern Uttar Pradesh (Poorvanchal). Further, this

---

[24] M. Chad Bauman, *Identity: Conversion and Violence: Dalits, Adivasis and the 2007–08 Riots in Orissa,* in Robinson (ed.), *Margins of Faith,* 263–7.

[25] *Times of India* (31 July & 4 August 2010) in the Varanasi edition.

[26] *Dainik Jagran* (17 August 2010) in the Varanasi edition.

study focuses on the manner in which tensions between religious and inherited social identities are being resolved, and how local *satsang* or *sangati* (fellowship) assists its members in coping with contentious situations and in withstanding the reaction of other local communities.

4. Background

In spite of grinding poverty and poor literacy, eastern U.P. has been politically very active and has made a significant contribution to the cause of national struggle. So far, it has produced four prime ministers and one vice-president, and is now spearheading Dalit empowerment and activism in almost all spheres of life. The region is bounded by Nepal to the north, Bihar to the east, Baghelkhand of Madhya Pradesh to the south, the Awadh region of Uttar Pradesh to the west and the end of Doab (at Allahabad) in Uttar Pradesh to its south-west. It has 17 districts with a population of 4,23,14,287, of which around 20% are designated as Dalit and less than 40,000 are registered Christians (0.09%).[27] The Dalits have come to realize the need to fight for their rights, having recently been galvanized by the BSP for political action. Kanshiram's concerted effort in implementing social programmes created awareness among the masses, as a result of which they are now in a better position to lay claim to their privileges and rights. However, the modicum of success achieved does not alter their current predicament as far as their present religious status is concerned.

Motivated by the sense of religious affiliation, many of them have joined syncretic cult groups like *Kabir Panth, Ravidas, Brahmakumari* and *Santoshi Mata*. Religion as a primary network of social relationships offers easy access to intra-communal action through *bhajans*, *kathas*, public discourses and other participatory activities. These activities are conducted not only for the spiritual need of congregations, but also to make their presence felt in the rural public space.

The indigenous church movement began in the late 1990s in UP, with a view to present the Gospel in a culturally sensitive manner. It

---

[27] Alex Abraham and H. Tony E. Semyel, *Serve India Harvest Field Hand Book* (New Delhi: National Resource Centre, 2009); Alex Abraham and H. Tony E. Semyel, *Serve-A-State Uttar Pradesh Hand Book* (New Delhi: National Resource Centre, 2007).

soon grew by leaps and bounds and penetrated deeply into the remote *bastis* of eastern UP, for the cause of the Gospel. Unlike in the past, there is openness to the gospel in this region, but the main respondents are mostly from the servile castes, through whom local *satsangs* are formed across villages.

5. Origin of the Indigenous Church Movement

The term 'Indigenous Church Movement' has been comprehensively used to refer to a range of agencies and independent workers who take the Gospel to the doorsteps of the ordinary masses and make them followers of Jesus Christ, without disrupting their socio-cultural set-up. Historically, the term refers to a departure from the conversion mode to an inculturational or contextualization mode, without diluting the essence of the Gospel.

There are hundreds of individuals and agencies currently involved in sharing the Gospel and forming local churches (*calishia*) across the region. While this socio-historical study attempts to cover the region on the basis of its socio-cultural formation, the primary data has been culled from the Full Gospel Church of the Living God, located in Seer Govardhan village, adjacent to Varanasi town; *Yesu Darbar* assembly, located in Kuddupur village, Mariahu block of Jaunpur; and *Yesu Darbar* assembly, located in Bujwa Chowki in Mirzapur. (The name *Yesu Darbar* is used by some churches for the sake of legal immunity. Rajendra B. Lal, the founder of the *Yesu Darbar* assembly in Allahabad, obtained the right to run village assemblies under the banner of *Yesu Darbar*, through a Supreme Court order. Apart from the name, these assemblies function independently in all respects). The Kachhwa Church Transformation Initiative (KCTI) has also provided much-needed input.

Scholars who worked on the movement of Christianity in India have made only passing remarks about mission activities in this region. G.M. Moras, Stephen Neill and C.B. Webster have furnished some preliminary data upto the colonial period, in their comprehensive works on Christianity in India.[28] Rev. M.A. Sherring, an acclaimed anthropologist who wrote on Hindu castes and tribes, had been associated with the city of Benares as mission staff of the Anglican Church for about three decades. He was perhaps the only missionary to make a social enquiry into the factors that impede the promotion of the Gospel in this region; his findings appear to be relevant even today. He argues that

> Hinduism is in its fullness and maturity of its strength in these upper provinces, where it has acquired a stony compactness and solidity of an almost impenetrable character. Hence the greater difficulty of the progress of Christianity is in the north-west . . . than anywhere else in India. Humanly speaking, it is the last tract in India which will submit to the gospel.[29]

Benares, the veritable cultural capital of India, attracts devotees from all walks of life and from all across the subcontinent throughout the year, injecting a sense of belonging to the hoary tradition of *sanatanadharma*. He also argues that, unlike Bengalis, the Hindustanis were very concerned with their 'blood, breed and pedigree caste as an encompassing principle governing their everyday life'.[30] Loss of caste identity confirms, in all its religious virtues, the social death of an individual.

Considering the enormity of social opposition faced by the converts, the Anglican Church had constructed a cluster of houses within the premises of its mission compounds for its believers. Thus, the Christians came to be identified as an appendage of the colonial mission enterprise. The remnants of the mission compound can be found, even today, in many of the northern cities; the city of Varanasi has two of them in extant. In the eyes of the locals, many of the churches seem to have foreign links and, of course, foreigners of American-European origin are common in the streets of Varanasi, searching for meaning in their lives. Given the social ambience, the need to redefine

[28] Stephen Neill, *A History of Christianity in India, 1707–1858* (Cambridge: CUP, 1985); G.M. Moras, *Christianity in India*, vol. I (Bombay: Manak Talas, 1964); C.B. Webster, *A History of the Dalit Christians in India* (San Francisco: Mellen Press, 1992); C.B. Webster, *A Social History of Christianity: North-West India Since 1800* (New Delhi: OUP, 1999).

[29] M.A. Sherring, *The History of Protestant Missions in India* (London: Religious Tract Society, 1884), 162.

[30] Sherring, *History*, 165.

the functioning of mission emerged as a matter of importance and the initiative for an indigenous church movement emerged out of such a concern.

6. The Evolution of the Indigenous Church Movement

Mohan Philips, a retired aeronautical engineer envisioned a project (U.P. Mission) to reach out to the whole of U.P. through church planting. It was started in the late 1990s, with a modicum of resources to realize its vision in about two decades. Soon U.P. Mission caught the imagination of like-minded people and churches that invested their resources and energy to advance the cause of the mission movement. Raju Abraham, a physician by profession, left his career in London and joined the task of completing the Great Commission of Jesus in eastern U.P.[31] He started a church planting mission on a small scale, with what may be called Kachhwa Church Transformation Initiative (KCTI), in an abandoned Christian hospital belonging to Emmanuel Hospital Association in 1999. It was started with a view to plant churches, equip servant leaders, assist the poor, care for the sick and educate the next generation. Today, it not only concentrates on the spiritual well-being of people but also aims to improve access to basic health, education and other facilities, to bring about holistic change in their lifestyle. The movement has become a transformational initiative by bringing people into right relations with God. Kachhwa, a small village (40 kms from Varanasi) has now become a nodal centre for the Church Transformation Initiative, partnering with Operation AGAPE.

KCTI initially focused on forming house churches through Gospel activities which, in due course, gave way to the emergence of village churches. These centers then became an important point for village gatherings, cutting across social differences. On special occasions, the village churches used to meet at the hospital campus in large numbers.

People gathering in large numbers was earlier the prerogative of political rallies and 'Rural Melas'. Today however, gatherings for the cause of the Gospel, once unimaginable, have become a feasible reality. The village churches are manned by local staff, trained for this purpose

---

[31] Based on oral interview with Rajiv Abraham at Kachhwan on 25 August 2000.

and designated as G-12 workers. KCTI has proper infrastructure with sufficient expertise to train its G-12 workers for its various ministries. Seminars, workshops and religious retreats are periodically organized for the G-12 workers to upgrade their understanding of the mission. Reading and referring to the Bible is encouraged at every level; besides conducting the Sunday service, the G-12 workers are involved in house visiting, organizing cottage prayers, sharing the Gospel with new contacts, conducting literacy classes and other incumbent activities depending upon local exigencies.

The members of the village churches primarily relate themselves to the church for spiritual needs. However, in times of distress, they looked for various forms of aid and assistance. Kachhwa Christian Hospital is where they can access medical aid as and when it is required. KCTI has now enlarged its scope of activities to include critical ameliorative ventures, such as setting up village pumps, constructing local lavatories, assisting women to form self-help groups, setting up village preparatory schools, conducting adult literacy programs, organizing medical camps, and improving local sanitation conditions, in order to bring about holistic transformation in the life of the rural people. Diploma courses in light engineering and paramedical courses for the youth are conducted to help them obtain gainful employment. Women are given training in tailoring, to help them improve their prospects of income. These activities have not only benefitted the members of the church, but also created positive environs across the village, through their spillover impact. KCTI is also exploring the possibility of partnering with the government in executing rural health projects on account of their field, knowledge and expertise.

The church planting mission thus has opened up new vistas for spiritual and material amelioration of village life in many respects. The KCTI mission activities already covers upto 60 blocks in this region, and the target is to reach 100 blocks within the next four years.[32] The initiative began primarily with the view to plant churches. Then, compelled by the prevailing social predicament, KCTI took on the task of rendering basic critical services to the masses that have hitherto been denied their rights by state agencies. However, such deeds are being

---

[32] Based on an interview with Sunil, one of the KCTI staff, on 15 September 2010.

seen as acts of allurement to conversion, and needs to be thoroughly critiqued. Converts are not the product of missionary machination. In fact, they are the catalytic agents of social regeneration, creating a possibility for a choice of faith.[33]

Mission as a social enterprise came into being as a result of an individual or institutional effort to share the Gospel with a community of people in a particular geographical context. It was evolutionary in nature but rarely took a radical course at the initial instance. The Kuddupur *Yesu Darbar* assembly, which was otherwise called *Prabhu Sewa Sangati*, came into being to meet the needs of the local people in 2002. Rajendra Chauhan, an unschooled painter, came under the influence of the Gospel and sought the gift of healing while he was working in Mumbai,. He did not use his gift there, but after returning to Kuddupur, his native village, he realized the need for praying for the sick.

Rajendra Chauhan administered a cup of water to the sick that came to him for prayer. As soon as they drank the water, they were reported to have experienced divine healing in their bodies. The news about this incident spread across the locality like wild fire, causing shock and awe. Many started coming to Rajendra Chauhan's place for prayers throughout the week. To serve the spiritual need of the people, he started a Sunday worship service in the open space close to his home. By the time, he was widely known as the *'Pani Baba'*, who was said to have released the power of Jesus through administering water.[34] The Sunday gathering grew enormous, causing immense disturbance to the routine life of the village. The dominant landowning caste of the village—the Rajputs—saw it as a violation of the existing social norm and resorted to violence. However, they were unsuccessful in controlling the village crowd, who were coming from all directions.

Following this, Rajendra Chauhan was implicated for disturbing communal harmony and charged with misleading people through water magic. He was arrested and put behind bars for a month. Subsequently, he was released with the order not to use water magic in his worship service. He was continuously challenged by the dominant

---

[33] Ryan Dunch, 'Beyond Cultural Imperialism: Cultural Theory, Christian Missions, and Global Modernity', *History and Theory* 41.3(2002): 301–25.

[34] Based on an interview with Rajendra Chauhan, 29 August 2010.

caste groups of village. Therefore, he sought a legal injunction under the banner of *Yesu Darbar* assembly to conduct his worship service. In a short time, his *Prabhu Sewa Samiti* grew in strength to overcome impending challenges. Today it is the fastest growing village church in the region, accounting for 27,000 members in about 12 assemblies in Mariahu block of the Jaunpur district. Besides, it also has assemblies at Azamgarh and Faizabad. The Kuddupur *Yesu Darbar* assembly conducts its weekly services on Sundays and Saturdays to minimize the crowd congestion in the village. Besides this, prayer meets and healing ministries are conducted throughout the week. Charismatic assemblies like these are in the process of evolving, and it may take some time to settle down to an organized form.

The *Yeesu Darbar* assembly located at *Bujua Chowki* near Mirzapur town was started by pastor Vijay Kumar from Kerala, in 2000. Though he has minimal school education, he learnt the art of conversing with people in their local dialects. In the beginning, the church faced severe local opposition and got involved in court cases. However, it successfully managed them all.[35] It maintains an informal link with the founder of the *Yesu Darbar* assembly in Allahabad, but for all practical purposes it functions as an independent church. Today, it has a membership of 1,500 and conducts weekly services, Bible Studies, cottage prayer meets and fasting prayer meetings. It has developed a cordial relationship with the local administrative authority. The local MLA Shailendranath Singh Yadav recognizes its visible numeric strength.

The Full Gospel Church of the Living God, located at Seer Govardhan, is an independent church which was started by Pastor Paul in 2007. From Tamil Nadu, he worked in the city for about a decade with other church movements. Currently, the church meets at his residence and has 60 members. The construction of the church building has already. These house churches show signs of progress in their missionary endeavour.

Most of the local churches mentioned above were the result of pioneering efforts in the virgin mission field. Though missions like KCTI were started in the old missionary field, it extended and enlarged

---

[35] Based on an interview with Pastor Vijay Kumar on 17 July 2010.

its scope of activities in the vicinity through its church planting mission enterprise. They were all manned by people who had a modicum of school education and no formal theological training. Yet they were competent enough to convey the Gospel message in the local language and dialects to the rural masses. They followed similar methods of sharing the Gospel to identical people groups, spread across the region. G-12 workers of the KCTI were initial trained in village church coordinating activities, but the workers of the Kuddupur *Yesu Darbar* assembly are in the process of learning through personal experience.

Considering the social profile of these congregations, it may be argued that Dalits of this region not only responded to the Gospel, but are also actively involved in the congregational programme. The people of intermediary castes showed keen interest in the Gospel message, but were unsure about identifying themselves with Dalit church groups. Caste Hindus showed initial resistance to the Gospel; however, in recent times, they have toned down their aggressive postures significantly. Caste Hindu women have shown some interest in the Gospel and taken part in services for festive occasions. Muslims and Jains have, by and large, remained indifferent to the Gospel; the churches did not make special efforts to reach out to them. People, irrespective of their social affiliations, earnestly seek prayer support, especially in times of physical ailments, from the members or workers. They have joined the fellowship after receiving miraculous healing.

7. Modes of Worship

All these churches follow similar patterns of worship, in which participation of the congregation is encouraged at every level. Songs, sung either in Bhojpuri or Hindi to local tunes, are accompanied by countryside drums and cymbals. This encourages the masses to engage in the act of worship. Sufficient time is allotted for narration of testimonies and public witnessing, in which people are encouraged to share their personal experiences of blessings and requests for prayer. An hour is earmarked for the sermon, which is delivered by the preacher; a simple, straightforward message pointing to the salvation offer or the miraculous interventions of Jesus, urging members to give up their bad habits as a precondition to divine blessing. The service ends with the receiving of offerings—most members give according to their means as a mark of respect to the God whom they worship, either in cash or kind.

Women always outnumber men in attendance and the youth participate with a sense of reservation, since they are concerned about their image and interest. Though there is no compulsion from any quarter, some members are under the grip of a lurking fear about their dual identity. Peer pressure, perceptions about one's public image and having to possibly forego future reservation benefits make them ponder over their acquired identity as against their ascribed one, as the acquired identity will have a de-stabilizing impact on their personality and social pedigree.

Given the high level of political consciousness, the Dalits of U.P. feel that they have already been liberated from the tyranny of caste oppression, if not from its discrimination. This was largely achieved by a process of political empowerment, through the sustained efforts of Dalit intellectuals to undermine the hegemony of the caste structure. Dalit mass consciousness reached its critical state with the formation of the Dalit-Brahmin *Bhaichara Samiti.* An organization for the promotion of Dalit-Brahmin brotherhood, it instilled a sense of hope and dignity among the Dalits about their social identity. The realization of the strength of collective bargaining made the youth believe that their future would be brighter within the Hindufold and that the search for an alternative identity would weaken their social solidarity.

However, most Christian converts seem happy with their dual identity and identify themselves as *Isai, Masiha, Yesu Bhakhtas* and Dalit-Christians, depending upon their socio-cultural milieu. This section of the Dalit community argues that the Dalit-Brahmin *Bhaichara* is an attempt to sell out the interest of the gullible masses to cunning Brahmins; Dalits would stand to gain nothing and their struggle for equality is one of resistance, as against collaboration and submission. Dalits were never hopeful of finding equal space within the Hindu spiritual domain and, therefore, they must look for one outside the Hindufold. According to one of the G-12 workers, 'Christianity has not only given them a sense of belongingness but also an opportunity to serve them as priests and bishops.' Further, he claimed that he had already led two Brahmin families to the saving knowledge of

Christ. 'For a Dalit,' he asserted, 'it was by no means an ordinary achievement.' According to a migrant labourer from Kuddupur, 'Caste has lost its grip over the rural life of the society and Dalits will throng to Christianity and make it their national faith.'

Dalits had already learned to live with overlapping identities and they stand to lose nothing by aligning themselves with the Christian faith, as it did not impose any restrictions on them. The Mala and the Madiga Christians of Andhra Pradesh, as Rowena argues, 'have learned to live with their professed identity, which is different from their declared identity. Though they they have been using their social identity for all legal and administrative purposes, they remain committed to their professed faith otherwise.'[36]

This arrangement of convenience seems to be working well in coastal Andhra Pradesh. However, this mode of ambivalence can at best be a stop-gap arrangement. It cannot be ideologically justified as a viable alternative, to avail reservation benefits for historical sufferings. Similarly, the inculturation process also tends to privilege the dominant functional worldview as a national culture, which has its own limitations. In either case, the Dalits have to negotiate with new social realities, while adopting the Christian identity. The duality of identity with regard to their everyday life entails innumerable obstacles, which they have to face time and again. Clash of interests sometimes leads to intra-communal conflicts, leading to the intervention by right-wing forces, which further communalises the issue.

From a radical Dalit point of view, anything that is Brahminical belongs to Hinduism, which does not represent the holistic national culture in the real sense. Therefore, the alternative must be inclusive in outlook, holistic in approach, and must resist all discriminatory tendencies and social exclusivity. Retaining caste titles can be culturally tolerable for a generation, but maintaining it beyond a period betrays the spirit of social egalitarianism. Justice cannot be sacrificed at the altar of sensitivity. Truth should not be relativized for the sake of accommodation. Cultural sensibility can only be a

---

[36] Ashok Kumar and Robinson, 'Legally Hindu: Dalit Lutheran Christians of Coastal Andhra Pradesh', in Robinson (ed.), *Margins of Faith*, 149–68.

guiding force but not a governing principle, as far as religious truth is concerned.

As a matter of fact, indigenous churches should follow a policy of zero tolerance towards caste discrimination and contending issues. If they do not, they will end up repeating the mistake of the south Indian churches. Given its political clout and internal strength, the Indian church must make a concerted effort to secure the legitimate reservation rights due to Dalit Christians for the historical wrongs they have suffered over generations. The State cannot continue to follow the dubious policy of permitting converts to Buddhism and Sikhism to avail such rights and preventing those converting to Christianity from doing the same.

Besides, the conjectural notion about conversion and its colonial predicament needs to be thoroughly critiqued. The Niyogi Report and its outdated statistics, and the Gandhian atavistic argument, can no longer stand the test of the day. In this age of globalization, where freedom of choice is the prerequisite for progress, the Indian Christian community must learn to aggressively promote its interests through legitimate means, by demonstrating its positive contribution to the process of nation building. The community must rise from its stereotyped sense of diffidence, timidity and servitude, and learn to articulate its interests. It must learn to present its case without yielding to the undue pressure of majoritarian community. As Nirad C. Chaudhari rightly observes, 'There is only one way in which a small minority can make itself respected by a majority. That is, by maintaining its integrity and showing legitimate spirit of independence.'[37] He continues, 'The Indian Christian has to show more of this spirit in religion, social life, and politics,' failing which it will 'remain the member of a client community', waiting to receive the order to execute with a sense of servile loyalty.

The Indian Christian community must assert its rights, present its identity and stake its claim to argue, in Mother Teresa's words, that 'no man, no law, no government, has the right to prevent me, nor force me, nor anyone, if I chose to embrace the religion that

---

[37] Ka Naa Subramanyam, *The Catholic Community in India* (Madras: Macmillan, 1970), iv–vi.

gives me peace, joy and love.'[38] Thus, the call for conversion should be stated in universal terms, without diluting its legitimate essence. The vacillating idea of dual identity can no longer be sustained in a democratic social milieu, since it violates the principle of trust. While church missions and congregations are making steady progress, community statistics remain static in government records and census reports—a fact that is not in conformity with the professed ideals of Christianity.

S.No.	District	Population	Christian population	Christian as %
1	Azamgarh	39,39,916	3,049	0.08
2	Ballia	27,61,620	2,913	0.11
3	Chandauli	16,43,251	1,196	0.07
4	Deoria	27,12,650	1,616	0.06
5	Ghazipur	30,37,582	2,227	0.07
6	Gorakhpur	37,69,456	6,576	0.17
7	Jaunpur	39,11,679	3,028	0.08
8	Kushinagar	28,93,196	1,372	0.05
9	Maharajganj	21,73,878	1,782	0.08
10	Mau	18,53,997	1,095	0.06
11	Mirzapur	21,16,042	1,008	0.05
12	Sant ravidas nagar	13,53,705	776	0.06
13	Sonbhadra	14,63,519	3,149	0.22
14	Varanasi	31,38,671	4,499	0.14
15	Siddharthnagar	20,40,085	1,280	0.06
16	Basti	20,84,814	1,511	0.07
17	Sant kabir nagar	14,20,226	707	0.05
Total		4,23,14,287	37,784	0.09

Source: Alex Abraham and H. Tony E. Semyel, *Serve India Harvest Field Hand Book* (New Delhi, National Resource Centre: 2009).

[38] *The Examiner* (31 March 1979): 193–4.

Select References

Augustine, Kanjamala (ed.). *Paths of Mission in India Today.* Mumbai: St Paul, 1997.

Bayly, Susan. *Saints, Goddesses and Kings: Muslims and Christians in South Indian Society 1700–1900.* Cambridge: Cambridge University Press, 1989.

Caplan, Lionel. *Studies in Religious Fundamentalism.* Albany: State University of New York Press, 1987.

Dirks, Nicholas B. *Castes of Mind: Colonialism, and the Making of Modern India.* New Delhi: Permanent Black, 2001.

Harper, Susan B. *In the Shadow of the Mahatma: Bishop V.S. Azariah and the Travails of Christianity in British India.* Richmond: Curzon Press, 2000.

Hobsbawm, Eric and Terence Ranger (eds). *The Invention of Tradition.* Cambridge: Cambridge University Press, 1992.

Kolenda, Pauline. *Caste and Christianity: Attitudes and Policies on Caste of Anglo-Saxon Protestant Missions in India.* London: Curzon Press, 1979.

Kolenda, Pauline. *Caste in Contemporary India: Beyond Organic Solidarity.* Jaipur: Rawat Publishers, 1997.

Manners, John (ed.). *The Oxford History of Christianity.* London: Oxford University Press, 1993.

Moras, G.M. *Christianity in India.* Vol. I. Bombay: Manak Talas, 1964.

Morrison, Karl. *Understanding Conversion.* Charlottesville: University Press of Virginia, 1992.

Neill, Stephen. *A History of Christianity in India, 1707–1858.* Cambridge: Cambridge University Press, 1985.

Oddie, G.A. *Religion in South Asia: Religious Conversion and Revival Movements in South Asia in Medieval and Modern Times.* New Delhi: Oxford University Press, 1977.

Oddie, G.A. *Social Protest in India: British Protestant Missionaries and Social Reforms 1850–1900.* New Delhi: Oxford University Press, 1979.

Raj, Sunder. *The Confusion called Conversion.* New Delhi: TRCACI, 1986.

Research Wing, Indian Bibliographic Centre. *Christianity and Conversion in India.* Varanasi: Rishi Publication, 1999.

Robinson, Rowena and Joseph Marianus Kujur (eds). *Margins of Faith: Dalit and Tribal Christianity in India*. New Delhi: Sage, 2010.

Robinson, Rowena. *Conversion, Continuity and Change: Lived Christianity in Southern Goa*. New Delhi: Sage, 1998.

Sebastian, Kim C.H. *In Search of Identity: Debates on Religious Conversion in India*. New Delhi: Oxford University Press, 2003.

Sherring, M.A. *The History of Protestant Missions in India*. London: Religious Tract Society, 1884.

Shourie, Arun. *Harvesting Our Souls: Missionaries, Their Design, Their Claims*. New Delhi: ASA Publication, 2000.

Subramanyam, Ka Naa. *The Catholic Community in India*. Madras: Macmillan, 1970.

Viswanathan, Gauri. *Outside the Fold*. New Delhi: Oxford University Press, 1998.

Webster, C.B. *A History of the Dalit Christians in India*. San Francisco: Mellen Press, 1992.

Webster, C.B. *A Social History of Christianity: North-West India Since 1800*. New Delhi: Oxford University Press, 1999.

Revisiting the Identity of Women

Jayakumar Ramachandran*

1. Introduction: Gender Issues and Women's Identity

One of the most enduring truisms about India is her contradictions. On the one hand, she advocates openness, equality and tolerance in all spheres of life, while on the other hand, she does not want to let go of outdated traditions. For the purposes of this paper, we consider in particular Indian women who are both oppressed and liberated. Urvashi Butalia, co-founder of India's first feminist publishing company, writes, 'It is true to say that they [Indian women] are among the most oppressed in the world and equally true to say that they are among the most liberated.'[1]

The last two decades have witnessed the growing mosaic of women's educational accomplishments, outstanding career achievements and professional milestones, and being a key role member in families, all of which promote the equal treatment of women. These avenues, along with and the passing of new statutory laws in support of women, have opened various doors of personal and professional development for women. The question, however, is: Have these changes contributed lasting benefits to the common woman in India? Much as a bright light cannot help a blind man see better, the aforementioned advances in women's development have not done much for women in the mainstream population. Many still practice paternalism with regard to women.

This paper will address this duality of development and discrimination, or fairness and bigotry, with respect to women, in order to enable the Church at large in India to respond adequately. A brief scrutiny of how women were treated in the past becomes indispensable for understanding this duality of fairness and bigotry that must be confronted within contemporary identity issues of Indian women.

* Dr. Jayakumar Ramachandran is the President of Bible Believing Churches and Missions/Academy for Church Planting and Leadership and the senior pastor of Calvary's Grace Bible Church in Bangalore.

[1] Urvashi Butalia, 'The Women's Movement in India: Action and Reflection', http://www.twnside.org.sg/title/india1cn.htm (accessed 8 June 2010).

2. Religions, Movements and Legislation Regarding Gender Issues and Women's Identity

The women's movement gained public influence in the 1920s, and steadily progressed through the period of strong nationalism and the freedom struggle. The movement itself was built on 19th century social reform movements.[2] This timeline helps understand the process of development of women identities in India, in order to find answers to the following queries: How did religions in general regard women? How were they treated, and why? What did women's movements accomplish for women at large in India? Is the present atmosphere of development for women a myth? Are we still sailing in the same vessel that was afloat prior to 1920?

From its genesis, the women's movement has testified repeatedly to the unacceptable and ongoing discrimination that women's roles and status have been subjected to from the earliest times. The grounds for such discriminatory practices are being studied in a dual manner.

2.1. The Impact of Religious Factors on Gender Issues and Women's Identity Prior to 1920

Religions, in general, possess texts which are considered sacred and unchallengeable in their respective spheres. These texts are the primary source of doctrinal and dogmatic formulations, religious instruction, and influence. They contribute significantly to the construction of each religion's cultural values and traditions. In the following sections, I make a few observations from teachings on women in the three major religions of India.

2.1.1. Hinduism, Gender Issues, and Women's Identity

General observation of Hinduism's perspective of women's identity is indistinct. Though many Hindu proponents argue that Hinduism reveres

---

[2] Samita Sen, 'Toward a Feminist Politics? The Indian Women's Movement in Historical Perspective', The World Bank Development Research Group, Poverty Reduction and Economic Management Network, April 2000, http://www.onlinewomeninpolitics. org/india/indian.pdf (accessed on 26 August 2010).

the role and position of women, their ill-fated state in general is obvious and undeniable. In order to have a vivid understanding of women's position in Hinduism, we must view it from various vantage points.

The Upanishads, the greatest of all *Sruti* scriptures, summarizes the concept of women in the four *Mahavakyas* as follows: *aham Brahmasmi* (I am the spirit, i.e., *atman*); *tat tvam asi* (That thou art); *prajnanam Brahma* (*Brahman* is pure consciousness); and *ayam atma Brahma* (This self is *Brahman*). Hindu teaching would commonly interpret these utterances as advocating that an individual, regardless of religion, race, culture, gender, colour, caste, creed or location, is *atman* clothed in a physical body.

The belief is also that, during the Vedic period, women acquired a status equal to that of the men in every political, social, economic and religious field. They were treated with equal dignity and respect.[3] Vedic history records that women pursued some of the highest learning opportunities, whereby many became seers and philosophers. *Ghosha, Apala, Lopamudra, Vishwvara, Surya, Indrani, Yami, Romasha* — all of these names highlight the position and esteem which Hindu women enjoyed in that period.[4] Supreme Goddess or the reat Mother Devi, the female aspect of the divine, received highest veneration, and without her, the male aspect was considered powerless. A famous Sanskrit *slokha* further depicts the significant status of women in religious settings: *'Yatra naryastu pujyante, ramante tatra devta.'* Loosely translated, these words tell that god himself would inhabit the places wherein women were worshipped. Various events from the *Smritis* illustrate the significant role of women: when Sri Rama was conducting the *Aswamethey Yagna*, he had a golden statue of Sita made, as a mark of her presence as he performed the *yagna*. Some of the *Smritis* speak about the valiant roles of women in stories, and tell of the freedom women had in choosing their husbands through *swayamvaras*.

However, other Hindu texts must be mentioned which provide a less positive view of women. In the Rigveda, many goddesses serve as the center of the religion. Yet, they play a minor role in comparison to the male gods.[5] Most texts and traditions understand male deities as

---

[3] Swami Abhdananda, *India And Her People* (New York: Vedanta Society, 1906), 253.

[4] Asha Lata Pandey, 'Hindu View on Women', *Dharma-marg* (July 2009): 43–5.

[5] Trilok C. Majupuria and Rohit K. Majupuria, *Gods, Goddesses & Religious Symbols of a Hinduism, Buddhism & Tantrism* (India: M. Devi, Lashkar, 2005), 100.

significant individual beings while females are not regarded as such.[6] In the later days however, Vedic Hinduism, which seems to observed religious concepts generally favourable to women, also incorporated censurable practices such as *sati, jauhar, devadasi, purdah,* inhumane treatment of widows and the denial of education to girls. One of the *Smriti* scriptures, *Manu,* describes the various developmental stages of women in society as follows: 1) in childhood, a female must be subject to her father; 2) in youth, she is subject to her husband; 3) when her lord dies, the widow is then subject to her sons. Thus, as one may observe, a woman was seldom to be considered fit for independence.[7] According to *Manu,* a woman needs the presence of a man if she is to possess an identity in society. Otherwise, her identity is in and of itself a non-entity. Women have never been independent of men and a woman's happiness depends on male control, as delineated in *The Code of Manu,* one of Hinduism's oldest foundational texts.[8]

2.1.2. Islam, Gender Issues and Women's Identity

Many passages in the Quran declare that God created man and woman. However, women are not considered significantly equal in essential aspects of life. They are equal when it comes to faith, obedience and beliefs. However, a dividing wall seems to exist between social and spiritual existence, in the teachings of the Quran concerning equality.

Insistence on equality is obvious in the following passages. Sura 4.124 declares: 'And whosoever doeth good works whether of male or female, and he (or she) is a believer, such will enter paradise and they will not be wronged the dint in a date-stone.'[9] Suras 74.38; 3.195; 16.97 and 4.124 are other passages found in support of equal religious obligations for women.

Though women are given equal religious obligations, they are not given equal privileges, such as daily prayers, fasting, alms-giving and pilgrimage. For example, women are excluded from observing

---

[6] Babita and Sanjay Tewari, 'The History of Indian Women: Hinduism at Crossroads with Gender', *Politics and Religions* 3.1 (2009): 30–31.

[7] *Laws of Manu*, verse 148.

[8] John Raines, *The Justice Men Owe Women; Positive Resources from World Religions* (Minneapolis: Fortress Press, 2001), 1.

[9] Mohamad Marmaduke Pickthall, *The Meanings of the Glorious Quran* (Delhi: Nusrat Ali Nasri, 1992).

the daily prayers. They are barred from fasting during menstruation and for forty days after childbirth, as they are considered unclean. They are also exempted from fasting during pregnancy and while nursing their babies. Further, if women miss fasting, they are expected to compensate for their missed days whenever they can. Quran 2.228 declares that women are under men in the context of the divorce: 'And they [women] have rights similar to those [of men] over them in kindness, and men are a degree above them.'[10] Suras 4.11 denies an equal share of ancestral wealth to women: 'The share of the male shall be twice that of a female.' Suras 2.282 states that women are forgetful beings; so, two women witnesses are insisted upon to settle a matter under dispute. 'And let two men from among you bear witness to all such documents. But if two men be not available, there should be one man and two women to bear witness so that if the woman forgets (anything), the other may remind her.' In spite of the whole chapter 4 in the Quran entitled *An-Nisa,* which exclusively deals with women—their social parameters, their relationships to the other gender, marriage, family rights for and obligations on each member—yet Islam does not practise equality.

Al-Aqqad, a well-lettered Arabian and a reformer who is being viewed as a genius, believes that a woman is a necessary evil, and that she does not possess any talent or virtue at all.[11] It is reasoned by a few that cultures and traditions of Islamic countries have caused these discriminations. Sarah Alaoui, a staff author with the journal *Prospect* says that Islam does give women and men equal human rights spiritually, financially and socially. It was the persistence of agrarian labor and tribal traditions of many Middle Eastern countries that created an imbalance and inequality of gender roles.[12]

In spite of various legislations which prevent discrimination against women in India, many Islamic women in the country are not given a fair chance. According to government reports, Muslim women are among the

[10] Pickthall, *The Meanings of the Glorious Quran.*

[11] Abbas Mahmud al-Aqqad, *al-Mar'a fi al-Qur'an* (Beirut, 1985), 24.

[12] Sarah Alaoui, 'Women's Status in Islam: The Line Between Culture and Religion', *Prospect Journal* (February 2011), http://prospectjournal.ucsd.edu/index.php/2011/02/womens-status-in-islam-the-line-between-culture-and-religion/ (accessed on 10 August 2011).

poorest being an educationally disenfranchised, economically vulnerable and politically marginalized group in the country.[13] Consequently, civil society and the state locate Muslim women's deprivation not in terms of the 'objective' reality of societal discrimination and faulty development policies, but in the religious-community space.[14]

2.1.3. Christianity, Gender Issues, and Women's Identity

The Bible emphatically insists on equality of women, in general. However, there are a few passages that appear to be advocating for their secondary status.

The Bible describes various positive roles of women. In 1 Thessalonians 2.7, a woman is expected to be a loving, caring, self-sacrificing wife and mother, while Proverbs 31.13–19 describes her as a faithful housewife who labours hard. Women are vessels of reverence that others may see (1 Pet. 3.2) and are considered noble and praiseworthy by society and family (Prov. 31). In relation to the body of Christ and the Church, the woman is skillful in doing God's work (Exod. 35.25; Luke 8.3; Rom. 16.3, 12; Phil. 2), equal with men in the body of Christ (1 Cor. 12.13; Gal. 3.28), and gifted with spiritual gifts for the purpose of the Church of God (Eph. 4.1–13). During the apostolic age, women were potential instruments, as illustrated by the effective roles of Mary (the mother of John Mark), Mary of Bethany, Priscilla of Pontus, Lydia of Philippi, Apphia of Colossae, the elderly lady of 2 John, and others.

On the other hand, there are scriptural passages that appear to confer on women an inferior status. (Gen. 3.16, Isa. 3.12 , 1 Cor. 11.3, 14.34–36, Eph. 5.22–24 , Col. 3.18, 1 Tim. 2.11–15 , Titus 2.4–5 and 1 Pet. 3.1). However, an exegetical understanding of these passages helps us understand that the Bible does not advocate any kind of inferior status for women. Apart from scriptural insistence on the dignified identity of women, noteworthy are the contributions of the Church and Christian individuals for women equality.

---

[13] Seema Kazi, *Muslim Women in India* (UK: Minority Rights Group International, 1999), 31, 98/2.

[14] Rajinder Sachar Committee, *Report of the Prime Minister's High Level Committee on Social, Economic and Educational Status of the Muslim Community of India to the Prime Minister of India* (Cabinet Secretariat Government of India, November 2006), 12–3.

The Church in India, as well as individual Christians, have significantly contributed to the upliftment of women and their identity. There are several noteworthy endeavours in this direction. Cornelia Sorabji, a Parsi Christian and a daughter of an ordained minister from what was formerly known as the Bombay Presidency, emphatically insisted on the need for formal education among women and helped to establish several schools for girls in Pune.[15] William Carey and the Serampore Mission have made a valuable contribution towards the uplifting of women. Hannah Marshman, the wife of Joshua Marshman, one of the founders of the Serampore Mission, worked tirelessly for female education. Through Hannah's efforts, several schools for girls were established, which enabled women to achieve to a great extent of their development and emancipation in this region.[16] Several other Societies engaged in imparting education to the women of Bengal were: Society for Promoting Female Education in the East, established in 1834; Ladies' Society for Female Education, Free Church of Scotland, established in 1837; Women's Union Missionary Society, established in 1861; Baptist Female Missionary Society, established in 1870; L.M.S. Ladies' Committee for Missions in India and China, established in 1875; and Church of England Zenana Missionary Society, established in 1880.[17] B.V. Subbamma, a convert in Andhra Pradesh who pioneered the Ashram Movement, advocated for women as educators, nurses, social activists, counselors, pastors, theologians, leaders and so on.[18] Pandita Ramabai was one of the greatest women produced by modern India. A champion of women's rights, she was a pioneer in the field of women's education and one of India's most influential women reformers. She was the first to promote the welfare and education of Indian widows. She had a charismatic personality and was passionately interested in the freedom and welfare of her countrywomen.[19]

---

[15] Suparna Gooptu, *Cornelia Sorabji: Indian Pioneer Women Lawyer* (USA: OUP, 2006), 74–9.

[16] T. Johnson Chakkuvaracka, 'Glimpses of the "Feminine" in Indian Religion and Society: A Christian Perspective', *Indian Journal of Theology* 44.1–2 (2002): 79–93.

[17] National Encyclopedia of Bangladesh, *Banglapedia*, http://www.banglapedia.org/httpdocs/HT/Z_0013.HTM (accessed on 20 August 2011).

[18] Leela Manasseh, 'Emancipation of Women and Nation Building: A Christian Perspective', *TBT Journal* 3.1 (2009): 69.

[19] Radha Kumar, *The History of Doing: An Illustrated Account of Movements for Women's Rights and Feminism in India 1800–1990* (London: verso. 1993), 26.

As I argue for women's equality from scriptures and contributions made by the Church and individual Christians, I do admit that there still are avenues in the Church at large where inequality of women can be found hibernating. The situation with regard to the identity and role of women in the Church is similar to that we find in society due to the fact that the culture from which Christianity originated was patriarchal. The identity and role of women in the Church in India is conditioned by Indian culture as well as by biblical tradition.[20]

2.1.4. Movements, Gender Issues and Women's Identity

The roots of the Indian women's movement go back to the early 19th century, to Rajah Ram Mohun Roy (1772–1833). He focused on issues concerning *sati* and *kulin* polygamy, and spoke in favour of women's property rights.[21] It was not only elite Indian men and women who worked for improvements related to the identity of women; Europeans aided this effort significantly. Between the 1820s and 1850s, reformers who favoured both legislative interventions by the colonial state and a wider program for female emancipation, set up organizations like the *Brahmo Samaj* in eastern India, the *Prarthana Samaj* in western India, the *Arya Samaj* in northern India, and the Theosophical Society in southern India.

The efforts of the *Brahmo Samaj* in promoting education for women resulted in the Hindu *Mahila Vidyalaya,* a school for educating their women. The *Prarthana Samaj* in Maharashtra and Gujarat focused on prohibition of child marriage, widow re-marriage, and on women's education. Annie Besant came to India in 1893, by which time she had worked with Charles Bradlaugh on the *National Reformer,* had become a critic of British colonialism, and had joined the Theosophical Society. In 1914, she joined the Congress and in 1916 was one of the founders of the Home Rule League. In 1917, she was elected president of the Congress. Under her influence, the Congress expressed the opinion that the same test be applied to women as to men in regard to franchise, and the eligibility to all elective bodies concerned with local government

---

[20] Nirmala Vasanthakumar, 'Role and Identity of Women in the Church in India', http://www.womenutc.com/nirmala.htm (accessed on 30 August 2011).

[21] Sakuntala Narasimhan, *Sati: Widow Burning in India* (India: Harper Collins, 1998), 31.

and education. In December 1917, she, along with Margaret Cousins, Sarojini Naidu and eight other Indian women, went to meet Mr. Montague to demand votes for Indian women.[22]

Remarkable individuals, such as Pandita Ramabai, Anandibai Joshi, Tarabai Shinde, Haimavati Sen and Saraladevi challenged patriarchal constraints,[23] at least in their own lives. Some went on to participate in the emerging nationalist movement. Another leader, Swarnakumari Devi, sister of the poet Rabindranath Tagore, formed the Ladies Society in Calcutta in 1882, for educating and imparting skills to widows and other poor women, to help them become economically self-reliant. The National Conference was formed at the third session of the Indian National Congress in 1887 to provide a forum for the discussion of social issues. The Bharat Mahila Parishad was the women's wing of this and was inaugurated in 1905.

2.2. The Impact of Women's Movements on Gender Issues and Women's Identity after 1920

In this section, I will analyze the role and status of women in India after 1920.

2.2.1. Responses from Select Social and Political Associations and Unions

From 1920 to 1970, Indian feminists focused on gaining equality by forming associations for women. Saraladevi Chaudhurani, a feminist and a nationalist who actively participated in both the social reform and nationalist movements, founded the Bharat Stree Mahamandal in Allahabad in 1910.[24]

In 1918, during the early spurt of nationalist agitation, a group of progressive women with the common goal of helping distressed women and children launched the Women's Indian Association at Visakhapatnam in Andhra Pradesh.[25] This remained highly limited in

---

[22] Kumar, *The History of Doing*, 48.

[23] Geraldine Forbes, 'Medical Careers and Health Care for Indian Women: Patterns of Control', *Women's History Review* 3.4 (1994): 519.

[24] Samita Sen, 'Toward a Feminist Politics? The Indian Women's Movement in Historical Perspective', in World Bank Report, *Policy Research Report on Gender and Development Series 9* (April 2000), 14.

[25] Women's Indian Association, 'About Us', http://www.womensindia.org/about_us (accessed on 10 August 2011).

class and caste composition, and failed to spread outside the Madras presidency. A branch of the International Council of Women, the National Council of Indian Women (1925) and All-India Women's Conference (1927) were born subsequently.[26] Mehribai Tata, the wife of Sir Dorab Tata and one of the richest women in India, along with other wealthy women, initiated the National Council of Indian Women in order to liberate women from the clutches of various social evils.[27]

As a result of various efforts made by the associations, women almost gained acceptance as equals in the political and social arenas in the nation-to-be. However, the hegemony of the associations was short-lived, as priorities changed with the gathering of momentum of the national freedom movement. By mid-1940s, the associations ceased to promote women's causes in a general sense because their ideology had turned Hinduistic, their membership was limited to the middle class, and their nature was too urban to appeal to or adequately represent all Indian women.[28]

In 1954, under the leadership of Aruna Asif Ali, the Communist Party of India developed the National Federation of Indian Women in order to speak up for women's freedom. *Shramik Sangathana* was formed in 1972 at Maharashtra, in order to protect women from domestic violence.[29] In the same year, Gandhian socialists broke away from the Textile Labor Association to form the Self-Employed Women's Association (SEWA) under the leadership of Ela Bhatt. It aimed to empower poor women working in the informal sector so that they could secure employment and self-reliance.[30] In 1973, Mrinal Gore from the Socialist Party joined women from the Marxist Communist Party of India to form the United Women's Anti-Price Rise Front, which turned into a mass movement of women seeking consumer protection. In 1973–1974, the women's sector of the Leninist Communist party in

---

[26] Sen, 'Toward a Feminist Politics?', 15.

[27] Sweta Narayanan, 'Women Taking Action: A Survey of Chennai Women's Organizations', 8, http://www.prajnya.in/chennaiorgs.pdf (accessed on 10 August 2011),.

[28] Geraldin H. Forbes, *Women in Modern India* (Cambridge: CUP, 1998), 83.

[29] Amirta Basu, 'Indigenous Feminism Tribal Radicalism and Grassroots Mobilization in India', in M.J. Diamond (ed.), *Women and Revolution: Global Expressions* (Netherlands: Kluwer Academic Publishers, 1998), 250.

[30] John Blaxall, *India's Self-Employed Women's Association (SEWA) — Empowerment through Mobilization of Poor Women on a Large Scale* (Washington: World Bank, 2004), 1.

India initiated efforts to protect women from various oppressions and discriminations. When the Indian government declared Emergency in June 1975, many of these associations began to actively challenge society's traditional attitudes, rejecting its unacceptable behaviours and practices toward women.[31]

2.2.2. Legislation in Favour of Women

The Constitution of India guarantees equality to all Indian women in Article 14, no discrimination by the State in Article 15(1), equality of opportunity in Article 16, and equal pay for equal work in Article 39(d). In addition, it allows special provisions to be made by the State in favour of women and children in Article 15(3), renounces practices that are derogatory to the dignity of women in Article 51(A) (e), and also allows for provisions to be made by the State for securing just and humane conditions of work and maternity relief in Article 42.

The Dowry Prohibition Act, No. 28 of 1961, was passed to prohibit the giving or taking of dowry, which is one of the most derogatory practices against women. In order to protect women better, this act was further amended by Amendment Acts 63 of 1984 and 43 of 1986.

The Department of Women and Child Development was set up in 1985, as a part of the Ministry of Human Resource Development, to give a much needed impetus to the holistic development of women and children. With effect from 30 January, 2006, the Department has been upgraded to a Ministry.

The National Commission for Women (NCW) was set up as a statutory body in January 1992 under the National Commission for Women Act No. 20 of 1990 of the Government of India. It was to review the constitutional and legal safeguards for women, to recommend remedial legislative measures, to facilitate the redress of grievances, and to advise the government on all policy matters affecting women.

The Department of Women & Child Development circulated the National Policy for the Empowerment of Women (2001) for implementation. The goal of this policy is to bring about the

---

[31] Lina Fruzzeti, 'Kinship Identity and Issues of Nationalism, Culture and Power and Agency', in Lina Fruzzetti and Sirpa Tenhunen (eds), *Culture, Power, and Agency: Gender in Indian Ethnography* (Kolkata: Stree, 2006), 16.

advancement, development and empowerment of women. The Protection of Women from Domestic Violence Act 2005 is an act to provide for more effective protection of the rights of women, who are victims of violence of any kind occurring within the family and for matters connected therewith or incidental thereto. At present, the Women Reservation Bill demands 33% reserved representation of women in the *gram-panchayat*[32] and municipal elections. This bill was passed by the Upper House (Rajya Sabha) on 9 March, 2010, and is awaiting approval of the Lower House (Lok Sabha).

3. Contemporary Gender Issues and Women's Identity in India

Identity and gender roles in India are influenced by two factors: the first is one's own moral voice and internal judgment;[33] the other involves societal pressures and cultural expectations.[34] It is important to note that women in certain cultures (so also men) tend to allow the society around them define them and thus determine who they are, what they can be and do. How much can an Indian woman's identity and role be precisely determined in India, in the context of changing societal pressures and cultural expectations? Understanding the realities of one's 'assigned' identity and 'asserted' identity will help us analyze the quandary of identity better.

3.1. *Assigned Identity and Gender Equality*

Assigned identity is an identity and description of self that originates outside the self.[35] Despite the fact that women have proved themselves equal to men in terms of their capability, the abuse of women in

---

[32] This refers to a village assembly, which is a form of local village government.

[33] A. Roland, 'The Self in Cross-Civilizational Perspective: An Indian-Japanese-American Comparison', in Rebecca C. Curtis (ed.), *The Relational Self Theoretical Convergences in Psychoanalysis and Social Psychology* (New York: Guilford Press, 1990), 160–80.

[34] Steve Derne, 'Beyond Institutional and Impulsive Conceptions of Self Family Structure and the Socially Anchored Real Self', *Journal of the Society for Psychological Anthropology* 20.3 (1992): 259–88.

[35] Richard Jenkins, 'Rethinking Ethnicity: Identity, Categorization and Power', *Ethnic and Racial Studies* 17.2 (1994): 197–223.

contemporary India highlights the fact that women continue to be considered inferior. Common forms of women abuse include female foeticide, domestic violence, dowry death or violent dowry harassment, mental and physical tortures, and sexual trafficking.

Under-utilization of women is another indicator of inequality. Though women's enrollment in professional schools has increased, as have the number of women graduates with honours from excellent business and engineering schools, women are still not adequately represented in the workforce. Most top positions in Indian corporations are still held by men.[36] The percentage of women in the management sectors of India is roughly 3% to 6%.[37]

A study of Indian women in the workplace notes the negative impact of stereotyping women managers. Male managers are viewed as able in the areas of sales, marketing and production, as being good leaders, decision makers and bosses, and as capable of handling challenging assignments. On the other hand, Indian women are viewed as able in areas of public relations, human relations and administrative positions at junior levels, or in fields such as fashion and beauty.[38] Kumar and Bhatia conclude as they write on women's entrepreneurship:

> women own tremendous potentials to contribute towards economic development. The question is to what extent the society can benefit from such potentials? The answer to this question lies on the way the society intends to harness such resources and policies and strategies it frames to incorporate female in the economic mainstream.[39]

Women are not considered as capable as men in the bureaucratic sector. The *Times of India*, a leading daily newspaper, notes that:

> The recent bureaucratic reshuffle has once again proved that the women IAS cannot be trusted to shoulder heavy responsibilities. Almost all the women IAS officers have been given light weight assignments and not a single officer

---

[36] Ashok Gupta, Manjulika Koshal and Rajindar K. Koshal, 'Women Managers in India: Challenges and Opportunities', in Herbert J. Davis, Samir R. Chatterjee and Mark Heuer (eds), *Management in India: Trends and Transition* (New Delhi: Response Books, 2006), 285–312.

[37] P.S. Budhwar, D.S. Saini, and J. Bhatnagar, 'Women in Management in the New Economic Environment: The Case of India', *Asia Pacific Business Review* 11.2 (2005): 179–93.

[38] P. Khandelwal, 'Gender Stereotypes at Work: Implications for Organizations', *Indian Journal of Training and Development* 32.2 (2002): 72–83.

[39] Jayant Kumar, 'Hitesh Bhatia, Employment to Entrepreneurship: Participation of Women in Indian Labor Force', *Women Link* 16 (2010): 15–21.

has been found fit to handle bigger command, despite the fact that four of the women officers are Principal Secretaries.[40]

Domestic service is emerging as the largest segment of female employment in India. Neetha writes:

> As per National Sample Survey Organization (NSSO) estimates in 2004–2005, the number of workers employed in private households, largely as domestic workers, are 4.75 million workers. Of these 3.05 million women are in the urban areas. The percentage of domestic workers in total female employment in the service sector increase from 11.8 per cent in 1999–2000 to 27.1 per cent in 2004–2005 — a phenomenal increase about 2.25 million in a short span of five years.[41]

The household sector shows a high degree of feminization with 87.4% of the workers being women. It was, however, a male-dominated occupation during the pre-independence period of India.[42] Increase in the percentage of women in the household sector denotes the intentional imposition of inferior status on women by society.

In the agricultural sector, women have a greater role. In the Indian Himalayas, a pair of bullocks works 1,064 hours, a man 1212 hours and a woman 3485 hours in a year on a one hectare farm. This illustrates the significant contribution of women to agricultural production.[43] In spite of women's high productive value, society still assumes that men are the farmers and women only play a 'supportive role', as a farmer's wife.

3.2. Asserted Identity and Gender Equality

Asserted identity is self-described and determines the sociality of self.[44] There are various arenas in society where women in India excel by virtue of their proven abilities. India had one woman Prime Minister and has at present two strong women in the offices of the President and the Chair of the Lower House of the Parliament. From 1962 till date, there have been thirteen democratically elected women chief ministers, who have administered their offices in ten states of India.

---

[40] [n.a.], 'No Woman on Top', *Times of India* (5 June 2003).

[41] N. Neetha, 'Domestic Workers: Profile and Emerging Concerns', *Labour File* (2010): 8.

[42] N. Neetha 'Making of Female Breadwinners: Migration of Social Networking of Women Domestic in Delhi', *Economic and Political Weekly* 39.17 (2004): 168–88.

[43] V. Shiva, *Most Farmers in India are Women* (New Delhi: FAO, 1991), 7.

[44] Richard Jenkins, 'Rethinking Ethnicity', 197–223.

The late Prime Minister Indira Gandhi was nicknamed *Iron Lady of India* for her courage and accomplishments.

There are eighteen Indian Administrative Service (IAS) women officers out of 160 officers, who serve in the Union Government of India.[45] Nine out of 165 university level institutions have women vice-chancellors. Out of 598 officers (Registrars, finance officers, librarians, deans, and directors of student welfare), 21 are female. Out of 446 heads of department and principals, 43 are women.[46]

The demographics of the Call Centre workforce in India confirms the effectiveness and courage of women, where late night shifts are an inevitable part of employment. Sahaya points out that, 'Amongst more than 1,60,000 men and women on the payroll of Call Centres in India, approximately 45 per cent are women. In some companies, the figure can be as high as 70 per cent.'[47]

Women of certain categories and societal classes (as mentioned above) remain as a signpost of their new identity in India today. These women are symbols of dignity, ability, courage, reverence, respect, honour and nobility.

3.3. Present Identity Ambiguities

Since the social system in India is rapidly changing, it certainly contributes to changes in the status of the individuals in society. Though this change has impacted women to a certain extent, it does not mean that women are out of the clutches of gender discrimination in society. The aforesaid dual realities of assigned and asserted realities, and the equal and unequal nature of women's status, are being increasingly manifested in society today.

3.3.1. Identity of Significance and Insignificance

Thirty-three per cent of women representation in civic government is an outstanding milestone in the journey of women equality, which

---

[45] [n.a.], '3 Women IAS Officers Promoted as Secretaries', *Times of India* (11 September 2004).

[46] Sowmini Sebastian, 'Higher Education and Violence Against Women', *Journal of Women Studies* 1 (2009): 56.

[47] Amita Sahaya, 'Call Centres—A Road to Empowerment', *Women's Link* (2010), 16.

was accomplished on 8 March, 2010. This denotes women's significant identity in society. On the other hand, sons are still preferred over daughters, which is women's insignificant identity in practice. Female infanticide has been a known practice in India for centuries. It is estimated that 5–7 lakh female foetuses are aborted every year, despite stringent laws prohibiting the practice.[48] In 2005, UNICEF reported that it was prosperity, rather than poverty, that supported son preference and female foeticide.[49] It supposes that sons are more likely to be of benefit than daughters to their parents in the society since they have religious significance, perform necessary funeral rites, and maintain the spiritual and physical lineage that preserves the important connection with previous generations.

3.3.2. Identity of Exaltation and Subjection

Venerating India by addressing *Bharatha Matha* and naming rivers with feminine names are exemplary acts of honouring the feminine gender. However, Renuka Chowdhury, the Minister for Women and Child Welfare, voiced the paradoxical reality that in India around 70% of women were victims of violent acts in one form or another.[50] Strong cultural biases and attitudes concerning male superiority are seen in many Indian men, who believe husbands are entitled to control their wives. Violence against women is partly the result of gender relations that assume men to be superior to women.

3.3.3. Identity of Invincibility and Vulnerability

Stories of Rani Samyuktha, Rani Mangamma, and Jhansi Rani remain symbols of the bravery and courage of Indian women. Late Prime Minister Indira Gandhi is another icon of the same kind. Ever since 1972, India has been served by several women IPS[51] officers in various

[48] Subodh Varma, 'A Million Mutinies Now', *Times of India* (14 August 2010), http://timesofindia.indiatimes.com/india/A-million-mutinies-now/articleshow/6308883.cms (accessed on 1 September 2010).

[49] UNICEF, 'Prosperity, Not Poverty behind Female Feticide', http://www.unicef.org/india/child_protection_948.htm (accessed on 2 September 2010).

[50] Delores Friesen and Mary Shamshoian, 'Peace Making in the Family: A Systemic View of Domestic Violence', in Frampton Fox (ed.), *Violence and Peace* (Pune: CMS, 2010), 204.

[51] Indian Police Service, which is one of the highest academic credentials for high level police officers in India.

capacities. The first woman IPS officer, Kiran Bedi, is an outstanding officer known for her courage and bravery. While narrations of the braveries of these invincible characters build a positive identity for women, accounts depicting women's vulnerability mars it considerably. Sexual harassments and rape are common abusive acts that women face in contemporary India. There were 18,233 rape incidents officially reported in 2004 and 21,467 cases in 2008; 34,567 cases of molestation were registered in 2004 and 40,413 in 2008.[52] Sexual harassment is commonly found in public transportations, auditoriums, work areas, and coeducational institutions. A staggering 44,098 incidents of sexual harassment were reported in 2002 with 121 women being sexually harassed every day and one every 12 minutes in 2002. An increase of 20.6 % was seen in incidents of sexual harassment between 1997 and 2002. Displaced aggression[53] is a common reason behind most of the rape incidents in India. The vulnerability of women, possible societal rejection of the rape victims, and societal shame are the factors why men have the gall to commit these atrocities.

3.3.4. Identity of Parity and Disparity

In no region of the developing world are women equal to men in legal, social and economic rights.[54] The Constitution and the judiciary, other than few religious personal laws, guarantee equality of women. Women have occupied the highest legislative offices in various capacities. Yet, there are few avenues where disparity is found unchallenged. Panvar, professor and an economist comments:

> Girls are compelled to limit their activities in society. A sense of insecurity is generated in them and thus limits the acquainting opportunities they could have availed interacting with opposite sex. They are advised to train themselves in managing household activities, this way their canvas of activities is contracted. They are not given an opportunity to develop their innate abilities and talent. What does this behavior towards woman-kind show? Putting restrictions on activities and desires to live life in a certain manner is

---

[52] National Crime Records Bureau Ministry of Home Affairs, *Crime in India 2008*, 81, http://ncrb.nic.in/cii2008/cii-2008/Chapters.htm (accessed on 21 August 2009).

[53] When a rapist uses the rape of a wife, girlfriend or mother, as an outlet for his anger.

[54] *Linking Gender Equality to the Millennium Development Goals*, a report by the Gender and Development Group, World Bank, Washington DC (4 April 2003), 4, http://www.worldbank.org/gender (accessed on 29 August 2011).

a symbol of manhood, it is so, and we still live in a patriarchal feudal society which does not want to disturb status-quo when it comes to gender equation.[55]

India has the largest recorded number of widows in the world — 33 million and growing. Widows remain oppressed by norms, traditions, and cultural expectations of the past.[56] Most of the widows remain single and work for a living, bringing up children, coping with loneliness and the pressures of life. Despite the fact that widows are lawfully permitted to remarry, this has not yet made a significant impact in the lives of Indian widows.[57] Widows, when they remarry, can still be refused the property of their first husband.[58] Remarriage by widowers is still more accepted in the society than widow remarriage.

4. Reflections

Gender and women identity issues, perspectives of religions, contributions of various movements and legislation, and contemporary status of women and their ambiguous identities have been discussed in this paper. Following are the reflections from the narrated background.

4.1. Women's Identity, Equality and Roles

'Citizen of India' is the foremost identity for men and women of India. This significant identity defines a promise of equality and justice for both men and women within the country's constitutional framework.

Certain gender inequalities victimize many women. Sen presents some of examples: (i) mortality inequality, (ii) natality inequality, (iii) basic facility inequality, (iv) special opportunity inequality, (v) professional inequality, (vi) ownership inequality, and (vii) household inequality.[59] Other than natality inequality, all other inequalities are often from identity issues.

---

[55] Shiv Prakash Panvar, '21st Century Perspective and Crimes Against Women', *Central India Law Quarterly* 12, 586.

[56] Pritha Das Gupta, 'The Unheard Voices Silent Stories of Widows in India', *Journal of Women Studies* 2 (2010): 4–5.

[57] Geraldine Forbes, *Women in Modern India* (Cambridge: CUP, 1998), 223–45.

[58] Uma Chakravarthy, *Gendering Caste Through a Feminist Lens* (Kolkatta: Stree, 2003), 125.

[59] Amartya Sen, 'Many Faces of Gender Inequality', *Frontline* (9 November 2001).

Distinct gender roles for common good do not necessarily mean inequality. Inequality is the fruit of intentional gender-biased discriminations. Any intentional act against women in this manner is a social and spiritual illness and is detrimental to society. The summary review of UNESCO's accomplishments since the Fourth World Conference on Women states: 'Gender equality means that the different behaviour, aspirations, and needs of women and men are considered, valued and favoured equally. It does not mean that women and men have to become the same, but that their rights, responsibilities and opportunities will not depend on whether they are born male or female.'[60] Distinct roles for men and women with no gender bias is possible. Distinct roles with impeccable equality is possible as well.

4.2. Women's Identity and Feminists

While most of the agencies of feminism intend to promote feminist solutions for gender discrimination, they often seem idealistic. Feminism is an inadequate solution to the real issue of inequality of women in a sinful society. It is essential for feminists to maintain an unambiguous distinction between equality and roles. Gender refers to the biological differences between men and women, and describes socially constructed roles, rights and responsibilities that communities and societies consider appropriate for men and women. Biological equality is impractical; so also, certain roles men and women hold are not transferrable. Feminists need to remember that the quest for the equality of roles should not lead to inter-role conflicts.[61] Equality in dignity, respect and justice should be retained in distinct roles held by men and women. Society must distinguish between the nature of the role and the person of the role. An ideal illustration could be drawn from the scriptures. It portrays equality by accounting that God made man and woman in his own image and likeness. The same scriptures categorically designate man as being invested with the

---

[60] *Gender Equality and Equity* (Paris: Unit for the Promotion of the Status of Women and Gender Equality, UNESCO, May 2000), 5, http://unesdoc.unesco.org/images/0012/001211/121145e.pdf (accessed on 26 August 2011).

[61] Uma Shankar Jha, Premalata Pujari (eds), *Inter-Role Conflict: Inside the House and Outside the Door in Indian Women Today*, vol. 3, (New Delhi: Kansihka Publishers, 1998), 149–226.

role of headship over his spouse. Headship does not make the wife inferior, since she is made in the same image of God that the husband is made. Headship and submission to the husband (Eph. 5.21, 23) is a biblical mandate. Headship essentially calls the husband to sacrificial love, which has none of the usual assumed actions of headship such as commanding, controlling, restricting activity, etc. Indeed, if Christ has assumed his headship to set us free with the truth, then the role of the husband in a patriarchal society is to free his wife in whatever way he can. Feminists must know that not all the roles of men and women are transferrable, but all the roles are significant, equal and complementary.

4.3. Status of Women at Present in the Religious Realm

I see discrimination of women having diminished since 1920. In particular, post-1970 has witnessed a dramatic revolution taking place in terms of the freedom and justice for women. Nevertheless, we cannot dogmatically declare that women are no longer considered inferior beings. While the society knows that women have the same potential and capability as men, it continues to not fully recognize and utilize this.

Certain Hindu and Jain temples and shrines in India still have restrictions and reservations against the entry of women. The role of Priestess in general is not yet recognized among the Hindus; women *Madathipathis* are seldom found in the Hindu sector. *Sharia* still curtails equality for women in certain areas; it is commented, 'Even though many changes have taken place in the role and status of women in India and also in the world, no spectacular transformation has taken place in the case of Muslim women.'[62] Contemporary Christian churches in India speak about equality of women but are far behind in practice; there are churches where the spiritual gifts and abilities of women are unused or under-used.

It is obvious that a wide gap still exists between the goals enunciated in the Constitution, legislation, policies, plans, programmes, and related mechanisms and the situational reality of the status of women in India.

---

[62] Saukath Azim, *Muslim Women* (New Delhi: Rewat Publications, 1997), 15.

4.4. Christian Response

Though the status of women has improved since 1920, gender discrimination continues to hibernate in all spheres of societal life. Identity issues breed broken homes, single parenting situations, lesbianism, increasing divorce rates, alcoholism, premarital sex, rape, women molestation, and suicide. It is my opinion that neither laws nor efforts made by the women movements can solve the issues before us.

Can religions ameliorate the marred identity of women in society in order to build equality? At the personal and familial levels, religions have a greater impact on the people of India when compared to the government. Therefore, I believe that the current challenges and injustices faced by women can most successfully be met by efforts in the religious sphere rather than through the work of feminist associations and statutory laws of the land.

As a Christian leader, I see that the Church in India can respond to women's issues of identity, equality and role development both from inside and outside the Church, with far greater efficacy than other religions can, since the scriptures do strongly advocate for gender equality. It is an undeniable fact that women are a great source of strength and are capable instruments for transformation in the local churches in India. An outstanding author and a faculty member of Boston University writes:

> the overwhelming impression based on a sampling of both regional and ecclesiastical studies is that women constituted roughly a two-thirds majority of practicing Christians in the growing world church in the late twentieth and early twenty-first centuries. From a demographic perspective, Christianity is a women's religion. Studies of world Christianity, either as global force or as local movement, need to put women's issues at the center of our scholarship about the growth of Christianity in Asia, Africa, and Latin America.[63]

The Bible portrays God's establishing equality[64] of men and women, women's dignity[65], divinely determined equally responsible roles for

---

[63] Dana R. Robert, 'World Christianity as a Women's Movement', *International Bulletin of Missionary Research* 30.4 (2006): 183.

[64] God's image and likeness in men and women.

[65] James A. Borland, 'Women in the Life and Teachings of Jesus', in John Piper and Wayne Grudem (eds), *Recovering Biblical Manhood and Womanhood: A Response to Evangelical Feminism* (Downers Grove: Crossway, 1991), 114.

a pleasant home and society,[66] and equally significant witnesses for Christ.[67] Hence, the Church at large can certainly contribute to women's equality and empowerment by making known to women (and men) in the world what the Bible says about their status and role. The Church has a critical role to play in delivering this goal, both within the church community and beyond.[68]

I have outlined ways in which I foresee the Church in India being able to respond to the changing identities of the 21st century Indian women:

1. Since the Bible consists of guidelines, apart from theology and doctrines, for mankind's holistic transformation, the church needs to find answers for contemporary social issues of various kinds, pertaining to women, through a comprehensive exegetical study of the Bible. These biblical solutions need to be made available for all men and women, irrespective of faith, creed and class, in their social and linguistic context and in an educative and accessible manner.

2. The situation with regard to the identity and role of women in the Church is not in any way different from what we find in society due to the fact that the culture from which Christianity originated was patriarchal. The identity and role of women in the Church in India is also very much conditioned by Indian culture as well as by the biblical tradition.[69] The accounts of Jewish patriarchal practices in the Bible led a few to subjugate women in Christian society. Christian couples need to demonstrate the distinction between submission and subjugation in order that non-Christian families may be educated in their neighborhood.

3. Churches may come forward and offer Christian forums and consultations on gender equality and women's roles. Non-Christians may be invited for programmes of this kind.

4. Churches can offer free legal opinions and directions to women victims in their respective pastorates, irrespective of faith and

---

[66] Larry Christenson, *The Christian Family* (Minneapolis: Bethany Fellowship, 1970), 18.
[67] Christenson, *The Christian Family*, 198.
[68] Liz Wade, 'Promote Gender Equality & Empower Women', *Aim* (January 2009): 11.
[69] Nirmala Vasanthakumar, 'Role and Identity of Women in the Church in India', http://www.womenutc.com/nirmala.htm (accessed on 29 August 2011).

244   *Indian and Christian: Changing Identities in Modern India*

creed. Since most of the victims are uneducated and economically weaker, most of their cries are unheard by the law and society.

5. Churches may enhance their ministries among women for a holistic development in a way that women are not only made stronger in spiritual disciplines but also in their holistic life development.

6. Christians must practice and promote widow re-marriages.

7. Churches need to give adequate representation to women in their administrative, pastoral and leadership positions, in order to display the biblical teaching of women equality.

8. Churches should stand alongside the efforts of legislation and other associations, in their efforts to achieve women's equality.

4.5. Conclusion

If one were to look for an image that best portrays an Indian woman, it would not be the gracious, sweetly smiling beauty with folded hands found on the travel posters. It would be a strong wiry woman, straight-backed under some heavy load balanced on her head (bricks, water pots, firewood, or grass for fodder).[70] Over the last five decades, there have been considerable advancements to empower and develop women.[71] Efforts to build appropriate women identity are not being defeated; yet we need to admit realistically that victory is far away.

Select References

Abishekananda, Swami. *India And Her People*. New York: Vedanta Society, 1906.

Arunachalam, Jaya. *Women's Equality: A Struggle for Survival*. New Delhi: Gyan Books, 2005.

Azim, Saukath. *Muslim Women*. New Delhi: Rewat Publications, 1997.

Chakrabarty, Renu. *Communists in Indian Women's Movement, 1940–1950*. New Delhi: People's Publishing House, 1980.

Chakravarthy, Uma. *Gendering Caste Through a Feminist Lens*. Kolkatta: Stree, 2003.

---

[70] Geetanjali Kolanad, *Culture Shock* (Singapore: Marshall Cavendish, 2005), 70.

[71] K.G. Gayathridevi, 'Contours of Women's Development: A Synthesis of Thoughts, Efforts, and Challenges', *Journal of Social and Economic Development* 11.1 (2009): 97–119.

Christenson, Larry. *The Christian Family.* Minneapolis: Bethany Fellowship, 1970.

Davis, Herbert J, Samir R. Chatterjee and Mark Heuer (eds). *Management in India: Trends and Transition.* New Delhi: Response Books, 2006.

Diamond, M. J. *Women and Revolution: Global Expressions.* Netherland: Kluwer Academic Publishers, 1998.

Forbes, Geraldine. *Women in Modern India.* Cambridge: Cambridge University Press, 1998.

Fox, Frampton (ed.). *Violence and Peace.* Pune: CMS, 2010.

Fruzzetti, Lina and Sirpa Tenhunen (eds). *Culture, Power, and Agency: Gender in Indian Ethnography.* Kolkata: Stree, 2006.

Gooptu, Suparna. *Cornelia Sorabji: Indian Pioneer Women Lawyer.* USA: OUP, 2006.

Joha, Uma Shankar and Premalata Pujari (eds). *Inter-Role Conflict: Inside the house and Outside the Door in Indian Women Today.* Vol. 3, New Delhi: Kansihka Publishers, 1998.

Kumar, Radha. *The History of Doing: An Illustrated Account of Movements for Women's Rights and Feminism in India 1800–1990.* London: verso. 1993.

Malone, T. Mary. *Women & Christianity.* New York: Orbis Books, 2003.

Manjapuria, Trilok C. and Rohit K. Majupuria. *Gods, Goddesses & Religious Symbols of a Hinduism, Buddhism & Tantrism.* India: M. Devi, Lashkar, 2005.

Narasimhan, Sakuntala. *Sati: Widow Burning in India.* India: Harper Collins, 1998.

Pickthall, Mohamad Marmaduke. *The Meanings of the Glorious Quran.* Delhi: Nusrat Ali Nasri, 1992.

Piper, John and Wayne Grudem (eds). *Recovering Biblical Manhood and Womanhood: A Response to Evangelical Feminism.* Downers Grove: Crossway, 1991.

Raines, John Raines. *The Justice Men Owe Women; Positive Resources from World Religions.* Minneapolis: Fortress Press, 2001.

Shiva, V. *Most Farmers in India are Women.* New Delhi: FAO, 1991.

Indian and European Muslim Identity: Possible Implications for Christian Political Thought

Sean Oliver-Dee[*]

1. Value and Hypothesis

This paper argues that the Christian communities in Europe have been directly and indirectly affected by the Muslim debates over the nature of their faith in relationship to questions of citizenship. As yet, there does not seem to have been a parallel discussion within the Indian Christian communities. Is there a reason for that, or is it simply a question of time?

In the context of this question, a difficult decision has had to be made, for the scope of this study necessitates omitting the valuable contributions of Muhammad 'Abduh, Sayyid Qutb and Fatima Mernissi amongst others. However, in the context of focussing on India and comparing it with European trends, geographical and cultural boundaries had to be declared.

2. Symmetries and Divergences for Indian and European Muslims

In India, Muslims have been present in significant numbers for almost a thousand years whilst in Western Europe Muslim immigrants came in significant numbers only following the Second World War. Given the differing periods of historical interaction between Islam and other faiths (and none) in the two continents, one would naturally assume that the Muslim minority communities in each continent would be in vastly dissimilar positions in relation to the majority cultures. For example, if we were to follow the model of integration that is assumed more

Sean Oliver-Dee is the Associate Researcher, Inter-Religious Affairs, for the Archbishop of Canterbury's Representative to the EU. He is also the Inter-Religious Advisor for the Diocese of Peterborough. This paper is based upon the research and writing done in his forthcoming book, *Muslim Minorities and Citizenship: Authorities, Communities and Islamic Law* (London: I.B. Tauris, 2012).

generally in Europe and the West, we would expect to see a gradual integration of cultures, even to a point of some synthesis, as successive generations of Muslims and Hindus grew up together over the course of time. That has not been the case. This is not the space to question why there has been this apparent lack of integration, or to even think about possible solutions to it. Rather, the focus for this paper is simply the existence of the dynamic.

Indian Muslims have found themselves in a position where they have had to deal with disempowerment, to a 'Christian' state initially, and thereafter to a secular state.[1] In coming to terms with this, they produced (and continue to do so) a flurry of ideological evaluation which fed into the broader 'Muslim Reformist movement'. These writings still impact the thinking of Muslims in the UK (and further afield), who continue to grapple with the same issues of citizenship, as well as the nature of the *ummah* and *shari'a* in a minority situation. Indeed, for British Muslims, many of whom have roots in the Indian Subcontinent, one might argue that those same questions of loyalty and citizenship to non-Muslim authority have simply been uprooted from India and re-planted in the UK.[2] Consequently, the questions of identity, which the Muslim reformers in India were asking during the British Raj, have a direct relevance to these communities (communities that constitute about 70% of the total Muslim population of the UK).[3]

The situation of Muslims in the UK and in continental Europe is slightly different from that of their Indian brethren.

Much of the past decade following the 9/11 attack and the other European attacks which followed it, has been spent in both refuting various understandings of Islam in the European media and, simultaneously

---

[1]   The October 2010 ruling of the Indian Supreme Court on Ayodhya also prompted the *Daily Times* to report on the lack of opportunities for Indian Muslims, citing two statistics: 'Muslims account for fewer than seven percent of public service employees, only five percent of railway workers and there are only about 30,000 Muslims in India's 1.3 million-strong military.' [n.a.], 'Muslims Angry with the Mosque Verdict, but India Calm' in *Daily Times* (6 October 2010).

[2]   One would suggest that a similar dynamic is being seen in Continental Europe. However, the essential difference is that Muslims in Continental Western Europe are mainly from North Africa and Turkey—countries which are Muslim majority states. They are therefore moving from majority to minority situations.

[3]   P. Lewis, *Young, British and Muslim* (London: Continuum, 2007), 22.

advocating on behalf of a greater integration of Islam within European public life.[4] At present, Islam is viewed with some suspicion; there has been a swing to the political right all over Europe and European politicians have responded to this by bringing in a series of draconian laws against veiling and, in Switzerland, a ban against the building of tall minarets.

Whilst this public battle is being fought, there has been extensive competition amongst differing groups and sects to become 'the public voice of Islam'.[5] Who will eventually emerge on top is impossible to predict, but the needs of the various European governments to bring Muslim communities into an 'integrated' national or transnational state means that the search for suitable representative voices will continue.

The issue of minority status for Muslims therefore contains common elements for both European and Indian Muslims. For both there is a sense of victimhood and concerns about insularity from the wider society. At the same time, there is a desire amongst Muslims to understand their situation in relation to expressions of their faith. One of the most visible expressions of public faith for Muslims on both continents is the place of *shari'a*. Given the importance of *shari'a* within Islam, it is natural therefore to ask how Muslims have engaged with their minority status and how their thinking might impact Christians on both continents, especially as Christians are a minority faith in secular humanist Europe, as well as in India.[6]

---

[4] Perhaps the best example of the dynamic is the publication of the 2008 *European Muslim Charter* which sought to be both a unifying document for the disparate Muslim communities as well as an 'outreach document to politicians and commentators, encouraging a greater role of Islam in Europe. The document can be found at http://www.google.co.uk/search?client=safari&rls=en&q=european+muslim+charter&ie=UTF-8&oe=UTF-8&redir_esc=&ei=55MJTsKxCpKGhQeKm8nrDw. The issue of training Imams for Europe, in Europe, is a very practical consideration, in which issues of identity and context are being worked on.

[5] The issues connected with this problem of multiplicity of 'Islams' are examined in A. Azmah and E. Fokas, *Islam in Europe: Diversity, Identity and Focus* (Cambridge: CUP, 2007), 91–3.

[6] Although they still constitute the largest faith group in Europe, figures suggest that generally atheism is on the increase over the continent as a whole. The Eurobarometer poll of 2005 asked a large sample whether they believed in a god: 52% across the continent said they did. The UN estimates that, of a total of 891 million people, approximately 300 million would be Christian and 37 million would be Muslim. See also P. Jenkins, *God's Continent: Christianity, Islam and Europe's Religious Crisis* (New York/Oxford: OUP, 2007), which is full of fascinating statistical data.

3. A Long-Standing Problem

At the heart of the issue of a Muslim's relationship with a non-Muslim state lies the fundamental question of whether a Muslim can give loyalty to a non-Muslim ruler. The question is intimately connected to the role of *shari'a* and the nature of the *ummah* because of the religio-political orientation of Islam in its early years: for theologically, the Caliphs, whilst not taking on the Muhammad's prophetic role, retained his headship of the burgeoning Imperial *ummah* which cast him as the implementer of *shari'a*.[7]

On the Subcontinent, this issue has taken on an even greater significance in relation to an Indian Muslim's attitude towards conflict between their national home and the Islamic Republic of Pakistan. For the Indian government therefore, there are natural concerns about possible divided loyalties amongst a large minority of their subjects (approximately 13% currently).[8] This issue of non-Muslim headship over Muslims is therefore not new on the Subcontinent. Instead the problems encountered by the Imperial British government, in relation to what became known as the 'Caliphate Question', have simply passed to the Independent one, but with the added issue of Pakistan on its borders.[9]

In Europe, there are no threats to national security of the nature that Pakistan presents to India. Nevertheless, intelligence analysts, government officials and media commentators in the UK as well as in continental Europe are concerned about their Muslim communities.[10] According to Emerson, these communities seem to be becoming increasingly, rather than decreasingly radicalised against the state.[11]

[7] See P. Crone, *Medieval Islamic Political Thought* (Edinburgh: Edinburgh University Press, 2005), 10–13.

[8] The Pew Forum's 2009 report on global Muslim populations put India's Muslim population at 13.4%. See http://pewforum.org/uploadedfiles/Topics/Demographics/Muslimpopulation.pdf .

[9] ,See M. Sageman, *Understanding Terror Networks* (Pennsylvania: University of Pennsylvania Press, 2004), 9; S. Oliver-Dee, *The Caliphate Question: British Government and Islamic Governance* (Lanham: Rowman and Littlefield, 2009), 43–51.

[10] See, for example, the British Government's paper *Prevent Review,* launched in May 2011.

[11] For more details and statistical data, see M. Emerson (ed.), *Ethno-Relgious Conflicts in Europe: Typologies in Europe's Muslim Communities* (Brussels: Centre for European Policy Studies, 2009).

The issue of Muslim citizenship has therefore become urgent on both continents for similar, though slightly differing reasons.

4. Muslim Debates on Authority and Obedience.

4.1. Theology and Political Theory

Central to the issue of authority, loyalty and the nature of the *ummah* is the teaching of Muhammad himself as found in the Qur'an and Sunnah. Amongst the *ayah*s and Hadith that have been quoted to justify differing positions, Qur'an Q4:59 is considered the most important:

> Believers, obey Allah, obey the Apostle and those in authority among you. Should you disagree about anything refer it to Allah and the Apostle, if you truly believe in Allah and the Last Day. This will in the end be better and more just. [12]

The focus of discussion for all Muslims living under non-Muslim authority is 'those in authority among you'. Argument has raged amongst Muslim theologians and scholars for centuries over what the correct interpretation should be. For many of the early Muslim exegetes, 'those in authority' was taken to mean specifically Muslim military commanders.[13] Later, the concept was broadened to include 'people that loosen and bind' (ahl al-hal wa-l-'aqd).[14] During this period one might say that headship of Muslim over Muslim was assumed rather than ever explicitly discussed. Indeed, it was not until the Mongol hordes swept out of central Asia and conquered Muslim lands that the issue of

---

[12] A.J. Arberry, *The Koran Interpreted* (London/New York/Karachi: OUP, 1964).

[13] Al-Tabari, *Commentary on the Qur'an: Abridged Translation with Introduction and Notes by J. Cooper*, vol. 4 (Oxford: OUP/Hakim Investment Holdings Limited, 1987), 150–51. Walid Saleh, in his book on the formation of Tafsir, is critical of al-Tabari's methods and findings. However, he does admit al-Tabari's *Tafsir* as the first comprehensive version of the Sunni tradition. W.A. Saleh, *The Formation of the Classical Tafsir Tradition: The Qur'an Commentary of al-Tha'labi* (Leiden: Brill, 2003), 133, 156.

[14] See J. Schacht, *An Introduction to Islamic Law* (Oxford: Clarendon Press, 1982), 110; D.B. MacDonald, *Development of Muslim Theology, Jurisprudence and Constitutional Theory* (New York: Clarendon Press, 1903), 23.

non-Muslim headship had to be raised.[15] In that period, the exegete Ibn Kathir, who also recorded the interpretations of his predecessors, made specific provision in his work for Muslim obedience to non-Muslim rulers, as indeed did Ibn Taymiyya.[16]

4.2. The Subcontinent

In the modern period, luminaries such as Sayyid Ahmad Khan and Muhammed Mujeeb have also come to the same conclusion. Their interpretations have been largely based upon the Hanafi *shari'a* that dominates in North India and it was Khan himself who encouraged the North Indian *'ulama* to publish a *fatwa* which proclaimed that the British Empire was *dar-al-Islam*. This fundamental Hanafi ruling was based upon the concepts articulated by al-Shaybani in his *Law of the Nations*.[17] The central premise of this developing body of legal theory was 'expediency'.[18] However, even though pious pragmatism appears to have central to this *shari'a* code, Abu Hanafi himself held to the principle that a Muslim should rather emigrate than live permanently under the authority of a non-Muslim. Al-Shaybani countered the teaching of his master and decreed that the necessity for emigration had ended in the lifetime of Muhammad himself. He stated that there was therefore no need for Muslims who found themselves under non-Muslim authority

---

[15] In 1258, when the Abbasid capital of Baghdad was captured, the theologian who became known as the 'Father of Revolutions', Ibn Taymiyya, advised Muslims who were under the rule of the new non-Muslim rulers—the Mongols—to obey their rulers on the basis that Q4:59 did not specify Muslim headship when enjoining obedience to authority. However, once the Mongols had converted to Islam, the same Ibn Taymiyya issued a *fatwa* against them for continuing to rule through the Mongol legal code, the *Yasa*, rather than through the *shari'a*. It was upon that basis that he called for Muslims to overthrow their leaders. See E. Sivan, 'Ibn Taymiyya: Father of the Islamic Revolution, Medieval Theology and Modern Politics', *Encounter* 60.5 (1983): 41–9.

[16] Ibn Kathir, *Tafsir*, Abridged English Version, trans. A. Daryabadi (Medina: Dar Ibn Kathir, 2004), 92–4. Firestone makes some interesting observations on Ibn Kathir's exegetical approach in the course of his article on the Qur'anic teachings on war. R. Firestone, 'Disparity and Resolution in the Quranic Teachings on War: A Re-Evaluation of a Traditional Problem', *Journal of Near Eastern Studies* 56.1 (1997): 1–19.

[17] M. al-Shaybani, *The Islamic Law of Nations: Shaybani's Siyar*, trans. M. Khadduri (Baltimore: John Hopkins Press, 1996).

[18] al-Shaybani, *Islamic Law*, 21–3. See also J. Rahmen and S.C. Breau (eds.), *Religion, Human Rights and International Law: A Critical Examination of Islamic State Practices* (Leiden: Martinus Nijhoff, 2007), 81–114.

to consciously seek to live under Muslim authority instead, especially if the non-Muslim authority allowed for freedom of Islamic practice and worship, as the British did.[19]

The Caliphal ambassador and reformer Jamal ad-Din al-Afghani, refused to accept the principle of obedience to non-Muslim rulers. His theories were based upon the *rashidun* period and is evident most clearly in his quotation of Q49:13, where he suggests that, in the original *ummah*, leadership was based on piety, rather than ancestry.[20] Al-Afghani does not specify whether British Rule would be 'religious' in his own sense, though the implication appears to be negative given the fact that his ultimate goal, as described by Goldziher, 'was to unite Muslim states (including Shi'i Persia) into a single Caliphate, able to repulse European interference and recreate the glory of Islam.'[21] In essence, al-Afghani's stance was one of temporary submission, whereas Sayyid Ahmad Khan saw loyalty to one's ruler as a guiding principle, with the renewing of Islamic strength purely within the context of that rule. It is therefore not surprising that al-Afghani attacked Sayyid Ahmad Khan as a tool of British imperialism when he visited India during the late nineteenth century.

More alluring to some Muslims than the thought of unqualified submission to non-Muslim authority has been the position espoused by Mushir ul-Haq (the murdered former Vice-Chancellor of Kashmir University), Benazir Bhutto (the former Prime Minister of Pakistan) and Sayyid Jalaluddin 'Umri (the Deputy Head of Jama'at-i-Islami Hind who published *Ghayr Islami Riyasat Aur Musalman [A Non-Islamic State and Muslims]* in 2005). All of them espoused the concept of temporary submission whilst working towards the regeneration of Muslim power.

In coming to their conclusions 'Umri, Bhutto and ul-Haq focus upon pointing the way forward, encouraging a positive response to

[19] M. Shatzmiller (ed.), *Nationalism and Minority Identities in Islamic Societies* (Quebec: McGill University Press, 2005), 16. See also A. El Fadl, 'Islamic Law and Muslim Minorities: The Juristic Discourse on Muslim Minorities from the Second/Eighth to the Eleventh/Seventeenth Centuries', *Islamic Law and Society* 1.2 (1994): 141–87.

[20] Jamal al-Din al-Afghani, 'Jinsiyah wa al-Din al-Islamiyah', *Al-Urwah al al-Wurthqa* 2 (20 March, 1884), in R.G. Landen (trans. and ed.), *The Emergence of the Modern Middle East: Selected Readings* (New York: Van Nostrand Reihnold Company, 1970), 108.

[21] I. Goldziher, 'Djamal al-Din al-Afghani', in B. Lewis, Ch. Pellat and J. Schacht (eds), *Encyclopedia of Islam*, 2nd edn (Leiden/London: Brill/Luzac and Co., 1965).

the situation from Muslims.[22] They argue that Muslims should be both grateful that India is a secular, rather than a constitutionally Hindu state, and discontented with Islam's current position. They share the view that Muslim submission to non-Muslim authority in the short-term is sensible, but that this does not mean that a Muslim cannot engage in the democratic process in order to change the position of Islam within society in the long-term.[23]

At the far end of the scale from Khan were Maududi, Iqbal and Mohammed Ali.[24] They argued that Muslims cannot be properly Muslim if they live under non-Muslim rule: 'you can see that it is impossible for you to follow more than one Din at a time. Of various rulers only one can rule your lives: of various systems of law, only one can be the law of your lives.'[25] Clearly this feeds into the calls for a Muslim homeland as far as Iqbal was concerned, but for Maududi himself, the idea of Pakistan was an anathema to him. He did not recognise state boundaries in the context of Islam at all and instead argued that the only identity that mattered to a Muslim was that of the ummah.

4.3. UK and Europe

In Europe, such debates are at a far more germinal stage. Ramadan himself has proposed active Muslim participation in European cultural, social and political life on precisely the same basis as that of Mushir ul-Haq and Sayyid Ahmad Khan: gratitude that freedom of religion is permitted and a political and cultural activism that is working for a more central role for Islam in Europe.[26] This view is shared by the prolific late Algerian-French scholar Mohammed Arkoun who deployed socio-historical arguments similiar to Khan, Muhammad

---

[22] S. Abid Husain, *The Destiny of Indian Muslims* (New York: Asia Publishing House, 1965) and B. Bhutto, *Reconciliation: Islam, Democracy and the West* (New York: HarperCollins, 2008), 275–318.

[23] M. ul-Haq, *Islam in Secular India* (Simla: Indian Institute of Advanced Study, 1972).

[24] Maududi argued that Q4:59 was 'the very cornerstone of the entire religious, social and political structure of Islam and the very first clause of the constitution of an Islamic state' (A. Maududi in Z. Ansari [trans. and ed.], *Towards Understanding the Quran* [Leicester: Islamic Foundation, 1989], 50).

[25] Sayyid Abul A'la Maududi, *Let Us Be Muslims*, ed. K. Murad (Leicester: Islamic Foundation, 1985 [orig. 1940]), 296.

[26] T. Ramadan, *Western Muslims and the Future of Islam* (Oxford: OUP, 2004), 113–4.

Mujeeb and Kalam Azad, to propose that Islam should not look back in order to progress, but rather see the religion as a narrative upon which all Muslims, whether in Europe, India or elsewhere, could write their own chapter.[27]

The spirit of Arkoun's work is exemplified in the 2009 report entitled '*Contextualising Islam in Britain: Exploratory Perspectives*' which was the outcome report of a series of research gatherings at Cambridge University under the Project Leadership of Professor Yasir Suleiman. The report exemplifies the deeper engagement that academic Muslims are having with the issue of citizenship in the UK.[28] The study attempts to engage with much of the same theological content as their fellow adherents on the Subcontinent had done, and continue to do. As such, it is not worth repeating their arguments once again, however, it is important to note that, unlike the majority of the Indian Muslim writers, Yasir Suleiman's team did not propose the idea of temporary submission, even by implication. Instead, they used some theological engagement to emphasise instead the concept of ongoing submission to non-Muslim rulers.

Theirs is by no means the only voice in the UK. Voices such as Anjem Choudhary have sought to advocate an Islamic state of the kind advocated by Maududists, but his following appears small and shrinking.

One might argue therefore, although hard evidence is difficult to find, that in the Muslim intellectual community, a relatively conciliatory and pragmatic approach to non-Muslim authority is dominating the discourse. That said, there are issues about the disconnection between Imams and their young Mosque congregations which, although being addressed slowly with regard to state-centred training programs, are leaving religious gaps which are being exploited by organisations that have a more Islamist ideology, such as Hizb ut-Tahrir, Tablighi Jama'at, the Muslim Brotherhood and clerics like Yusuf al-Qaradawi.[29]

---

[27] M. Arkoun, *Islam: To Reform or to Subvert?* (London: Saqi Books, 2006).

[28] Professor Suleiman is the Director of the Prince Alwaleed Bin Talal Centre of Islamic Studies, Cambridge.

[29] Several works such as Phillip Jenkins' *God's Continent* and Phillip Lewis's *Young, British and Muslim* also discuss the impact of these groups. There is also a book by the RAND Research Fellow Lorenzo Vidino, *The New Muslim Brotherhood in the West* (New York/Chichester: Columbia University Press, 2010), which explores the impact of the 'Federation of the Islamic Organisation of Europe'.

4.4. Summary

The choice being laid before Muslims in both Europe and India is therefore one of developing a local narrative, versus developing a re-constituted Muslim Imperialism that attempts to reverse the flow of history.

5. The Role of the *Ummah* and the Place of *Shari'a*

The plethora of answers in relation to a Muslim's relationship to non-Muslim authority appear to leave the modern Muslim with even more questions. For, there is the group who argue that Muslims must work to overthrow non-Muslim authority. Then, there are those who advocate political activism through peaceful means to promote Islam to the centre of political and social life of the state they happen to be living in. Yet another group of scholars are telling Muslims that it is perfectly acceptable to live as Muslims in a minority situation without any need to work for change at all.

In the context of these divergent answers therefore, what should define 'Muslim identity'? How can the concept of an *ummah* be maintained when the physical demarcations of an Empire no longer exist?

5.1. The Subcontinent

Faruki's book *The Evolution of Islamic Constitutional Theory and Practice* proposes that Hindus and Muslims lived as two distinct groups before 1947.[30] By this he meant that the two groups were identifiable because of the differing religious rules and practices they followed.

On the other hand, the passage of the Shariat Act 1937 demonstrates that Muslim politicians such as Jinnah and Muhammad Ali felt that there was no sense of corporate Islamic identity in India and that they authored and promulgated the Bill for the precise purpose of creating that '*ummah*' identity.[31]

---

[30] K.A. Faruki, *The Evolution of Islamic Constitutional Theory and Practice* (Karachi: National Publishing House, 1971), 203–37.

[31] Oliver-Dee, *Muslim Minorities*, ch. 5.

However, for the Indian Muslim reformers the observation itself was irrelevant. The bar was raised a good deal higher in their eyes, for it was not simply about whether the community was 'identifiable' or not, but whether it could be 'Muslim', to the extent that the Qur'an and Muhammad would require it. The acid test therefore was whether Muslims feel that the system in their home state permits the full expression of their faith.

Unsurprisingly, Maududi argued that *shari'a* should find expression at the global level as the source of law for all.[32] His position was based upon the sovereignty of God being divinely delegated to his rulers on earth, on the basis that they rule through His law—the law of God as encapsulated in the *shari'a*.[33] However, Al-Afghani's stance was surprisingly different from that of Maududi, for, whilst agreeing on a need for a universally acknowledged Muslim community, he was happy for individual states to determine *shari'a* matters rather than have some global council do so.[34] He therefore brought the notion of a 'global identification' down to a series of more localised community identities under the umbrella of the *ummah*.

For Sayyid Ahmad Khan, there was no sense that the *ummah* could exist in anything other than a metaphysical realm. His argument was that the Caliphate, even when it did exist, was simply a monarchy by another name and that therefore the *ummah*, over which the Caliph should theoretically rule, could exist only in a theoretical world.[35] This observation was confirmed and developed by Muhammad Mujeeb. According to Mujeeb there was no sense in attempting to forge a global Muslim *shari'a* state, when Indian Islam had its own identity and history.[36] In such reasoning, the notion of a single *ummah* on

---

[32] Maududi, *Islamic Law and Constitution*, 148–50.

[33] Maududi, *Islamic Law and Constitution*, 148–50. He cites Q24:55 as theological justification. Maududi is engaging in the debate of the role of the Caliph here. However, the nature and role of that office theologically and historically is a matter of contentious debate. See A.K.S. Lambton, 'Khalifa', in *Encyclopedia of Islam*, vol. 4, 947.

[34] Landen, *Emergence*, 108–9. An interesting theory on the attraction of al-Afghani's message for Muslims in India (as well as other parts of the world) is given in A. Jalal, *Self and Sovereignty: Individual and Community in South Asian Islam since 1850* (London/ New York: Routledge, 2000), 188–9.

[35] Khan, *Khalifat*, 6–17.

[36] Mujeeb, *Indian Muslims*, 555.

anything other than a 'personal belief' level was not just unrealistic, it was not even to be desired. As a consequence, national identity became important, not just in terms of being one facet of a person's identity, but in defining that individual's religious identity as well. This view is underlined by Fazlur Rahman, the Pakistani scholar, who argued for a more flexible approach to definitions of all terms such as the *ummah* and *shari'a*.[37] For Rahman, the problem for Islam was not one of facility in relation to adapting to changing circumstances, rather it was the rigidity of orthodox definitions that had become a block to effective engagement with the modern world.

Interestingly, the view of one of the chief theologians of the 'Khilafat Movement', Abu'l Kalam Azad straddles both approaches. He agreed with the notion of a supreme global Caliphate. Azad proposed that the Caliph should indeed be the supreme ruler and that each country with a large Muslim population should have an Imam who would represent them on a Caliphal council.[38] At the same time he echoed Mujeeb's ideas in his concept of 'dual identity'.[39] Azad was deeply proud to be both Indian and Muslim. He therefore highlighted those parts of the Qur'an that he believed taught participation in human affairs.[40]

5.2. Europe

One might argue that similar positions to each of these Indian authors have been found in modern European Islamic thought, for opinion polls in the UK consistently show that their Islamic identity is more important for Muslims than Christian, Jewish and Hindu identity is for those faiths.[41] Yet, there are relatively few, either in Continental Europe

---

[37] See F. Rahman Malik, *Islam and Modernity: The Transformation of an Intellectual Tradition* (Chicago: University of Chicago Press, 1984), 43, 144.

[38] For a fuller description of Azad's ideas, see A. Ahmad, *Islamic Modernism in India and Pakistan 1857–1964* (London/Bombay/Karachi: OUP, 1967).

[39] K. Cragg, *The Pen and the Faith: Eight Modern Muslim Writers and the Qur'an* (London: G. Allen and Unwin, 1985), 25–8.

[40] Troll, *Islam Subcontinent*, 6.

[41] Internal Department of Communities and Local Government (UK) Survey carried out in 2008–2009 asked respondents to rate their faith on a scale of 1 (most importance) to 10 (no importance) in their identity and daily lives. Muslims consistently rated at '3', whereas other faiths rated around about '7'.

or in the UK, who agitate actively for either some unified '*Khilafah*-led *ummah* state' or even an increased role for *shari'a* within European legal systems. That said, there is said to be a growing radicalisation amongst European Muslims under the influence of the Muslim Brotherhood, Hizb-ut Tahrir and Tablighi Jama'at, all of whom are known to be very active throughout the continent.[42] However, leading theologians and activists such as Ramadan, Arkoun and lately, Ed Hussain, have been keen to downplay the role of *shari'a* whilst not suggesting that it is irrelevant. In this respect Ramadan and Hussain appear to still be in the process of defining a suitable role for *shari'a* and a definition for the *ummah* in an European context.[43]

5.3. Summary

Even though the British and European debates on these questions are at an earlier stage than those of their South Asian counterparts, it can be seen that many of the arguments used in India are being re-deployed in the European context. It is also important to note that none of these Muslim reformers engage with the pragmatic and theological issue of a single identity for the *ummah*, when there are different schools of *shari'a* prevailing in different geographical locales within both Europe and the Subcontinent.

6. Christian Engagement with Identity and Citizenship Issues

6.1. Europe

For Western European unfamiliar with the public expression of faith for over a century at least, having Islam in such close proximity has prompted fears about the re-emergence of religion on the continent that

---

[42] R. Coolsaet, *Jihadi Terrorism and the Radicalisation Challenge in Europe* (Farnham: Ashgate, 2008), 113–9.

[43] See for example, Ramadan's interview with Open Democracy in 2004 at http://www.opendemocracy.net/faith-europe_islam/article_2006.jsp.

have crystalised around fears of an 'Islamic Conquest' of Christendom.[44] This fear has fed an increasingly strong anti-religion sentiment that has sought to remove any form of public expression of faith relegating religion back into the private sphere and removing any collective consciousness that might become a competitor to the state identity.[45]

As a result, there has been a noticeable rise in the number of Christian political and social think-tanks which have engaged with issues of faith-state relations for Muslims and Christians and the place of religion in the public sphere. These think-tanks have sought to engage with the idea that religion must be returned to the private sphere alone, whilst at the same time, they have sought to contribute to the wider debate on Islamic impact on the continent. Significant amongst them has been the work of *Theos* who are based in Westminister, as well as other established Christian agencies who are taking on advocacy and research in this area, in both London and Brussels.[46]

This political engagement has also been reflected in a number books from within the Christian community that have sought to re-evaluate the nature of Christian engagement with political authority. Significant contributions in the field have come from Alan Storkey, Nick Spencer, Jonathan Chaplin and Luke Bretherton.[47] The approaches each of these authors have taken regarding issues of political engagement have frequently been within a framework of historical, theological and the philosophy of ethics standpoint. Clearly these authors do not come to exactly the same answers in respect to all aspects of faith-government relations, but it is important to note that the majority of publications came in the last decade. Of course, this does not mean to say that there

[44] Many differing voices are jostling to be heard in Europe amongst the differing groups, all involved in inter-faith or inter-cultural work. For example: EKD, CEC-KEK, KAS and COMECE have all been producing publications and conferences on inter-faith work at a furious pace over the last five to six years.

[45] See M. Jordan, 'In Europe and the U.S., Nonbelievers are Increasingly Vocal', *The Washington Post* (15 September 2007).

[46] For example, CARE and Evangelical Alliance now have political units established for both capitals. *Theos* has published a number of reports and, most recently, a book which examines the interrelationship of church and state from a Christian perspective. These can all be found at www.theosthinktank.co.uk.

[47] A. Storkey, *Jesus and Politics: Confronting the Powers* (Grand Rapids: Baker Academic, 2005); N. Spencer and J. Chaplin (eds), *God and Government* (London: SPCK, 2009); L. Bretherton, *Christianity and Contemporary Politics* (London: Wiley-Blackwell, 2010).

was no exploration of faith-government relations before the impact of Political Islam was felt in the West. Rather, it seems clear from the volume of material now being published that the discussions that Muslims have had in relation to authority in a minority situation have also stimulated an increased debate within Christian circles in Europe.[48]

This re-engagement with faith-state relations dynamic is all the more marked because, in the US, unlike in Europe, religion never disappeared from the public sphere. In Europe, liberal secular elites had striven for centuries to encase the power of the church within the private sphere and to some extent, evangelicalism in Europe had also either withdrawn from, or avoided engagement with, the public square and the political process.

It seems therefore that the advent of Islam and the activities of the *salafi* Muslims in Europe have become a stimulant for fresh Christian engagement in the same field. Much of this self-reflection has been around the question of dual loyalism versus 'mono-loyalism', once again as the state, whether it be the European Union or a national government, demands 'mono-loyalism' in the face of terrorist threats.[49]

6.2. The Subcontinent

Indian Christians have been a minority in a way that European Christians had not begun to experience until relatively recently. That said, the government of Manmohan Singh has shown signs of making a determined effort to bring Christians into the mainstream of political life in India in a way not previously seen.[50] Indeed, public reports on the plight of Christians and the institutional disadvantages they suffer in India have also served to suggest an improved outlook for Indian Christians in their homeland.[51] Many reasons, such as India's desire to 'put its house in order' before emerging fully onto the world

---

[48] See, for example, Oliver O'Donovan's *The Desire of the Nations* (Cambridge: CUP, 1999).

[49] See T. Wright, 'Neither Anarchy nor Tyrany: Government and the New Testament', in Spencer and Chaplin (eds), *God and Government*.

[50] As reported on the *Asianet* website at http://www.asianews.it/news-en/Four-Christians-in-Manmohan-Singh's-governing-team-15380.html.

[51] See *The Hindu*'s article on Dalit Christian reservation at: http://www.hindu.com/2011/03/13/stories/ 2011031355071000.htm.

stage, might be behind it however, whatever the political or social motivations, it seems that there are opportunities opening up for Indian Christians to have a voice in the public and political process in a way unseen in recent history. Should that prove to be the case, Christian leaders in India may face some of the same questions about the place of Christians in relation to government that British and European Christians have been facing. In that eventuality, looking from the outside, there does not seem to have been the kind of theo-political discussions taking place there, as there have been in Europe.

On the face of it, this is surprising given the undoubted intellectual and literary tradition within the Indian Christian communities. Indeed, given that Islam and Christianity have been living side by side in a minority situation far longer than European Christians and Muslims have, one might have expected the highly influential discussions amongst Muslims in India to have stimulated a discussion within the Indian church far earlier than European Muslims did for European Christians. Yet this does not seem to have been the case.

Reasons for this are not immediately apparent, but it seems appropriate that, should the present trend of cautious encouragement into political life continue, then thinking on the nature of Christian-government engagement in the Indian context will be vital. Once such thinking becomes published into the wider Christian and general public domain, the material will provide a tremendous stimulant to theo-political thinking across the global church.

7. Conclusions

The question of religious identity in a minority situation has stimulated debate amongst Muslim theologians and politicians ever since the European colonial periods. Indeed the debates had existed before that time, but it was the onset of European domination that caused Muslims in India and in the Middle East to start asking both why this had been allowed to happen, and how to react in the face of this new reality. In broad terms, the Indian Muslims who drove much of the debate, and indeed continue to do so, fell into two broad categories in terms of their answers to the questions of obedience to non-Muslim authority and the nature of the *ummah*, particularly the role of the *shari'a*, in this minority situation. On one side were those such as Maududi, Iqbal and Muhammad Ali who took a visionary path, reacting against the present reality in order to call Muslims to work for a return to the early model of the Islamic Empire. On the other side were scholars such as Sayyid Ahmed Khan and Muhammed Mujeeb who also called for the revival of Muslim energy and faith on the Subcontinent but who proposed instead a pragmatic, developmental model of a specifically Indian Islam in order to achieve that end.

In Europe, many of these Indian thinkers have had a profound effect on the Muslim communities throughout the continent and have also, indirectly, forced the Christians there to re-examine their own theology in relation to 'mono-loyalism' and community identity. It remains to be seen whether the present upheavals in the Muslim communities in India will have the same effect for Indian Christians, especially given the prospect of political engagement in the 'New India' in a way that has not been previously experienced.

Select References

Abid Husain, S. *The Destiny of Indian Muslims.* New York: Asia Publishing House, 1965.

Ahmad, A. *Islamic Modernism in India and Pakistan 1857–1964.* London/ Bombay/Karachi: OUP, 1967.

al-Din al-Afghani, Jamal. 'Jinsiyah wa al-Din al-Islamiyah'. *Al-Urwah al al-Wurthqa* 2 (20 March 1884). In *The Emergence of the Modern Middle East: Selected Readings.* Translated and edited by R.G. Landen. New York: Van Nostrand Reihnold Company, 1970.

al-Shaybani, M. *The Islamic Law of Nations: Shaybani's Siyar.* Trans. M. Khadduri. Baltimore: John Hopkins Press, 1996.

Al-Tabari. *Commentary on the Qur'an: Abridged Translation with Introduction and Notes by J. Cooper.* Vol. 4. Oxford: OUP/Hakim Investment Holdings Limited, 1987.

Arberry, A.J. *The Koran Interpreted.* London/New York/Karachi: OUP, 1964.

Arkoun, M. *Islam: To Reform or to Subvert?* London: Saqi Books, 2006.

Azmah, A. and E. Fokas, *Islam in Europe: Diversity, Identity and Focus.* Cambridge: CUP, 2007.

Bhutto, B. *Reconciliation: Islam, Democracy and the West.* New York: HarperCollins, 2008.

Bretherton, L. *Christianity and Contemporary Politics.* London: Wiley-Blackwell, 2010.

Coolsaet, R. *Jihadi Terrorism and the Radicalisation Challenge in Europe.* Farnham: Ashgate, 2008.

Cragg, K. *The Pen and the Faith: Eight Modern Muslim Writers and the Qur'an.* London: G. Allen and Unwin, 1985.

Crone, P. *Medieval Islamic Political Thought.* Edinburgh: Edinburgh University Press, 2005.

El Fadl, A. 'Islamic Law and Muslim Minorities: The Juristic Discourse on Muslim Minorities from the Second/Eighth to the Eleventh/Seventeenth Centuries'. *Islamic Law and Society* 1.2 (1994): 141–87.

Emerson, M. (ed.). *Ethno-Relgious Conflicts in Europe: Typologies in Europe's Muslim Communities.* Brussels: Centre for European Policy Studies, 2009.

Faruki, K.A. *The Evolution of Islamic Constitutional Theory and Practice.* Karachi: National Publishing House, 1971.

Firestone, R. 'Disparity and Resolution in the Quranic Teachings on War: A Re-Evaluation of a Traditional Problem'. *Journal of Near Eastern Studies* 56.1 (1997): 1–19.

Goldziher, I. 'Djamal al-Din al-Afghani'. In *Encyclopedia of Islam.* Edited by B. Lewis, Ch. Pellat and J. Schacht. 2nd edn. Leiden/London: Brill/Luzac and Co., 1965.

Jalal, A. *Self and Sovereignty: Individual and Community in South Asian Islam since 1850.* London/New York: Routledge, 2000.

Jenkins, P. *God's Continent: Christianity, Islam and Europe's Religious Crisis.* New York/Oxford: OUP, 2007.

Jordan, M. 'In Europe and the U.S., Nonbelievers are Increasingly Vocal'. *The Washington Post* (15 September 2007).

Kathir, Ibn. *Tafsi.* Abridged English Version. Trans. A. Daryabadi. Medina: Dar Ibn Kathir, 2004.

Lewis, P. *Young, British and Muslim.* London: Continuum, 2007.

MacDonald, D.B. *Development of Muslim Theology, Jurisprudence and Constitutional Theory.* New York: Clarendon Press, 1903.

Maududi, A. *Towards Understanding the Quran.* Translated and edited by Z. Ansari. Leicester: Islamic Foundation, 1989.

——. *Let Us Be Muslims*. Edited by K. Murad. Leicester: Islamic Foundation, 1985 [orig. 1940].

O'Donovan, O. *The Desire of the Nations*. Cambridge: CUP, 1999.

Oliver-Dee, S. *The Caliphate Question: British Government and Islamic Governance*. Lanham: Rowman and Littlefield, 2009.

——. *Muslim Minorities and Citizenship: Authorities, Communities and Islamic Law*. London: I.B. Tauris, forthcoming 2012.

Rahman Malik, F. *Islam and Modernity: The Transformation of an Intellectual Tradition*. Chicago: University of Chicago Press, 1984.

Rahmen, J. and S.C. Breau (eds). *Religion, Human Rights and International Law: A Critical Examination of Islamic State Practices*. Leiden: Martinus Nijhoff, 2007.

Ramadan, T. *Western Muslims and the Future of Islam*. Oxford: OUP, 2004.

Sageman, M. *Understanding Terror Networks*. Pennsylvania: University of Pennsylvania Press, 2004.

Saleh, W.A. *The Formation of the Classical Tafsir Tradition: The Qur'an Commentary of al-Tha'labi*. Leiden: Brill, 2003.

Schacht, J. *An Introduction to Islamic Law*. Oxford: Clarendon Press, 1982.

Shatzmiller, M. (ed.). *Nationalism and Minority Identities in Islamic Societies*. Quebec: McGill University Press, 2005.

Sivan, E. 'Ibn Taymiyya: Father of the Islamic Revolution, Medieval Theology and Modern Politics'. *Encounter* 60.5 (1983): 41–9.

Spencer, N. and J. Chaplin (eds). *God and Government*. London: SPCK, 2009.

Storkey, A. *Jesus and Politics: Confronting the Powers*. Grand Rapids: Baker Academic, 2005.

ul-Haq, M. *Islam in Secular India*. Simla: Indian Institute of Advanced Study, 1972.

Vidino, L. *The New Muslim Brotherhood in the West*. New York/Chichester: Columbia University Press, 2010.

PASTORAL THEOLOGY
and PSYCHOLOGY

Religious Conversion and Dual Identity: A Phenomenological Perspective

Joshua Iyadurai[*]

'A man has as many social selves as there are
individuals who recognize him and carry
an image of him in their mind' —William James

1. Introduction

Religious conversion in India occupies centre stage not only in religious circles but also in politics and media. The emergence of the right wing political parties to power kindled the anti-Christian sentiments among the fundamental elements. The anti-conversion legislations in some states and the increased violence against Christians further complicated the lives of the Christian converts in India. Conversion is a complex issue which cannot be defined simplistically. Classical conversion studies define conversion as an event; but contemporary studies have established that conversion is a process. However, my study on conversion from an inter-disciplinary perspective has demonstrated that conversion is both an event and a process.[1] Only converts to Christianity in India are the subjects of this paper; conversion is viewed both as an event where a convert experiences Jesus and as a process in which transformation is sparked off.

The purpose of the study is to show how converts manage dual identities by retaining their socio-religious identity as Hindus or Muslims to avoid conflicts in a multi-religious context. They define a new identity in conversion as a spiritual identity: the followers of Jesus. Converts see the religious identity of their birth more as a social identity than attributing any religious significance to it due to conversion. I am

[*] Joshua Iyadurai, PhD, is Director of the Mylapore Institute for Indigenous Studies, Chennai, Guest Faculty of the Department of Christian Studies, University of Madras, Chennai, and Associate Editor of *Dharma Deepika: A South Asian Journal of Missiological Research*.
    [1] J. Iyadurai, 'The Step Model of Transformative Religious Experiences: A Phenomenological Understanding of Religious Conversions in India', *Pastoral Psychology* 60.4 (2011): 505–21.

using the term 'social/religious identity' in order to make this sense clear. When the terms 'social identity' and 'religious identity' are used independently, they refer to the social aspect of identity and religious aspect of identity respectively. The scope of the paper is limited to the issue of dual identity of the converts to Christianity from a phenomenological perspective and is from the actor's or converts' point of view. The phenomenological approach demands that the researcher avoids the temptation of evaluating the phenomenon under study from his/her ideological or theological position. Instead of looking at the data from a particular theological perspective, I choose to look at it as it appears, bracketing my theological perspective. 'Bracketing', in a phenomenological research, is making the ideological position of a researcher known in order to demonstrate objectivity in the research process. My ideological or theological position is based on the spiritual roots that have been built in an evangelical student movement. My theological foundation was shaped by an evangelical seminary in India and I had my higher education in a Catholic arena in a state university. This should enable the readers to understand my biases and prejudices as I try consciously to avoid being evaluative of the phenomenon under study. Social psychological identity theories are discussed here and the converts' management of dual identity is interpreted in the light of these theories. Finally, the trend of retaining social/religious identity in conversion in the global context is presented in order to draw some implications for pastoral theology.

Early converts to Christianity in India, in the last century, felt that it was legitimate for them to be 'Hindu' socially and culturally, while being followers of Jesus in their faith.[2] Chenchiah, as a convert, felt it was sufficient for him to encounter Christ; being part of the Christian church was not considered imperative. He held the view that the essence of Christianity is the experience of Christ and that baptism is a ritual similar to many rituals in Hinduism but prevents many Hindus from accepting Christ due to the public perception that baptism is switching loyalty from one's community to the Christian community. Manilal Parekh was another convert who was of the same opinion.

---

[2] Robin Boyd, *An Introduction to Indian Christian Theology*, rev. edn (Delhi: ISPCK, 1975).

He took baptism but was never part of the Church. He emphasized the spiritual aspect of baptism while discounting the social aspect of joining the Christian community. This paper aims at highlighting how contemporary converts retain a dual identity—socially/religiously as Hindus/Muslims and as followers of Jesus for their spiritual identity in order to avoid conflicts and this phenomenon appears to be transitory.

2. Social Psychological Perspective on Multiple Identities

Social psychology is a discipline which studies human behaviour in a social context. Personal identity is understood as the aggregate of one's unique characteristics of the person, and social identity is grounded on one's association with a group. Identity is one's sense of himself or herself. James Marcia defined identity as a 'self-structure—an internal, self-constructed, dynamic organization of drives, abilities, beliefs, and individual history'.[3] This structure is constantly modified by taking new elements while leaving out some old elements. This indicates that there is no one fixed identity for a person.

Erik Erikson's theory of identity from a psychoanalytic perspective linked developmental stages of an individual with identity formation. The process of identity formation begins at childhood and reaches a crisis at adolescence. In an identity crisis, an adolescent explores various options of identifying himself or herself. An individual is able to resolve the identity crisis by recognizing his/her own sense of uniqueness, continuity, ego completeness and the ideals of a group one belongs to. One's ability to resolve this identity crisis is based on various factors such as trust, autonomy and initiative, in which the individual grew in the previous developmental stages. In the absence these factors, one struggles with an identity crisis.[4] However, it is acknowledged that an identity crisis is not limited to this stage alone and changing situations in one's life demand change in perceptions of oneself. Similarly, conversion is a major change of situation in one's life

---

[3] James E. Marcia, 'Identity in Adolescence', in J. Anderson (ed.), *Handbook of Adolescent Psychology* (New York: Wily & Sons, 1980), 159.

[4] Erik Erikson, 'Identity/Identity Formation', *Gail Encyclopedia of Psychology* (April 2001), http://findarticles.com/p/articles/mi_g 2699/is_0001/ai_2699000172/ (accessed 02 June 2010).

that creates an identity crisis where the converts form a new identity based on their conversion experience.

Bailey Gillespie draws a parallel between identity experience and conversion experience. He observes that in both instances lives are changed — there are behaviour changes due to a 'changed frame of reference,' change of ethical values, and the core of a person is affected. Religious conversion is concerned about identity; a new identity is formed based on a relationship with God. He asserted, 'knowing God through religious conversion is identity producing'.[5] Converts acquire a new, spiritual identity in conversion through their newfound relationship with Jesus.

Social psychological identity theories emphasize one's membership in a group and the role that plays in a social context in identity formation. Social identity theory was developed by Tajfel and Turner to explain the relationship between the personal and social. Tajfel defines social identity as, 'the individual's knowledge that he/she belongs to certain social group together with some emotional and value significance to him/her of his/her group membership.'[6] Social identity comprises one's membership and emotional attachment to the group with its status. Marilynn B. Brewer specifies social identity as 'an extension of the self-concept that entails a shift in the level of self-representation from that of the individual self to that of the collective self'.[7] For Brewer, social identity is based on the shared beliefs, values and practices of a group. An individual draws on elements from the group membership to understand the self. As a member of a group one tries to promote the positive image of the group so that in turn the membership in the group could enhance one's self image. Social identification involves social categorization, social identity and social comparison. Social categorization is marking the boundaries of the in-group. In social identification, one begins to think and act in the same way the members behave; the self appropriation of

---

[5] V. Bailey Gillespie, *The Dynamics of Religious Conversion: Identity and Transformation* (Birmingham: Religious Education Press, 1991), 191.

[6] Tajfel, cited in Michael A. Hogg, 'Social Identity', in Mark R Leary and June Price Tangney (eds), *Handbook of Self and Identity* (New York: Guilford Press, 2005), 462.

[7] Marilynn B. Brewer, 'Optimal Distinctiveness, Social Identity, and the Self', in Mark R Leary and June Price Tangney (eds.), *Handbook of Self and Identity* (New York: Guilford Press, 2005), 480.

the collective identity is the social identity. Social comparison is viewing the in-group positively while discriminating against the out-group[8].

Group membership is one of the influential factors through which others perceive an individual; on the other hand, the group influences the individual in perceiving the self. Michael Hogg points out, 'our sense of self derives from the groups and categories we belong to, and in many ways individuality may "merely" be the unique combination of distinct groups and categories that define who we are'.[9] Marilynn Brewer argues that social identity is person based, role based and group based.[10] Person based social identity is derived from the fact of the membership in a social group. Role based social identity is based on inter-personal relationships where one's role determines identity. Group based social identity is where the self and other members are dominated by the differences between in-group and out-group and the attributes and behaviours of individuals are absorbed into the group which brings cohesiveness and uniformity.

However, Marilynn Brewer also claims that studies have pointed out that everyone derives social identity from more than one social group and everyone manages multiple social identities according to social contexts. She explains:

> On an ongoing basis, the individual (either consciously or subconsciously) weighs and assesses available aspects of the self to determine which are activated or engaged as guides to behavior in the current situation. The individual may be aware that different identities have conflicting implications for behavior, in which case self-expression reflects some choice or compromise among different aspects of the self-concept. Actualization or enactment of different identities is influenced by the demands of the situation or social context, but the process is one of selecting from a repertoire of identities or self-representations that reside within the individual.[11]

She observes that handling multiple identities in a conflicting context, an individual has the option of adopting four kinds of strategies.[12] First, the individual could commit to one dominant group identification

---

[8] Brewer, 'Optimal Distinctiveness', 480.

[9] Michael A. Hogg, 'Social Identity', in Leary and Tangney (eds.), *Handbook of Self and Identity*, 462.

[10] Marilynn B. Brewer, 'The Many Faces of Social Identity: Implications for Political Psychology', *Political Psychology* 22.1 (2001): 117–21.

[11] Brewer, 'Faces of Social Identity', 117–21.

[12] Brewer, 'Faces of Social Identity', 117–21.

and ignore all the other group identities. Second, one could insulate different group identities in different environments and be alert that multiple identities are not simultaneously activated. The third strategy could be that of adopting an inclusive strategy when group identities overlap.

Similarly, Galen V. Bodenhausen argues that people adopt three kinds of strategies in handling multiple identities: dominance, compartmentalization and integration. When a person adopts dominance he or she activates only one identity while suspending all other identities. In compartmentalization, different contexts activate different identities and there is no one dominant identity. By integrating multiple identities, one is able to use multiple categories to define the self. He argues that greater integration results in well being and smooth functioning. He claims, 'Individuals with integrated social identities . . . may be in the best position to deal with group diversity, because they can find bases for social self-verification in many diverse ways and may not experience any sense of inherent oppositionality in the situation.'[13] When groups are in conflict, managing multiple identities becomes problematic. Dora Capozza and Rupert Brown observe, 'the adoption of more inclusive levels of categorization can, with appropriate safeguards, contribute to the reduction of intergroup discrimination.'[14] When their allegiance to each identity is strong, they try to work out compromises and develop tolerance. On the other hand, removing a person from conflicting demands leads to intolerance.

Identity, whether personal or social, is not fixed; personal identity changes in different life situations and social identity changes in different social contexts. Better integration of multiple identities leads to well being and smooth sailing in social functions. Integrated identities draw elements even from conflicting social groups to present a multi-faceted self to negotiate conflicting contexts. Arthur L. Greil and Lynn Davidman claim that people creatively adapt traditional identities to

---

[13] Galen V. Bodenhausen, 'Diversity in the person, diversity in the group: Challenges of identity complexity for social perception and social interaction', *European Journal of Social Psychology* 40 (2009): 1–16. http://www.interscience.wiley. com, DOI: 10.1002/ejsp.647.

[14] Dora Capozza and Rupert Brown, *Social Identity Process: Trends in Theory and Research* (London: Sage, 2007), 189.

new situations.[15] If this is how individuals determine social behaviour based on their multiple identities in different social contexts, a close look at how converts to Christianity in India deploy different identities in different social contexts is necessary.

3. Conversion and Dual Identity

Converts realize that conversion means potentially much trouble in Indian society. I have used the qualitative data from my doctoral research for the purpose of writing this paper.[16] The data is analysed from a phenomenological perspective, in other words 'as it appears' or from the actors' or the converts' point of view. In this section, I would like to discuss various reactions to conversion from family and friends and how the converts negotiated various hostile contexts by retaining their dual identity.

3.1. Reactions to Conversion

In the interviews, converts reported various kinds of reactions to conversion from family and friends. Some family members reacted with shock and even tears. The immediate response from the families was to persuade the converts to renounce their new faith. In other cases, there were extreme reactions expressed by the spouses even threatening to commit suicide. In some families, the members felt ashamed to relate with the converts, as Christianity was perceived as a religion of the lower castes. Some were perplexed at how a person could change his religion! Family members blamed the converts for any mishap in the family. They accused the converts to be the cause of the tragedy or crisis in the family, saying that the family deities were displeased. Some converts were mocked and publicly humiliated. Family members and friends also reacted with shock, anger, irritation, hatred, unhappiness, mockery and worry.

---

[15] Arthur L. Greil and Lynn Davidman, 'Religion and Identity', in James A. Beckford and Nicholas Jay Demerath (eds.), *The Sage Handbook of the Sociology of Religion* (London: Sage, 2007), 549–65.

[16] Joshua I., *Self-transformative Religious Experiences: A Phenomenological Inquiry*, unpublished PhD dissertation (Chennai: University of Madras, 2008).

Some thought the converts were out of their mind. Sania,[17] an engineer from a Muslim family, reported that her father thought she had become mentally ill. She was given electric shock treatment to cure her mental illness.[18] Nambiar, a medical doctor, also reported a similar reaction in his family when his brother converted.[19] In other cases, the converts were forced to practice the religion of their birth. Parents threatened to stop paying for studies. In some cases they withheld financial support to their children who wanted to continue their studies. Some of the extended family members resorted to witchcraft against the converts and their families. The converts had to face physical threats on many occasions from family and community members.

Marriage was a crucial issue in a convert's family. If the converts were single, then it became a big issue between the family and the converts when choosing a life partner. Converts insisted on marrying a Christian; this meant crossing the caste barrier against the family's objections. In many cases the converts did not insist on crossing the caste barrier; however, within the same caste, the converts insisted on finding a Christian. This was the compromise arrived at in the family. Rekha, a high caste Hindu girl, could not convince her parents on her stand of marrying a Christian. She reported, 'They didn't agree to my marriage. They said, "If you want to marry in this manner, go and marry, but we won't come and participate in it."'[20] Therefore, she walked out of the house and married a Brahmin convert.

Some of the converts did not make an issue that they would marry only a Christian. They obeyed their parents in marrying a person of their choice. They did not object to the marriage being conducted in accordance to their religious tradition. After marriage, either they followed Jesus secretly or they discussed with their spouses their belief in Jesus and sought permission to follow him. The converts were quite comfortable in this manner. Then slowly, over a period, they influenced their spouses.

If the converts were elderly, then the children's marriage became a big issue. The relatives exerted a lot of pressure on the converts to

---

[17] The names of the interviewees are changed to protect their identity.

[18] Sania, a business person (India, Interview, Sep–Dec 2005).

[19] Nambiar, a doctor from a Namboodri Family (Chennai, Interview, Sep–Dec 2005).

[20] Reka, a Hindu girl (Chennai, Interview, Sep–Dec 2005).

marry off their children to a person from their own religion. However, the converts were firm in delaying the marriage, waiting and hoping for a suitable match. The relatives and friends ridiculed them for taking such a stand. However, the converts claimed that though there was a delay, their stand was honoured by Jesus and they found the right match. Some of the same people who ridiculed them expressed surprise in the manner in which some of the weddings took place.

In some cases, parents disowned their children or threatened to disown them. The converts had to suffer financially as the parents stopped financial support. The converts were denied access to the Bible, any Christian fellowship or even a friend.

In some cases, the family members, despite knowing about the conversion, did not react or just ignored the issue. The converts also did not feel the need to inform the family about it. But both the parties deliberately did not make an issue out of it. Some have accepted the conversion but did not support openly or encourage it. Nevertheless, some family members accepted it as a reality and were even indirectly supportive. Some accepted it with a warning not to practice Christianity publicly.

Converts had to face different kinds of crises: losing family and friends, going without food, without money, fear of future troubles, being disowned by parents, anxiousness in finding a suitable life partner and public humiliation. Some were pushed to a situation where they even contemplated suicide at some point. Life became far more difficult for many due to conversion. These instances show that conversion in India leads to more problems and even life-threatening situations.

3.2. Converts' Responses

Converts adopted different mechanisms to tackle the situations in the family. Some of the converts practiced their newfound faith secretly. They were scared to come out openly and declare their change of religion. Fear of being caught practicing Christianity determined the converts' behaviour and movements. For some, the time spent in the family circle was horrible and intolerable, so the converts avoided being with the family. Some never informed the family members of their conversion or baptism and did not feel the need to inform their family. Some of the converts avoided situations where they would have to participate in religious rituals. Some had the courage to resist the pressure to practice the rituals of the religion of their birth.

3.2.1. Continuity of Religious Practices

The converts' spiritual identity is changed in the conversion experience as a follower of Jesus; however, some of them retain the social/religious identity based on the religion of their birth. Converts continued the previous religious practices externally and attributed new meanings to some of the cultural practices, and cultural or religious symbols. They adopted this strategy to maintain peace in the family hoping that someday the family would convert. The following narrative illustrates this factor.

Janaki, a house wife who was a secret follower of Jesus for about thirty years, narrated her ordeal, 'Whenever he [husband] called me to the temple, I would go there and stand behind him. Whenever he gave me *prasadam* which was offered in the temple, I would throw it or I put it in my mouth and spit it out later . . . Sometimes I had to eat it and then I prayed "Lord please protect me."'[21] Komala, a retired government employee, gave biblical basis for continuing her Hindu religious practices:

> I had to go to the temple. The very first thing I came to know from the Bible was about Naaman. Somehow, from somewhere, I heard. He said, 'When my master enters the temple I will bow down in the temple, the Lord should forgive this.' Like that I had also decided, I would go because they [family members] were calling me. I would tell the Lord, 'You are only everything for me.' I would say this always; then I would be satisfied and I didn't feel guilty. I had taken part in all our family functions.[22]

Balan, a software engineer, reported that he would take part in *Pujas,* but, in his heart, he would pray to Jesus.[23] School teachers in a focus group interviews brought to light how they negotiated such situations. The following excerpts indicate various strategies adopted by these women.[24] One of the teachers reported, 'There was a festival and my father called me to the temple. I went there but I was praying to Jesus.'

---

[21] Janaki, a housewife (Sivakasi, Interview, Sep–Dec 2005).
[22] Komala, a retired govt employee (Chennai, Interview, Sep–Dec 2005).
[23] Balan, a software engineer (Chennai, Interview, Sep–Dec 2005).
[24] Focus Group of Teachers (Sivakasi, Interview, Sep–Dec 2005).

Another one said, 'There were occasions that I couldn't avoid. I went there. There was no other way. Inside my heart I prayed to Jesus.' Another teacher said, 'When *prasadam* was offered, I just prayed and ate it; because I didn't want to hurt my family members.' Another teacher recalled an incident, 'I was asked to clean the *Puja* vessels. I couldn't refuse it so I did it. I was praying "Lord I have no other way. But I love you."' Wearing a *bindhi* on the forehead is another issue. One of them said, 'I just tell Jesus, "what to do I have to put this." We can't be stubborn in such issues, we want see that there should not be trouble for us in following Jesus.' Selvi, a business person, recalled, 'I used to go for the family deity worship. I had shaved my children's hair in the temple. I did all these, as I was afraid of my mother-in-law.'[25]

3.2.2. Secret Following

One of the women in her 40s in a focus group interview said, 'I don't tell others about going to Church or Bible study, because people would look down on us.'[26] Another woman in the same group said, 'We hide the Bible and go.'[27] Samsudeen, a convert from Islam, reported that he used to read the Bible in the bathroom.[28] Janaki, a woman who practiced her faith secretly for 30 years, narrated her daily routine:

> He [my husband] goes for a morning walk. The moment he goes out, I would lock the door and pray for forty minutes. Then I would start doing the household works. Around 9 o'clock he would leave for the office, and then I would have bath and immediately start reading the Bible and meditate on it till 11 o'clock. Then I would start my cooking along with praise and worship. Then at 12 noon, I would go around my house; as I walk, I praise Him and claim His promises like, 'I will satisfy you with long life and I will show you my salvation.' Then I pray with thanksgiving. God has blessed me with the gift of tongues; I pray and praise Him in other languages. When my husband is expected, I would sit on the dining chair, which was near the window; I would pray with my eyes open; because I was scared of him. Even if I delay for a few seconds in opening the door, he would question me.[29]

Venkat, an assistant professor in a college, said, 'My mom is sensitive, she tells me, "Do not stand in the street corner and shout Hallelujah

---

[25] Selvi, a business person (Sivakasi, Interview, Sep–Dec 2005).
[26] Focus Group of Women in their 40s (Sivakasi, Interview, Sep–Dec 2005).
[27] Focus Group of Women in their 40s (Sivakasi, Interview, Sep–Dec 2005).
[28] Samsudeen, a convert from Islam (India, Interview, Sep–Dec 2005).
[29] Janaki, a housewife (Sivakasi, Interview, Sep–Dec 2005).

and Praise the Lord; do not distribute tracts. And if you want to pray, read your Bible, listen to music whatever you want to do, do it within the four walls, nothing outside of it.'"[30] Converts were adopting this strategy to hold on to their new found faith by following secretly rather than jeopardizing their spiritual journey.

3.2.3. Attending Church

Some of the participants struggled a lot to attend a church. Kushbu, a convert from Islam, reported her difficulties in attending Church:

> As a convert it was very difficult for me to go to church. We [Muslim converts] very secretly go. So I used to dress as if I am going to the market in a very simple way so that my husband would not notice and my relatives wouldn't know. And I would go to any church which was open and nearby. I don't go to church on Sundays . . . He [my husband] said 'You are spoiling my name by going to the church and they are telling me that I am a fool. So I want to be strict with you now.' But I could not keep myself away from the fellowship. I tried different routes every time to go to church because my brothers were following me wherever I went. I took a roundabout route to reach the Church which was very near. I hid myself because I didn't want to hurt my husband and I wanted to satisfy my spirit also. I was rejoicing in my spirit.[31]

The converts were determined to hold on to Jesus in spite of the troubles and found ways to strengthen them, as Kushbu did.

Some of them did not or could not attend a church for some time. Janaki could not attend Church for about 30 years, but she was able to hold on to her faith. Balan was quite content with his experience of Christ for the first 1½ years without being part of a church. Sania was under some sort of house arrest for 1½ years and could not attend a church. She did not even have the Bible with her during this period. Her only help in surviving in her faith was prayer. Still, in spite of the hostile atmosphere at home, she was able to hold onto her newfound faith. Mohan, a young Brahmin priest, claimed that he was following Jesus for about four years but no one knew about it. Rekha, another participant in the study, did not attend Church for about a year after her conversion. Vinodha, a house wife, never attended a church; she used to visit a Catholic church whenever she got time; however, she did not attend the mass but she simply went, prayed alone and came back. Balan, a software engineer, articulated his thoughts on attending church:

---

[30] Venkat, Assistant Professor (Chennai, Interview, Sep–Dec 2005).
[31] Kushbu, a convert from Islam (India, Interview, Sep–Dec 2005).

It was just the relationship with Christ . . . I was not even going to church; nobody even knew that I was a Christian. Somehow didn't want to lose the experience I had . . . At one point of time, I thought 'let it be secret all through my life. Maybe I will stay on like this and even marry a girl my parents choose and probably live this life like this and still be God's child.'[32]

Similarly, Venkat, an assistant professor in a college, said, 'My faith was secret at home. I used to read the Bible and pray in my room.'[33] These converts felt their conversion was total, even without being part of a church. Initially they did not consider participation in the church as an essential element of following Jesus. They identified the church with institutionalized Christianity. They were content to define their spirituality through prayer and reading the Bible. Their perception of Christian spirituality is maintaining a relationship between Jesus and the individual — nothing more. They consider all other religious requirements as non-essentials. They held the view — or some still hold the view — that a personal experience of Christ or following Jesus is the essence of conversion.

3.2.4. Baptism as a Ritual

Kavia, a professor in a college says 'Baptism is not important. It's my personal relationship with God. As far as my faith is concerned, I felt I was right with God. So I didn't bother.'[34] Initially, converts consider taking baptism and participation in the church as external rituals and later many change their views.

3.3. A Reflection

In spite of all these problems, the converts were not willing to give up their new found faith. At one point or the other, some contemplated returning to the religion of their birth and some even felt suicidal because of unbearable situations. However, they found the strength to cope with those situations through prayer, reading the Bible, and the support given by fellowship. Some felt that Jesus wanted them to go through this path.

---

[32] Balan, a software engineer (Chennai, Interview, Sep–Dec 2005).
[33] Venkat, Assistant Professor (Chennai, Interview, Sep–Dec 2005).
[34] Kavia, a retired professor (Chennai, Interview, Sep–Dec 2005).

The converts reported that when they went through such situations they prayed for their family members. They were firm in their conviction and in their commitment to love the family, in spite of all the troubles caused by the family. They were ready to forgive what the family members did to them. They were eager to please the family members in all other aspects other than giving up Jesus. They loved the family but had a greater love for Jesus. Sania, a convert from Islam, had to flee from her home because of her conversion; she was clear in her choice that she loved her dad, but she had greater love for Jesus.

These converts experienced self-transformation and acquired a new self-identity. This was a spiritual identity but they retained the social/religious identity as Hindus or Muslims to maintain peace in the family and in the community. They were comfortable in maintaining this dual identity. However, the desire to come out into the open was present and they eagerly waited for an occasion. Some reported that when there was a crisis in the family, the converts began to assert their belief in Jesus. They invited the family members to try Jesus. Such crises gave them the opportunities to come out openly and sometime resulted in the conversion of the family members.

The converts adopted these kinds of strategies to safeguard their interest in following Jesus. Their motives in adopting these strategies were to survive physically and spiritually, avoid conflicts and convert the rest of the family. They were maintaining dual identity for physical, psychological, sociological, and missiological reasons till they found a receptive situation to declare their conversion openly. These strategies were not permanent, only transitory.

4. Social Psychological Interpretation

As we have seen earlier, the social psychological identity theories point out that an individual draws from elements of the in-group to enhance the self image. In social identity formation, the individual uses various social categories to mark the boundaries of in-group and out-group. One's behavior is chosen to maintain uniformity and cohesiveness within the group. By social comparison the individual attaches greater positive image to the in-group. I would like to discuss here how the converts use these elements in managing identities in conflicting social contexts.

Arthur L. Greil and Lynn Davidman claim that people creatively adapt traditional identities to new situations.[35] This is very true in the case of converts in India. Although the boundaries between Christianity, Hinduism and Islam are clearly marked, a convert redraws the boundaries so that he or she can cross them by creating a dual identity.

The converts articulate that they continue the religious practices of Hinduism/Islam for social reasons, not for religious purposes. They offer new meanings to the same practices which they have been following as the religious practices of their own religion. When the boundaries are loosely marked, it is easier for them to move from one identity to another identity. Maintaining uniformity and cohesiveness is very important for membership in a social group. When the family invites them to go to the Temple/Mosque, the converts go with them and activate the identity of Hindus/Muslims. However, they try to maintain their new identity as followers of Jesus by injecting new meaning to the practice of going to the Temple/Mosque; they go there and pray to Jesus.

The converts adopt another strategy to redraw the boundaries of religions by differentiating between religious identity and spiritual identity. They see their conversion experience as a religious experience of Jesus and Christianity as the institutional form of religion. This way they deploy their religious identity as Hindus/Muslims while claiming to have a spiritual identity as the followers of Jesus by virtue of their religious experience.

According to social identity theories, the self is enhanced based on the positive image of the in-group. Converts are members of both groups, Christianity and Hinduism/Islam which are inherently in conflict. They compare both groups and based on social contexts, they activate one identity over the other. Christianity is viewed as a foreign religion and/ or the religion of Dalits in India. Hence, by activating only the Christian identity, the convert is unable to enhance the self image. On the other hand, because of the religious experience of encountering Jesus in their conversion, they do not give up the Christian identity either. Therefore they juggle the two identities according to social contexts.

In handling multiple identities, Marilynn Brewer listed four strategies[36] and Galen V. Bodenhausen highlighted three strategies.[37]

---

[35] Greil and Davidman, 'Religion and Identity'.
[36] Brewer, 'Many Faces', 121.
[37] Bodenhausen, 'Diversity in the Person'.

We find the converts adopting some of these strategies in handling their dual identity. In conflicting or threatening situations, the act of continuing religious and cultural practices by the converts show that they commit to the dominant group identification as Hindus/Muslims, by underplaying the identity of the newfound faith in Jesus. In this context they activate the dominant identity as Hindus/Muslims while underplaying the Christian identity.

The strategy of following Jesus secretly falls in the category of compartmentalization or insulation of multiple identities. Converts are cautious that dual identity is not simultaneously activated. In this instance, the social context determines which identity is activated. When they are with the families, they activate the identity of Hindus/Muslims and when they are away from them, they activate their Christian identity.

When they are among fellow converts to Christianity, they use the inclusive strategy to identify all of them as Christians in general, including secret Christians, converts from Hinduism and Islam. But in a larger social context, converts from Hinduism may identify only with secret Christians from Hinduism rather than with secret Christians from Islam. Though the group identity of 'secret Christians' overlaps with that of converts from Islamic backgrounds, they would prefer to exclude secret Christians from Islam. When adopting a conjunctive strategy, it is easier for them to connect with secret Christians from Hinduism rather than including those from the other group, the secret Christians from Islamic backgrounds.

Bodenhausen's integration of multiple identities is not found amongst those I studied. Integration is where a convert simultaneously activates the identity of a Hindu and as Hindu-Christian. He argued that the integration of multiple identities will enable one to bring tolerance and harmony. The classical Indian Christian theologians activated such an identity. We find various movements emerging along this line, which will be discussed later.

Geoffrey A. Oddie, in his study of conversion movements in South Asia, observed, 'it was not a case of either/or but of striking the balance between the old and new, or perhaps of adopting an additional identity.'[38] The concept of converts juggling different identities in different social

---

[38] Geoffrey A. Oddie (ed.), *Religious Conversion Movements in South Asia: Continuities and Change, 1800–1900* (Richmond: Curzon, 1997), 6.

contexts is not something unusual because, we all juggle multiple identities (Indian, Christian, Professor, Pastor, caste identity etc.) in various social contexts. Dual identity in conversion is not an anomaly but a core element of managing self in a multi-religious context. If so, what are the implications for pastoral theology?

5. Implications for Pastoral Theology

We have found that converts use dual identity more as a strategy to manage the self in a multi-religious context. The data indicates that it is only a transitory phenomenon. When the situation changes, the converts are willing to join mainstream Christianity. Theologians and church leaders may insist that once a person is converted to Christianity, s/he must forego the former social/religious identity. But when does conversion culminate? My study on conversion from a phenomenological perspective has demonstrated that conversion is both an event and a process.[39] Conversion is a complex phenomenon and it is very difficult to pin point a moment where conversion culminates. Transformation is an ongoing process which begins at the religious experience when one experiences Jesus personally. It is a spiritual journey where the convert moves at a speed in which the Spirit of God leads him/her. Theologians and church leaders cannot decide when a convert should break his/her family ties. Moreover, breaking of a family or community link is from the Western individualistic perspective of conversion, not suitable for India.[40]

As theologians, how do we perceive what the Spirit of God is doing out there, which appears contrary to our theological paradigm? Should we reject them altogether saying that they are not loyal to Jesus? Should we judge them as wanting to enjoy both worlds? Is it theologically appropriate to encourage this trend? These questions are to be pondered over and be wrestled along with the theological concepts that we hold close to heart. There are no categorical answers

[39] Iyadurai, 'The Step Model'.

[40] For a detailed discussion on individualistic verses community approach in mission, see Joshua Iyadurai, 'Mission in Postmodernity: An Asian Perspective', http://edinburgh2010.oikoumene.org/fileadmin/files/edinburgh2010/files/Study_Process/Iyadurai%20Study%20Theme%203.pdf.

to these questions. However, this phenomenon should open our eyes to see beyond our theological paradigms in order to understand what God is doing out there; because God is not bound by our theological paradigm which we may claim to be normative.

This phenomenon of following Jesus while not being part of an institutionalized church is not an isolated one; it is quite widespread in India and abroad. *Kristubakthas*[41], in Varanasi, a movement initiated by a Catholic priest is one of the movements in North India, brings Dalits and Other Backward Castes (OBCs) together in the name of Jesus. They do not have any structured form of worship or rituals; but they devotedly read the Bible and pray. In terms of social customs they follow their traditions. The 'churchless Christians' in Tamil Nadu[42] and 'non-church movement' is spreading fast in many places.[43] Based on a extensive research, Dasan Jeyaraj identified four reasons for its growth:[44] (1) in order to avoid rejection and exclusion from the family; (2) fear of losing one's role and identity in the community; (3) fear of breaking the family traditions; and (4) ignorance of the need to be part of a church.

Similarly, such movements are growing among Muslims not only in India but worldwide and it is known as 'Insider Movement'.[45] Rebecca Lewis defines Insider Movement as:

> any movement to faith in Christ where (a) the gospel flows through pre-existing communities and social networks and where (b) believing families, as valid expressions of the Body of Christ, remain inside their socio-religious communities, retaining their identity as members of that community while living under the Lordship of Jesus Christ and the authority of the Bible.[46]

[41] Jerome Sylvester, *Hermeneutics of Khristbakta Movement: A Subaltern Reading of Religio-Cultural Phenomenon in Varanasi*, unpublished PhD dissertation (Chennai: University of Madras, 2010).

[42] Herbert E. Hoefer, *Churchless Christianity* (Pasadena: William Carey Library, 2001).

[43] For detailed discussion on non-church movement see: Dasan Jeyaraj, *Followers of Christ Outside the Church in Chennai, India* (Zoetermeer: Boekencentrum Academic, 2010).

[44] Jeyaraj, *Followers of Christ*.

[45] John J. Travis and J. Dudley Woodberry, 'When God's Kingdom Grows Like Yeast: Frequently-Asked Questions About Jesus Movements Within Muslim Communities', *Mission Frontiers* (Jul–Aug 2010): 24–30.

[46] Lewis, 'Promoting Movement to Christ within Natural Communities', *IJFM* 24.2 (2007): 75.

Mazhar Mallouhi, an Arab Syrian novelist, a Sufi Muslim follower of Jesus, claims, 'I was born into a Muslim context and I don't wish to reject my heritage. Islam is my heritage and Christ is my inheritance.'[47] Based on his association with other Muslim followers of Jesus, he argues that the same Holy Spirit who works among Christians only transforms the Muslims within Muslim contexts. If this is what the Spirit of God is accomplishing, how do theologians respond to this trend?

Dasan Jeyaraj argues that this phenomenon is a manifestation of Christ outside the church and is continued in the relationship between Christ and His followers. Christ continues to manifest himself through the lives of the believers who are not part of the church. He emphatically states:

> The followers of Christ outside the visible church are a proof of Christ's manifestation outside the church, which joyfully needs to be recognized by those who follow Christ inside the church. The dynamic of Christ's presence among followers of Christ outside the church is both a promise and a challenge to those inside the church, which too often manifests itself as static and inward-looking.[48]

Rebecca Lewis, a promoter of Insider Movement, articulates that the fellowship of believers in their pre-existing communities becomes the church which is similar to the household churches in the New Testament. The social/religious identity is retained while their lives are being transformed through Jesus. She argues that this is in line with the paradigm shift the apostles experienced in accepting the Gentiles as part of the church without making them to be Jews through circumcision. She resolutely argues:

> Just as the Apostles freed the Gentiles from any perceived need to convert to the Jewish religion, today we should likewise free people groups from the counter-productive burden of socio-religious conversion and the constraints of affiliation with the term 'Christianity' and with various religious institutions and traditions of Christendom. We must once more affirm with Paul and the Apostles that the obedience of faith in God through Christ alone is sufficient for salvation and that His Word, His Spirit, and the fellowship of the saints is sufficient for spiritual growth.[49]

---

[47] Mallouhi, 'Comments on the Insider Movement', *St Francis Magazine* 5.5 (2009): 13.

[48] Jeyaraj, *Followers of Christ*, 419.

[49] Lewis, 'Promoting Movement', 76.

I think, there should not be any problem for us to recognize that this is a work of God. Salvation is through Jesus Christ, not through any religion either Judaism or Christianity. Paul says that without the Spirit of God, no one can confess Jesus Christ is Lord; it implies that the Spirit of God works among the people who are outside the church. It results in the transformed lives of people who in the process join the institutional church. So the work of the Spirit is not limited to the institutionalized church.

Social identity theories have pointed out that integration of multiple identities increases tolerance and reduces intergroup conflicts. Religious harmony is very much the need of the hour in India; conversion to institutionalized Christianity triggers communal tension and conflicts. If the Indian Church adopts the strategy of encouraging converts to retain their social/religious identity while acquiring the spiritual identity as the followers of Jesus, it would make conversion less threatening and make it expedient for those who want to follow Jesus in India. Let the converts have the right to manage their identity.

References

Primary Sources (names are changed to protect identity)

Balan, Software Engineer, Chennai, Interview Sep–Dec 2005.
Focus Group of Teachers, Sivakasi, Interview, Sep–Dec 2005.
Focus Group of Women in 40s, Sivakasi, Interview, Sep–Dec 2005.
Janaki, Housewife, Sivakasi, Interview Sep–Dec 2005.
Kavia, Retired Professor, Chennai, Interview Sep–Dec 2005.
Komala, Re retired Govt. employee, Chennai, Interview, Sep–Dec 2005.
Kushbu, Housewife, India, Interview, Sep–Dec 2005.
Nambiar, Doctor, Chennai, Interview, Sep–Dec 2005.
Reka, Housewife, Chennai, Interview, Sep–Dec 2005.
Samsudeen, Convert from Islam, India, Interview Sep–Dec 2005.
Sania, Business Person, India, Interview, Sep–Dec 2005.
Selvi, Business Person, Sivakasi, Interview Sep–Dec 2005.
Venkat, Assistant Professor, Chennai, Interview Sep–Dec 2005.

Secondary Sources

Bodenhausen, Galen V. 'Diversity in the Person, Diversity in the Group: Challenges of Identity Complexity for Social Perception and Social Interaction'. *European Journal of Social Psychology* 40 (2009): 1–16. http://www.interscience.wiley.com, DOI: 10.1002/ejsp.647 (accessed 18 August 2010).

Boyd, Robin. *An Introduction to Indian Christian Theology.* Rev. edn. Delhi: ISPCK, 1975.

Brewer, Marilynn B. 'The Many Faces of Social Identity: Implications for Political Psychology'. *Political Psychology* 22.1 (2001): 115–25.

——. 'Optimal Distinctiveness, Social Identity, and the Self'. Pp. 480-91 in *Handbook of Self and Identity.* Edited by Mark R Leary and June Price Tangney. New York: Guilford Press, 2005.

Capozza, Dora and Rupert Brown. *Social Identity Process: Trends in Theory and Research.* London: Sage, 2007.

Gillespie, V. Bailey. *The Dynamics of Religious Conversion: Identity and Transformation.* Birmingham: Religious Education Press, 1991.

Greil, Arthur L. and Lynn Davidman. 'Religion and Identity'. Pp. 549–65 in *The Sage Handbook of the Sociology of Religion.* Edited by James A. Beckford, Nicholas Jay Demerath. London: Sage, 2007.

Hoefer, Herbert E. *Churchless Christianity.* Pasadena: William Carey Library, 2001.

Hogg, Michael A. 'Social Identity'. Pp. 462–79 in *Handbook of Self and Identity.* Edited by Mark R Leary and June Price Tangney. New York: Guilford Press, 2005.

Iyadurai, Joshua. *Self-transformative Religious Experiences: A Phenomenological Inquiry.* Unpublished PhD Thesis. Chennai: University of Madras, 2008.

——. 'Mission in Postmodernity: An Asian Perspective'. http://edinburgh2010.oikoumene.org/fileadmin/files/edinburgh2010/files/Study_Process/Iyadurai%20Study%20Theme%203.pdf.

——. 'The Step Model of Transformative Religious Experiences: A Phenomenological Understanding of Religious Conversions in India'. *Pastoral Psychology* 60.4 (2011): 505–21.

Jeyaraj, Dasan. *Followers of Christ outside the Church in Chennai, India.* Zoetermeer: Boekencentrum Academic, 2010.

Lewis, Rebecca. 'Promoting Movement to Christ within Natural

Communities'. *IJFM* 24.2 (2007): 75–6.

Mallouhi, Mazhar. 'Comments on the Insider Movement'. *St Francis Magazine* 5.5 (2009): 3–14.

Marcia, James E. 'Identity in Adolescence'. In *Handbook of Adolescent Psychology.* Edited by J. Anderson. New York: Wily & Sons, 1980.

Oddie, Geoffrey A. (ed.), *Religious Conversion Movements in South Asia: Continuities and Change, 1800–1900.* Richmond: Curzon, 1997.

Sylvester, Jerome. *Hermeneutics of Khristbakta Movement: A Subaltern Reading of Religio-cultural Phenomenon in Varanasi.* Unpublished PhD dissertation. Chennai: University of Madras, 2010.

Travis, John J. and J. Dudley Woodberry. 'When God's Kingdom Grows Like Yeast: Frequently-Asked Questions About Jesus Movements Within Muslim Communities'. *Mission Frontiers* (Jul–Aug 2010): 24–30.

Identity and Conflict: A Pastoral Response

Ravi David[*]

1. Introduction

A few years ago, after long-haul flights through several airports of the world, I landed in Mumbai's international airport just after midnight. My connecting flight to Bengaluru was several hours later, but the transit time was not long enough to go into town and find a place to sleep. My options were to either sleep sitting on a seat in the common area of the airport or find a place in the often booked up retiring rooms. I was pleasantly surprised to find that there was a vacant bed at the retiring rooms and began to fill out forms to complete the check-in process. On scrutinising my form, the officer-in-charge, with a strange expression on his face, said, 'Your name is Ravi David?' I replied in the affirmative. He went on to say that while 'Ravi' was a common Indian name, he wondered where the name 'David' came from, which he said was 'not Indian'.

More recently, I was on a bus in Bengaluru, travelling from Kothanur to KR Market, conversing with the person sitting next to me. In the middle of the conversation, he enquired after the caste I belonged to. Identity is a significant factor in India, and is often defined by caste, profession, family history, religion, economic status, ethnicity, language and a host of other categories.

India is changing rapidly. The changes critically influence and impact lifestyles, priorities and the overall quality of life. Change affects identity, both individually and collectively. In a country with huge disparities in caste, class and education, identity is an important part of the ongoing upheaval in society. An understanding of who we are in Christ is foundational for self-worth and self-esteem, which in turn influences self-identification.

Christians have always been a small minority of the Indian population and have generally lived peacefully in a multi-religious,

[*] Ravi David is Professor of Pastoral Theology and Counselling at South Asia Institute of Advanced Christian Studies (SAIACS) in Bangalore.

multicultural and multilingual context, while proactively contributing to nation building in several ways. However, a growing intolerance towards religious pluralism is resulting in the subtle sidelining, alienation and, at times, aggressive persecution of minorities, with a tendency to equate allegiance to the majority religion as patriotism and nationalism. This subtly affects and questions the identity of Indian Christians in their own country. What does the Bible say about identity as individuals and as a community, and about identification with one's motherland? The section entitled 'Indian and Christian' examines biblical concepts that shed light on these questions.

Identity-related conflicts can be both internal to the individual and external to the community. The wider community plays a critical role in addressing issues arising out of individual and collective identity conflicts. The section entitled 'Shalom in Koinonia' explores therapeutic characteristics of the community that the Lord intends to build, wherein individual identities are both nurtured and nestled within the wider community of faith.

2. India Booms

India has changed in many ways and continues to change. India is now portrayed as the third most powerful country in the global power line-up, surpassed only by the United States and China.[1] 'Global Governance 2025' (a follow-on to the NIC's 2008 Report) was jointly issued by the National Intelligence Council (NIC) of the Office of the Director of National Intelligence and the European Union's Institute for Security Studies (EUISS). The report states that, in 2010, the United States topped the list of powerful countries/regions, accounting for nearly 22 per cent of the global power. It was followed by China (more than 12 per cent), the European Union (more than 16 per cent), India (nearly 8 per cent), and Japan, Russia and Brazil (less than 5 per cent each).[2]

Thus, the India of today has been described as a rapidly modernising country which is adjusting to its new-found status as a global power;

---

[1] 'From Third World Country to Third Most Powerful Nation', *The Times of India* (22 September 2010).

[2] An article on the report can be viewed at http://www.ndtv.com/article/world/india-third-most-powerful-nation-us-report-53548 (accessed on 26 September, 2010).

a country which is proud of its culture and heritage and continues to embrace these; a country of unparalleled diversity amongst its people and environment; a hotbed of entrepreneurialism, from the individual to a multinational scale; and a country which is leading by example.[3]

India has made significant progress in several areas: education, agriculture, science, technology, information technology, telecommunications, nuclear programmes, space programmes, health care, infrastructure development and transportation to name a few. She has become an important nation on the global stage, a key player in international economics, politics, technology and business. A three hundred million strong middle-class with significant purchasing power and an ever-expanding base of brand-conscious youth makes India a prime and profitable market for multinational companies, who are making substantial investments in the country. India has also made an indelible mark on the global IT industry and, in the process, created several jobs, produced considerable wealth, and even contributed to the English language by the creation of a new slang word—'bangalored' (referring to 'overseas unemployment due to jobs outsourced to India').

3. India Booms, but for Whom?

What makes a country modern or developed? The former President of India, Dr A.P.J. Abdul Kalam sought to address the issue in his book entitled '*India 2020: A Vision for the New Millennium*'. Some indicators are (1) the wealth of the nation, (2) the prosperity of its people, and (3) its standing in the international forum. Economical indicators are the Gross National Product (GNP), the Gross Domestic Product (GDP), the balance of payments, foreign exchange reserves, rate of economic growth, per capita income and so on. (The per capita income indicates the wealth in the hands of the people, but does not indicate in whose hands how much of the wealth is concentrated).[4]

India no doubt booms, but the question is, for whom? Are all the one billion plus Indians benefitting from the modernisation of

[3] More details can be viewed at http://www.thisismodernindia.com/this_is_modern_india_our_objective.html (accessed on 8 September 2010).

[4] A.P.J. Kalam, *India 2020: A Vision for the New Millennium* (New Delhi: Penguin Books, 2002).

India and the resulting economic growth? There is no doubt that significant progress has been made in alleviating extreme poverty through the efforts of the Government, NGOs, businesses and the efforts of international agencies, such as the United Nations through their Millennium Development Goals (MDGs). The progress that has been made often tends to get buried under the tasks that are yet to be accomplished. Nevertheless, credit needs to be given where credit is due. However, the hard questions still need to be asked and addressed: Does every Indian village have access to clean drinking water, nutritious food, electricity, equal opportunities for employment, basic health care and sanitation, and basic education? Has the discrimination and oppression of the Dalits reduced and are they being benefitted in any way by 'booming' India? Mahatma Gandhi*ji* asserted that only when we have wiped the tears from the faces of all, have we truly arrived as a nation.

Nobel Laureate, Bengali poet and writer, Rabindranath Tagore (1861–1941) in his poem-prayer, envisioned and prayed for an India:

> Where the mind is without fear and the head is held high;
> Where knowledge is free;
> Where the world has not been broken up into fragments
> By narrow domestic walls;
> Where words come out from the depth of truth;
> Where tireless striving stretches its arms towards perfection;
> Where the clear stream of reason has not lost its way
> Into the dreary desert sand of dead habit;
> Where the mind is led forward by thee
> Into ever-widening thought and action—
> Into that heaven of freedom, my Father, let my country awake.[5]

Dr Kalam states that a nation without a vision is like a ship cruising on the high seas without any aim or direction. He argues that the first vision, set by the people for the nation, was 'freedom for India'. Dr Kalam calls for Indians to collectively set the second national vision for a 'developed India' and to work towards its realisation by shedding cynicism and initiating concrete actions.[6]

---

[5] See http://oldpoetry.com/opoem/25043-Rabindranath-Tagore-Where-The-Mind-Is-Without-Fear (accessed 6 September 2010).

[6] Kalam, *India 2020.*

4. Change and Identity

Mental, emotional, physical, social, spiritual and psychological well-being, dignity, self-worth, self-esteem, unity, liberty, respect, reason, growth, freedom and identity, both for individuals and for communities, are important indicators of the health of a person or a community. These are topics that pastoral theology is concerned with.

As the nation goes through unprecedented changes, issues related to the well-being of its citizens are important. Much can be said on a topic as vast as the one we are exploring and more so in a nation as diverse and complex as India is. However, I would like to restrict the rest of this paper to address some of the identity conflicts that individuals and communities experience in this India that I have described, and propose a pastoral response for a way forward in the changing context of South Asia in general, and India in particular.

5. Who Am I?

Self-identification is closely related to self-worth and self-esteem. The way a person perceives themselves influences their feelings about themselves, which in turn has potential to affect the way in which they relate to others. In the India of today, a person's identity tends to be defined more by their positions, connections and possessions than their true inner self. The business world, through their advertisement campaigns urges and ensures that expensive branded products are purchased in order to make a statement of identity. For example, you are a 'complete' man only when you wear an expensive Raymond suit.

Self-esteem is a term used in psychology to reflect a person's overall evaluation or appraisal of his or her own worth (self-worth, self-respect, self-regard). A person's self-esteem may be reflected in their behaviour, such as in assertiveness, shyness, confidence or caution.

American psychologist Abraham Maslow included self-esteem in his hierarchy of needs. He described two different forms of esteem: the need for respect from others and the need for self-respect, or inner self-esteem. Respect from others entails recognition, acceptance, status and appreciation, and is believed to be more fragile and easily lost than inner self-esteem. According to Maslow, without the fulfilment of the self-esteem need, individuals will be driven to seek it and unable to grow and obtain self-actualization.

5.1. Low Self-Esteem

Low self-esteem comes from a poor self-image. Self-image is based on how a person sees himself or herself. Low self-esteem also depends on other factors like a person's job or job title. For example, do you value the job you do? Does the job you have help you be happy with who you are? Do the others in your office respect you? Low self-esteem feeds negative thinking.

Does identity come with positions and possessions? I have come across scores of individuals whose entire lives have been defined and controlled by their jobs, resulting in disastrous consequences both for themselves and their families. A person who derives their identity from their job title undergoes an identity crisis when they lose their position or when they retire. In modern India, is the issue of work-life balance being adequately addressed? How are families being affected by jobs that require long hours of work or long periods of absence from home? How are marital relationships affected? How are children affected by absent parents? Can money and things compensate adequately for an absent parent? Prosperity in modern India is evident, but at what cost? Are multinational companies and businesses aware of how their policies and expectations damage families and relationships? Do they care or is money always the bottom line? Is this modern day slavery?

When Jesus was asked to give a summary of his teachings, he urged his disciples to love God wholeheartedly and to love their neighbours as themselves. Persons who are not at peace with themselves will find it challenging to love others. A person's self-perception is a significant factor, which affects their own mental, psychological and emotional well-being, as well as their relational abilities. The scriptures exhort us not to think of ourselves more highly than we should, but to develop a self-perception based on our identity in Christ.

5.2. Our Identity in Christ

In the context of change, an individual's identity can be secure and firmly rooted in that which remains unchanging—God and his word. Gen. 1.26–27 reminds us that we are created by God in his image. If we were to pause for a moment and reflect on the implications of this fact, it would greatly enhance our identity (knowing that we are created by God) and our self-worth (knowing that we are created in his image). John 3.16 affirms that we are loved by God and that he sent his son to die for us. Reminding ourselves that we are loved by God, created by him and made in his image, are truths that can counter low self-esteem, provide a sense of meaning, self-worth, dignity and purpose in life, without being dependent on the 'esteem' that fleeting positions and possessions may temporarily provide.

In Paul's letter to the Ephesians, he reminds his readers of the many spiritual blessings that are theirs in Christ. The fact that we are chosen (1.4) enhances our self-worth, and our adoption as his sons and daughters (1.5) is sufficient for our identity. The fact that we have been redeemed (1.7) enhances our self-esteem; our hope in Christ (1.12) promises us a future; and all of this is secured and sealed by the Holy Spirit (1.13–14). We, who were dead, in sin are now made alive in Christ (2.1–5). We, who were separate from Christ, excluded from citizenship, foreigners to the covenants of promise, without hope and without God, have been reconciled to God through the blood of Christ (2.11–13). We are now no longer foreigners and aliens, but fellow citizens with God's people and members of God's household (2.19). An understanding of our position and possessions in Christ helps diminish the need for seeking, or being dependant, on human approval to feel significant and accepted. A person whose identity is securely rooted in Christ need not feel insecure when other identities are challenged, lost or dishonoured, as the core identity of being sons and daughters of God, created by him in his image and loved by him, is eternally secure. This does not preclude the fact that even Christians can experience low self-esteem, which often is the result of ignoring or being unwilling to receive the gift of wholeness that God makes available to all of his children.

5.3. Identity of Dalit Christians

The Dalit Christian community forms the largest group of Christians in India and, hence, the Dalit Christian identity in modern India needs to be explored. Despite many changes in modern India, there are some things that have not changed. Because of their conversion to Christianity, millions of Dalit Christians are deprived of the benefits accorded to Dalits from other religions, such as Hinduism, Buddhism and Sikhism. On 10 August 1950, the then-President of India signed and issued the Constitution (Scheduled Castes) Order, 1950 which precludes Schedule Caste converts to Islam and Christianity from eligibility for benefits of affirmative action.[7]

Despite some affirmative measures, the majority of Dalits are still in social bondage and experience violence, murder, rape and other atrocities, which often go unreported due to their powerlessness. The Tribal Dalits have been deprived of basic survival needs such as food, shelter, health, education, employment and freedom.[8]

The National Commission on Religious & Linguistic Minorities, headed by Justice Ranganath Mishra (a former Chief Justice of India) submitted its report to the Prime Minister on 22 May 2007. It recommended that 'Para 3 of the Constitution (Scheduled Castes) Order 1950—which originally restricted the Scheduled Caste net to the Hindus and later opened it to Sikhs and Buddhists, thus still excluding from its purview the Muslims, Christians, Jains and Parsis, etc.—should be wholly deleted by appropriate action so as to completely de-link Scheduled Caste status from religion and make the Scheduled Castes net fully religion-neutral like that of the Scheduled Tribes.'[9] No action has been taken on these recommendations thusfar.

The Catholic Bishops Conference of India (CBCI) Commission for SC/ST/BC asserts that the denial of Scheduled Caste status to Dalit Christians and Dalit Muslims constitutes a violation of Articles 14

[7] See http://www.churchnewssite.com/portal/?p=24640 (accessed on 4 September 2010).

[8] J.M. Razu, 'Dalits-Tribals as Victims of Asymmetries: A Liberative Mission Perspective', in S. Prabhakar (ed.), *Missions in the Past and Present: Challenges and Perspectives* (Bangalore: BTESS/SATHRI, 2006), 56–76.

[9] See http://minorityaffairs.gov.in/newsite/ncrlm/ncrlm.asp (accessed on 3 September 2010).

(equality before the law); 15 (prohibition of discrimination on grounds of religion); and 25 (freedom to profess and practice any religion) of the Constitution of India. To voice their protest, the CBCI Commission for SC/ST/BC had called for an observance of 10 August 2010, as a 'Black Day' and suggested that 'a black flag be hoisted on all our churches and institutions, rallies and public meetings be held in District and Taluk head quarters [sic] submitting memoranda to the District Collectors and Thashildars and Press Meets.'[10]

Relentless efforts are being made to extend the benefits to all Dalits, irrespective of their religion. The campaign of Dalit Christians for the Scheduled Caste status took an interesting turn recently with a sceptical Supreme Court responding to their demand by asking whether Christians also practised the caste system. 'Would Christians admit that they practice caste system and that Dalits (among them) face social discrimination requiring reservation to uplift their cause?', asked a Bench headed by Chief Justice K.G. Balakrishnan (2007).[11] The matter is currently pending before the Supreme Court and there is a considerable dialogue taking place both within and outside the Christian fold.

What are the pastoral and psychological needs of the Dalit Christian community in India, as they continue to face social alienation, economical deprivation, emotional trauma, psychological damage, physical abuse, mental torture and identity crisis? What kind of pastoral care and counselling is being offered to this large section of the body of Christ in India? What theology has undergirded the actions or inactions, responses or non-responses, of the urban, elite church? Like the Good Samaritan, has there been interest in, awareness of, solidarity with, and hands-on involvement with Dalit issues? Or has the urban and elite church in India crossed over to the other side of the road and walked away, instead of identifying with the Dalit church in India? The remarks of Bishop Devasahayam at the Global Ecumenical Conference on Justice for Dalits (held in Thailand in March 2009) best answers

---

[10] See http://www.churchnewssite.com/portal/?p=24640 (accessed on 30 August 2010).

[11] K.G. Balakrishnan (2007), 'Do Christians practice caste system [Electronic Version]', *Times of India*. http://timesofindia.com/India/Do_christians_also_practice_caste_system_ask_SC/articleshow/2218560.cms (accessed on 2 September 2010).

the question as to how both the Government and the church in India have dealt with the Dalit issue. He urged the Government of India to acknowledge the existence of caste-based discrimination, expressed particularly through the failure of providing justice for the Dalits. He also urged the Indian church to confess their sins of casteism and identify with the Dalits, by encouraging expressions of Dalit culture in church life, worship and theology.[12]

6. Indian and Christian? Who Are We?

It is generally believed that Christianity has existed in India since the year 52 CE. Christians in India are a minority and comprise only about 2.3% of the total Indian population (2001 census figures). Despite being a small minority in a large nation, Christians in India have contributed immensely to nation building and have served the nation in several ways, especially in the field of education, health care and social development. Indian Christians have provided decades of sacrificial service without practising discrimination on grounds of caste, language, creed or religion. However, the church in India has not adequately interacted with the social, political and cultural processes of Indian societies and the prophetic voice of the church has not been audible in the public square.

The words 'Christian' and 'Christianity' are loaded with meanings of more than what it means to be a follower of the Lord Jesus Christ.[13] In the recent past, there has been an open challenge to any form of mission work in India, and laws have been passed to restrict and make impossible the work of many churches and Christian mission agencies. The misuse, rather than the use, of the Freedom of Religion Bill is the cause of increasingly violent opposition towards various forms of Christian ministry, wherein false cases of forced conversions are reported to the authorities. Though many of the cases are subsequently dropped, significant damage is already done in the process, and several new 'cases' continue to emerge.

---

[12] See http://www.lutheranworld.org/News/LWI/EN/2359.EN.html (accessed on 5 September 2010).
[13] K. Rajendran, 'The Identity of Christians', a paper presented at AICOCIM, 2009.

Brian Wintle describes the context in which the church exists in India today as characterized by religious and cultural plurality, economic divide, corruption, political parties challenging the secular character of the nation's Constitution with openly communal agendas, and gender- and caste-based discrimination and oppression.[14]

In response to the increasing number of attacks on Christians, a commission of inquiry was set up in Karnataka, headed by Justice B.K. Somashekar. Among many other petitions submitted to the Commission was a demand to 'Indian-ise' Christianity and to 'edit' the Bible by removing portions which are 'offensive' and 'unconstitutional' in a pluralistic society. The question of Christian identity was explored at the All India Congress on Church in Mission (AICOCIM 2009), organised by the Evangelical Fellowship of India. Bishop CV Matthew, in his paper entitled 'Christian Identity: To Be or Not To Be', made reference to the various 'calls' that have been made to the church in India: 'The first call was to give up our theology, the very foundation of our faith. The second call was to give up our mission, the very reason for our existence, and now the call is to give up our identity as an integral part of the Universal Body called the Church and to merge with the "mainstream".'

The call to give up our theology comes with the advice to stop making exclusive claims about Jesus Christ as the only Saviour. Instead, Jesus can be located as 'one among many saviours'. The call to desist from mission was because conversion is an anti-national and subversive act and charitable social services are unethical and motivated programmes inspired, funded and controlled by nefarious foreign powers that work towards the disintegration of our glorious country. Merging with the mainstream implies celebrating local festivals and considering as heroes the deities of the majority.[15]

How then are Christians expected to live in India? How can we be identified as 'Indian Christians'? What are the possible ways in which the Indian church can respond to the changes and challenges that emerge from the changing context of modern India? I suggest four

[14] B.C. Wintle, 'Evangelicals and the Bible', *Dharma Deepika* 9 (2005): 9–19.
[15] C.V. Matthew, 'Christian Identity: To Be or Not To Be', a paper presented at AICOCIM, 2009.

notions in tension with each other, but which when held together in balance, produce valuable creative tension for the church in India, as she strives to be both Indian and Christian.

6.1. Incarnational Ekklesia

God himself came into our world and lived among us. Jesus' incarnation is an important biblical truth that demonstrates how God identified with the human race, lived among us as one of us, served us selflessly and, ultimately, died for us. Establishing our roots and living among a people demonstrates identifying with the people and grappling with the same issues that they face. Incarnational living involves experiencing with others in the community the same concerns and challenges that emerge from the particular context and location in which they live.

The Greek word used for the church is '*ekklesia*', which means 'those called out'. This might seem contrary to the concept of incarnation. How is it possible to be closely identified with and at the same time be called out of a system or structure? To be Indian and Christian is to understand the implications of being firmly rooted in both the nation and the church. Often the emphasis is more on being 'called out' rather than on being a 'part of', resulting in the neglect of our 'Indian-ness', which in turn, alienates the church from the rest of the community within which she exists and seeks to serve.

6.2. In the World and Not of the World

The scriptures exhort us to be a part of the world in which we live—to actually live in it. Christians have often been accused of being heavenly-minded and not of much earthly use. Living in India involves grappling with contextual realities which we need to constantly address and engage with. It involves a long journey on bumpy roads and often under a hot scorching sun. The Christian faith is lived out with our feet on the ground, seeking to engage practically with ground realities that confront us on a daily basis. Has the Indian church demonstrated how our faith informs and influences our life in the real world, or has there been a convenient separation of spiritual matters and 'worldly' matters without their intersection?

The scriptures exhort Christians to be 'in the world, but not of the world' — another seemingly contradicting statement. Again, often the emphasis has been 'not of the world' rather than 'in the world'. Identifying with the world is not the same as being a part of the evil systems that prevail in our fallen world. Has the Indian church demonstrated this distinction clearly? Has our identity been marked as people who are in the world but who operate very differently, or are the issues, practices and systems of the church same as that of the world around it? A boat is meant to be in the water but it gets dangerous when the water enters the boat. Is the Indian church sailing in the water or has the water entered and endangered the church? What would be the identifying marks of a church and a Christian who is in the world and not of the world? What would that look like in the changing contexts of modern India?

6.3. Resident Pilgrim

A resident is not a visitor, but is one who belongs to the community where he or she lives. The identity of residents is defined by their location, and their interaction with the rest of the community. Residents live with the people and share in all the joys and sorrows of the community. There is a sense of belonging when others in the community see you as 'one among us'. Have Indian Christians merged into the communities in which they live in or again, has the emphasis been more on being a 'pilgrim' rather than a resident? Communicating and relating to a community as a non-resident has its limitations and does not foster a sense of belonging and oneness.

The scripture also exhorts Christians to live as pilgrims and aliens in this world, implying that we are on a journey which will eventually take us out of this world. 'This world is not my home. I'm just a passer through' are the words of an old, popular song which emphasizes the temporary nature of our life here on earth. What would life look like when the concepts of resident and pilgrim are balanced and how will this affect our identities in modern India?

6.4. Locally Universal

A local person is someone who lives in the locality and is familiar with the people who live there. A local person understands the culture, the language, the unwritten rules of the society and knows how things are done. Each locality is unique and has its own subculture and nuances. Effective communication and interaction can only happen when the appropriate language is used and actions are congruent with the local culture. Does the church in a given location understand the locality in which it is located? Can the church identify with the people who live in the locality and relate to the wider community, in culturally appropriate ways? Do Christians participate in and engage with the issues that the locality faces, such as bad roads, poor water supply, erratic power supply, crime, transportation needs, etc.? Or is the church so universal that the unique local issues are overlooked?

Yet, the church is the body of Christ and every local church in India is part of the universal church. Our local uniqueness is important but not to the point of exclusivity, wherein the universal church is overlooked. The universality of the church does not negate the uniqueness of a local church. Neither does the uniqueness of a local church exclude the universal church. What does this mean for the church in India today? How can the uniqueness of a local church be enriched by the universal church and how can the universal church express itself locally? These are critical questions for the church in India to grapple with, as we seek to be simultaneously Indian and Christian.

6.5. Shalom in Koinonia

Identity, identification and identity crisis are significant life issues which, when not handled properly, can result in conflicts that are relational, psychological and emotional. How can pastoral theology and psychology address the identity challenges that emerge out of the changing context of modern India? I suggest a fresh examination of two passages from Acts, namely 2.42–47 and 4.32–35.

After the resurrection and just before his ascension, Jesus spoke to his disciples about the power that the Holy Spirit would give them to be witnesses in Jerusalem, in all Judea and Samaria, and to the ends of the earth (Acts 1.8). This promise was fulfilled on the Day of Pentecost, when Peter stood up and addressed the crowd, testifying boldly about Jesus and inviting them to receive forgiveness of sins. About three thousand people responded that day to Peter, as he spoke empowered by the Holy Spirit (Acts 2.14–41).

Following a period of Spirit-empowered proclamation and miraculous healings, Peter and John were seized and put in jail (Acts 4.3). When questioned by the rulers, elders and teachers of the law about their preaching and the source of their power, they courageously testified to the death and resurrection of Jesus, asserting that 'Salvation is found in no one else, for there is no other name under heaven given to men by which we must be saved' (Acts 4.12). After being threatened of dire consequences if they continued to proclaim Jesus, they were released. They returned to their own people who, on hearing their report, gave themselves to fervent prayer.

Persecution of Christians in contemporary India and South Asia is on the rise. Christian activities are being perceived in some quarters as anti-national activities. What can we learn from the early church as they responded to the persecution and prosecution of their day?

- **Unity**. Acts 4.32 indicates that all the believers were one in heart and mind. Unity in the body of Christ is a powerful and compelling witness. In his high priestly prayer, Jesus prayed that we would be brought to complete unity to let the world know about his love for people (John 17.21–23). Fragmentation and divisions are like a house divided against itself, and the house is bound to fall. There needs to be intentionality in our efforts to maintain unity in the body of Christ. A strong identity in Christ unites the household of faith as it transcends other identities that tend to divide. This is a simple but significant truth, familiar yet far-reaching.

- **Selflessness**. No one claimed that any of his possessions was his own. The blessings of God on Abraham were not to make him a blessed person but to be a blessing to others (Gen. 12.2–3). In a world that tends to be consumed with the self, selflessness is almost an alien thought. Selfless stewardship of God's blessings ensures the well-being of the entire community. Paul exhorted the church in Galatia to do good to all, especially to those of the household of faith (Gal. 6.10).

- **Sharing**. They shared everything they had with each other. A willingness to share can be developed only when God is acknowledged as the source of all our possessions. Stewardship requires both faithfulness and accountability, and it is the Lord who gives us the power to produce wealth (Deut. 8.18).

- **Power**. Their testifying to the resurrection of the Lord Jesus was done with great power. In the context of a modern and changing world, new challenges constantly emerge. The apostle Paul realised that human energy alone is not sufficient to complete his God-given task. He laboured with God's energy that was powerfully at work in him (Col. 1.29). The Lord has not left his people stranded and powerless in this world. He has made available to them the power of the Holy Spirit, to be effective witnesses for him (Acts 1.8).

- **Grace**. Much grace was upon them. As our world changes, people under various pressures tend to become easily irritable, as is evident in increasing road rage and other conflicts that emerge out of seemingly small issues. Grace seems to be a rare commodity in the modern world. How is grace demonstrated in the church and in the world at large?

- **Caring**. They cared for each other's needs and there were no needy persons among them. 'I don't care' and 'who cares?' are common phrases today. There are several 'one another' passages in the Bible that exhort us to care for each other. What does care look like in the real world? What are the challenges and hindrances to genuine care and how can they be overcome?

- **Community**. There was a sense of belonging, community and family among them. In our changing modern world, community is being replaced by individualism, to our detriment. Hectic lives have resulted in relationships that are shallow. A caring community is a therapeutic community, which brings wholeness and well-being to all of its members. It takes time to invest in relationships and to build trust. This requires a commitment and the intentional setting apart of time and energy.

- **Love**. All of this is undergirded by love. Jesus said 'a new command I give you, love one another as I have loved you. By this all men will know that you are my disciples' (John 13.34–35). Paul explained to the Corinthian church the meaning and definition of love (1 Cor.13). What hinders the church in India or South Asia from being a community that is recognized by love? What will it take to make the Indian church identifiable as a loving community?

In such a *koinonia* (communion by intimate participation), the early church experienced *shalom* (peace, welfare and completeness). They spoke the word of God boldly, empowered by the Holy Spirit, and the church grew exponentially. All of this was happening in a context of persecution and threats as they continued to live as disciples of the risen Lord, unapologetically. Their identity came from Christ and, in the context of community, their bio-psycho-social-spiritual needs were met.

Even such a community was not without its share of identity-related conflicts. Acts 6.1 describes a situation in which a conflict arose between the Greek Jews and the Hebraic Jews. Could identity conflicts emerge even in such a wonderful and caring community? Yes, indeed. In our struggling human frailty there is bound to be conflict, but it can be resolved. The leadership gathered all the disciples together to address the conflict and identify a solution, by setting up a team to deal with the cause of the conflict. The decision was communicated to all concerned and the conflict was resolved, freeing up the disciples to continue their God-given task, which resulted in the number of disciples increasing rapidly. Identity-related conflicts are inevitable, but resolution is possible, for 'in Christ there is neither Jew nor Greek, slave nor free, male nor female, for you all are one in Christ Jesus' (Gal. 3.28).

7. Conclusion

What will it take for Christians in India to be unashamedly and unapologetically Indian and Christian? It would take individuals with a strong identity in Christ, living in harmony with themselves and with each other as members of one family under the headship of Christ. It demands intentionality to resolve inevitable identity conflicts, through a commitment to live out practically our theologies, which are held in high reverence. It needs a balanced understanding and praxis of being in the world and not of the world; of being an incarnational *ekklesia*; of being resident pilgrims and of being locally universal. It requires a fresh devotion to the apostles' teachings and doctrines, lived out in fellowship with God and with each other (Acts 2.42). Finally, it involves being prepared to face new issues that would inevitably emerge out of our praxis of the above, in the changing realities of the vibrant Indian and South Asian context.

References

Balakrishnan, K.G. (2007). 'Do Christians Practice Caste System' [Electronic Version]. *Times of India*. http://timesofindia.com/India/Do_christians_also_practice_caste_system_ask_SC/articleshow/2218560.cms (accessed on 2 September 2010).

http://www.ndtv.com/article/world/india-third-most-powerful-nation-us-report-53548 (accessed on 26 September 2010).

http://www.thisismodernindia.com/this_is_modern_india_our_objective.html (accessed on 8 September 2010).

http://oldpoetry.com/opoem/25043-Rabindranath-Tagore-Where-The-Mind-Is-Without-Fear (accessed on 6 September 2010).

http://www.churchnewssite.com/portal/?p=24640 (accessed on 4 September 2010).

http://minorityaffairs.gov.in/newsite/ncrlm/ncrlm.asp (accessed on 3 September 2010).

http://www.churchnewssite.com/portal/?p=24640 (accessed on 30 August 2010).

http://www.lutheranworld.org/News/LWI/EN/2359.EN.html (accessed on 5 September 2010).

Kalam, A.P.J. *India 2020: A Vision for the New Millennium*. New Delhi: Penguin Books, 2002.

Matthew, C.V. 'Christian Identity: To Be or Not To Be'. Paper presented at AICOCIM, 2009.

[n.a.]. *Times of India* (22 September, 2010).

Rajendran, K. 'The Identity of Christians'. Paper presented at AICOCIM, 2009.

Razu, J.M. 'Dalits-Tribals as Victims of Asymmetries: A Liberative Mission Perspective. Pp. 56–76 in *Missions in the Past and Present: Challenges and Perspectives*. Edited by S. Prabhakar. Bangalore: BTESS/SATHRI, 2006.

Wintle, B.C. 'Evangelicals and the Bible'. *Dharma Deepika* 9 (2005): 9–19.

Human Identity from the Perspective of Hinduism (*Sanātanadharma*)

Kiran Kumar K. Salagame*

1. Introduction

Identity formation is a bio-psycho-social process. Biologically, our experience of our body is the foundation; we develop a 'self-sense' out of bodily experiences. Then our emotions and feelings, imaginations, likes and dislikes, interests, abilities, etc., which are psychological in nature, contribute to the process. Simultaneously, many socio-cultural factors like family, community, educational background, religion and nationality also influence our sense of identity. We can distinguish four components of identity or 'self-sense' according to the Hindu tradition: *sense of differentiation, sense of agency, identification* and *individuality*. Each human being develops his or her identity with respect to these four components. However, individual differences exist because all human beings do not have an uniform amount of these components developed in them. Further, identity formation is a dynamic process and the structure of our identity keeps changing as we grow and pass through major developmental stages of life. The dynamic process of identity formation and development mentioned applies only to the bio-psycho-social aspect of being. In addition to this, Hindu tradition also recognizes that identity is multidimensional; besides and beyond the bio-psycho-social aspect, it acknowledges our spiritual identity, which is unchanging and permanent. Therefore, the Hindu tradition urges everyone to realize that which is permanent (*nitya*) and real (*satya*), by giving up that which is impermanent (*anitya*) and not real (*asatya*). This paper will explicate some of these ideas from the perspective of transpersonal psychology.

*Dr Kiran Kumar is Professor of Psychology at the University of Mysore.

2. Human Identity

The problem of human identity is an age old one and wise men all over the world have pondered about the nature of self and identity. While the ancient Greek tradition urges 'know thyself', seers and sages of ancient India asked the question *'ko'ham'* ('who am I?'). While the dictum 'know thyself', is an injunction from the 'other', *'ko'ham'* is an inquiry from 'within'. Both the traditions have pointed out that our true identity is beyond the realm of ordinary awareness, and mystics from all the cultures across the globe agree on this point.[1]

In India, for five thousand years and more, rishis of the ancient, medieval, and modern periods have unequivocally declared that human beings have the capacity to transcend narrow self-definitions (with reference to caste, creed, religion, nationality, language, and so on), to know their 'real self', which is not characterized by any psychological or social attributes. Thus, pursuit of self-inquiry has been a central preoccupation in Indian traditions. This is best expressed in the Upanishads. Two major schools of Indian tradition — *Sāmkhya* and *Vedānta* — both of which have their origins in the Upanishads, have dealt with the problem of human identity extensively. While the former termed it as *purusha,* the latter termed it as *ātman.* However, the term *ātman* has gained currency in Indian tradition and *ātma sākshātkāra* (self-realization) is regarded as the highest goal of human existence (*parama purushārtha*). Though there are certain differences in how the nature of *purusha* and *atman* is conceptualized in different schools, there is no doubt regarding their centrality in human life. In view of this, in understanding Indian perspectives on self and identity, it is always important to keep the distinction between spiritual and bio-psycho-social aspects of human existence in focus.

Modern psychology, which developed within the scientific mould, primarily focused on bio-psycho-social aspects of human existence (the notable exception being the works of Carl Jung) and the issues of self and identity were accordingly limited by this. On the other hand, the Indian traditions in general, and *Sanātanadharma* in particular, takes into account the transcendental dimension of human

---

[1] William James, *The Varieties of Religious Experiences* (The Fontana Library, 1971); Charles T. Tart (ed.), *Transpersonal Psychologies* (New York: Dutton Paperbacks, 1975).

existence and the nature of human identity. With the emergence of transpersonal psychology in 1960s, the problem of human identity has been revisioned to incorporate the transcendental dimension as well. In this context, the Indian approach to the understanding of self has gained significance among researchers. Recent developments within our country, encouraging the presentation of traditional ideas under the banner of 'Indian Psychology', have further helped in approaching the issues of self and identity more comprehensively[23]. This article is an attempt to present the essential arguments on the nature of human identity and self as found in Hinduism (*Sanātanadharma*). Since there are six perspectives (*darshanas*), there are certain differences in the views regarding the nature of transcendental identity. The contents of this article rely heavily on the Vedānta.

3. Hinduism (*Sanātanadharma*)

Before we discuss the issue of identity further, a few words of clarification on the usage of terms 'Hinduism' and '*Sanātanadharma*' would help understand the position of the present paper better. Though it has become customary to refer to Hinduism alongside other traditions like Christianity and Islam as a religion, scholarly opinion differs on this point. Historically, the term Hinduism is a misnomer. It is a result of the distorted pronunciation of the Sanskrit name for a river, *Sindhu*, on whose banks the Vedic *Rsi* tradition flourished. The early tourists to this sub-continent pronounced *Sindhu* incorrectly, as 'Hindu' and 'Indus'. From this distortion, the country came to be known as 'India', and the tradition of the Vedic people, 'Hinduism'.

Hawkins, an expert on Asian religions, notes that in the monotheistic religions there is a general agreement as to the nature of God and to the content and status of the core scriptural foundations of the religion. But, in the case of Hinduism, it is not so. As an illustration he points out that 'a devout Indian [Hindu] can believe that there is one God (in

---

    [2] Anand C. Paranjpe, *Self and Identity in Modern Psychology and Indian Thought* (New York: Plenum Publishers, 1998).

    [3] Kiran Kumar Salagame, 'Ego and Ahamkāra: Self and Identity in Modern Psychology and Indian Thought', in Matthijs Cornelissen, Girishwar Misra, Suneet Varma (eds), *Foundations of Indian Psychology*, vol. 1 (New Delhi: Pearson, 2011), 133–45.

the monotheistic sense of the word espoused by Christians, Jews and Muslims), many gods, or no gods at all . . . This has led to considerable difficulty in defining the basic parameters of this tradition, with some scholars arguing that there is no such thing as "Hinduism" . . . [instead there is] a constellation of "Hinduisms" sharing a common cultural matrix, but different enough from one another to be considered separate religions.'[4]

According to Dandekar, two 'patterns of life and thought' existed in ancient India: a non-Aryan, pre-Vedic pattern (the *Muni-yati* tradition) and, the other, an Aryan Vedic pattern (the *Rsi traditions)*.[5] The *Muni-yati* tradition was primarily characterized by (1) the prevalence of the Siva religion and the practices and cults associated with it; and (2) the glorification of a life of renunciation, asceticism, wandering mendicancy, and severe austerities. It was an 'iconic religion' and idol worship was its chief feature. Rituals *(pûja)* and offerings *(bali)* were part of this. Yoga practices, involving 'concentration' aimed at 'mental control' was another feature.

In contrast, the *Rsi* tradition of the Vedic people was characterised by (1) *homa*, offering oblations to God through fire; and (2) an ideal of a materially secure and prosperous family life. In the course of time, the elements of the two traditions mutually influenced each other. Dandekar states, 'a large number of elements in the classical Hindu way of life and thought clearly betray a pre-Vedic non-Aryan origin' and 'the Aryan Vedism may be regarded as a grand interlude in the continuity of ancient Indian thought.'[6] What is contemporarily known as Hinduism is a compound of these two traditions. The Vedic religion did not believe in a personal God. Nevertheless, what was once a pattern of life and thought later acquired the connotation of an organized faith or belief system, as in the sense of Christianity, Islam, and other monotheistic religions.

From the ancient to the modern period, India has moved away from spirituality to religion, and the many foreign invasions that occurred have also been responsible for this. These invasions brought

---

[4] Bradley K. Hawkins, *Asian Religions: An Illustrated Introduction* (New York: Pearson Longman, 2004), 13.

[5] R.N. Dandekar, *Exercises in Indology* (Delhi: Ajanta Publishers, 1981).

[6] Dandekar, *Exercises in Indology*, 339.

other religions into the country and forced the formation of a 'religion', which otherwise did not exist in this land. It is instructive to note what one scholar of religion has to say about this. Swami Harshananda states, 'this religion had no particular name since the most ancient days, because there existed no other religions from which it had to be distinguished.'[7] Some scholars prefer to use the term *Sanātanadharma* to emphasize this. References to *Sanātanadharma* can be found in such ancient sources like *Matsyapurana* 143, 30-32, *Bhagavata* 7.11.2, *Brahmandapurana* 2.33.37-38 and *Khānāpura* plates of *Mādhavavarma* assigned to the sixth century CE.[8]

The American scholar and Indologist David Frawley translated *Sanātanadharma* as 'the eternal tradition' which literally means the 'eternal or universal truth' and is 'sometimes translated as the "perennial wisdom" . . . a tradition conceived as inherent in the cosmic mind, arising with creation itself . . . [it] is a set of teachings which comprehend Universal Life and Consciousness, including religion, yoga and mysticism, philosophy, science, art and culture as part of a single reality.'[9] Frawley identified the following characteristics of *Sanātanadharma*: (a) It is not limited to any messiah, prophet, scripture, or church; (b) It is not restricted to any particular community or looking toward any particular historical end; (c) It embraces all aspiration toward the Divine or Supreme Being by all creatures, not only human beings but also plants and animals and the creatures, godly or ungodly, of subtle worlds beyond our physical senses; and (d) It maintains our connection with the universal tradition through all worlds and all time, to the ancient past and the distant future 'in the vision of a timeless self-renewing reality (Brahman)'.[10]

Hence, what is commonly known as Hinduism may be considered as a meta-perspective on the nature of reality, the universe, and the beings in it. I prefer to use the term *Sanātanadharma*, rather than Hinduism.

---

[7] Swami Harshananda, *Encyclopedia of Hinduism*, vol. 3 (Bangalore: Ramakrishna Mutt, 2008), 183.

[8] See *Epigraphica Indica*, vol. 27, 312, and Swami Harshananda, *Encyclopedia of Hinduism*.

[9] David Frawley, *Hinduism: The Eternal Tradition (Sanātana Dharma)* (New Delhi: Voice of India, 1995), 18.

[10] Frawley, *Hinduism*, 20–21.

4. Human Identity according to *Sanātanadharma*

Sanātanadharma, by emphasizing the eternal, has employed 'discrimination between the permanent and the impermanent' (*nityānitya viveka*) as the tool to arrive at Truth. This is applied to all phenomena in the universe, and understanding of the nature of self is no exception. Vedic and Upanishadic seers and sages inquired into the nature of self and identity using this tool, and attempted to know what remains as against what perishes about human beings, or beings in general. Such an inquiry led them to postulate that all identities that develop with reference to body and mind undergo change and do not last forever. Therefore, they postulated the existence of *jīva* and *ātman*. *Jīva* undergoes reincarnation but even *it* has to cease undergoing the cycle of birth one day. *Jīva* thinks, feels, and acts. *Jīva* is the person of modern psychology. There are many equivalent terms for *jīva* and they represent different states and aspects of a person. They include the following: *sansārin* (involved in worldly enjoyment and activity), *sārīrin* (one who is embodied), *purusa* (human being), *kartā* (self as agent), *bhoktā* (self as experiencer/enjoyer/sufferer), *Ksetrajña* (knower of the field), *prajñā* (self as cognizer), *samprasāda* (the 'self-sense' present in dream), *vijñānātman* (prime mover of discriminatory knowledge).

According to the Upanishads, *ātman* is beyond and behind *jīva* and it is described as *sat, chit, ānanda* (existence, consciousness and bliss). *Ātman* is neither born nor dies. But *ātman* 'is'. To realize that as one's true nature and identity is called *ātma sākshātkāra*. It involves transcending all the limiting conditions of human existence, including the notions of time and space. Thus, a person may consider himself to be a body, soul or Self, and one may say *'aham deha'* ('I am body'), *'aham jīva'* ('I am soul') or *'aham ātma'* ('I am Self'). The term *aham* is a generic one and it only means 'I'. These are different loci of human identity. The Upanishads urge one to move from one locus to the other till one realizes one's true identity, *ātma vid.* At this state, knowing and being are the same. In order to attain this stage, one has to overcome the tendency of identifying with biological, psychological and social aspects of one's existence. In other words, one has to transcend the feeling of 'me' and 'mine', known as *abhimāna* and *mamkāra.* As long as one remains with the feelings of such identifications, one's identity is anchored in the material and social reality. But it is only when one consciously attempts to move beyond that one has any chance of realizing one's identity as nothing but *ātman*.[11]

Such a person is striving to move away from what a British psychologist termed as 'belonging identity' towards an 'awareness identity.'[12] Throughout our lives, we reinforce our self or identity in terms of belongingness; either belonging to something or making something to belong to us. To what we belong, or what belongs to us, maybe of a material or non-material nature. It may be as substantial and concrete as a building or it may be as abstract as faith in God. As long human beings remain in this 'belonging identity', they are bound to suffer.

Curle points out that we can have an 'awareness identity' in two ways. One is achieved through self-analysis or undergoing any of a number of psychotherapeutic procedures that enhance our self-awareness in terms of our psychological characteristics. This he terms as 'psychological awareness'. It is in contrast to the 'supraliminal awareness' of a mystic. Awareness identity that is emphasized in *Sanātanadharma* is of the latter type, and it is described as 'pure awareness' or as 'contentless consciousnesses' by some. The words *chetana, shuddhātma, chaitanya, shuddhachaitanya* and such others convey this sense. The term *ātman* refers to awareness-identity that is rooted in supraliminal awareness. A person who is established in such an identity is described as *stithaprajna* in the Bhagavad Gita (2, 54–72). *Sanātanadharma* holds that every person has the potential to attain this highest state and one has to strive to realize it. A person who has known his real identity is called *ātmajñāni* or *jñāni*. The term *jñāni* commonly refers to one who has this Self-knowledge and *jñāna* (spiritual knowledge), which is also called *parā vidya* (knowledge par excellence). In contrast, all empirical knowledge is called *ajñāna* or *aparā vidya*. Therefore, Indian traditions concentrate more on the former than on the latter. Not knowing one's true nature is called *avidya*.

[11] Kiran Kumar Salagame, 'Concept *Ahamkāra*: Theoretical and Empirical Analysis', in K. Ramakrishna Rao, Sonali Bhatt Marwaha (eds.), *Spiritual Psychologies: Essays in Indian Psychology* (New Delhi: Samvad India Foundations, 2005), 97–102.

[12] Adam Curle, *Mystics and Militants: Awareness, Identity and Social Action* (London: Routledge & Kegan Paul, 1972).

If one realizes one's true Self in one's lifetime, he/she is a liberated person, a *jīvanmukta*. That is why it is said '*sā vidyā yā vimuktaye*' ('that is knowledge which liberates'). Such a liberated being is beyond all limitations and conditionings, and hence a universal being (maybe called '*vishwamānava*', '*vishwabandhu*', '*vishwapremi*'), and so on.

5. Modern Psychology and Transpersonal Psychology

Modern psychology, having embraced the paradigm of physical sciences, has failed to grapple with fundamental problems of human identity. Modern psychology as a scientific discipline has not recognized the spiritual dimension of human existence and thus contemporary mainstream psychological discourses on self and identity often revolve around bio-psycho-social aspects of human nature alone, or (as Curle termed them) around 'belonging identity' and 'awareness identity' of the psychological kind. There was no room for 'awareness identity' of the supraliminal kind in modern psychology, till recently.

To fill this void, a new movement emerged within psychology five decades ago, known as 'transpersonal psychology'. This movement, ushered in by Abraham Maslow, attempts to grapple with all that is considered spiritual, mystical, religious, ecstatic and psychical in human nature. Transpersonal psychology, as the term implies, is an attempt to move beyond the personal, to connect with the larger whole that includes the whole of humanity and the cosmos. Transpersonal psychology recognizes and affirms the human impulse for 'self-transcendence' as a 'meta-motivation' beyond self-actualization. While the latter refers to development certain potentialities and abilities and identifying oneself in terms of those developments, the former is an urge to move away from all such strivings to realize the nature of true identity.[13] Transpersonal psychology is informed by all the religious and spiritual traditions of the world. It attempts to draw the essence of all the traditions to arrive at a universal conceptualization of the core values of human existence and the transcendental possibilities intrinsic to human nature.

---

[13] Abraham Maslow, *Farther Reaches of Human Nature* (New York: Bantam Books, 1971).

However, as of now, even transpersonal psychology does not completely do justice to the notion of *ātman* as espoused in the Upanishads, because in that state of realization there is no concept of the personal. The concept of 'I' cannot exist without its complementary aspect, the 'Other'. But the Upanishads speak of a condition of human existence which goes beyond this dualism, hence 'non-dualism' or *Advaita*. Nevertheless, the transpersonal psychology movement has enabled psychologists to move beyond the narrow and limited views of self proposed by different thinkers and researchers.

The different views on self and identity prevalent in modern psychology can be understood with reference to the Indian concept *ahamkāra*. In Sanskrit, this term means 'I am the doer' ('*aham karta iti ahamkāra*'). It also conveys the idea of one who experiences reality. It has four aspects: *sense of differentiation, sense of agency, identification,* and *individuality*. Individual differences arise because of the relative predominance of these aspects in the configuration of 'self-structure'. Thus, one may have much identification, another person a greater sense of individuality, a third feels highly differentiated and a fourth is bogged down by the sense of 'doer-ship'. Our daily existence is impelled by these aspects of self; we are motivated by them. Our actions are guided by our identifications, our sense of agency, our sense of differentiations and our strivings for expression and development of individuality.

Our religious faith and associated beliefs and practices give us an identity and, therefore, it differentiates us from others. We tend to identify with our religion as it contributes to a belonging identity. However, when our primary identification is with our religion and some of us fail to develop our self-structure with respect to the other aspects of self, then there is a danger of losing this identity anchor, and one may feel insecure constantly. Then one is likely to act out of anxiety and indulge in behavior that may lead to what is known as 'fundamentalism'.

The issue of Indian and Christian identity, and for that matter Indian and Hindu, Indian and Muslim, Indian and Buddhist, Indian and Parsi, and so on, hinges on to what extent one's sense of self is coloured by the factors of identification and differentiation, and to what extent they serve as moorings for one's identity formation. If one does not identify excessively with one's nationality and religion, and appreciates other views and perspectives, there is no conflict of interest.

As a result, one may feel at ease with both and also live in harmony with other nationals and religious people. But the problem starts when nationality or religion become the exclusive determinants of one's 'self-sense', leading to rigid identifications and differentiations. Since religion is essentially a path towards transcendence to realize God or Self, as you like it, transpersonal psychology and psychotherapy can be an antidote in helping such persons who have excessive identifications, to move beyond the narrow concepts of self (transpersonal), so that one is not overweighed by them.

References

Curle, Adam. *Mystics and Militants: Awareness, Identity and Social Action.* London: Routledge & Kegan Paul, 1972.

Dandekar, R.N. *Exercises in Indology.* Delhi: Ajanta Publishers, 1981.

Frawley, David. *Hinduism: The Eternal Tradition (Sanātana Dharma).* New Delhi: Voice of India, 1995.

Hawkins, Bradley K. *Asian Religions: An Illustrated Introduction.* New York: Pearson Longman, 2004.

James, William. *The Varieties of Religious Experiences.* The Fontana Library, 1971.

Maslow, Abraham. *Farther Reaches of Human Nature.* New York: Bantam Books, 1971.

Paranjpe, Anand C. *Self and Identity in Modern Psychology and Indian Thought.* New York: Plenum Publishers, 1998.

Salagame, Kiran Kumar. 'Concept *Ahamkāra:* Theoretical and Empirical Analysis'. Pp.97–102 in *Spiritual Psychologies: Essays in Indian Psychology.* Edited by K. Ramakrishna Rao and Sonali Bhatt Marwaha. New Delhi: Samvad India Foundations, 2005.

——. 'Ego and Ahamkāra: Self and Identity in Modern Psychology and Indian Thought'. Pp. 133–45 in *Foundations of Indian Psychology.* Edited by Matthijs Cornelissen, Girishwar Misra and Suneet Varma. Vol. 1. New Delhi : Pearson, 2011.

Swami Harshananda. *Encyclopedia of Hinduism.* Vol. 3. Bangalore: Ramakrishna Mutt, 2008.

Tart, Charles T. (ed.). *Transpersonal Psychologies.* New York: Dutton Paperbacks, 1975.